THE APPEASERS

Martin Gilbert is one of the foremost historians of the 20th century. In 1968 he succeeded Randolph Churchill as the official Churchill biographer, writing six volumes of narrative and editing ten volumes of Churchill documents. He has also published a definitive history of the Holocaust and twelve historical atlases, including those on British, American and Russian history. He is married with three children and lives in London. Since 1962 he has been a fellow of Merton College. He was knighted in 1995.

Also by Martin Gilbert

Churchill: A Life
First World War
Second World War
The Holocaust: the Jewish Tragedy
The Boys: Triumph over Adversity

Richard Gott is a well-known journalist and critic. He was for many years a senior editor at the *Guardian* newspaper, working as a leader-writer, foreign correspondent, features editor and literary editor. In the 1960s he worked at the Royal Institute of International Affairs, and later at a comparable institute at the University of Chile. He has also been the foreign editor of the state newspaper in Tanzania, the editor of the Pelican Latin American Library, and a director of Latin American Newsletters. He is married, with two children and five grandchildren, and lives in London.

Also by Richard Gott

Guerrilla Movements in Latin America
Land Without Evil: Utopian Journeys across
the South American Watershed
In the Shadow of the Liberator: Hugo Chávez
and the Transformation of Venezuela

Alice laughed.

"There's no use trying," she said; "one can't believe impossible things."

"I daresay you haven't had much practice," said the Queen.

—Through the Looking Glass

THE APPEASERS

Martin Gilbert
and
Richard Gott

PHOENIX
PRESS

5 UPPER SAINT MARTIN'S LANE
LONDON
WC2H 9EA

FOR A.J.P. TAYLOR
HISTORIAN, TEACHER AND FRIEND

A PHOENIX PRESS PAPERBACK

First published in Great Britain
by Weidenfeld & Nicolson in 1963
This paperback edition published in 2000
by Phoenix Press,
a division of The Orion Publishing Group Ltd,
Orion House, 5 Upper St Martin's Lane,
London WC2H 9EA

A CIP catalogue record for this book
is available from the British Library.

Printed and bound in Great Britain by
Butler & Tanner Ltd, Frome and London

ISBN 1 84212 050 6

Contents

v

PART FOUR

PART FIVE

Acknowledgments

WE HAVE been inspired by the example of Englishmen who refused to be bullied by Nazi bombast; who saw German threats for what they were, the brash noises of a successful bully; who determined to stand up to that bully, and by firm words to caution him; and who urged England not to compromise with evil, but to face the dictators with courage and conviction. These men were not warmongers. But they were quite willing to face war if the alternative were a dishonorable peace, bought at the expense of others. We owe a special debt to these men who, by their example, convinced us of the need to tell this sad story of British weakness, not haltingly, but forthrightly. For it is also a story of British strength in the end; of the defeat of appeasement; of the triumph of honor. To the men who helped make this triumph possible, and who, by according us the privilege of lengthy discussion, enabled us to understand how the political and diplomatic struggle was waged, we give our thanks: Sir Norman Angell, Lord Boothby, Philip Conwell-Evans, Lord Harvey of Tasburgh, Sir Reginald Leeper, Sir Con O'Neill, Sir Harold Nicolson, Sir Clifford Norton, Duncan Sandys, Sir Orme Sargent, Frank Savery and Lord Strang.

Many other people have helped us, guided the direction of our researches, and given us the benefit of their knowledge of the period. Sir Horace Wilson described many of the moods and activities of appeasement. Sir Alexander Cadogan and Sir Ivone Kirkpatrick answered our queries about the working of the British Foreign Office; Sir Isaiah Berlin gave us an insight into the character of Lord Halifax; A. I. Polack enabled us to understand more about Leslie Hore-Belisha; Frank Ashton-

Gwatkin, with his unrivalled knowledge of pre-war economic policy, told us more in one day than innumerable archives could have done in months; David Dilks gave us the benefit of his researches into Lord Avon's career; and Count Edward Raczynski helped us understand British policy towards Poland. Lady Diana Cooper, Lady Vansittart, Lord Norwich, The Hon. Margaret Lambert, James Joll, F. W. Deakin, Nicholas Kaldor and Lord Salisbury gave us of their wisdom; Mr. and Mrs. Emmanuel Kaye, and Mr. and Mrs. Robbins Milbank gave us their hospitality; and Michael Kinnear and Richard Gombrich gave us their time, in correcting typescripts and reading proofs.

To the above is the credit for what is good in these pages; the errors are all our own.

M.G.
R.G.

Introduction

When *The Appeasers* was first published in 1963, a Fifty-Year Rule for publication of government documents was in force. Two years later the closure period was reduced to thirty years. The documents then made available highlighted the portrayal of the appeasement policy as presented here. Among the new documents were those that pinpointed the government's neglect of defences. On 16 February 1938, as Hitler threatened Austria, Lord Swinton, Secretary of State for Air, warned the Cabinet that the existing air expansion scheme 'to speak quite frankly, was inadequate vis à vis Germany'. The First Lord of the Admiralty, Alfred Duff Cooper, commented: 'It was all very well to have a five years' programme, but we should not have five years for it.' Neville Chamberlain insisted, however, on maintaining the existing scheme until 1941.

Following the German annexation of Austria, the Labour Party demanded an enquiry into Britain's air defences. Chamberlain's principal adviser, Sir Horace Wilson, noted on March 10: 'The Prime Minister decided that an inquiry should be refused and should be refused flatly and firmly, the decision to be adhered to notwithstanding any criticisms that may be raised during the debate.'

On March 18 the Cabinet's Foreign Policy Committee discussed Hitler's pressure on Czechoslovakia. Sir Thomas Inskip, Minister for Coordination of Defence, called Czechoslovakia 'an unstable unit in Central Europe'. He could 'see no reason why we should take any steps to maintain such a unit in being'. The Lord Chancellor, Lord Simon, agreed. Czechoslovakia was 'a modern and very artificial creation with no real roots in the past'. Chamberlain criticized French support for Czecho-slovakia. He 'wondered whether it would not be possible to make some arrangement which would prove more acceptable to Germany'. The Foreign Secretary, Lord Halifax, warned that 'the more closely we associated ourselves with France and Russia the more we produced on German minds the impression that we were plotting to encircle Germany'.

Halifax explained that he 'distinguished in his own mind between Germany's racial efforts, which no one could question, and a lust for conquest on a Napoleonic scale which he himself did not credit'. As to British policy: 'We should try to persuade France and Czechoslovakia that the best course would be for the latter to make the best terms she could with Germany while there was yet time and that we would use any influence we might have with Germany to induce her to take up a reasonable attitude. If in the result a satisfactory solution of the Sudeten problem was reached we might offer in that event to join with Germany in guaranteeing Czechoslovakia's independence.'

On March 14 Chamberlain told the Commons that defence spending would be reviewed. Members assumed that 'reviewed' meant 'increased'. Eight days later, however, the Cabinet minutes recorded: 'The Cabinet were reminded that at the present time the Defence Services were working under instruc-tions to cut down estimates, and it was suggested that this was hardly consistent with an announcement that we were accel-erating our armaments.' In Cabinet on July 20, Duff Cooper protested against the Cabinet decision to ration the Service departments, pointing out that there was a Budget surplus of £20 million, and that sixpence had been added to the income tax. If, he said, it was believed that 'owing to financial con-siderations, the Government were rejecting the advice of their naval experts as to the minimum needed for security, there would be such a storm in the House of Commons that the Government could not hope to survive'.

Hitler's demands on Czechoslovakia grew. On August 30

Halifax told the Cabinet he had spoken to Churchill, who suggested 'a joint note to Berlin from a number of Powers'. Halifax disagreed. 'If we were to invite countries to sign a joint note,' he warned, 'they would probably ask embarrassing questions as to our attitude in the event of Germany invading Czechoslovakia'. At Cabinet on August 30, Duff Cooper wanted to send the Fleet to Scapa Flow as a sign of preparedness. It was decided no such move should take place, and no multi-Power cooperation attempted. On September 10 the Dominion Prime Ministers were told of Halifax's message to France, that 'although Great Britain might feel obliged to support France in a conflict, if only because our interests were involved in any threat to French security, it did not mean that we should be willing automatically to find ourselves at war with Germany because France might be involved in discharge of obligations which Great Britain did not share and which a large section of opinion in this country had always disliked'. Those 'obligations' were the territorial integrity of Czechoslovakia.

Following the first of Chamberlain's three visits to Hitler, the Secretary of State for War, Leslie Hore-Belisha, told the Cabinet he doubted Czechoslovakia's ability to survive without the largely German-speaking Sudeten region. Chamberlain replied that Hitler had assured him Germany had no designs on Czechoslovakia, and 'would not deliberately deceive a man he respected'. After Chamberlain saw Hitler a second time, he reported back to the Cabinet's 'Situation in Czechoslovakia Committee'. The minutes noted: 'The Prime Minister thought that he had established some degree of personal influence over Herr Hitler. The latter had said to him, "You are the first man for many years who has got any concessions from me." Again he had said that if we got this question out of the way without conflict it would be a turning-point in Anglo-German relations. To the Prime Minister that was the big thing of the present issue. He was also satisfied that Herr Hitler would not go back on his word once he had given it to him.'

At Munich, Hitler assured Chamberlain he had no more territorial demands. Chamberlain told the Cabinet on his return:
'He thought that we were now in a more hopeful position, and
that the contacts which had been established with the Dictator
Powers opened up the possibility that we might be able to reach
some agreement with them which would stop the armaments
race.' Britain must continue to 'make good our deficiencies' in
armaments. 'That, however, was not the same thing as to say
that as a thank offering for the present détente we should at once
embark on a great increase in our armaments programme.'

On October 31, Kingsley Wood, Secretary of State for Air,
warned the Cabinet the air force was 'seriously deficient as
compared with Germany'. He added: 'Our weakness might be
said likely to provoke aggression by others'. Chamberlain
remained reluctant to authorize a substantial increase in armaments, telling the Cabinet: 'There had been a good deal of talk
in the country and in the press about the need for rearmament
by this country. In Germany and Italy it was suspected that this
rearmament was directed against them, and it was important
that we should not encourage these suspicions.' Chamberlain
added: 'A good deal of false emphasis had been placed on rearmament, as though one result of the Munich Agreement had been
that it would be necessary for us to add to our rearmament
programmes. Acceleration of existing programmes was one
thing, but increases in the scope of our programme which would
lead to a new arms race was a different proposition.' On November 1 Horace Wilson told Kingsley Wood that the Air Ministry's
proposed increase in the productive capacity 'to a level equal
to the estimated German capacity' was unacceptable because
Germany would 'take it as a signal that we have decided at once
to sabotage the Munich agreement'.

On November 1 Simon told the Cabinet's Committee on
Defence Programmes and Acceleration: 'Germany was
extremely unlikely to violate the neutrality of Belgium.' Six
days later, when Kingsley Wood asked for greater air defence

spending, Simon warned the Cabinet that the 'rash outlay' of such spending might lead to inflation, 'a rise in prices, in wages, in interest rates', and involve 'some real injury to our financial strength'. Chamberlain explained: 'In our foreign policy we were doing our best to drive two horses abreast, conciliation and rearmament. It was a very nice art to keep these two steeds in step. It was worth remembering that it was by no means certain that we could beat Germany in an arms race.'

On 1 January 1939 an Advisory Panel of Industrialists, set up to examine delays in the existing rearmament programme, reported that British industry was 'operating, it must be remembered, on a peace-time basis'. Horace Wilson insisted these words be cut out from the published version of the report. 'There are previous references to the peace-time basis,' he explained, 'and I do not see any point in rubbing it in quite so much. Repetition rather invites comment that it might be a good thing to put the country on a war footing and we do not want to do that just yet.'

On March 31, two weeks after Hitler occupied Prague, Chamberlain gave a guarantee to Poland, explaining to his sister: 'It was unprovocative in tone, but firm, clear but stressing the point (perceived alone by *The Times*) that what we are concerned with is not the boundaries of States but attacks on their independence. And it is we who will judge whether this independence is threatened or not.' That summer Chamberlain put pressure on Poland to make concessions to Germany over Danzig. 'If Dictators would have a modicum of patience,' he wrote to his sister on July 15, 'I can imagine that a way could be found of meeting German claims while safeguarding Poland's independence and economic security.' On July 23 Chamberlain told his sister why pressure was being put on Poland: 'I heard last week that Hitler had told Herr Forster the Danzig Nazi Leader that he was going to damp down the agitation. True the German claim that Danzig should be incorporated in the Reich was to be maintained but that could wait until next year or even longer. Meanwhile the city would

be demilitarized and the press muzzled but particular stress was
laid on the necessity for secrecy at present and for restraint on
the Polish side. Accordingly we sent all sorts of warnings to the
Poles accompanied by exhortations to let nothing leak out.'

Chamberlain then explained his wider hopes: 'One thing is I
think clear namely that Hitler has concluded that we mean
business and that the time is not ripe for the major war. Therein
he is fulfilling my expectations. Unlike some of my critics I go
further and say the longer the war is put off the less likely it is
to come at all as we go on perfecting our defences and building
up the defences of our allies. That is what Winston and Co.
never seem to realise. You don't need offensive forces sufficient
to win a smashing victory. What you want are defensive forces
sufficiently strong to make it impossible for the other side to win
except at such a cost to make it not worthwhile. That is what
we are doing and though at present the German feeling is it is
not worth while yet they will presently come to realise that it
never will be worthwhile, then we can talk.'

British pressure on Poland failed. As German demands intensified, Britain's guarantee was turned into a Treaty. Last-minute
British efforts to secure Polish concessions were rebuffed by the
Poles. Nor had Hitler been persuaded to talk as a result of
Britain 'perfecting' its defences. On September 1 he invaded
Poland. Britain issued an ultimatum calling on him to halt or
face war with Britain. On the following day Chamberlain went
to the Commons and spoke of the possibility of further negotiations. 'If the German Government should agree to withdraw
their forces,' he said, 'then His Majesty's Government would be
willing to regard the position as being the same as it was before
the German forces crossed the Polish frontier.' If German troops
withdrew 'the way would be open to discussions' between
Germany and Poland, discussions with which the British Government would be 'willing to be associated'.

Hitler's troops drove on to Warsaw.

MARTIN GILBERT
RICHARD GOTT
January 2000

Foreword to the First Edition

THIS IS a history of British policy towards Nazi Germany, and of the men who supported and opposed it. It shows in some detail how British policy was formed, how it was carried out, and why it was misconceived, in the light of warnings received at the time from trained diplomats like Vansittart, Rumbold, and Kennard; and from experienced politicians like Amery, Eden, and Duff Cooper. British policy, far from appeasing Hitler, showed him that the British Government were willing to come to terms with him at the expense of other nations. It is our intention to show what the appeasers sought, and what methods they were prepared to use in order to attain their ends.

We have given prominence to certain aspects of British policy which have not been widely studied. Colonial and economic appeasement are two such aspects. Anglo-French dissension is another. So too are the continual and often bitter conflicts within the Government and Cabinet, and the widespread fear of Communism that heavily weighted the scales in favor of a pro-German policy.

We have consulted the available diplomatic documents. The pre-war decade is perhaps better documented than any other period in modern British history. The official documents are readily available. We have also used memoirs, biographies and private papers. At the end of the book are biographical sketches which contain details of the careers of the leading appeasers and their opponents.

Those who supported appeasement after October, 1938, did so for two reasons. Munich "bought" a year of peace, in which to rearm. It brought "a united nation" into war, by showing

XV

Hitler's wickedness beyond doubt. Both these reasons were put forward by the Government, and accepted by many who could not check them. Both were false.

If a year had been gained in which Chamberlain could have strengthened Britain's defences and equipped the country for an offensive war, there should be evidence of growing strength, growing effort, and growing Cabinet unity. But while some members of the Government sought to use the "bought" year, others did not. Chamberlain and his closest advisers were unwilling to allow the Minister of War, Hore-Belisha, to introduce conscription. The Air Minister, Kingsley Wood, failed to achieve the needed air parity with Germany. Machines were not lacking. Will-power was. Germany, not Britain, gained militarily during the extra year. German forces were strengthened by Czech munitions, western forces weakened by the loss of the Czech Army and Air Force.

Munich showed the Soviet Union that western resolve could be broken. By sacrificing Czechoslovakia, democracies had sacrificed one of their number. In England the First Lord of the Admiralty, Duff Cooper, resigned. He saw the moral as well as the military implications of the "betrayal." In 1938 France had been willing to fight. But again and again Chamberlain poured scorn on this willingness, and forced Daladier to accept British policy. In the "bought" year, French courage failed. Britain, having abandoned Anglo-French interests once, could abandon them again. France lapsed into defeatism.

Chamberlain and his advisers did not go to Munich because they needed an extra year before they could fight. They did not use the year to arouse national enthusiasm for a just war. The aim of appeasement was to avoid war, not to enter war united. Appeasement was a looking forward to better times, not to worse. Even after the German occupation of Prague, Chamberlain and those closest to him hoped that better times would come, and that Anglo-German relations would improve. They gave the pledge to Poland, not with enthusiasm, but with embarrassment. They wanted to befriend Germany, not anger her.

Firm public statements were disavowed in private. The Germans were told there would be peace. Chamberlain fought against time, and asked the Germans to help him. He wanted an Anglo-German agreement *before* public passion made one impossible. His efforts, between Munich and the invasion of Poland, were made to avoid war, and to convince the Germans that if they accepted British friendship, great would be the benefits to both nations. Chamberlain wanted to solve first the Czech, then the Polish problems, so that the field would be clear to solve Anglo-German problems. He wanted to be on good terms with Germany, not to defend Czechoslovakia or Poland. He had little sympathy with either small nation. With Germany he sought closer bonds. Sometimes he and his advisers spoke of the possibility of an Anglo-German alliance. This was their dream. Anglo-German co-operation, they hoped, would touch every aspect of life—political, economic, imperial. The appeasers failed because in 1939 parliamentary pressure forced them into war in defence of Poland, and in 1940 removed them from office. They neither declared war, nor left office, willingly. War delayed the chances of Anglo-German agreement; May, 1940 destroyed them. Appeasement had been an attempt to move closer to Germany, despite German domestic brutality and eastward expansion. It failed. We have shown how serious the appeasers were, and how they nearly succeeded.

Much of our material comes from the *Documents on British Foreign Policy, 1919-1939*, edited by E. L. Woodward and Rohan Butler. These documents, published after the war, contain the letters and telegrams which the Foreign Secretary sent to his Ambassadors abroad, and the replies and reports which they sent home. This publication is one of the most remarkable windfalls that has come into the hands of the historian. It gives a clear and detailed picture of the working of the Foreign Office day by day, often hour by hour. It contains a much fuller selection of documents than the comparable *Origins of the War, 1898-1914,* edited by G. P. Gooch and Harold Temperley. It lacks the minutes written by Foreign Office officials on various dispatches, and contains no inter-departmental communications. But in Woodward and Butler's volumes we have an excellent collection of documents.

In England official documents cannot be seen by historians until fifty years after they have been written. For this reason, material not published in Woodward and Butler is closed to the public gaze. But even in England, there are whispers, carbon copies, and individual memories. No law can lock away what a man remembers. Some of our material is from sources which cannot be revealed. Only when the fifty-year rule allows, or when it is swept away, will the documents be officially, and legally, available. What we offer here without source we offer on trust.

In implementing his foreign policy, Neville Chamberlain did not always use the Foreign Office. The threads of British policy must therefore be taken up in the *Documents on German Foreign Policy, 1918-1945,* edited by a number of American, British, and French historians. These volumes often reveal details of Anglo-German meetings of which no record was sent to the Foreign Office. Among these are the meetings which Chamberlain's *éminence grise,* Sir Horace Wilson, had with German diplomats, politicians, and officials.

We have drawn on memoirs, biographies and private papers. Most good memoirs contain not only emotions recollected in tranquillity but also the *actual words* written or spoken at the time: in the Cabinet, at private meetings, in letters and in diaries. On its own a memoir illustrates only a few isolated incidents. Combined with documentary evidence memoirs show something closer to reality. There comes a time when enough is known to begin. The story we have pieced together ought to be known.

MARTIN GILBERT
RICHARD GOTT

PART ONE

There could have been no greater misfortune for England than that the period of inactivity which was superintended by Lord Baldwin should have so perfectly resembled in outward appearance that period which would have been a necessary preliminary to her regeneration . . . But the quietness lasted too long. The new forces did not emerge. The obsolete party did not mean to yield power. On the contrary, it gripped the nation's throat with a tenacity that was terrifying, for it pertained to another realm than life. For the grip of a living man must relax if he grow tired; it is only ghostly hands that, without term, can continue to clench. But these were not honest ghosts, for had they been such they would have re-enacted the pomp of Elizabeth's power, even if the dust lay thin on the national stage; they would have repeated the imperturbable insolence of Victoria, even if the words came hollow from the fleshless thorax. They were, however, as much strangers to all tradition of English pride as though they were alien in blood . . .

— REBECCA WEST
Black Lamb and Grey Falcon

CHAPTER 1

The Birth of Appeasement: 1933

THE GREAT WAR ended in 1918. The slaughter on the battle-fields, which had lasted four years, had been greater than any since the seventeenth century. In London and Paris the desire for revenge increased with each year of the war. Lloyd George believed the war "had poisoned the mind of mankind with suspicions, resentments, misunderstandings and fears."[1] The Treaty of Versailles embodied all these. It cut back Germany's frontiers in the east; it forbade German union with Austria in the south; it demilitarized a large industrial area in the west. It brought the German army and navy to an end and imposed severe conditions to prevent their being built up again. It took away all Germany's colonies, and gave them as mandates to Britain, France, Japan, South Africa, New Zealand, and Australia. Germany agreed to pay a large cash indemnity.[2] The legacy of the Treaty was bitterness in Germany, and a sense of guilt in Britain.

J. M. Keynes said the Treaty was filled with clauses "which might impoverish Germany now or obstruct her development in future."[3] Many Englishmen read, and accepted, his criticisms. Ashamed of what they had done, they looked for scapegoats, and for amendment. The scapegoat was France; the amendment was appeasement. The harshness of the Treaty was ascribed to French folly. But nobody could deny that Britain had supported France. France was blamed for having encouraged Britain in an excess of punishment. Justice could only be done by helping Germany to take her rightful place in Europe as a Great Power.

Appeasers turned to Germany with outstretched arm, hoping for a handshake. But the Germans hesitated. The war had embittered them too. They believed Britain was as responsible as France for asserting their "war-guilt." The British denied that the Treaty contained an accusation of German guilt; but denial was not enough. The more reluctant Germany proved to accept an Anglo-German *rapprochement*, the guiltier the appeasers felt. They wanted German friendship, and resented Germany's unwillingness to consider it. During the years of the Weimar Republic, Germany's internal troubles prevented a closer link between the two countries, each a parliamentary democracy, each unwilling to accept the political uncertainty that democracy entailed. By 1933, the alternation of Left and Right in Britain seemed to have ended. Many assumed that the National Government, dominated by Conservatives, would be in power for many years. And in 1933 German instability was also coming to an end.

The year 1933 introduced a new régime to Europe. Its doctrine and first public acts were autocratic. Its form was not new. The collapse of parliamentary government had already taken place eleven years earlier in Italy, seven years earlier in Poland. Bulgaria, Hungary and Portugal had likewise abandoned democratic forms. Knowledge of how dictators worked was widespread, for dictatorship had become something of a commonplace in post-war Europe. Its violence was feared; its efficiency admired.

There was no unanimous response in England to the growing brutality of European politics. England had been wise in her history and had thrown off the despotism of an alien church and autocratic and unsuitable kings. These battles were over. The passions that directed them were no longer understood. Men need strong stirrings within them before they challenge the existing order. European conflicts were less tragic for being far away; other men's tears aroused resentment as often as sympathy.

Once the excitement and confusion of British intervention in Russia and the Middle East had passed, Englishmen sought a quieter life. Germany had been the old enemy, the evil spirit across no-man's-land, the destroyer of English youth. When the war had ended men talked of hanging the Kaiser. But the mood of anger passed. Forgiveness was a Christian virtue; hatred was not. Germany lay on many consciences. Her defeat in war had been just; it was wrong to crush her further.

Keynes explained the folly of the Treaty, and criticized both the way it had been drawn up and the restrictions it imposed.[4] Whether the appeasers read his books with any particular care is difficult to discover. But it mattered little whether they knew his actual words or arguments. They needed no professor to show them that Versailles had been unduly severe. Appeasement was an affair of the heart, intuitive, not taught; a strong emotion, not an academic speculation.

Europe had been the center of English thought for almost a decade before 1914. When the war ended Englishmen tried to forget continental quarrels and edged towards the pre-war "posture" of isolation. But the nation against whom so much effort had been spent could not be ignored. Attitudes hardened, some in the direction of further hostility towards Germany, others in the direction of friendship. Hugh Dalton said Englishmen were divided in their prejudices. "Some became stupidly anti-French; others stupidly anti-Russian; others reverted to a sentimental pro-Germanism, based on some myth of special kinships or national resemblance, or in the sporting habit of a handshake after a fight." [5] The appeasers were pro-German. They turned to Germany in hopeful mood, hoping by their own honesty to make the Germans honest. They wanted Anglo-German relations to be close and friendly. Appeasement was an attitude of mind rooted in pro-Germanism. It was both moral and realistic. It was close to Christian sentiments of fair play and forgiveness. It was often arrogant, but not always sentimental. For the appeasers it was the height of "realism" to criticize the Versailles Treaty, and to show that all Germany's grievances in the 1930's sprang from the injustices of that Treaty. It was "practical politics" to advocate Treaty revision in Germany's favor. Englishmen should abandon the wicked mood which blamed all European tensions on Germany. Germany made wild demands; it was the duty of Englishmen to realize that those demands were reasonable, however wildly put forward. Lord Lothian* wrote that "the root of the present difficulty is that the Germans have got a case, but nobody is really willing to make the concessions necessary to meet their claims." [6]

Reluctance to meet German claims was widespread in England. The stronger it became, the more the appeasers sought to erase it. Some of their enemies were the anti-Germans to whom it was immaterial whether the German Government were overtly democratic or dictatorial. Such historical hatreds were common; the Eyre Crowe tradition in the Foreign Office lived on. Nazism was grist to its mill. The mill ground on regardless of political changes. Sir Robert Vansittart, very much a "professional" anti-German, explained that it was not only Nazism that he disliked. He did not hate all Germans: only "the bloody-minded bulk." [7]

Dislike of Germany sprang from the Nazi record, as well as from attitudes rooted in the past and incapable of moderation. Anti-Germanism and pro-Germanism had practical as well as sentimental origins. Appeasers ignored the Nazi record, and made Anglo-German relations seem more capable of successful evolution than the record gave reason to suggest. Many were revolted by stories of Nazi brutality. But those who considered Anglo-German friendship a vital interest were willing to close their eyes to excesses. Such men sought excuses for the barbarism of 1933, and tried to move closer to Germany in the years that followed. Sometimes the evils of the new régime were condoned, sometimes ignored, sometimes wished away. Like alcohol, pro-Germanism dulled the senses of those who overindulged, and many English diplomats, politicians and men of influence insisted upon interpreting German developments in such a way as to suggest patterns of co-operation that did not

* For details of Lord Lothian's career, see Biographical Sketches at the end of the book.

exist. Only by ignoring what was happening in Germany could those patterns be found.

Those who regarded Anglo-German friendship as possible were optimists. They sought to ignore the lessons of the past. Those who regarded that friendship as desirable, and were prepared to sacrifice common sense for the sake of their desire, were appeasers. Appeasement was a passion which ignored the rules, for it sought to create new ones.* It saw the possibility of European peace and prosperity arising out of Anglo-German cooperation. Appeasement sprang from sympathy, as well as from fear. Often it was the sympathy of men in a slow, sluggish society for the dynamism of autocracy. Mussolini had already been admired for his firm, progessive rule:[8] a rule impossible within a democratic framework. Sympathy thus aroused for Mussolini's Italy could easily be transferred to Hitler's Germany. It was a sympathy that sought more than a casual friendship. Co-operation is of value only when it produces results. The appeasers hoped for widespread and lasting results once they had won Germany's favor.

Nazi Germany was new, active, outspoken; a nation which had emerged from defeat, and economic and social chaos. It sought inner discipline and external power. German power in Europe attracted the appeasers. A strong Germany would prevent the spread of communism in Europe. It would help create a European economic bloc with which it would be an advantage to trade. Britain through her overseas empire, Germany in Europe would make common cause. America was too isolationist to be an ally; Russia was poisoned by communism. Germany's revolution had made her friendship suddenly worthwhile.

Many Englishmen knew less of communism than they knew

---

* Many knew what these rules were. Sir Harold Nicolson told the Commons on October 5, 1938: "For 250 years at least the great foundation of our foreign policy, what Sir Eyre Crowe called 'a law of Nature,' has been to prevent by every means in our power the domination of Europe by any single Power or group of Powers. That principle has necessarily had the corollary that we shall always support the Small Powers against the strong."

of Nazism. Fears thrived on ignorance. Even when Germany was at war with England, a prominent philosopher could write that he had "no doubt that the Soviet Government is even worse than Hitler's, and it will be a misfortune if it survives." [9] Wise men as well as appeasers saw communism as the greater menace. For the appeaser Anglo-German friendship was an essential counterweight to the harmful influence of Russia. With Russia went France. These two powers, by their prewar alliance, had helped lead Europe into war in 1914. If such a combination were repeated, England would be no partner to it.

Lothian told Eden, the Foreign Secretary, in 1936, that Britain must abandon the "policy of drift" which France and Russia were supporting in order to deny Germany her rightful position in Europe; a position "to which she is entitled by her history, her civilization and her power." Russia and France wanted to maintain an "overwhelmingly military alliance" against Germany. Britain should have nothing to do with it. Instead, it was our duty to help the Germans to "escape from encirclement to a position of balance." [10]

Appeasement was a call to action. The appeasers hoped for new alliances to replace the old, and for Anglo-German co-operation to break the pro-French "bias" that still survived in high places. Lothian knew Anglo-German co-operation would annoy many members of the Foreign Office. It was an annoyance he wished upon them. For he regretted that they were "pledged to the French view of European politics," a view he abhorred.[11]

If Germany was to be won for friendship, France's friendship must be discarded. Dislike of France ran deep in English life: Lothian was not alone. He often dined at Cliveden, the home of Lord and Lady Astor. Lady Astor was known to be "obsessed with a vivid personal dislike of the French." [12] It was a dislike shared by her circle: by Thomas Jones, the close friend of Baldwin, by Lloyd George, and by Barrington-Ward, who wrote many of The Times' leaders on foreign policy.

While Germany gained a new master and a new discipline in

1933, France remained slovenly, excitable, under the influence of left-wing politicians. "Rather Hitler than Blum" — the cry had many English supporters. German excesses there indeed were, but French weakness was as great a crime. It was a weakness the communists could exploit; a weakness which offered a chance of power to the agents of Moscow. A deal with France would be a deal with danger. But the Germans were wiser and stronger, and anti-communism was a leading point in Hitler's program.

Where the Nazi program was violent, Germany was not alone to blame.* It was England who had helped to drive Germany into confusion and anarchy, by agreeing with France to the severe terms of Versailles. By a policy of understanding and conciliation England could remedy her fault. A sense of guilt drove the appeasers into a one-sided relationship with Germany, in which Germany was always to be given the benefit of the doubt. Hitler's outbursts were not treated as the ravings of a wicked man: they were the understandable complaints of a man who had been wronged. He was a man who had been a wild revolutionary, but now, in power, he had surely acquired the responsibility that comes with power. He was older now, and had long mixed with statesmen. With age and wise companions, there is always maturity and moderation.

Diplomats challenged the appeasers from the first weeks of the Hitler régime. They denied that the Germans would make excellent friends, or allies. Two months after Hitler had come to power Sir Horace Rumbold, British Ambassador in Berlin, reported that the Nazis were cowing the population.[13] "Prominent adherents of the Left" had been forced to flee for refuge "to places on or beyond the frontier."[14] The new government had brought to the surface "the worst traits in German character,

---

* Lothian wrote in 1939: "I do not think it possible to understand British policy without realizing the fact that a great many people including, I think, Mr. Chamberlain, felt that the internal persecution in Germany was in great part the result of the denial to Germany of the rights which every other sovereign nation claims." (Quoted in J. R. M. Butler: Lord Lothian.)

i.e. a mean spirit of revenge, a tendency to brutality, and a noisy and irresponsible jingoism." [15]

Rumbold saw everything. It was said of him: *"Malgré sa mine idiote, c'est un homme intelligent."* [16] Curzon had once described him as "not alert enough for Berlin"; but, as Sir Robert Vansittart noted, "little escaped him, and his warnings were clearer than anything we got later." [17] Those warnings were indeed persistent. Rumbold informed Vansittart that Brüning, a former Chancellor, had "thought it wiser to change his quarters when he learned that a man resembling him had been attacked in the street." Brüning's caution was not unwarranted, said the Ambassador, for although reports of atrocities might be exaggerated, it was undeniable "that a great deal of injustice has been done." There was no sense in minimizing the nastiness of events. Rumbold informed the Foreign Office:

> The departure from Germany of so many writers, artists, musicians, and political leaders has created for the moment a kind of vacuum, for whatever may have been the shortcomings of the Democratic parties, they numbered among their following the intellectual life of the capital and nearly all that was original and stimulating in the world of art and letters.[18]

The future was uncertain. It was rumored in Berlin that Hitler might call back the ex-Emperor, William II, from his exile in Holland. Rumbold hardly knew. "Stranger things might come to pass," he commented.[19]

Rumbold was shocked by the anti-semitic policy of the new régime. He reported that Jews were being "systematically removed from their posts" throughout the public services. Disabilities were the result of "the accident of race." [20] Nor was it Jews alone against whom the hatred of the régime was set. Social Democrats, Communists, and non-political critics of Nazi policy, were likewise deprived of both work and liberty. Rumbold was aware that "large concentration camps were being established in various parts of the country." [21]

The observer in Berlin could not avoid seeing the terror in the streets, or hearing of the fate of those whose views, or whose race, had turned the régime against them. In England the stories of brutality were listened to with a certain incredulity. London, awakening to a gentle spring, hoping for a restful summer, refused to believe eyewitnesses. Rumbold lamented that "foreign opinion does not appear to have fully grasped the fact that the National-Socialist party programme is intensely Anti-Jewish." It was neither a brief nor passing phenomenon. "The imposition of further disabilities . . . must therefore be anticipated, for it is certainly Hitler's intention to degrade, and if possible expel the Jewish community from Germany." [22]

Liberty of the individual was an easy ideal, but like many ideals it flourished mainly in an abstract world. To speak of Jewish disabilities was not always to evoke disgust. The Jews were an unsympathetic, unloved people, and their presence in the capitals of Europe was frequently resented. They were uncouth, loud-mouthed, "flashy," alien. They interfered in government and grew rich in trade at other men's expense. When Europe learned how Germans reviled them, it often laughed. Even England was not free from anti-semitism. Terror could be ridiculed, even if it could not be minimized. Dislike, as well as laughter, accompanied the anti-semitic jokes of Western Europe. Not all Hitler's criticisms of Jews were discounted as absurd. Rumbold hated the anti-semitism of the new Germany; other Englishmen were less certain in their condemnation.

Gilbert Murray learned from an acquaintance that "as for the Jews, I begin with no aprioristic ideas on this point; but experience has more and more taught me that they are in some peculiar and exceptional way a pernicious element in any country of the West . . . I understand perfectly the German attitude towards these people, and I approve it fully." [23] Lord Londonderry, a former Minister for Air, wrote to Ribbentrop in 1936: "As I told you, I have no great affection for the Jews. It is possible to trace their participation in most of those International disturbances which have created so much havoc in different countries." [24]

Londonderry went on to admit the existence of good Jews, as well as "malevolent and mischievous" ones. But his admission came after his condemnation. Such welcome words lay on Ribbentrop's table, and encouraged him to believe that many upper-class Englishmen were as sensible as the Irish Lord. Through private channels the Germans frequently learned that Englishmen did not really oppose their aims, even if their methods were causing concern. Nazi aims were praised, according to Hoesch, the German Ambassador in London, even by the clergy, some of whom had expressed "boundless admiration for the moral and ethical side of the National-Socialist programme, its clear cut stand for religion and Christianity and its ethical principles, such as its fight against cruelty to animals, vivisection, sexual offences etc." [25]

Nazis behaved with violence and brutality. Yet such methods were neither new to postwar Europe, nor regarded with automatic hostility. Gilbert Murray, a man of conscience and far-sightedness, pleaded in a public speech in October for the widest possible liberty of the individual within the confines of the state.[26] A friend reminded him that people seemed "astonishingly ready to forget" the need for liberty. "If a Dictator of any type seizes power and continues to crush opposition, the methods and consequences of his tyranny are airily dismissed." [27]

Rumbold did not tolerate attempts to whitewash the régime. He had made up his mind that it was evil, and repeated his views in every dispatch. For him:

> One of the most inhuman features of the present campaign is the incarceration without trial of thousands of individuals whose political antecedents have rendered them obnoxious in the eyes of the new régime. The establishment of concentration camps . . . on a wholesale scale is a new departure in civilized countries.[28]

One of Rumbold's dispatches gave so vivid a picture of how the parliamentary régime had been replaced by one of "brute force" that it was shown to the Prime Minister, Ramsay MacDonald, and circulated to the Cabinet.[29] Rumbold made two main assertions. By reading *Mein Kampf*, he claimed, the evils of the régime were easily forecast. Nor were those evils to be perpetrated for a day. They would be repeated again and again, without modification. Rumbold quoted from *Mein Kampf* to prove his points. Hitler, he insisted, was not a moderate man.

An expert on German affairs, J. Wheeler-Bennett, had disagreed. Speaking to a gathering in London in April he said:

> Hitler, I am convinced, does not want war. He is susceptible to reason in matters of foreign policy. He is greatly anxious to make Germany once more self-respecting and is himself anxious to be respectable. He may be described as the most moderate member of his party.[30]

It was only during question time after the talk that it was revealed that Wheeler-Bennett had not as yet read *Mein Kampf*.[31] Had he done so, he might still have asserted that Hitler's foreign policy would be pacific, at least for some years. But he could hardly have attributed moderation to the author in internal affairs.*

Rumbold was uncompromising on foreign policy. For him the régime would prove as aggressive abroad as it had already shown itself at home. Even before he met Hitler he wrote, "Germany's neighbours have reason to be vigilant." He claimed that the need for vigilance was urgent. Hitler would turn against his neighbors "sooner than they may have contemplated." Hitler, he wrote, was an extremist, in complete control of his party. Attempts to divide him from his fellow revolutionaries were bound to fail, being based on a total misconception of the nature of Nazi power.[32] Rumbold's attitude hardened even further after he met Hitler. He no longer doubted "that Herr Hitler is himself

---

* Wheeler-Bennett soon became one of the most informed and outspoken critics of Nazism. He was also a stern critic of appeasement.

responsible for the anti-Jewish policy . . . it would be a mistake to believe that it is the policy of his wilder men whom he has difficulty in controlling." [33] /

Rumbold was in Berlin during the first five months of Hitler's rule. The forceful tone of his many dispatches echoed in the Foreign Office in London. Nor was it from Rumbold alone that warnings came. At Geneva the Disarmament Conference was in session; and from Geneva came the reports of delegates who, having wrangled long and acrimoniously *before* January, 1933, found themselves confronted, in the first months of the new year, with a Germany even less willing to reach agreement than they themselves had been earlier.

The German grievance was an easy one to understand, and found many sympathizers. Lord Lothian defended it in *Round Table;*[34] *The Times* gave it good coverage. Germany could hardly be expected to promise not to arm further, when she had no arms whatever. Only once she had *re*armed would it be either feasible or just to ask her to *dis*arm. If Germany were allowed to rearm, this would give her an "equality" that would enable her to sit without any sense of weakness or inferiority at the Disarmament Conference. As Lothian wrote to a friend: "The first condition to reform (inside Germany) is that we should be willing to do justice to Germany." Equality in arms would be such justice.[35]

Philip Conwell-Evans, a Welshman who lectured at Königsberg University, told Gilbert Murray that "Germany's claims must be satisfied, and then we can begin to build up a new cooperation between the nations." But if Germany were denied equality there would be trouble. It was wrong to expect the Germans to "adopt the virtual Quaker philosophy of life while other nations rely on the tank and the big guns." [36] Gilbert Murray was worried by Conwell-Evans' argument. He thought that there was a flaw somewhere, though it seemed reasonable on the surface. Murray replied that the Nazi Government "make a pride of refusing to co-operate, and . . . are besides in a wild state of emotion."[37] He thought it was impossible to discount that wildness when talking of arms equality.

A. C. Temperley, one of the English delegates at the Disarmament Conference, insisted that disarmament was impossible while Germany continued to rearm. No conference would stand for it. In a memorandum in May, 1933, Temperley asked: "What then is to be our attitude? Can we too go forward as if nothing has happened? Can we afford to ignore what is going on behind the scenes in Germany?" His answer was — no. Germany should be urged to stop all military preparations, and told that if she refused to do so, Britain would use force against her. In Temperley's opinion the "hint of force" would be enough to call Germany's bluff. It *was* a bluff.

> She is powerless, before the French army and our fleet. Hitler, for all his bombast, must give way. Strong concerted action . . . should prove decisive, even though the threat of military pressure might have to be maintained for years, calling for fresh monetary sacrifices, until Germany is brought to her senses . . . There is a mad dog abroad once more and we must resolutely combine either to ensure its destruction or at least its confinement until the disease has run its course.[38]

This was the strongest action that could be demanded. It assumed that if Germany were allowed to rearm she would one day seek the mastery of Europe. It was a view supported by all "anti-Germans."

Vansittart, the most vociferous of anti-Germans, was Permanent Under-Secretary for Foreign Affairs. He noted "his entire agreement" with Temperley's memorandum. Cadogan, who later succeeded Vansittart, considered it "of the utmost importance and interest." It was shown to Eden, and then, on Vansittart's advice, circulated to the Cabinet. Vansittart said it was read in the Cabinet "to no effect."[39] The Foreign Office took it more seriously. Allen Leeper, to whom it had originally been sent, was himself anxious to expose Germany's clandestine rearmament, and to urge the French and British Governments to combine in doing so. What better moment, suggested Leeper, than at the Disarmament Conference itself? After the German representative had made one of his speeches "in the best Hitlerian manner" expounding Germany's peaceful intention, the British and French representatives "should stand up one after another" and denounce the German rearmament. The breach of the Versailles Treaty which this involved should be brought before the League of Nations. Leeper realized this was a "sensational step" to propose. But without it, he claimed, the Disarmament Conference would "drift to its certain death," and Germany would continue to rearm.[40] Leeper's remedy was an extreme one. But the events he forecast soon took place. In December, 1933, Germany walked out of the Conference, and her rearming, though much denied, continued.*

In June, 1933, Rumbold reached the age of retirement, and wrote his last dispatch from Berlin. Vansittart discussed it with Sir John Simon, the Foreign Secretary, who said it would be "of great and permanent value to His Majesty's Government in determining their policy towards Germany."[41] Rumbold stressed the abnormality and probable permanence of Nazism. Hitler, Göring and Goebbels were three "notoriously pathological cases . . . One looks in vain for any men of real worth" among the leaders. The German domestic scene had passed out of control; wisdom would no longer guide it. "The average German does not appear to possess a true sense of proportion." Rumbold viewed the future

---

* J. H. Herring, the British Air Attaché in Berlin, sat next to the wife of an important German air official at the Tempelhof air display, hoping to see, in the display itself, some indication of the illegal rearmament program. Not the display, however, but the lady, gave him his clue.

The lady did not appear to be very interested in the proceedings, and, in an attempt at relieving the tedium, I pointed to the new Heinkel and Junkers *express postal aircraft* and said: "those are two of the newest types in Germany." She turned slowly to her husband and, still slightly bored, said: "Oh those will be two of the new *single-seater fighters*, I suppose." (Brit. Docs. Series 2, vol. V, no. 127, Note 1. May 10, 1933.)

with great uneasiness and apprehension . . . it would be misleading to base any hopes on a return to sanity . . . Unpleasant incidents and excesses are bound to occur during a revolution, but the
deliberate ruthlessness and brutality which have been practised
during the last five months seem both excessive and unnecessary.
I have the impression that the persons directing the policy of the
Hitler Government are not normal. Many of us, indeed, have a
feeling that we are living in a country where fantastic hooligans
and eccentrics have got the upper hand.[42]

Rumbold had not always been so outspoken, though he had always reported his opinions more fully than most diplomats. During a diplomatic career of forty-one years he had been little prone
to emotional outbursts, and was noted for his "apparent bland-
ness." [43] But he had an alert and critical mind. He had mastered
Arabic and Japanese as well as German, and sought as profound
an understanding of the nations he knew as of their languages.
He had been an "assiduous reporter" for the Foreign Office, and
within his own embassies had organized Embassy Press surveys
"day in and day out." Wise men can be violent when provoked,
and their violence is more valuable for being well-grounded. "In
the long run the Nazis both upset and angered him;" [44] it was
the anger of a man who refused to treat the Germans in any
arrogant spirit, but who refused equally firmly to fawn on them.

Rumbold left Berlin. His Third Secretary, Duncan Sandys,
returned to the Foreign Office in London, to work under Ralph
Wigram in the Central Department. What Sandys had seen in
Berlin convinced him of the need for a positive British policy.
Sandys was too junior for his opinions to carry much weight,
yet he wanted to be heard. He knew that any minutes he might
write upon an incoming dispatch could be read, not only by the
Permanent Head of the Foreign Office, Vansittart, but also by
the Foreign Secretary, Sir John Simon. Sandys decided to take
action. A dispatch from Berlin late in 1933 provided him with
his opportunity. On it he expressed, at some length, the fears
that had been troubling him.[45]

The Government, wrote Sandys, must think ahead. The Rhineland was clearly a potential problem. The Germans, when they felt strong enough to do so, would seek to re-militarize it. Britain and France must decide what their attitude would be when Hitler's troops marched into the Rhineland. If we intended to do nothing, it was better to concede the point to the Germans before they took it from us. If this were handled properly, some *quid pro quo* might be obtained. But if the Western Allies were determined to resist re-militarization they should make their determination quite clear to the Germans. They should also work out some plan of action with France, should Germany decide to move. A firm stand by the British and French Governments would impress the Germans, and deter them. The absence of any agreed plan for joint Anglo-French action would encourage the Germans to take advantage of Western indecision.

Sandys was a realist, not a visionary. He saw the danger into which Britain would fall: the danger of not knowing its own mind, and of not concerting action with the French. It was French troops who would have to be ready to cross the frontier the moment Hitler's troops crossed the Rhine.

Simon was unimpressed by Sandys' farsightedness. It was not in his nature to try to anticipate events. He commented drily on Sandys' minute: "We cannot consider hypothetical issues." [45]

Realizing that he could not hope to exercise any influence from his lowly position inside the Government machine, Sandys resigned from the Foreign Office, at the age of twenty-five, and made up his mind to enter politics. Wigram knew Sandys was right to go. "I wish I'd done it long ago," he told Sandys. "I left it too long." [45] Wigram remained in the German Department, and tried to infuse the Foreign Office with a sense of urgency.

In Vansittart, Wigram had a powerful ally.

Vansittart never ceased to condemn the inner workings of Nazism. He deplored the growing English tendency to divorce

German domestic brutality from possible aggression abroad. Nazism, he claimed, knew no such division.

> From the very outset of the régime I have felt, with all deference to those who with more sweet reasonableness were disposed for at least a little to wait and see, that there was no doubt whatever about the ultimate intentions of the Nazis . . . It is an open secret that anything peaceful said by Hitler is merely for foreign consumption and designed to gain time . . . Nothing but a change of heart can avert another catastrophe; and that change of the German heart is unlikely to come from within, for the true German nature has never changed.[46]

Here was crude racialism. Though it offended many, it found sympathizers. Churchill had gone as far as informing the German Press Attaché in London that there was only one possible solution of the "German problem." "If," said Churchill, "a mad dog makes a dash for my trousers, I shoot him down before he can bite." [47] The Attaché, Fritz Hesse, looked elsewhere for the pro-German sentiment which he felt it his duty to foster. Unwisely, he approached Vansittart, who was "a little taken aback" when told that Hesse intended "to work for a better understanding between Germany and England." Vansittart replied:

> But my dear Mr. Hesse, you will not be able to prevent the war . . . Hitler wants to make Germany the first power in Europe. I think our information on this subject is correct. We shall certainly try to get him to abandon this policy, but I fear we shan't succeed.[48]

Hesse's disappointment was short-lived. The evils of Nazism had not turned all Englishmen into implacable enemies of Germany. Its chief success had been to confirm old enemies in their prejudices. But it was one thing to confirm and strengthen well-established prejudices; another to destroy the faith and hope of would-be friends.

Appeasement was a search for friendship; an unwillingness to pass hurried judgment; a desire to make the best of difficult times by offering the hand of friendship. Baldwin, who succeeded MacDonald as Prime Minister, told Hoesch that England was "entirely willing to continue to work closely even with a Germany under the new order." [49] The past history of Germany must be taken into account. As Lord Londonderry told an audience at Newcastle, Germans "have passed through a tribulation which we have never known. We should receive in no niggardly spirit the offers made to the world by Herr Hitler." It was wrong of Englishmen to "refuse to believe in the sincerity of Germany." [50]

The desire to be fair to Germany was often endangered by German actions. Nazi brutality offended the upholders of the liberal democratic tradition. Basil Newton, who was in charge of the Berlin Embassy until the arrival of Rumbold's successor, tried to *explain* German actions where Rumbold had condemned them. "German susceptibilities" should be borne in mind, he wrote, before German policy was criticized too sharply.[51] Sharp criticism would arouse only hostility, and a hostile Germany would be less amenable to reason than one which had not been offended. Newton's desire to be objective revealed the gulf between plain speaking and diplomacy. Rumbold, speaking his mind, had failed as a diplomat, however much he had succeeded as an observer. Vansittart had been criticized, by Baldwin, because he "hates the Germans." Baldwin's friend Thomas Jones had agreed that "diplomats should have nothing to do with hatred of anybody. It is both silly and dangerous." [52]

Although to be too outspoken was to incur, as Vansittart had done, the hostility of enemies and the embarrassment of friends, there was an equal danger in keeping silent. By being too cautious, and too eager to excuse German actions, diplomats lost the power of influence through criticism which was, even in diplomacy, a real power. Halfhearted censure and timid praise only encouraged Hitler to disregard what criticism there was from England. At the same time, he lulled the English into a drowsy if not uncritical acceptance of him and his régime. At every interview he gave he described himself as a moderate man, spoke of his liking for England, and dangled before his listener the most succulent fruit of all, an Anglo-German *rapprochement*. There it was for the asking. It could be picked with evident ease. Many who saw it were tempted to eat. "Rightly or wrongly," wrote Jones, "all sorts of people who have met Hitler are convinced that he is a factor for peace." [53]

Even those who had seen neither Hitler nor his even more amiable friends interpreted German actions in as favorable a way as possible. *The Times* reported German claims and threats in some detail; then commented on them, with less wisdom than its long experience of Europe might have led one to expect. Much of the "shouting and exaggeration" in Germany were, it decided, "sheer revolutionary exuberance." Those Germans who "felt themselves to be the only true patriots are enjoying the sound of their own unrestrained voices." The noise and threats could continue — *The Times* would not be hastened into criticism. "Anxious Germans may rest assured that all this is not deliberately misconstrued by foreigners whose home has been Germany for the last decade." [54]

Vernon Bartlett, a well-known English journalist, admitted that Germany was a dictatorship. But he asked his readers to remember that Englishmen "have never yet been able to realize that a form of government which suits us, and which we have been able to adapt through centuries, may not suit other people." Here was a wise appeal to the problem of environmental pressures on forms of government. If the more immediate evils were discussed, apologists for Nazism could always find some simple answer. The concentration camps were unpleasant, wrote Bartlett, but "the Government now propose to get rid of the concentration camp without much delay." [55] It was a proposal which had escaped Rumbold's hostile gaze, and remained below Newton's more cautious horizon.

It was easy to be an apologist, less easy to be alert. Bartlett, having spent forty minutes in Hitler's study, remembered Hitler's "large, brown eyes — so large and so brown one might grow lyrical about them if one were a woman." Four years later Lord Halifax looked into those same eyes, "which I was surprised to see were blue." They were indeed blue.[56]

Bartlett mistook the nature of the régime with equal certainty. He feared an alternative to Nazism that would be more extreme still — either militarism or communism. Hitler was the balance, the mean, the best that could be expected. We must make our peace with him, and befriend him, as soon as possible. The evidence that he wanted war was "extremely slight." *Mein Kampf* included expansionist passages, but it was "unfair" to quote from it, since it was written after the failure of a revolution, ten years earlier. It was wrong to expect from a young, embittered revolutionary "the reflections . . . that might be jotted down by a respectable politician with a distinguished university career behind him and a whiskey and soda by his side." Hitler must be treated as a mature statesman, not as a frustrated revolutionary. It was wrong to forbid German rearmament. A disarmed nation would never feel secure, and would resent being treated like a spoiled child. "How could Germany be expected not to worry about her security when her neighbours, so much better armed and equipped, talk all the time about *theirs*." [57]

Here was the crux of the rearmament argument; one which continued throughout 1933. Germany could not be expected to remain disarmed when all around her there prowled such well-armed, hostile neighbors. Journalists were convinced where politicians wavered. A. L. Kennedy, of *The Times*, expounded, privately and in print, the same thesis as Bartlett. It was "essential" to allow Germany "to build the forbidden weapons at once." Most urgent, she should be allowed, "immediately," to construct fortifications, and equip herself with anti-aircraft guns.[58] If Britain would only have the sense to allow and to encourage German rearmament, Germany, with her new feeling of security, would then agree to disarm in company with Britain. In March, 1933, Kennedy explained his thesis to leading politicians. Arthur Henderson, who had led the British team to the Disarmament Conference, was openly sceptical;* Ramsay MacDonald, the Prime Minister, less so.[58]

MacDonald showed little hostility towards the new Germany. He was unwilling to protest against Germany's illegal rearming, and told Hoesch that he disagreed with the views of his advisers on the need for a British initiative. MacDonald told the Ambassador outright that:

> From the very start he had not believed the reports of excesses and moreover he understood very well the character of and circumstances attending a revolution. He also understood the movement of young Germany and did not criticize it.[59]

In April, MacDonald told Hoesch that he feared lest young Germany's "desire for action" might "in the end" be imposed on the Government. But by November, MacDonald's doubts had been dispelled. Hoesch reported him as showing once more "a great deal of understanding for German complaints and of sympathy for German wishes."[60]

MacDonald wanted to show the Germans that they were not to be treated as renegades on account of the internal affairs of the régime. He had a plan for a *détente*. It was a plan, he told Hoesch, "which the English Cabinet knew nothing about." Hitler should visit England. He would "receive a most friendly reception from the people and the Government."[60] Yet how could MacDonald know? Neither the people nor the Government had been told of the visit. MPs in a number of debates had shown marked hostility towards Nazism. Might not that hostility be increased if Hitler were to visit England? It was not an entirely hypothetical objection. The visit of Rosenberg in May, 1933, had shown something of the strength of popular dis-

---

* Henderson told Kennedy: "I am presiding over a disarmament conference, not a rearmament conference." (Kennedy: *Britain Faces Germany*.)

approval. A wreath he laid at the Cenotaph had been removed, as a protest against Nazi racial doctrines. Rosenberg was the leading theorist of those doctrines. But it was clear that it was Hitler who allowed them to be put into practice, in the streets and on the statute book.

The German Government had noted how, with Rosenberg's visit, the English "saw all at once . . . the incarnation of the new Germany right in England itself and took up arms against it." [61] But MacDonald still argued that Hitler would be well received and spoke of his visit as a chance to improve Anglo-German relations. Von Neurath, the German Foreign Minister, noted in the margin of MacDonald's suggestion:

"Absurd." [62]

CHAPTER 2

Hitler's Visitors

"Daily life here is full of the strange conduct of civilized people."
— Ambassador Dodd, Berlin, August 7, 1934

THE WARNINGS and optimisms of 1933 came in equal measure. The outright pessimism of Rumbold and Vansittart was no less extreme, in origin and expression, than the hopeful forecasts of those anxious to be on good terms with Germany. Between 1934 and 1937, both sets of attitudes hardened. With greater knowledge of German affairs came a greater determination either to oppose with every means possible, or to appease. Appeasement was free from the overtones the word later acquired. It meant neither cringing, nor acting through fear. It was a mood of optimism. Its future model was an Anglo-German *rapprochement*, even an Anglo-German alliance. Both partners, in return for not molesting each other, would gain mutual benefits of every sort: colonial, economic, even "spiritual."

The European enemy was communism. Only Britain and Germany, united, could challenge the foe. Anglo-Saxondom was revived as a concept of racial and ethical solidarity. Evils lay in the East, and against the East Britain and Germany could together erect their defenses. France was too weak, too riddled with communist and "Left" sympathies, to be of use. William II had seen the dangers thirty years earlier, and had told Queen Victoria that Britain and Germany:

Must stick together. There are only two races in the world: the Teutonic and the Slavs. The Latin race is dropping down the ladder and we need take no account of it. But the Teutonic people must stand shoulder to shoulder or the Slavs will destroy us.[1]

25

Here were the very images, the very fears, that Hitler produced when talking to his English visitors. Nor were they unattractive to many of those that heard them. Anti-communism, like anti-semitism, and like francophobia, was never far below the surface of appeasement. Each provided a common ground for Anglo-German contact, if not for co-operation. Each, in whatever measure it was present, could be exploited. Hitler told most of his listeners exactly what they wished to hear.

Hoesch found that many Englishmen admired the autocratic nature of Nazism.[2] German discipline and efficiency impressed them; England was indolent and lazy. But autocracy found critics as well as admirers. Austen Chamberlain asked in the Commons:

> What is this new spirit of German nationalism? The worst of all Prussian Imperialism, with an added savagery, a racial pride, an exclusiveness which cannot allow to any fellow-subject not of "pure Nordic birth" equality of rights and citizenship within the nation to which he belongs. Are you going to discuss revision with a nation like that? [3]

Appeasement resulted from mental laziness, not from political immorality. Even Vansittart, who never ceased to fulminate against the harm which the appeasers' views were doing, admitted that their error "was no crime but a misfortune shared by the country." [4] The appeasers saw only what they wished to see. They refused to condemn Germany out of hand, and tried to adopt as fair an attitude as possible towards a phenomenon about which they knew little.

The violence of the régime was explained away, either as a temporary exuberance, or as a necessary adjunct to any revolution. It would soon disappear. If Britain were kind to Germany, and offered her the hand of friendship, German internal "contradictions" might resolve themselves. Lothian wrote to Eden in 1936:

I believe that if we assist Germany to escape from encirclement to a position of balance in Europe, there is a good chance of the twenty-five years peace of which Hitler spoke. British public opinion, with its traditional sagacity, feels that Germany has not yet had justice.[5]

Lothian regarded Anglo-German friendship as necessary to balance Franco-Russian dominance in Europe. Hitler himself was anxious to give the impression that Anglo-German unity was an essential preliminary to European peace. France and Russia were his enemies. He could point to *Mein Kampf* as proof that he had always wanted Anglo-German understanding. Without it France would dominate Europe. Lothian thought Britain must be "wise, resolute and strong enough to break away from the Russian-French combination sufficiently to make possible those re-adjustments in Eastern Europe" which would bring an end to the "encirclement" of Germany.[6] The Germans exploited such views. The German Embassy in London tried to soothe over the more obvious causes of friction. Hoesch noted: "It must be our task to promote relations with England and protect them from unnecessary damage."[7] He was an ideal man for such a task; a diplomat of the Stresemann era, popular with journalists, "as he was amongst society ladies."[8] *

On October 30, 1936, Joachim von Ribbentrop became German Ambassador in London. He had been in England the previous May, when he had visited Lord Londonderry, whom he found a sympathetic host. On his way back to Germany he had called at Downing Street, but "found nobody to receive him."[9] The snub was considered to be of Vansittart's making. But Ribbentrop had little difficulty in making initial contacts. He' had accompanied Lloyd George on a visit to Hitler in September,

---

* Hoesch did not impress everyone whom he met. The historian H. A. L. Fisher found him "an exultant Nazi, apologizing for everything, even for the exile of Einstein! These Germans always go off the deep end. They are a real danger." Curiously, Hoesch was not a member of the Nazi Party. (*Fisher Papers*, Bodleian Library, Oxford.)

and in the Embassy itself had, among his advisers, a relation of the Mountbattens called Doernberg.

When he arrived in London, Ribbentrop spoke of the danger of communism for Britain and Europe. Hitler had helped avert the communist menace. England and Germany should co-operate "in our common struggle for upholding our civilisation and cultures." Among his English friends, Ribbentrop found Lord Londonderry one of the most appreciative of German fears of communism, and not without fears of his own. The two men were on Christian name terms — "Charlie to Joachim" [10] — and Londonderry had no objection to Ribbentrop's scheme of per-suading Britain to "make common cause" with Germany "in fighting communism." Londonderry deplored the "indifference" with which Englishmen regarded, or rather disregarded, the problem. By appearing to ignore, and even to condone, com-munism, England spoiled her chances of progressing towards an Anglo-German *rapprochement*. Londonderry could not under-stand

> why we could not make common ground in some form or other with Germany in opposition to communism . . . The anti-com-munist platform was . . . invaluable; and I am quite sure that if we could have gone forward and made Germans understand that while we deprecated and in fact condemned a great deal of what they were doing, still they could rely on us to be whole-heartedly associated with them in their attitude towards communism.[11]

Some Englishmen found this anti-communism the least attrac-tive aspect of any proposed Anglo-German activity. Austen Chamberlain answered Ribbentrop's advances in *The Daily Telegraph*:

> If our friendship is to be sought, let it be for its own sake.
> Common sympathies, common interests and a common purpose are a more stable and a healthier foundation for friendship than prejudice and passion . . . Communism is alien to our tradition and as incompatible with our institutions as Nazism itself. The

encirclement of Russia has as little attraction for us as the encirclement of Germany. The verbal contests of Nazi and Bolshevik are
not worth the bones of a British Grenadier.[12]

Gilbert Murray also denied that communism was the greater
danger. In 1937 he drew up a draft resolution for the May assembly of the National Liberal Federation. Liberals, he wrote,
"rejected with ridicule the propagandist legend that 'communism' is the sole enemy of society, and 'fascism' its destined
saviour." [13]

Germans in England insisted that Hitler wanted British
friendship. Sir Eric Phipps, who succeeded Rumbold in Berlin,
considered such a friendship possible. After his first meeting
with Hitler, "an hour's *tête-à-tête*," Phipps told Simon that
"cold, hard, logical reason" would produce no effect on the Nazi
leader. He would answer only with "windmill gestures and
'storm' eloquence." But there was still a chance of influencing
the dictator. Hitler "may possibly respond to some rather the-
atrical personal appeal to his emotions." The moment and
manner of the appeal would have to be chosen carefully, "but
the possibility may be worth bearing in mind." [14] The French
Ambassador, François-Poncet, had found Hitler "more ready to
reciprocate to a generous gesture" than the "more civilized and
more calculating" Neurath had been.[15]

Both Phipps and François-Poncet became disillusioned with
the possibilities of Nazism. Further acquaintance with it led
them to abandon the slender hopes that had arisen from first
impressions. It was the disillusionment of the "man on the
spot," who was prone to both exaggeration and invention, but
more aware of realities than were the smoking-room observers of
the international scene. The latter leaned towards Germany as
a tired man towards the mantelpiece, seeking a resting place
where none was to be found. The "Cliveden set" were weary in
this way, though they included more women than would be
seen in any smoking-room. Mussolini, who sought to explain all

things simply, ascribed female appeasement to the widespread sexual frustration that he knew to exist in England. "Four million surplus women. Four million sexually unsatisfied women, artificially creating a host of problems in order to excite or appease their senses. Not being able to embrace one man, they embrace humanity." [16]

Mussolini's simplifications were not enough. Appeasers were to be found everywhere, without distinction of sex, party, or club. "Right or Left, everybody was for a quiet life," wrote Vansittart;[17] and in this broad category he included Cliveden. There was no organization binding the "set," no rules and no specific program. But some were "spontaneously inclined to criticize France rather than Germany." [18] They resented the anti-Germanism of Vansittart and those, equally unorganized, who were considered Vansittartites.

Much of Cliveden's anger was reserved for Vansittart personally. The more he was criticized, the more extreme became his anti-Germanism. It eventually drew upon him the criticism of friends as well as the scorn of enemies.

From Cliveden the Astors sent out the invitations that brought together "Tories and Liberals of distinction." [19] Dislike of Vansittart's outspokenness was common ground. He was a man who would alienate Hitler by being too rude to him. Dictators should not be criticized. Unlike democrats, they resented such criticism, and it was important not to rouse their resentment. Mutual hatred was evil. The Christian virtue was of meeting enmity with love. Margot Asquith put it succinctly when she wrote:

> There is only one way of preserving Peace in the world, and getting rid of yr. enemy, and that is to come to some sort of agreement with him — and the *viler* he is, the more you must fight him with the opposite weapons than his . . . The greatest enemy of mankind today is *Hate*. . . .[20]

When Thomas Jones attacked Vansittart's hatred of Nazism, Baldwin commented: "I've always said you were a Christian." [21]

Appeasement was no hole-in-the-corner creed, but the belief of well-meaning men who spoke their minds to the world, and hoped to win in the end a peaceful Europe, if not a just one.

Much has been written about the weekend parties at Cliveden where the guests made up the "set." They were an easy target. Maisky argued that the Cliveden set were among Hitler's "real accomplices." [22] Others who were called its members denied that it existed. Both were wrong. It did exist, but was innocent of the guilt Maisky claimed for it. Despite the social status of those who dined there, Cliveden was responsible for very little. There was much talk, and some of the talkers hoped to influence those in power. Their success, where it existed, was the result of general dispositions among the mighty rather than of Cliveden's wine. The disposition to appease was widespread. It needed no half-hidden cabalistic social gathering to enforce it. The talk at Cliveden was certainly of appeasement, but it was a sideshow. Were the archives of Cliveden ever on view, they would be more useful to the novelist than to the historian.

Westminster was as much a hive of appeasement as the country houses to which MPs retired for the weekends. Sir Thomas Moore and Sir Arnold Wilson were typical of parliamentary appeasers. Neither obtained Cabinet office. Both supported appeasement in every possible way. In October, 1933, Moore said: "If I may judge from my personal knowledge of Herr Hitler, peace and justice are the key-words of his policy." [23] In 1934, he wrote of Hitler as "absolutely honest and sincere." His article was headed: *Give Hitler a Chance*.[24] Arnold Wilson knew Germany as well as Moore. In 1935, he described how his own visits to Germany "had given him the impression that there was almost no Great Power with which we were less likely to become involved in war than Germany." [25] On his travels Arnold Wilson was impressed by the changes brought about by Nazism. "There was very little drinking now, and less womanizing." He told a German audience: "There are things in the new Germany which we should do well to study, adapt, adopt. I have seen German youths displaying in work and play an energy and burning flame of patriotism which, because it is wholly unselfish, is wholly good." [26]

Not all Englishmen looked so kindly on Nazi Germany. Most members of the Anglo-German Association disliked Hitlerism. In 1934, the German Embassy refused to give it further financial support. It dissolved. H. A. L. Fisher, H. G. Wells and Archibald Sinclair had been members. Other Englishmen were less critical of Nazism. They established the Anglo-German Fellowship. Members often visited Hitler, and had their own magazine, the *Anglo-German Review*. Moore was on the Council of the Fellowship. In 1933, he explained that if Britain "were to isolate Germany," Hitler would suffer, and the Germans would "seek another God." There was only one alternative to Nazism — "the anti-Christ of communism." [27] Arnold Wilson told the President of the Fellowship, Lord Mount Temple, that the Franco-Soviet Alliance was "a grave blow." It endangered an Anglo-German *rapprochement*. German hostility to France would increase German criticism of Britain. "The real danger to the world today" came from Russia.[28] Mount Temple himself said that "if another war comes . . . I hope the partners will be changed." [29] The search for German friendship involved turning old allies into enemies.

The appeasers were shortsighted. They tumbled over themselves in an attempt to pacify Hitler at every turn, without seeing that such a blind riot of pacification was not the final peace which they sought, but a means of destroying it. Hitler expected them to pacify him whatever his crime.

Most appeasers agreed that Hitler was wild, vicious, and unpredictable. But they argued that his viciousness would modify, that his aims would eventually clarify, and that his wildness would end. Abrupt criticism would only anger him. Patience and kindness would bring him to reason. The Germans were not evil racially, as Vansittart seemed to argue. At bottom they were kind, wise, cultured, efficient — charming friends and possible allies, less excitable than the French, more upright than the

Italians. If sensible Englishmen could meet Hitler at the right moment, and speak to him in the right tone, he would be equally sensible. Once he could be persuaded to be reasonable there was a good chance of reaching agreement with him, and an Anglo-German agreement would prove as trustworthy as any agreement between two sovereign states. More so perhaps, for Englishmen and Germans were nearer to each other in temperament and in aspirations than Englishmen and Frenchmen or Englishmen and Slavs. Such was the logic of appeasement, defended with the fanaticism of a faith.

The German Ambassador in the United States learned from Cordell Hull, the U.S. Secretary of State:

> The more intelligent and thinking people in this country looked upon these racial and religious occurrences more as a matter of temporary abnormality or the outcroppings of highly wrought up emotions, especially in view of the past history of the German people . . . .
>
> People here still prefer to think of this people as the German people of the days of Schiller and Goethe and of the other famous philosophers and teachers of the past rather than in terms of what they conceive to be the temporary abnormal situation of the present day . . . .
>
> People here are, therefore, still hoping and believing that the old German type will reassert himself in Germany.[30]

Hitler was not "the old type" for Cordell Hull. But for English appeasers there was no reason why he should not prove to be so. He and his advisers were sensible men. The excitement of revolution had unbalanced them for a while, but it was a balance that could be restored. A chance to do so presented itself when Ribbentrop came to England as Ambassador. He was known to be close to Hitler. If he could be influenced favorably, he would surely pass on his impressions. Appeasers often met him. Londonderry knew him well; Lothian was a frequent and appreciative listener; Conwell-Evans was a close friend, willing to arrange further contacts.

Ribbentrop felt drawn to Cliveden. "It was the kind of world he would cherish, the world he always wanted to frequent — rich, substantial men, members of the best clubs, accustomed to traditional deference from the lower order." [31] It was, unfortunately, a world that failed to take kindly to Ribbentrop. He was not a likeable character. Lady Astor once called over to him at dinner: "Aren't you a damned bad Ambassador?" On asking why, he was told he had no sense of humor. He had the wit to reply: "You should see me telling jokes to Hitler, and how we both roar with laughter." [32]

Ribbentrop did joke in England, and not always wisely. Lord Mount Temple was married to Sir Ernest Cassel's daughter. Cassel was a Jew. Ribbentrop's comment on this was typical of his coarse and unappreciated humor. "This Temple," he said, "should not be destroyed in spite of the Jewish wife because its influence is not yet exhausted." [33] Mount Temple, a man of honor, resigned from the Anglo-German Fellowship in November, 1938, as a result of the anti-Jewish pogrom.

The rudeness of an emissary could not weaken the resolve of appeasement. J. L. Garvin, editor of *The Observer*, which Astor owned, wrote that one of the conditions for "constructive peace" was that "a large part of 'Eastern Europe' proper should be reconstructed under German leadership." The states of Eastern Europe, territorially small, economically weak, politically disrupted, "ought to be as efficiently connected with Germany along the whole course of the Danube as are the American States along that other 'ole man river,' the Mississippi." [34]

The States of Eastern Europe, some of them set up only in 1918, and looked on with a somewhat dubious paternity by liberal England, were to be ignored, insulted and betrayed by the appeasers. It was difficult enough for Englishmen to find an interest in the affairs of *Western* Europe. "If France and Germany want to blow each other to pieces," a Labour candidate at a by-election was reported to have said, "let 'em. There is no reason on earth why Britain should be forced to join in such a suicidal conflict." [35] There was even less reason, on such reckoning, for Britain to be concerned about *Eastern* Europe. Those distant states could be in danger only from Germany, and Germany's drive to the east was welcome for a number of reasons. At the least, it would divert German attention from Britain. At best, it would bring a new unity and a new order to the chaos and weakness of Eastern Europe. If Russian pressure westwards was a danger, any strong bloc between her and the West was to be welcomed. Germany could create just such a bloc, if given a free hand to her east and south. Lord Allen of Hurtwood, a Labour peer, told a group of friends in All Souls' that he "would let Hitler have whatever he wants in Eastern Europe." [36] Lothian argued that "we should be under no pledge to go to war with Germany, if Germany attacked Russia or Czechoslovakia." [37] An independent Eastern Europe was nothing but an obstacle to appeasement. Independence for its own sake was absurd, even dangerous. The British were often closer adherents to a German expansionist policy than the Germans themselves.

In order to discover whether Germany could be appeased successfully, the appeasers arranged the *visit to Hitler*. Anyone who thought that Germany deserved Britain's friendship was well advised to tell Hitler direct. Not only generalities, but specific likes and dislikes could be discussed. Hitler was never averse to hearing from others what his next moves ought to be. Perhaps he had decided upon them long ago, in his fortress prison, or in the ante-rooms of the Chancellery and the President's House. But it was no burden to hear them again, from the lips of such persistent, if unnecessary, allies.*

Hitler had no aversion to receiving visitors, nor they to accept-

---

* One *visit to Hitler* surpassed them all. The full details are in Thomas Jones: *Diary with Letters*, pp. 239-265. It was arranged by Conwell-Evans. Lloyd George was the visitor of honor. Jones also went. Lloyd George "was impressed by the Führer's brilliant exposition of the finance of public works," and thought Neville Chamberlain "could be closeted with him for an hour." Jones thought "Hitler does not seek war with us. He seeks our friendship. If we fail him he will turn to Italy and elsewhere and we shall be sorry to have refused him."

ing his invitations. Looking back to the pre-1939 era Vansittart wrote: "I frequently said that those who ask to be deceived must not grumble if they are gratified." [38] The visit to Hitler rarely failed to produce some gratification. Lloyd George found Hitler "the greatest living German," [39] and told him so to his face. Returning to England after his visit, he informed readers of the *Daily Express* "He is a born leader. A magnetic, dynamic personality with a single-minded purpose." [40] Germany no longer desired "to invade any other land." Greater knowledge did not alter Lloyd George's view. A year later he wrote to Conwell-Evans of "the admiration which I personally feel for [Hitler] . . . I only wish we had a man of his supreme quality at the head of affairs in our country today." [41]

The *visit to Hitler* was a curious anomaly. Governments normally learn about other governments through their ambassadors. It is the ambassador's job to become acquainted with the leaders of the state to which he is accredited. But the Berlin Embassy sadly disappointed the appeasers. First Rumbold and then Phipps reported details and convictions that the appeasers were unwilling to hear. Ivone Kirkpatrick, the First Secretary, was equally worried about the dangerous trends in German policy.

In 1933, Rumbold had informed the Government that "it would be misleading to base any hopes on a serious modification of the views of the Chancellor and his entourage. Herr Hitler's own record goes to show that he is a man of extraordinary obstinacy." [42] Phipps, who had at first believed Hitler could be reasoned with, changed his views completely during the course of his four years as Ambassador. Bullitt, the American Ambassador in Paris, noted in Phipps "a hostility to Germany and the German Government surprising to me." Phipps had told him that he considered Hitler "a fanatic who would be satisfied with nothing less than the dominance of Europe." Germans had actually suggested the division of European dominance between Germany and England. Phipps described such a division as "the end of international morality." [43] In 1935 Phipps told Dodd, the American Ambassador in Berlin, that Germany would not make war before 1938, but that "war is the purpose here." [44] Kirkpatrick made a point of taking English visitors to see evidence of German rearmament.[45]

The appeasers rejected such alarms. War was not inevitable. Certainly Hitler had no grandiose scheme for it, and would only be tempted to aggression if provoked. It was the very hostility of such men as Phipps that prevented an Anglo-German *rapprochement*. Hitler told Lord Londonderry that he "could not stand the looks of Sir Eric and would like nothing more than to see him replaced by a 'more modern' diplomat who showed, at least, some understanding of the changes which had taken place in Germany." [46] Hitler was not alone in his dislike. Nevile Henderson, then Ambassador in Belgrade, regarded Phipps as too pro-French to understand Germany objectively, and had written to him on hearing of his appointment to Berlin:

> Dear Eric,
>   I shan't congratulate you, because I think you are going to the wrong capital. You should be going to Brussels, where you would be much closer to your spiritual home.[47]

Any chance to criticize Phipps was enough for the man who later succeeded him in Berlin. Henderson told Dalton that he considered Phipps a "most unsuitable appointment" and spoke of "common talk that there was no British Embassy in Berlin at all, only a branch of the Quai d'Orsay." [48]

Hostility to Phipps was as common to the appeasers as hostility to Vansittart. He and Vansittart had married two beautiful and charming sisters. The two men, with their strong anti-Germanism which they refused to disguise, were a plague in the corridor of conciliation. Baldwin was embarrassed by their presence. "What are we to do?" he asked Jones in 1936. Jones' mind was already made up.

> If it is our policy to get alongside Germany, then the sooner Phipps is transferred elsewhere the better. He should be replaced by a man of the d'Abernon or Willingdon type, unhampered by pro-

fessional diplomatic tradition, able of course to speak German, and to enter with sympathetic interest into Hitler's aspirations.[49]

With Phipps growing increasingly hostile towards Germany, and deprecating the possibility of a *détente*, the need for private visits to Hitler increased. Visits whose overt function was purely social gained political importance. The appeasers wanted to hear that Hitler was reasonable. If their Ambassador would not tell them they must look elsewhere for confirmation. The Embassy could be ignored. The airplane made swift and unpublicized journeys comparatively easy. Hitler was a ready host, and there was no shortage of would-be guests.

In the councils of influential men Lord Lothian stood high. He had been a member of Milner's "Kindergarten," a group of young men thrown early into the responsibilities of government in South Africa. He had edited *Round Table* for seven years. In 1916, he had joined Lloyd George's Secretariat, where he remained for five years. He entered the House of Lords in 1930, and held office in the National Government in 1931. Samuel Hoare and Geoffrey Dawson were his friends. So too was Jan Smuts, who agreed with him about the dangers of treating Germany "as a pariah in Europe."[50] Lothian first visited Hitler in 1935. He was given a lecture on the evils of communism. In return he informed Hitler that he "did not rule out" a change in the political status of Austria. Hitler spoke of Anglo-German co-operation as one of the things he had always hoped would come about. Lothian said he would tell MacDonald, Simon and Baldwin that Britain and Germany ought to begin conversations "with a view to a plan designed to stabilize Europe for ten years."[51] Hitler thanked Lothian for his kindness. On his return Lothian told Simon that his chief impression had been that "here was a chance of a political settlement which would keep the peace for ten years." What was essential was for "frank discussions" to be held between the two countries.[52] "The central fact today," Lothian wrote to *The Times*, "is that Germany does not want war and is prepared to renounce it absolutely as a method of settling her disputes with her neighbours." [53]

Here was the trust in Hitler's word that the appeasers believed both necessary and wise. Behind it lay the feeling that Britain had been unfair to Germany in the past, and would make a grave mistake if she persisted in her unfairness. Lothian, who "saw a good deal" of Ribbentrop during the summer of 1935, was more impressed with him than Lady Astor had been and "became obsessed with the idea that Germany had been denied justice." [54] Nazi brutality, he told a friend, was "largely the reflex of the external persecution to which Germans have been subjected since the war." [55] Germany's aims were sensible ones, and Britain should not stand in the way of her achieving them. What Hitler wanted was "a peace for Germany commensurate with its real strength and quality." Hitler was no absolute ogre; possibly no ogre at all. "I am pretty sure he doesn't want war." [56]

Lothian met Hitler a second time in May, 1937, and told him that "Britain had no primary interests in Eastern Europe";[57] exactly what the British Government told Stalin in 1945. It was information that could only have a single thought behind it — recognition of Germany's (or Russia's) right to political dominance. But in 1945 Stalin's armies were already in control, or on the verge of it. Soviet tanks were in the capitals of Eastern Europe, Soviet airplanes on its airfields. In 1937, Hitler had no such power, nor any immediate chances of it. To point out Eastern Europe as an area in which he would be unmolested by Britain was to invite him to hurry on his plans, and to make them more grandiose than they might have been. Gafencu, the Rumanian Foreign Minister, asked plaintively: "Germany has her plans: have other countries their plans? If the other powers have no plans we must of necessity go with Germany." [58] There was no question of Britain being without plans. But those she favored were the ones most suitable for Germany to take up.

As at his first meeting, Lothian spoke to Hitler about Austria, and told the Chancellor that he considered the "obstacle" in the way of an Austrian solution to be, not England, but Mussolini and the Pope. "The Pope certainly," said Hitler. The two men were amused — Lothian the former Catholic, Hitler the man whose parents had needed a Catholic dispensation in order to marry. "After this diversion the atmosphere became considerably lighter, and there were smiles all round." [59] Such *camaraderie* gave the impression that Hitler was easy to befriend. Dodd, a stubborn anti-Nazi who refused to make the slightest concession towards the régime, and accused all who looked with the slightest kindness upon it of being "fascists," met Lothian and was scandalized.

Lothian, he wrote,

> praised Hitler for saving Germany in 1933. . . . His hatred of France was revealed twice. . . . I could hardly make out just where he belonged in European alignments. He seemed to be more a Fascist than any other Englishman I have met. Recent English criticism of Italy and especially Germany with reference to their barbarism in Spain bothered him.[60]

Dislike of France; anxiety when Germany was criticized — here were two of appeasement's mainstays. In February, 1936, Jones wrote: "I keep on and on preaching against the policy of ostracising Germany." It did not matter how "incalculable" Hitler and his followers might be. What was important was to resist Vansittart's "pro-French bias." Whatever the anti-Germans might say, "we have abundant evidence of the desire of all sorts of Germans to be on friendly terms with us." [61]

Two weeks later Jones went to Lord Lothian's home at Blickling where the "Cliveden set" had gathered, among them Lord Astor, Sir Thomas Inskip and Arnold Toynbee. Toynbee had just returned from a visit to Hitler. While most of the party were playing golf, Jones took Toynbee aside. The two men discussed the visit. Toynbee had been favorably impressed by Hitler, and was "convinced of his sincerity in desiring peace in

Europe and close friendship with England." [62] Jones asked Toynbee to put his impressions in writing. They were typed out and shown to Baldwin "first thing" the following morning. The Blickling meeting was also productive in another way. The assembled company drew up a series of suggestions under the heading: "How to deal with Hitler." The Germans had just sent troops into the Rhineland, which Versailles had declared a demilitarized zone. [63] At the same time, Hitler had offered to discuss a proposal for twenty-five years' peace in Europe. The offer impressed the appeasers so much, and so fell in with their picture of the reasonable statesman that Hitler at heart must be, that they were willing to ignore the breach of the Treaty* in order to take advantage of the peace offer. They telegraphed their conclusions to Baldwin. "Welcome Hitler's declaration whole-heartedly." They condemned the march into the Rhineland, but refused to take it "tragically" on account of Hitler's offer. "Versailles is now a corpse and should be buried." [64]

Londonderry and Lothian were reported to have sent a letter, on behalf of the Anglo-German Fellowship, congratulating Hitler on his success. [65] Lothian's own description of the re-militarization was that Hitler was entering his "back-garden." [66] There was no crime; hardly a fault. *The Times'* leader of March 9 was headed: *A Chance to Rebuild.* The following day Eden told the Commons that "there is, I am thankful to say, no reason to suppose that the present German action implies a threat of hostilities . . . If peace is to be secured, there is a manifest duty to rebuild." What Dawson saw as a "chance," Eden translated into a "duty." "No opportunity must be missed," he continued, "which offers any hope of amelioration." Eden went to Paris, hoping to find the French in conciliatory mood. He

---

* Under Articles 42 to 44 of the Versailles Treaty "Germany is forbidden to maintain or construct any fortification either on the Left bank of the Rhine or on the Right bank to the west of a line drawn fifty kilometres to the East of the Rhine." A violation "in any manner whatever" of this condition "shall be regarded as committing a hostile act . . . and as calculated to disturb the peace of the world."

was taken aback by the strength of French feeling. Under pressure he gave the French "positive assurances of his support in the settlement of the question." [67] But Eden's offer came to nothing. "Diplomats, like women and crabs, go when they seem to be coming, and when they seem to be going they come." [68] So it was with Eden. He may indeed have "tried his best" to help France, as Paul-Boncour wrote,[69] but Eden's "best" was not enough. He did not act alone. Eden urged staff talks. Baldwin told him, "The boys won't have it." [70] Paul-Boncour saw that Neville Chamberlain "seemed to take particular care not to hurt Germany's feelings." [71]

The promptings of Cliveden had their effect. But Cliveden's thoughts and telegrams introduced no new course into foreign affairs. They merely confirmed the appeasers in a course that was already set. Claud Cockburn, editor of *The Week*, wrote about a "shadow cabinet" that had directed Rhineland policy. Astor, Dawson and Ormsby-Gore were supposed to be its leaders. They had played an "almost decisive role." [72] But the realities of which these men were shadows already existed: a very visible cabinet. There was no need for shadow promptings. Cliveden's thoughts were marginal. The prompter at the theater does not write the play, though he can often speed it on its way.

Cliveden's role might be *almost* decisive. It was never entirely so. For those at Blickling, convinced of the importance of their views, the move into the Rhineland was, in the words of their telegram to Baldwin, a "demonstration of recovered status of equality and not an act of aggression." [73] Jones had been impressed by Toynbee's assertion that Hitler could be trusted. He wanted to visit the man on whose goodwill the appeasers were so reliant, and in whom they had such faith. The chance of a visit was not long denied him. The *visit to Hitler* had become too established a ritual to be withheld from so persistent a believer. The visit was arranged. Jones flew to Germany on May 16. He had breakfast with Ribbentrop, in a room that opened, as Jones noted, on to a large square lawn "surrounded by birches and willows, lilac and laburnum. One might be in Surrey or Sussex, so English did it seem." Ribbentrop told Jones that he could not talk to Phipps "without reserve," and would like Jones to give Baldwin a message direct. The Ambassador, whose job it was to pass on such messages, would know of neither its contents, nor even of its existence. The *visit to Hitler* would bypass the more critical channels of diplomacy. The main point of the message was that Ribbentrop wanted Baldwin to meet Hitler. There was no need for Jones to be alarmed at the prospect of such a meeting. Hitler, Ribbentrop assured him, "is not the Dictator in conversation. He is like Mr. Baldwin . . . Hitler would speak to him with complete candour." Jones might be interested to know, in passing, that Hitler "lives the life of an artist and is devoted to music and pictures." [74]

Two days later Jones was given the chance to verify Toynbee's appraisal and Ribbentrop's portrait. He could meet Hitler. Unfortunately Hitler's chauffeur had died, so that Hitler had left Berlin unexpectedly. He was in Munich. Jones flew to Munich, and drove rapidly "in an open Mercedes car" to Hitler's flat in the city. The waiting-room, with its "solid and Victorian" furnishings, boasted a small portrait of Wagner, a half-length of Bismarck by Lenbach, and other pictures including some by Breughel, Feuerbach and Cranach.

Ribbentrop introduced Jones to Hitler. Jones noticed that Hitler was "dressed in his Sunday best, all fresh from the laundry." The conversation lasted an hour and a half. Jones' picture of Hitler was one of a reasonable man. Jones knew none of the fears and hesitations of those who had been told Hitler was an ogre who monopolized all talk, and shouted interruptions down. In case Hitler should think Jones to be a man of no importance, Jones emphasized that he had been at the Cannes Conference, "when we tried to scale down German reparations," and that he himself had "arranged the famous golf match which brought Briand down." Later Jones had been in Paris with Bonar Law, when the latter had "entreated Poincaré not to enter the Ruhr."

Jones, it would seem, had played his part in helping Germany escape the shackles of Versailles. Hitler "urged the importance of an alliance with England." Jones had already explained that it was one of Baldwin's desires "to get alongside Germany," a reference that had "obviously pleased Hitler." The conversation took a constructive turn. Hitler expressed "his great desire to meet Mr Baldwin."

> *Jones:* Mr. Baldwin was a shy and modest statesman who had never entirely got over his astonishment at finding himself Prime Minister.
> *Hitler:* And I also.

Hitler signed a copy of some of his speeches, one of which was on Art. Jones assured him that Baldwin would be "particularly interested," as he was "acutely sensitive to all forms of beauty, especially in nature and language." [75] The interview ended.

On his return Jones breakfasted at 10 Downing Street and told Baldwin of the meeting. "We must talk all this out," said the Prime Minister. Next day Jones saw Dawson, who was "all for collaboration with Germany, but worried over S.B.'s inertia, as we all are." Jones tried to break the inertia, and after interrupting Baldwin's game of patience talked "with gusto" about the proposed meeting. "Would Hitler be willing to fly and land at Chequers or in Thanet?" Baldwin "did not fly and did not like the sea." If Hitler would agree to come over in August the two statesmen could choose a "mountainous rendezvous," in the Lake District perhaps. These enthusiastic imaginings continued into the night. "Then some more Malvern water, and so to bed." But Jones had not finished. He wrote down "the epitome of my various harangues," and forced Baldwin once more to contemplate ending the gentle inactivity of his quiet life. It was one thing to doze and yawn at Cabinet discussions of foreign policy; quite another to escape the questions of the eager Welshman.

Jones' new suggestions duly appeared on Baldwin's desk. "Hitler believes in you. . . . He wants to meet you to tell you this face to face. This secret visit should be arranged without too much delay, and a communiqué issued shortly after saying it had taken place." [76] Here were too many complications and evasions for Baldwin. Intrigue abroad held little attraction for him. Domestic maneuvers were more to his liking. Jones advocated a visit to Hitler. Baldwin was not interested. Jones urged the dismissal of Phipps, as a preliminary to Anglo-German understanding. Baldwin, through inertia rather than loyalty, stood by his Ambassador. Jones' plans failed.

Appeasement was garrulous and inventive but power was denied it. Unable to exert direct influence over foreign policy, the appeasers could not prevent that policy from drifting uncertainly, without shape or aim. From one side Eden, after his Rhineland hesitations, demanded firmness and decision, a reliance on the League of Nations and an attempt to try to make Collective Security work. From the other side lesser men, soon to be greater, sought an Anglo-German *rapprochement*, and cast France and the League of Nations in the roles of villain and stooge. Eden's promptings failed. As Austen Chamberlain told the Commons:

> Contradictory positions are taken successively . . . the attitude varies from day to day according to the sentimental considerations which affect us, rather than being governed by a clear outlook on the world and a steady appreciation of certain principles which should govern our policy in relation to it.[77]

Though Eden wanted those principles defined and then followed, the weight of appeasement was too strong for him. Within the Cabinet the plant had taken root, though it had yet to show its blossom. Neville Chamberlain, Austen's half-brother, disliked Eden's insistence on treating dictators firmly and directly. Between 1934 and 1937, he had not the power to give action to his dislike, but power was not denied him in the end.

Austen Chamberlain deplored the visit to Hitler, and realized that, whatever it might accomplish, it could not replace the well-tried, more critical channels of diplomacy. He told the Commons: "These are grave days. We are anxious in this country, I think a little over-anxious, to enter into new conversations with Germany." [78] But the re-occupation of the Rhineland was condoned by the appeasers, who looked forward to further German successes with equanimity. Austria was really German, in spite of Bismarck's skill in keeping her out of the Empire. Eastern Europe was a German sphere of interest from the moment the Austro-Hungarian Empire collapsed. Kirkpatrick wrote, "It would have been better to have told Germany quite bluntly what we would tolerate and at what point we would resist." [79] But the appeasers hardly set a limit to their toleration, and looked with horror at every suggestion that resistance might one day be necessary. If Germany would co-operate with Britain, both countries would be satisfied, and war avoided.

Jones and Ribbentrop met again. It was clear that neither Baldwin nor Hitler was willing to fly to the other's country. Ribbentrop offered to persuade Hitler "to come quite close to our coast, two or three miles from Dover or Folkestone." The statesmen should meet at sea. Jones repeated that Baldwin "does not much like the sea." The meeting was abandoned. The two men had been lunching, alone, at the Carlton. Jones persuaded Ribbentrop to go with him to Nancy Astor's house at Sandwich where they would meet a Cabinet Minister "in the shape of Inskip," Lothian and the Astors. It was to be a south coast Cliveden. Ribbentrop went, and lectured the group on "the importance of a collaborating England and Germany forming a new centre of crystallization for the smaller powers in Europe." Inskip told Jones that the arguments had impressed him. With Inskip and the Astors in bed, Jones and Ribbentrop then spoke privately with Lothian. The subject was Austria. Lothian hoped that if Austria fell to Germany it would not cause a "breach of faith" between Britain and Germany. Ribbentrop agreed. Anglo-German friendship was too valuable to be lost on account of Austria. German pressures and threats would be overlooked. Britain would not defend Austria. As Jones had told Baldwin a week earlier:

> We should not be compromised into undertaking to protect Austria from falling in the lap of Germany. We do not mean to fight for Austria any more than for Abyssinia. We are not going to impose sanctions against Germany under any formula of collective security. Has this been made crystal clear to France? [80]

Always France must suffer; must be coerced, or ignored.

In 1935, the Government produced a White Paper on rearmament. It was an opportunity to point out the spirit as well as the factual details of Germany's growing military and air strength. Not only the number of guns, but the whole burden of militaristic propaganda could be described. Englishmen could then see more clearly what was being said and done in Germany. But the White Paper, while advocating armaments on a larger scale than hitherto, was weaker in tone than it might have been. Vansittart had pressed for "a passage on the [militaristic] spirit pumped into German youth." [81] But his efforts, spread over a whole winter, were in vain. Labour and Liberal leaders joined with the Conservatives in refusing to recognize the need for greater military preparedness. "There is no security in armaments," said Clement Attlee, a Labour Party leader, "and we shall be no party to piling them up." Archibald Sinclair, the Liberal, found even the moderate proposals of the White Paper "dangerous and wasteful." [81]

One man, braver than diplomacy demanded, insisted upon informing the Government of the state of German rearmament. He pointed out, in a letter to the Berlin Embassy, the extent and fervor of German preparations. Captain Aue was an Englishman — Vice-Consul in Hanover. He was a businessman, not a diplomat, and approached politics with the pragmatic commonsense of business. Diplomatic subtleties and deceptions passed him by. The German Government, anxious to keep its new strength hidden, asked for Aue's recall. The British, unwilling to believe that Germany had ulterior motives, and caring only to preserve Anglo-German friendship, accepted the German request without protest. Aue's information was forgotten. So too was his right, if not his duty, to forward it to his own Government. German susceptibilities could not be ignored. Aue was withdrawn from Germany. Kirkpatrick wrote, "I have never heard such nonsense. He had only reported what he had seen." [82] But officialdom was unmoved. Eyes were being closed to realities, and a chance had been found, thanks to the German protest, to remove an eye that refused to close.

Pro-Germanism began as an open and well-argued attitude. But the more it was opposed and the more it was shown to be inadequate, if not erroneous, the more it transformed itself into a hidden obsession. The public desire for peace was vocal and widespread, reflected in Peace Polls and Oxford Union debates. But these were children playing with something they hardly knew. The appeasers were in earnest. And they knew the caliber of their would-be friends. As a result they began to act behind closed doors, and to scheme in the dark. The public knew little of how the appeasers acted before 1937; in the three years that followed they were to discover almost nothing at all. Originally a mood to be proud of, appeasement became, with the brutalization of German politics, a mood of whispers and cabals.

It was the wise, the far-sighted and the sceptical who talked of resisting Germany. The appeasers resented such wisdom, and sought greater power than Baldwin had allowed them in order to belie it. Before 1937, appeasement was active at party and hunt; in 1937 it moved, with Neville Chamberlain, into Downing Street. The vagaries of a mood became the realities of a policy.

CHAPTER 3

The New Men

> With aeroplanes circling round the hilltop, with church bells
> clanging and salvos of gun and musketry fire coming from the
> fields below, King Alexander was laid to rest in the crypt of
> the church of the Karageorgevitches at Oplenatz, after a
> pageant of mourning the like of which Yugoslavia had never
> seen.
>
> — *The Times*

IT WAS October, 1934. A dictator of the old world was buried;
one to whom men looked as wise and statesmanlike. When
they sought a mental image for a dictator, they did not see
Mussolini ranting or Hitler wheedling, but Alexander lying as-
sassinated in his open carriage at Marseilles.

Among those at his funeral were the Duke of Kent, Marshal
Pétain, General Göring, and Nevile Henderson. The latter,
British Ambassador at Belgrade, later found in Göring a new
shooting companion. Accustomed to shooting in the company
of Prince Paul of Yugoslavia, Henderson exchanged his Balkan
hunting lodge for that of Prussia. "After a brief holiday at Belje
in Yugoslavia, shooting stags in my old haunts at the invitation
of the Prince Regent, I proceeded to Rominten, to stay with
Göring as he had suggested." [1]

The attitude of different people towards Göring is illuminating. He was known to be responsible for the killings of June 30,
1934. History may have absolved him from the major part in
that event, but to contemporaries he carried the blame. Arrivi: 3
late at a dinner party one evening he apologized to Phipps: "I've
been shooting." Phipps replied: "Animals *this time* I hope."
Dodd met him at dinner in February, 1937, and "could not talk
freely with him, being unable to forget these things." [2] Dodd

noticed at the same dinner that the "French and British Ambassadors were most unrestrained in their apparent happiness." Lord Halifax, who met Göring in November, did not share Dodd's moral disgust. "I was immensely interested at meeting the man. One remembered all the time that he had been connected with the 'clean-up' in Berlin on June 30, 1934, and I wondered how many people he had been responsible for getting killed." [3]

Göring gave Halifax "a composite impression of film-star, gangster, great landowner interested in his property, Prime Minister, party manager, head gamekeeper at Chatsworth." Henderson had a "real personal liking" for Göring,[4] and in his dispatches always portrayed him as a moderate, jovial statesman with whom England would be wise to deal. Henderson, Halifax and Londonderry had all toured his estate, and inspected his wild animals. If ever a *camaraderie de la chasse* was inaugurated, it was on Göring's estate.

Göring was Game-Warden of the Reich. On his estate at Karinhall he had introduced elk, bison, and the wild horse. His game laws were a model for the protection and improvement of animal life. The hunting exhibition he planned for the autumn of 1937 was the greatest of its kind since that held in Vienna in 1910. Henderson asked the British Government if they would contribute towards a British section. His request was answered, and at the exhibition there was a "highly satisfactory collection of African, North American and Asiatic trophies, including heads shot by Their Majesties the King and Queen and HRH the Duke of Gloucester." [5] Britain won first prize for its overseas collection, though this victory was overshadowed by the presence of the German colonial section of the exhibition, complete with a map of the pre-war colonies.

As Master of the Middleton Hounds, Lord Halifax received an invitation to attend. He thought that he would "accept it for the pleasure of shooting foxes in Saxony, as a change from hunting them in England." [6] Nothing but good could come of this visit. Jones thought that "if we can confine our mutual slaughter to animals and satisfy the honour of the two nations that will justify once and for all the addiction of statesmen to sport." [7] But however much diplomatic and political life might hover about the hunting lodge, and fidget with a gun as something stirred in a nearby copse, politics was more than an outdoor sport.

In May, 1937, Neville Chamberlain became England's Prime Minister. Not, as Maisky said, on account of "internal struggles in Britain," [8] but because Stanley Baldwin had outlived his useful span. The "dear vicar" was exhausted. Although Baldwin remained in office until after the coronation of George VI, Chamberlain had been his chief adviser for some months, and was his natural successor. Baldwin's foreign policy had been passive, lifeless, and without initiative. Chamberlain provided it with the drive that was lacking.

The new Prime Minister had been considered by his father, Joseph Chamberlain, as entirely unsuitable for a political career. Lloyd George remarked that in outlook Neville Chamberlain did not rise above a "provincial manufacture of iron bedsteads." [9] As his policy of appeasing the Germans developed, he was to earn a French title: Monsieur J'aime Berlin.

Baldwin had favored appeasement; Chamberlain was determined to put it into practice. He excluded Russia from this general prospectus. It was the Treaty of Versailles that had to be rectified, not that of Brest-Litovsk. Russia remained outside Europe. She did not represent a potential help in solving European problems. She was an eventual threat. In seeking friendship with Germany, Chamberlain regarded Russia with coolness. When Chancellor of the Exchequer, he had told Maisky that he considered the USSR to be Britain's enemy.[10] Cliveden had not been alone in its bias, though it helped spread apprehension. "Dined at the Astors'," wrote Jones. "Bullitt, the USA Ambassador at Moscow there, and made our flesh creep with his Bolshevik stories." [11]

Chamberlain's desire to secure friendship with Germany mirrored his positive dislike of Russia. "If only," he told Maisky in July, 1937, "we could sit down at a table with the Germans and run through all their complaints and claims with a pencil, this would greatly relieve all tension." [12]

His policy was not new. Such thoughts had already crossed the minds of many people both in and out of politics. Chamberlain's innovation was to introduce a note of efficiency into Baldwin's policy of drift.

After Chamberlain had been Prime Minister for a year, Dirksen, who had succeeded Ribbentrop as Ambassador, wrote a report on the political situation:

> The present British Cabinet is the first post-war Cabinet which had made agreement with Germany one of the major points of its programme . . . It has come nearer to understanding the most essential points of the major demands advanced by Germany, with respect to excluding the Soviet Union from the decision of the destinies of Europe, the League of Nations likewise, and the advisability of bilateral negotiations and treaties.[13]

Dirksen believed that Chamberlain had a "concrete programme of international security based on definite action," and that he "concentrated, stage by stage, upon carefully selected points in the foreign front." [14] Chamberlain, not Hitler, was the far-sighted planner.

Within Government circles the voice of caution, even of sanity, was stilled; often purposely excluded. Those like Phipps, who had a story to tell, were disregarded as fools; those like Vansittart, who warned of Hitler's schemes, were dismissed as "hysterical." The Prime Minister pursued an independent foreign policy. There was no room for "independents." With the new reign came the new men.

Ramsay MacDonald and Walter Runciman left the Government at the same time as Baldwin. With their departure the National Government was dominated by an almost exclusively

Conservative Cabinet. Both MacDonald and Austen Chamberlain (who had been out of the Government for some years) died in 1937, and the Government felt the subsequent loss of elder statesmen. Runciman's absence was less noticed. He was a man "cursed by laziness." Lloyd George told Jones that Runciman

> never really knew his brief but impressed people who did not know the case. He never said a ship discharged her cargo, but broke bulk. This impressed the landsman. He talked as a yachtsman which meant that he wore a yachting cap and gave orders.[15]

Nonentities left the Government. They were replaced by equally docile characters.

In March, 1937, Chamberlain told Simon that he would like him to be Chancellor of the Exchequer. Simon warned him that he had "no special knowledge of national finance." He contemplated the thought of this office "with humbleness." "Not a bad qualification to start with," was Chamberlain's reply.[16] Kordt, an official in the German Embassy, described Simon as "one of the most prominent representatives of that typically British mentality which prefers a bad compromise to a straight solution, if that solution involves the assumption of any responsibility." [17] Lloyd George said that "the right hon. Gentleman has sat so long on the fence that the iron has entered his soul." [18] Chamberlain had no desire for men who might show anger or emotion.

Many people thought a place should have been found for Churchill in the Cabinet. With his continued exclusion Chamberlain had no potential successor. Perhaps this was the cause of the almost unnatural loyalty shown to him by his colleagues. Though often discontented by his methods, the Cabinet rarely questioned his policies. Perhaps they had no other policy to suggest. They were undoubtedly shocked by the situation in France, where lack of unity often prevented policy from being effective. The Cabinet did not sympathize with French difficulties.

As so little is known about Cabinet Government in this century, and about the distribution of power within the Cabinet, Chamberlain's treatment of his Ministers must be studied without the necessary historical background. Although he took great interest in the individual problems of each Minister, he did not regard their collective views as important or relevant. He conducted his foreign policy with the intermittent aid of an ever-decreasing group, which did not include the Defense Ministers, Hore-Belisha and Duff Cooper. He persistently ignored the advice of his permanent officials. In the crises which were to come, he made many moves without consulting either his Ministers or the Foreign Office.

Chamberlain's behavior was not unappreciated. Many thought his coming would be marked by greater firmness. Eden told Halifax it would be a great relief "to have a Prime Minister who would take some interest in the foreign side." [19] Eden could hardly know that the week before he came to power, Chamberlain had told Nancy Astor that he meant to be his *own* Foreign Minister. Jones commented that Chamberlain "is still rather a dark horse, especially in Foreign Affairs." [20] The Foreign Office regarded his lack of experience with concern.*

Chamberlain began his career as Prime Minister without sensational changes or noteworthy exclusions, apart from that of Churchill. Duff Cooper moved from the War Office to the Admiralty. He wrote in 1938: "Looking back on it now I was much nearer being dropped (when the new Cabinet was formed) than I thought at the time." [21]

A newspaper editor assumed he would be excluded, and offered him a job. But Chamberlain moved him to the Admiralty in order to give Hore-Belisha the War Ministry. This

---

* Strang wrote in retrospect:

> It can fairly be said of Neville Chamberlain that he was not well versed in foreign affairs, that he had no touch for a diplomatic situation, that he did not fully realise what it was he was doing, and that his naive confidence in his own judgment and powers of persuasion and achievement was misplaced. (*Britain in World Affairs*.)

excluded Churchill from the Ministry where he could have been most effective. Hore-Belisha's efficiency made further change unnecessary.

The retention of one appointment later aroused much resentment and concern. A small notice appeared in *The Times* of May 31: "The Prime Minister has decided to continue the arrangement under which Sir Horace Wilson, GCB, GCMG, CBE, has been seconded to the Treasury for service with his predecessors."

Horace Wilson was, according to Hoare, "in every respect the orthodox, conscientious and efficient Civil Servant." [22] At the Treasury he had shown himself an absolute master of decisions and men. He would have preferred to return to the Treasury. But having come to 10 Downing Street he proved indispensable in preparing difficult questions for ministerial decision. He was useful in other ways. Chamberlain used Wilson for unofficial meetings and initiatives. Wilson could be given assignments without fear of undue publicity. As Chamberlain wanted to deal directly with the Dictators, he also sought intermediaries to avoid the more critical ways of the Foreign Office. Wilson found those intermediaries, and used them when they were needed.

Chamberlain's Cabinet contained two ex-Foreign Secretaries; Simon and Hoare. He could therefore ignore Eden. He also received informed advice from his own intimate circle. In this circle Wilson predominated. We do not know whether he was a policy-*maker*, but clearly his presence was indispensable. Chamberlain could not have kept such a tight hold on the affairs of the various departments unless Wilson had continually interviewed the Ministers concerned, and vetted their memoranda for the Cabinet.

As Chamberlain chose to be his own Foreign Minister, it was essential that he should have adequate information on the subject. For this he used Wilson, who was always ready to interview officials of the German Embassy in order to explain Chamberlain's latest idea, or to secure some hint of German wants and desires. Kordt described Wilson as "averse to all outward show, he is a man who compels respect from everyone who comes into contact with him. He is an embodiment of Moltke's ideal: 'Be more than you seem.' " [23] The legend of the *éminence grise* dies hard. Some contemporaries regarded Horace Wilson as something more than a civil servant. For "Cato" he was very much Polonius, hiding behind the arras.[24] For this criticism, Strang later provided a partial explanation:

> The work of a civil servant in putting public business through is not performed merely by writing words on pieces of paper. It means also seeing the right people at the right time and saying the right thing to them in the right way.[25]

Whether Wilson shared Chamberlain's ideas, or shaped them, is difficult to ascertain. He certainly promulgated them. Without him Chamberlain would have been in a much weaker position. Lord Woolton, who was a close personal friend, wrote of Wilson:

> I suppose he had more detailed knowledge of what was happening in Government circles than anyone else. He was deeply conscious of the strain under which Prime Ministers work, with the perpetual flow of papers, minutes, and reports coming to them from every department. His insight and his high competence as a civil servant were invaluable, but I believe the greatest help he gave to the Prime Minister was that of his sympathy. The nature of the Prime Minister's position inevitably leads to loneliness: he has to keep a balance of judgement on the often conflicting interests and opinions of members of the Cabinet, which makes it difficult for him to have intimate friendships inside the Cabinet. Sir Horace Wilson, with his knowledge and his understanding, enabled the Prime Ministers to have somebody to whom they could talk and on whom they could rely.
>
> Wilson was in a position of much strain: on the one hand he found himself enjoying tremendous power — in fact *a power un-*

equalled by any member of the Cabinet except the Prime Minister . . . but there was, I am sure, another factor that determined his subsequent action. He was indeed, at heart, a civil servant, over long years trained to render service to his political masters without regard to their politics. Nobody ever needed such unbiased devotion more than Neville Chamberlain, who, outside of his ideal domestic life, was a lonely man. I remember Wilson, after dining with me one night, leaving me early and saying, "I must go and look after my master: he's feeling very lonely just now." [26]

Whether Chamberlain was lonely, or angry, Wilson was at hand to help him. Fewer and fewer people saw Chamberlain. When they came to 10 Downing Street with suggestions or complaints, they saw Wilson. When Chamberlain had messages to be delivered, Wilson delivered them, with tact and persuasion.

Twice in one week Wilson summoned Reith, head of the BBC, to No 10. On the first occasion Wilson passed on Chamberlain's complaint that the BBC, by broadcasting excerpts from speeches in the Commons attacking Chamberlain, gave those attacks undue publicity. Reith replied that "the balance could easily be adjusted if some Conservative leaders made speeches in defence of him." Five days later Wilson telephoned Reith, and asked him to call again. Wilson asked if he had his handkerchief with him. Reith replied that he had. "Anyhow, why?"

"Because I want you to weep with me." [27] Wilson and Chamberlain had been upset by a criticism of the Air Ministry in a news bulletin. Only the BBC and the *Daily Herald* had carried the story.

The job of running busy departments kept Chamberlain's Ministers from rivaling his knowledge and control of foreign affairs. Simon at the Exchequer and Hoare at the Home Office were both deeply involved in their new posts. The Exchequer has always been potentially the most important of Cabinet tasks, although in the inter-war years the combined financial acumen of its Chancellors was not great. At the Home Office, Hoare had to deal with the manifold disturbances of a restless age. Fascist marches in the East End and IRA bombs were among his troubles. Yet, despite the problems that beset them in their own fields, Chamberlain retained these two as advisers on foreign affairs. They had both had spells of varying success at the Foreign Office and were older, though not wiser, than Eden.

The grouping of Chamberlain, Simon, Hoare and Halifax became, in the popular imagination, "the Big Four." This inner Cabinet had, wrote Hoare, a "typically English beginning." [28] In early September, 1938, he had been shooting at Balmoral. On his return to London he came to the Prime Minister to report the Royal Family's reactions to the European crisis. While he was talking to Chamberlain, Halifax and Simon came in. Hoare was asked to join them in discussion. He never left. Even before September, 1938, Chamberlain used Hoare's services to solve international problems. "Both by instinct and training," wrote Hoare, "I was bound to find myself in accord with Chamberlain's ideas." [29] Every morning the two men walked round the lake in St. James's Park, followed by wives and detectives.

Lord Halifax, the fourth member of this Inner Cabinet, did not become Foreign Secretary until 1938, and did not walk through St. James's Park with the others. The King had given him the key to the gardens of Buckingham Palace, which provided him with a short cut from his home to the Foreign Office.[30] He walked alone. In 1937, he was Lord President of the Council. In his own words:

> I was untrammelled by any immediate administrative duty, and therefore able to do any other work which the Prime Minister might wish me to help. In this way I came to be a good deal associated with what Eden was doing at the Foreign Office.[31]

Lord Halifax never emerged from the myths that surrounded his name. He listened carefully to what his officials said, but rarely told them what his own thoughts were. Aloof and elusive, his wisdom was accepted by all. But he kept his criticisms to himself. Poised between Chamberlain and a hostile Foreign Office, he rarely showed where his sympathies lay. They lay with Chamberlain. Hoare described Halifax as:

> Pre-eminent among the Conservative Ministers for character and judgment. In India he had shown his wisdom in reconciling bitter differences. Communal troubles had become less acute under his mediating influence. Gandhi had become his personal friend. Might he not have the same success in Europe that he had won in Asia? [32]

In the autumn of 1931, Ramsay MacDonald had offered him the post of Foreign Secretary. He refused it. His name had been put forward to Carson and Milner in 1916 as a likely candidate for the War Cabinet. He was the most aristocratic member of the Cabinet, in temperament if not in origin. On his first visit to Hitler he mistook the Führer for a footman, and waited for him to open the door of his car. Only a hoarse prompting by Neurath saved the situation.[33] Had Anglo-German relations remained on this level, Hitler might have been less disgusted by the subservience of the Englishmen who came to see him.

There were many servile Englishmen in politics and diplomacy. Nevile Henderson, Ambassador in Berlin, was among them. Josiah Wedgwood, an MP for whom appeasement was abhorrent, saw how Henderson

> smiled, fraternised with evil, and did not stand apart with nose in air. Hitler thought he was the genuine article. The MPs who flocked to Germany at Hitler's invitation, in like manner, forgot their duty and their country's standards. The Americans were more squeamish and did not join in the fun: but, by those silly British of some social standing, he was mistaken for a new crowned head at whose fancy cruelties they might giggle and from whom they might not differ with propriety.[34]

Hitler delighted in their company. Foreign sycophants were far more appetizing than those at home. "Please invite a number of foreign guests for my fiftieth birthday," he commanded Ribbentrop in April, 1939, "and among them as many as possible cowardly civilians and democrats whom I shall show the most modern of armies." [35]

Democrats, without displaying cowardice, did tend to have a marked respect for autocratic armies. Cabinet members did not always condemn autocracy as such. Many of them condemned nothing. They stood waiting in the shadows of power. Prospective Prime Ministers did not like to alienate those from whom they expected support.

In a debate held in February, 1938, to discuss the merits of having a Foreign Secretary in the House of Lords, Churchill summed up the other candidates for the post, and criticized members of the Government for their lack of drive:

Obviously . . . the mind is first attracted to the ex-foreign Secretaries, but there, I agree . . . in respect to the Chancellor of the Exchequer (Simon) we should all feel that it would be a very serious thing to interrupt his preparation of the Budget. That disposes of that. It is quite true that no such disabling preoccupation affects the Home Secretary (Hoare). He has taken over a new department in which the principal and most urgent subject is the preparation of our air-raid precautions, but there, of course, one must feel that so much of that work was done by his predecessor, and our arrangements are so far advanced that he really has to put only a few finishing touches upon the work. Therefore he could not be liberated from his task. But I understand there is another obstacle to the right hon. Gentleman being appointed Foreign Secretary, namely, that nothing in the world would induce him to accept the office again. Once bitten, twice shy. It is a case of the burnt child dreading the fire. . . .

There are the Minister for the Co-ordination of Defence (Inskip) and the Minister of Health (Kingsley Wood), two most able Ministers, very impressive, physically, in their different ways . . . Having revived our Defences, co-ordinated them and brought this great matter into a thoroughly satisfactory position, with the as-

sistance of only a single secretary and a lady typist, I think it would
be very inadvisable to remove him (Inskip) from the sphere in
which the full fruition of his labours is about to be achieved.

As to the Minister of Health (Kingsley Wood), I should very
much have liked to see his cherubic, bland smile confronting the
smiling dictators; but in his case he is absolutely necessary where
he is. The fact is that we never begin to realize how good these
Ministers are in their jobs until we begin to think of them for some
other job.

This was Chamberlain's team. One of his closest friends in the
Cabinet was Kingsley Wood. For four years in the nineteen-
twenties he had been Chamberlain's Parliamentary Private Secretary. He had gone to the Post Office in 1931 and been very
successful there. At Chamberlain's suggestion he was given a
seat in the Cabinet in 1933. After a period at the Ministry of
Health, he became Air Minister in May, 1938. *The Times*
hoped he would "increase the number of aeroplanes with the
same bright suavity with which he has increased the number of
telephone subscribers." His outlook on foreign affairs was shared
by the majority of Cabinet members. "He clings to the idea of
friendship with Germany," Duff Cooper wrote of him in May
1938, "and hates the thought of getting too closely tied up with
the French." [36]

The individual biographies of Chamberlain's Cabinet show
little evidence of obvious incompetence before 1937. Some were
sound administrators and distinguished lawyers. Halifax and
Simon were Fellows of All Souls'. Seven members of the
Cabinet had the Military Cross. Yet those who showed independence and efficiency had to go: Eden, Duff Cooper, and
Hore-Belisha. Public outcry disposed of those that were unpopular: Swinton and Inskip. The path of a Minister in Chamberlain's Cabinet was fraught with difficulties. The over-zealous
and the inefficient were cast out. The ciphers remained. They
were "like a nought in arithmetic that makes a place but has
no value of its own." [37]

If Jones had been successful, Halifax would have succeeded

Phipps at Berlin. Jones was urging Baldwin and Chamberlain to visit Hitler at the beginning of 1937, and suggested that either Willingdon or Halifax should be "planted" in Berlin "for a few months." [38] Unintentionally the Foreign Office sent out the one man who faithfully pursued Chamberlain's policy without questioning to the end. Whereas it was no accident that Chamberlain surrounded himself with Wilson, Halifax, Simon, and Hoare, the appointment of Nevile Henderson was entirely fortuitous.

Before Baldwin retired, Jones asked him why he had appointed Henderson to Berlin. Baldwin replied that he had gone into the matter with Eden and Vansittart. They had been unable to find anyone in the Foreign Service better than Henderson, who was, incidentally, "a good shot." [39] Vansittart often told the story of this disastrous appointment with wry amusement.[40] At least Henderson was a diplomat. Vansittart may well have feared a political appointee who would deal directly with the Prime Minster, and avoid the Foreign Office. He could not know that Henderson would assiduously devise policies of his own and bypass official channels. Those in the Foreign Office who found Henderson personally obnoxious thought the Germans would soon dislike him in the same way.[41]

Henderson had once been recommended to Hoare as "the coming young diplomat in the Foreign Service." [42] Hoare found him alert, sensitive, and agreeable, "by nature emotional and expansive." Unlike Rumbold, no one could say that Henderson's appearance gave any impression of stupidity. Hoare thought "he was obviously very intelligent." But he did not give a good impression to Dalton "either of political intelligence or character." [43] Weizsäcker described him as "slim, elderly and a bachelor. He was also a lady's man, displayed a careless elegance, was never without a red carnation in his button-hole, was a sportsman, especially keen on blood sports, hated crowds. . . ." [44]

Sir Orme Sargent, one of his colleagues at the Foreign Office, wrote that "affection for his mother played a large part in his life, as did also certain female friendships." [45] Sargent failed to explain what part these relationships played. Henderson had curious habits. At Himmler's Camp Supper Party at Nuremberg in 1938 he met Unity Mitford. It was raining. "When she squeaked out 'Heil Hitler' to me, I was so dumfounded that I forgot my usual retort which is 'Rule Britannia.' . . ." [46]

Henderson felt himself to be the pre-ordained instrument of Anglo-German friendship. In his book, *Failure of a Mission*, he attempted to give the story of the pre-war years the quality of a Greek tragedy: great men struggling against fate. In a strange way this idea of the inevitability of the war of 1939-1945 has come to be accepted by men who would not normally regard themselves as determinists. Henderson, wrote Sargent,

> had no preconceived dislike of authoritarian government as such, and was therefore ready to believe that Great Britain and Germany could be reconciled even if this meant tacit acquiescence by Britain in the adoption by Germany of the Nazi philosophy of life and system of government as well as the aggrandisement of Germany in Central Europe.[47]

This was not a very friendly criticism from a man who had to read his dispatches. There were few in the Foreign Office who admired these dispatches. Sargent was Henderson's most trenchant critic.

Henderson arrived in Berlin at the end of April, 1937. On June 1, he made a speech at the dinner given in his honour by the *Deutsch-Englische Gesellschaft*. "In England," he told the assembled company of diners, which included Himmler and Rosenberg,

> far too many people have an erroneous conception of what the National-Socialist régime really stands for. Otherwise they would lay less stress on Nazi dictatorship and much more emphasis on the great social experiment which is being tried out in this country . . . It is regrettable to see how much concentration is applied to save

trees which appear misshapen in English eyes and how little appreciation there is of the great forest as a whole.

"Guarantee us peace and peaceful evolution in Europe," he continued, "and Germany will find that she has no more sincere and I believe, more useful, friend in the world than Great Britain." [48] Not for nothing was he nicknamed "Our Nazi Ambassador in Berlin." His namesake, Arthur Henderson, raised the question of this speech in the House of Commons:

> Is it an erroneous conception of what the National-Socialist party in Germany stands for to allege that they have oppressed the Jews, suppressed all political opposition, placed many of their opponents in concentration camps, and destroyed free trade-unionism? [49]

Dodd, Nevile Henderson's American colleague in Berlin, had observed him closely in 1937. Dodd wrote that Henderson disliked France and had "informed the German Government that England would make no objections if Hitler seized Austria and Czechoslovakia." [50] In conversation, he told Dodd:

> Germany must dominate the Danube-Balkan zone, which means that she is to dominate Europe. England and her Empire is to dominate the seas along with the United States. England and Germany must come into close relations, economic and political, and control the world. [51]

In a letter to Victor Gollancz in 1941, Henderson denied the exact words of these exchanges. But he passed on similar comments to many of his friends.

It was unfortunate for Henderson that his arrival in Germany coincided with renewed persecution of the Christian churches. Here was one topic the appeasers could not ignore. At Cliveden, on Sundays after breakfast, "the guests disposed in the lounge behind copies of The Observer and The Sunday Times before going off to Church." [52] A secular element had crept in, but the spiritual aspect of weekend life had not wholly disappeared.

German religious repression could not be ignored. Church-going might be a façade, or an institution, but it was still an integral part of British life. Arnold Toynbee wrote of the Big Four that

> a living religious tradition was the common influence that made these four men of one mind in taking their hazardous course. Halifax and Hoare were active lay members of the Established Episcopalian Church of England; Simon was the son of a Congregational Minister; Chamberlain was the child of a Unitarian family.[53]

The religious problem in Germany could not be ignored, but it could be evaded. At the Church Assembly in June, 1937, Bishop Headlam, a Fellow of All Souls', rebuked all those who criticized the Germans for restricting religious liberty:

> It was only fair to realise that a great majority of the people in Germany who accepted National-Socialism did so in the belief that it represented a strong spiritual influence and that it had saved their country from a feeling of despair. They looked upon it as a real representation of Christianity . . .
> He did not think there was persecution of religion in Germany. It was persecution of political action. He believed that, in all cases where a pastor had been arrested, it had been due to the fact that the pastor had disobeyed a definite order. That could not really be called an attack upon the spiritual character of the German religion.[54]

Such speeches reassured those who were perturbed by Nazi repression. "Herr Hitler has given the Church a free hand," Baron de Ropp told the Anglo-German Fellowship in February, "he is a very religious man himself." [55]

Lord Londonderry noted that 1937 witnessed "no marked improvement in Anglo-German relations." [56] If this was so, it was almost entirely because of events in Spain. It was generally conceded by Conservatives that the sooner Franco won, the better.

The frequent embarrassments caused by the Civil War only impeded progress towards European co-operation. Conwell-Evans made this point to Hitler extremely cogently when he and Lord Lothian saw Hitler on May 4.

> The British people yearned for good relations with Germany. When the situation had so greatly improved, as at present, some mischance such as press reports (Guernica) gave certain evil forces an opportunity to check progress, but the growing strength of British opinion regarding friendly relations with Germany was such that he felt he wished to confirm if possible the convinced beliefs of the Chancellor regarding our future relationship.[57]

Certainly press reports must bear their share of responsibility for the failure of an Anglo-German alliance. The messages of Ebbutt, *The Times'* correspondent in Berlin, caused as much annoyance to the Germans as those of his predecessors Chirol and Saunders had done at the end of the nineteenth century.* But journalists could not refrain from reporting facts. However much a correspondent might favor the Nazi régime, and discuss its ideology in glowing terms, he could not altogether ignore the day-to-day brutality, the permanent discrimination against minorities, and the propaganda speeches of Göring and Goebbels. It was not the *reporting* of Guernica that caused the friction, but the *bombing* itself. German airplanes had bombed a defenseless Spanish town.

Much of the British press sympathized with Germany. Geoffrey Dawson, editor of *The Times*, contrived in his newspaper to give qualified approval to the Nazi régime. Yet even he was more concerned than Bishop Headlam with the Nazi attitude towards the Christian Church. When Ebbutt was expelled from Berlin in the summer of 1937, Dawson could hardly believe it. In a leader, he wrote of the Germans:

> *The Times* has stood rather conspicuously for an attitude towards their country which is by no means universal in England . . .

* William II often criticized the strong anti-German tone of the reports Chirol and Saunders sent home.

There is too much reason to believe that Mr. Ebbutt's main offence has been his repeated exposure of these persecutions of religion which are the worst feature of the Nazi régime and which
are bound to be a perpetual stumbling-block in the path of international friendship.[58]

Dawson had refrained from printing much of Ebbutt's material.
It was a blow to find that even this stringent censorship in Lon-
don was not sufficient. He wrote to his correspondent in Geneva,
H. G. Daniels,

> It would really interest me to know precisely what it is in *The
> Times* that has produced this new antagonism in Germany. I do
> my utmost, night after night, to keep out of the papers anything
> that might hurt their susceptibilities. I can really think of nothing
> that has been printed now for many months past to which they
> could possibly take exception as unfair comment . . . I shall be
> more grateful than I can say for any explanation and guidance, for
> I have always been convinced that the peace of the world depends
> more than anything else upon our getting into reasonable relations
> with Germany.[59]

Dawson knew Chamberlain well, was a Fellow of All Souls',
and a close neighbor of Halifax in Yorkshire. "Personally I
am," he wrote, "and always have been, most anxious that we
should 'explore every avenue' in the search for a reasonable
understanding with Germany." [60] *The Times* had no Foreign
Editor. The responsibility for foreign affairs rested on Dawson.
His close associate and leader writer was Barrington-Ward, who
was given a free hand. For German matters Dawson relied for
much of his information on Lothian, although Evelyn Wrench
recalled that Lothian "did not pretend to be an expert on German affairs, apart from his visit to Hitler." [60]

The appeasers turned their attention to the Foreign Office,
where fortune aided their plans. Henderson had been sent to
Berlin; no one questioned his suitability. One of the most forthright permanent officials in the Foreign Office was Ralph Wigram, who was close to Churchill and Vansittart, and a great

friend of France. He had spent nine years in Paris before returning to the Foreign Office in 1934. He visited Berlin, where Kirkpatrick took him on a tour of German rearmament activities. Even Wigram, who was under no illusion about German plans, was horrified to see children playing "grenades" with snowballs. After the Germans had remilitarized the Rhineland, and the British Government had done nothing, Wigram was broken and disillusioned. His wife described how he had returned home "and sat down in the corner of the room where he had never sat before." He said to her:

> War is now *inevitable*, and it will be the most terrible war there has ever been. I don't think I shall see it, but you will. Wait now for bombs on this little house. All my work these many years has been no use. I am a failure. I have failed to make the people here realise what is at stake. I am not strong enough, I suppose. I have not been able to make them understand.[61]

Wigram died in December, 1936. His death, as Churchill saw, "played its part in the miserable decline of our fortunes." He was only forty-six years old. Had he lived longer the appeasers would have had to remove him. Instead they turned their attention to Vansittart.

A German official wrote of Vansittart:

> He is not so anti-German as he is always said to be, but to the Cabinet he seemed, as I definitely know, too pro-French, that is, he was too much under the charm of the French style of diplomacy and of handling European affairs. For that reason he was . . . removed from the Foreign Office.[62]

On January 1, 1938, the Government replaced Vansittart as Permanent Under-Secretary at the Foreign Office by Alexander Cadogan. Cadogan did not dissent from Chamberlain's policy, and was in Wilson's confidence. Vansittart was given the newly-created post of Chief Diplomatic Adviser to the Government.

Selzam, an official of the German Embassy, wrote that people with knowledge of politics saw the appointment as "intended in a way to sidetrack Vansittart." [63] There was, he thought, a chance that Vansittart would be in a vital position. Unlike the Foreign Secretary, he would not be responsible to Parliament. He would be able to conduct foreign negotiations, and might possibly exert as strong an influence as Wilson. Woermann, in the German Foreign Ministry, thought this unlikely. He considered that Vansittart's "one-sidedly French orientation of British foreign policy . . . did not fit in with Chamberlain's attempts to promote better relations with other countries." [64]

Woermann was right; Vansittart's new post had grave disadvantages. He could no longer give direct instructions to British Embassies abroad. As the official announcement said, problems would no longer be sent to Vansittart on a daily basis, but "as required." [65] The appeasers' greatest enemy had been pushed aside. Wilson had been active and influential in removing him from power. As early as May, 1937, Wilson had told Eden's Parliamentary Private Secretary "that Vansittart was an alarmist, that he hampered all attempts of the Government to make friendly contact with the dictator states and that his influence over Anthony Eden was very great." [66] Eden did not defend Vansittart as he might have done. Perhaps he resented Vansittart's overpowering outspokenness; perhaps he felt the natural jealousy of a young man placed in apparent "tutelage." Together these two might have rallied the anti-appeasers. Friends warned Eden that if Vansittart were allowed to fall by the wayside, Eden himself would not survive long. But Chamberlain "was insistent" that Vansittart go, and Eden, unwisely and rashly, bowed to the wind.[67]

Von Neurath's projected visit to London, planned for summer, 1937, had been abandoned. But Chamberlain explained that such visits would become important elements in his future policy. In a speech which he gave at a rally of the three parties supporting the National Government, on July 8, he said:

I *do* place great reliance upon personal contacts between influential statesmen, and I fully share the hope of the Foreign Secretary that some other occasion will offer itself for discussions which may lead to a better understanding on each side of the other's point of view.[68]

Eden was in favor of discussions, but as he later told Ribbentrop, he did not want conferences or ministerial visits, but discussions through "diplomatic channels." [69]

Eden's views were diverging rapidly from those of Chamberlain and his supporters. The Spanish Civil War dominated political arguments in 1937. Though the Left severely criticized Eden, he was at least a sincere supporter of non-intervention. But the Government, though officially neutral, contained a number of prominent supporters who sympathized with Franco. These men had no emotional or rational barrier against coming to terms with Italy or Germany. For them Spain was not the issue that marked the difference between right and wrong. In the Lords in October, Halifax suggested that it might be possible

to clear up a great many misunderstandings that have arisen out of the difficulties of the Spanish problem . . . and I can myself look forward — I do not want to be unduly optimistic — to the gradual establishment of a new and healthier atmosphere in which it would be possible to reach the position where Anglo-Italian conversations might be held.[70]

At the end of the month Eden gave his answer to this in a speech at Llandudno: "I am as anxious as anybody to remove disagreements with Germany or Italy, or any other country, but we must make sure that in trying to improve the situation in one direction it does not deteriorate in another." [71]

Lloyd George indicated the conflicts within the Cabinet by contrasting the "first-class chauffeur," Eden, with "the assembly of nervous wrecks at his elbow . . . I can see that he is not having his own way in the matter." [72]

When the split in the Cabinet was becoming clear to all, preparations were being made for Halifax to visit Hitler. The preparations were secret. Jones heard a rumor in October that Eden and the Prime Minister were at "cross-purposes." [73] Eden doubted if Halifax's visit would serve a useful purpose. Jones dined at Cliveden:

> I sat between (Eden) and Henderson after the ladies left last night and found they differed widely in policy. Henderson struck me as sensible and informed without distinction. He has lived in the countries we talked about and Eden has not and this was apparent.[74]

Jones was told that Vansittart wanted to bring Chamberlain round "to the secular Foreign Office view." Baldwin's comment on Cliveden was that "it was most foolish of Eden to tire himself out at the weekends by going to such crowded and exciting parties." [75]

In case Eden should disapprove of the proposal to send Halifax to Berlin, he was "packed off" to Brussels for a nine-power conference, the last attempt to enforce collective security in the Far East. Eden was not averse to meeting German officials. On October 27, he said he "would be very glad to meet the Reich Foreign Minister . . . for a conversation" in Brussels.[76] On a diplomatic level it would be foolish not to maintain regular contacts with the Germans. Eden objected to seeing them singled out for special treatment by casual visitors.

On November 11, during the Service of Remembrance at the Cenotaph, a man ran out of the crowd shouting, "Cease this hypocrisy. You are conniving in a new war." In the Commons, Hoare stated that the man was suffering from delusions.[77]

Such strange events could not prevent Halifax from going to Berlin. On November 15, he saw Ribbentrop and expressed his "pleasure at having the opportunity of becoming acquainted with the Führer . . . whose work he admires." [78] He also told him that "he considered the Rome-Berlin Axis and the London-Paris Axis to be realities." After the English and the Germans had discussed mutual problems he hoped it would then be possible "to bring our friends along" (meaning France and Italy).

On November 13, the *Evening Standard*'s diplomatic correspondent wrote,

> The British Government have information from Berlin that Herr Hitler is ready, if he receives the slightest encouragement, to offer to Great Britain a ten-year "truce" in the colonial issue. During the "truce" the question of colonies for Germany would not be raised. In return for this agreement Hitler would expect the British Government to leave him a free hand in Central Europe.

The European press exploded at such a suggestion. That England should declare her lack of interest in Central Europe was anathema both to the French and British public. It brought hasty denials from the Foreign Office. The German newspapers were equally horrified that Hitler should even *contemplate* not pressing for the return of the colonies immediately. The atmosphere for Halifax's visit was thus not wholly favorable. On November 15, George Ogilvie Forbes, Chargé d'Affaires in Berlin, discussed the press with Mackensen. Ogilvie Forbes "condemned the attitude of the British press severely" as it amounted to a "stab in the back" for the British Government. He agreed with Mackensen that "the root of the trouble" lay in the fact that the British press "had been permitted to discuss the subject at all." [79]

George Steward, Chamberlain's Press Secretary, discussed this with Fritz Hesse.[80] Chamberlain, he said, was "exceedingly angry" about the article in the *Evening Standard*. He had made "exhaustive investigations" into its origins, and was convinced that it had not been inspired by the Foreign Office, Cabinet members, or Parliamentary circles. Steward then discussed the importance of Halifax's visit to Berlin. Chamberlain thought Halifax "the most important statesman and politician England had at the present time. He was completely independent and without any personal ambition whatever."

An Anglo-German *rapprochement,* said Steward, could be brought about only "very slowly and gradually," but when it was achieved "it could be counted on to last." On November 19, Hitler met Halifax at Berchtesgaden. Arnold Toynbee described the hopes that had been placed on the visit:

> Mr. Gandhi and Herr Hitler were two hardly distinguishable specimens of the same species of foreigner . . . both of them superlatively exotic, and the average member of a British Cabinet may have reasoned in November 1937 that the guileless tamer of Gandhi had at any rate "a sporting chance" of taming Hitler likewise. Were not both these political "mad mullahs," non-smokers, non-drinkers of alcohol, non-eaters of meat, non-riders on horseback, and non-practisers of blood-sports in their cranky private lives? [81]

Hitler told Halifax which films he liked. He said *Lives of a Bengal Lancer* was required viewing for the SS "because it depicted a handful of Britons holding a continent in thrall." [82]

If the British had followed Hitler's advice for dealing with Gandhi when dealing with Hitler himself, they would soon have solved the Nazi Problem. "Shoot Gandhi," said Hitler,

> and if that does not suffice to reduce them to submission, shoot a dozen leading members of Congress; and if that does not suffice, shoot two hundred and so on until order is established. You will see how quickly they will collapse as soon as you make it clear that you mean business. [82]

For the rest of the morning Halifax and Hitler discussed the press. Hitler argued that agreement was impossible between Germany, where the press was rigidly controlled, and a democracy like Britain where it was not. Hitler was right. It is difficult to carry out an unpopular foreign policy if the country you wish to befriend is sensitive to the remarks of a free press. Hitler did not see democracy as it really was, autocratic at the center. He understood only democratic theory. He believed democracy was susceptible to changes of direction at the whim of the people or the press. For that reason he despised it.

Halifax did not understand the full import of Hitler's remarks. He said that if they were going to discuss matters in those terms, further talks were useless; he might as well not have come. But instead of leaving promptly, Halifax remained. The appeasers never took "no" for an answer. Perhaps Hitler exaggerated. Perhaps the British press could be encouraged to play down the atrocities. Dawson was a sound man. So was Barrington-Ward.

When Brüning, a former German Chancellor, had been dining in Oxford that summer, he told the Fellows of All Souls' that "there might be 4,000 now in concentration-camps and that the maximum had been between 150,000 and 200,000. Signs were increasing that young university graduates were against Nazism. [It] was certain that the German General Staff did not desire war." [83] If things were really improving, the press could be encouraged to say so. Halifax therefore continued his discussions with Hitler.

He stayed because he had important things to say. He thought the British press not only said too much about the unpleasant aspects of Germany, but also too little about the good things that were being done there. The British public were unaware of the remarkable material advances that had been made under National-Socialism. Halifax told Hitler,

The view was held in England that it was perfectly possible to clear out of the way the misunderstandings which existed at the present moment; the great services which the Chancellor had performed in the reconstruction of Germany were fully recognised, and, if the public opinion of England took up an attitude of criticism from time to time towards certain German problems, it might no doubt be in part because people in England were not fully informed of the motives and attendant circumstances of certain measures taken in Germany. Thus the Church of England followed with anxiety and disquiet the development of the Church question in Germany; and Labour Party circles were critical of certain action taken in Germany. In spite of these difficulties, he (Halifax) recognised that the Chancellor had not only performed great services in Germany but also, as he would no doubt feel, had been able, by preventing the entry of communism into his own country, to bar its passage further west.[84]

The communist menace excused many things.

Halifax said that Chamberlain would appreciate "further conversations between representatives of the two Governments" on "questions of detail." Hitler replied that "for the present he had in mind the diplomatic channel as a means for carrying the Anglo-German contacts further."

Hitler had no more desire than Eden to use these extra-diplomatic channels. If he could secure an agreement with Britain, well and good. But he was not going to go out of his way to get it. Anglo-German agreement was secondary for Hitler.

For Chamberlain it was fundamental. After lunch, Halifax again asked about the possibility of further talks. Hitler was unenthusiastic. They would need "careful preparation . . . If this or that question appeared difficult, they should first wait for two or three years."

Halifax met Goebbels. According to Henderson "the reasonableness and logic which Dr. Goebbels always displayed in private seemed to make, in spite of his reputation, quite a good impression upon Lord Halifax." [85]

Halifax had sown extensively. The stoniness of the ground had scarcely been understood. At lunch a month later with Ribbentrop he gave the impression that he thought negotiations would proceed slowly. Ribbentrop wrote home that Halifax had "only a rather vague idea of the course and the outcome of the negotiations and is, if not exactly pessimistic, at least sceptical about the prospects." [86]

Halifax had reason to be pessimistic. Hitler's lack of enthusiasm was now coupled with a rift in the British Cabinet over the means of continuing the conversations. The idea of the group led by Eden was to "broaden the number of States participating in the conversations as soon as possible, above and beyond the four great Western Powers." [87] Eden wanted some form of collective action which would strengthen the League. The group led by Hoare wished to proceed "from bilateral German-British conversations merely to a four-power discussion." [87] The specter of a four-power conference haunted Chamberlain's foreign policy. Only once did the four powers unite: to dismember Czechoslovakia.

At the end of 1937 there was only one question for the British Cabinet to face: how to remove Eden. Every remark he made seemed a rebuke to Chamberlain and appeasement. In February, 1938, Eden said at Birmingham that "in any agreements we make today there must be no sacrifice of principles and no shrinking of responsibilities merely to obtain quick results . . . It is not only by seeking to buy good-will that peace is made, but on a basis of frank reciprocity with mutual respect." [88] A week later he resigned.

Eden had resigned, not over a detail of policy, but because of a fundamental conflict with Chamberlain's attitude of mind and aspirations. He made this clear in his resignation speech:

> I do not believe we can make progress in European appeasement . . . if we allow the impression to gain currency abroad that we yield to constant pressure. I am certain in my own mind that progress depends above all on the temper of the nation, and that temper must find expression in a firm spirit. That spirit, I am confident, is there. Not to give voice to it is, I believe, fair neither to this country nor to the world.

Chamberlain had no answer. It was easier to attack elsewhere. Eden, supporter of the League and of collective security, had spoken, but power was no longer his. The League's advocate having fallen, Chamberlain proceeded to attack the League itself:

> You cannot expect a League constituted originally to perform certain functions, on the assumption that if it did not embrace every nation in the world, it embraced practically all the powerful nations in the world — you cannot expect a League which has been given a function corresponding with that state of things, to be able to exercise that same function if nearly all the Great Powers have left it.

Noel-Baker jumped to his feet. "Is it not a fact that membership of the League is the same as it was at the time of the last General Election, except for Italy, which had then been declared an aggressor?" The National Government had returned to power pledged to a policy of resistance to aggression under the League of Nations. Without appealing to the electorate, it had decided to renounce that policy. Bitter were the attacks which greeted this change. Kingsley Griffith told the Commons that Chamberlain claimed

> that, as a result of our increased military strength, we are listened to by foreign nations now. That may be true, but what do we say to them? If all that we have to say is *"Heil Hitler"* or *"Viva il Duce,"* I have no doubt that they are very ready to listen, but I would suggest that it is not necessary to go armed to the teeth to the meeting of a mutual admiration society.

Eden had resigned. Cranborne (later Lord Salisbury), the Under-Secretary for Foreign Affairs, resigned with him. Many people thought Duff Cooper would also resign. He did not. He remained in the Cabinet, to work against Chamberlain's policy from within. But it was a policy that resisted criticism and pressure. Eden was succeeded by Halifax, Cranborne by R. A. Butler. The way was clear for new European alignments.

On February 24, Butler called at the German Embassy. He

emphasized that he had "learned to know and appreciate Germany" from his travels, and to illustrate this "he spoke a part of the time in rather good German." Butler desired a "close and lasting co-operation" with Germany and said he would "do all he could" to promote it. He explained that many Foreign Office officials had "a biased attitude in favour of France." R. A. Butler said,

the generation of officials occupying the key positions in the Foreign Office today had grown up during a time when French was the language of diplomacy. For this reason it necessarily followed that the officials of the foreign service, both before and after they entered this service, attached, and were forced to attach, importance to spending several years in France to study the language. The result was that these officials very frequently acquired a biased attitude in favour of France, which they always retained, even after they had gradually been promoted to higher positions during the postwar years. In addition, they had obtained in Eden a young Foreign Secretary who obviously shared this attitude. On the other hand, Baldwin as Prime Minister had concerned himself with foreign policy only to the degree that was absolutely necessary, and consequently the predominant, pro-French element in the Foreign Office had been able to exert its influence to the fullest extent. . . . The generation which had come up in the foreign service in recent years, on the other hand, was free from any pro-French leaning. But this group in the Foreign Office had never really made much headway, and the first real break in the French line had come with Sir Nevile Henderson. It had been perfectly plain, however, to all intelligent observers, that there would have to be a showdown between these two groups after Baldwin left, and the first indication of this had been the sidetracking of Sir Robert Vansittart.

Butler also announced that, when Eden's resignation had been discussed in Cabinet, "all the members of the Cabinet had arrayed themselves on Chamberlain's side, and not a voice had been raised in favour of Eden."

Butler stressed Wilson's influence, but the Germans already had concluded that Wilson was "decidedly pro-German." They summarized Butler himself as having "no prejudices against us." [89]

A. L. Rowse, a young Fellow of All Souls', asked Dawson, "Look, can't you let up on your campaign against the Italians? It isn't they who are the danger. It is the Germans who are so powerful as to threaten all the rest of us together." Dawson replied, "To take your argument on its own valuation — mind you I'm not saying that I agree with it — but if the Germans are so powerful as you say, *oughtn't we to go in with them?*" [90]

Chamberlain intended to go in with them. In order to secure their co-operation, he offered to solve their problems for them. He offered Germany colonies, his to give and those of others. He offered them far-reaching economic agreements. He offered to help them deal with the Czechs. Within a year he was entrenched in power. Surrounded by his friends, there was no one left to oppose him. And Sir Horace Wilson, in the room next to him, was always ready with advice.

CHAPTER 4

Colonial Appeasement

In 1919, Germany, defeated in Europe, renounced "all her rights and titles over her oversea possessions." [1] She surrendered Tanganyika, South-West Africa, Togoland and the Cameroons. South-West Africa went as a Mandate to South Africa; Tanganyika and parts of Togoland and the Cameroons to Britain.

Before 1933, German politicians occasionally demanded the return of the lost, or "stolen" colonies. As a result some Englishmen insisted that the British Government must at no stage ever consider returning the Mandated Territories to Germany. L. S. Amery was the most vocal of the group. When Colonial Secretary he had stated the Imperial case:

> Our Mandate in Tanganyika is by no means a temporary tenure or lease from the League of Nations. It is "servitude," an obligation to observe certain rules of conduct . . . We hold Tanganyika not from the League of Nations . . . but in our own right under the Treaty of Versailles.[2]

The Joint Parliamentary Committee on Closer Union in East Africa sought every possible means of Parliamentary pressure and political influence to bring Tanganyika into a closer constitutional relationship with Kenya and Uganda. Amery told Sir Edward Grigg, a former Governor of Kenya: "You need not contemplate any possibility of Tanganyika ceasing to be permanently British." [3]

Tanganyika seemed the Mandated Territory that the Germans would be most likely to demand. It was important both as a market and as a base. If Britain were ever a potential enemy, or East Africa an area in which wider German penetration were planned, Germany would want Tanganyika first. In 1931, with the Nazi party growing in importance, *The Times* sent a correspondent to Germany to discover what colonial policy the party had adopted. The inquiry was encouraging. Tanganyika was the only colony the Nazis wanted. But, they said, "a demand for it would earn the enmity of England, the friendship of which was particularly desired." The return of Tanganyika must therefore be forgotten.

In 1933, the third German "Empire" came into existence. All that was imperial — national pride and the new-found fervor of a totalitarian régime — was to be devoted to European ambitions. Conscious of her ability to dominate Europe, economically if not politically, the new Germany cast no envious eye over the vast lands of Africa or Asia. Hitler sought to become the arbiter of European politics — a more adventurous Bismarck, a more successful William II. Africa held no attraction for him.

Even towards those Germans who demanded the return of colonies no kind words were spoken. It was the Jewish press, according to Hitler, which protested against the "theft" of colonies, in order to concentrate German hatred on England. The Nazis were not England's enemies. The colonial question was nothing but a "Jewish swindle," aimed at diverting the public from the real issues, chief of which was the rôle of the Jews in German public life.[4] Hitler's lack of an imperial sense mirrored the dull and feeble imperialism of the German public before 1914. Imperial ventures had been chiefly concerned with influencing domestic or European politics. Germans did not want new territory.* No German imperial statesman or poet could boast the energy, following or success of his English or French contemporaries. Yet however little sense of Empire there might be, an Empire had existed, and in 1919 it had been taken away.

---

* Academics often prove the exception to general moods. The historian Mommsen told Amery in 1899 that Britain had "filched an Empire" while Germany was weakened by the Thirty Years' War, but that Germany would soon displace Britain from her "ill-deserved supremacy in the world outside." L. S. Amery, *The German Colonial Claim*, p. 11.

With so many grievances discovered in the Versailles Treaty it was hardly to be expected that the lost colonies would stand foremost among them. There was no great ex-colonial pressure group in Berlin to demand the return of lost wealth and property with sufficient backing to win headlines in a party program. To those who claimed Germany needed "living space" Hitler answered that land was *not* to be found "in the Cameroons, but almost exclusively in Europe," and at the expense of Russia. It was the wartime Treaty of Brest-Litovsk, not the prewar agreements for the partition of Africa, that provided the new Empire with attractive precedents. Even if some overseas expansion were possible, wrote Hitler, it could not be started "until the confines of the Reich included every German." [5]

Von Papen, Hitler's Vice-Chancellor, was the first German politician to show an interest in the colonial question after the Nazi victory. "Germany," he told a London newspaper, "definitely wants to develop Africa in the same way as Great Britain, France, Italy, Belgium and Portugal do." [6] But the colonial question failed to come to life: a certain firmness on the part of the British Government may in part have been responsible. The British Government was more concerned to allay the fears of its own imperial-minded back-benchers than to clarify its position with the new German Government. It declared that it had "never contemplated any surrender of the Tanganyika Mandate." [7]

In June, 1933, at the World Economic Conference in London, Hugenberg, the German Minister of Public Economy and Agriculture, advocated "the return of Germany's African colonies," and a further grant to the "nation without space" of "territories for the settlement of its active race and for the construction of great works of peace." [8] The proposal found little support at the conference. It was disowned, somewhat belatedly, from Berlin, and ascribed to Hugenberg's personal views.

A number of Germans in the Mandated Territories had themselves been active in advocating their return to Germany. Nazi groups had been formed in the late nineteen-twenties with the express purpose of using a Nazi Government to obtain a reversal of the Versailles Treaty. Within the territories the groups wanted to organize themselves as potential Nazi Governments that could take over power once Berlin's diplomacy had brought an end to Mandates. One of the leading Nazis in South-West Africa wrote to the German Consul in Pretoria: "Everybody is anxiously looking to Germany. When will our Home Country fetch us back?" [9]

The Home Country was reticent. Another Nazi in South-West Africa noted that "the position taken by the Imp. Chancellor towards the colonial problem is, at present, a very circumspect one." [10] It remained circumspect. Pressure from the colonial Nazis failed to awaken any ambition in Berlin. E. W. Bohle, the head of the "Foreign Department" of the Nazi party, made the position clear in a letter to the senior Group Leader, Major Weigel:

> I have had fairly lengthy discussions with von Neurath about South-West Africa and the Union but cannot say in a letter what transpired. I have always been of the opinion that the colonial problem will ultimately be decided in Europe and not in the various Mandated Territories. I, therefore, consider it wrong to broadcast that South-West Africa must return to Germany . . .
>
> The present Government leaves none of its people in the lurch, but it would do no harm if the people of South-West Africa were to take a broader view of matters . . .
>
> It will be my first duty to put the party in order in this respect and to teach Party members to keep quiet.[11]

Berlin's warnings to South-West Africa's Nazis had their effect. In Tanganyika the local Nazis remained active. Propaganda and recruitment had been surprisingly successful. But increased Nazi activities angered Berlin. The German Consul in Pretoria told the Nazis to show proper courtesy to their British hosts, and uphold Germany's good name by economic, social and sporting co-operation. "Do as you are ordered, and do not undertake independent and embarrassing actions." [12]

If Berlin looked harshly on its African compatriots, London sought to win Berlin's confidence by showing that the return of the Mandates was still possible from the British side. Sir Thomas Moore suggested in July, 1933, that Germany "should be given back her own colonies" in West Africa, as an "outlet for her energies." [13] In December, 1933, Kirkpatrick told Ribbentrop that he had an "open mind" about colonies. Ribbentrop did nothing. Kirkpatrick, later, felt "ashamed" of his remark.[14] Yet his "open mind" was no isolated phenomenon. Many Englishmen felt it fair and wise to consider the return of some, if not all, of Germany's former colonies. It would be politically wise, for it would win the confidence of the Nazi régime. It would show the Germans that Britain wished to be friendly. It would also be morally right: the Versailles Treaty was an injustice which should be corrected.

Lord Allen of Hurtwood told a gathering at All Souls' that Germany should not only be given the colonies that had been hers before 1918, but also others.[15]

Clement Attlee opposed this. But he never addressed the august dons of All Souls'. Attlee's view, though unheard in Oxford, could not be silenced in London. Three months after Hitler came to power he made his position clear in the Commons. "We should say quite frankly to Germany that at the present moment no one in this country would propose to entrust any minority to Germany, seeing how she was treating her own minorities." It was a bold man who pointed to German domestic brutality and drew an international moral, but Attlee knew that ideological ruthlessness would not end within European frontiers. Imperial rule is usually an exaggeration, not a modification, of domestic rule.

Harold, 1st Viscount Lord Rothermere, who had many friends in Germany, claimed that Versailles had deprived Germany of "sources from which before the war she imported fifty per cent of her raw materials." Amery refuted him by pointing out that according to the German Statistical Yearbook for 1915 colonial imports were only 0.5 per cent of the total.[16] Rothermere ignored him. He was determined to destroy the Treaty. Through his newspaper, the *Daily Mail*, he advocated the return of Tanganyika, Cameroons and Togoland to the League "in order that they may be transferred to Germany." He explained:

> Though this proposal may not be so popular, I am convinced that it is wise. We cannot expect a nation of he-men like the Germans to sit forever with folded arms under the provocations and stupidities of the Treaty of Versailles . . . To deny this mighty nation, conspicuous for its organising ability and scientific achievements, a share in the work of developing backward regions of the world is preposterous.[17]

Rothermere's offer received neither acclaim nor support from Germany. But he persisted in trying to interest Britain, and Germany, in the idea of a colonial settlement.* In August, 1934, Hitler agreed to talk to a *Daily Mail* correspondent about colonies. His reply disappointed those Englishmen who tried to persuade their friends that Britain ought to return the Mandates, in order to win German friendship. Hitler said: "I would not sacrifice the life of a single German to get any colony in the world. We know that former German colonies are costly luxuries, even for England." [18]

Hitler showed no interest, but others were willing to show it for him. Lord Lothian, in *Round Table*, suggested the need for Germany to have access to colonial raw materials. Such a suggestion found many supporters. In May, 1935, Eden and Simon visited Hitler. According to their report they "made it perfectly plain to Herr Hitler" that the transfer of Mandates "is not a dis-

* In mid-April, 1934, the *Daily Mail* asked its readers if they considered it reasonable to return Germany's colonies to her. Two-thirds of those who replied said "yes."

cussible question." Simon claimed that it was Hitler who had broached the subject. But the Imperial lobby saw, in the very mention of the question, the hint of a British offer. Suspicion that Eden and Simon had not been as firm to Hitler as they might have been revealed itself in a heated exchange in the Commons.

> *Sir John Simon:* We pointed out [to Hitler] . . . that the distribution of Mandates is not a question for any individual member of the League. It is a question for the League itself.
> *Sir Austen Chamberlain:* No, certainly not.
> *Sir John Simon:* Not originally, but surely the Mandates Commission did at any rate ——
> *Sir Austen Chamberlain:* This is very important. If [your] words stood unqualified it would give rise to a wholly false impression, and indicate an entirely new departure on the part of the Government.[19]

Simon insisted that Hitler had been left in no doubt as to British determination not to leave the Mandates. His insistence was not entirely believed.

South-West Africa was a tricky problem for the Imperial lobby at Westminster. South-West Africa was a Mandate of South Africa, and Oswald Pirow, Defense Minister of South Africa, was well-known for his sympathies towards the Nazi régime. In January, 1935, he was reported to have told a group of German officers:

> For us in South Africa the maintenance and spread of white civilisation is a question of life and death. In this sense I express the hope that Germany will again soon become a Colonial Power, and, moreover, a Colonial Power in Africa.[20]

German politicians took up the colonial chorus. At the Leipzig Fair in March, Schacht pointed out the need for colonies — a "purely economic" one, but no less real for that.[21] In August, Frick, the Minister of the Interior, described Germany as "a nation sadly lacking in elbow room . . . We shall not permit others to ignore our vital necessities." [22] There was no official German move. But the British press took up the German claims. The *Sunday Dispatch* considered that a British refusal to return the German colonies "will have the gravest consequences," [23] and the *Daily Herald* thought it "grimly obvious enough" that the present unequal distribution of colonies endangered world peace.[24]

In September, the British Government was willing to discuss the colonial question, and to "share in an investigation" of the problem of access to colonial raw materials. Sir Samuel Hoare told the League of Nations that his Government wanted "to take their share in any collective attempt to deal in a fair and effective way with a problem that is certainly troubling many people at present and may trouble them even more in the future." [25] Any colonial investigation, he told the Commons, would require "sincerity and goodwill." [26]

The Economist advocated a super-mandate in Africa, with the Germans participating. At a meeting of the National Peace Council Lothian pressed German claims. Britain, said Lothian, "must be prepared to make sacrifices." "If only we could get into conference with the Germans," he wrote to Lord Allen of Hurtwood, "on the fundamental problems of today . . . we could influence them, I think, to moderate the brutality of their practice." [27]

Men of influence pressed for a solution. Lord Downe told an audience at York: "I wish our Government would screw themselves to the point of returning to Germany the colonies taken from her after the war." [28] Still the Germans were unsure of what attitude to adopt. Goebbels declared that "the time would come" when Germany would demand the return of her colonies.[29] It was not an urgent statement. In January, Lord Londonderry visited Germany, and asked the Nazi leaders about their attitude to colonies. Göring told him that Germany's increased population made the colonial question important. Hesse insisted that the need for raw materials made a return of colonies essential. Hitler spoke of a nation of sixty-eight millions needing colonies for "certain necessities of life;" but what those necessities were he did not say. Ribbentrop weakened the arguments of his friends by having admitted to Londonderry that the colonial demand was "a question of prestige." [30]

On February 5, 1936, the Commons debated the colonial question. Lloyd George, speaking as "one of the three or four who were responsible" for drafting the Versailles Treaty, stated that the German colonies "were not given to us as British possessions; they were given to the League of Nations, and the legal right is vested in the League . . ." Churchill interrupted — "No" —, but Lloyd George went on to inform the House: "I do not believe that you will have peace in the world until you recognize the Mandates." The German claims, for a return of the Mandates, did not seem to him "to be very extravagant."

The Imperial lobby was indignant. Page Croft went so far as to say that any Government that sought to return the Mandated Territories to Germany in order "to placate those who are doing wrong in the world . . . would be kicked from power by an indignant people." Sufficient outcry was raised for the Government to declare: "His Majesty's Government have not considered, and are not considering the handing over of any of the British colonies or territories held under British Mandate." [31] It was a definite assurance.

Still the pressures increased for a return of the Mandates. Speaking at Hamburg in March, Arnold Toynbee said of the colonial question: "We British are not so foolish as to think things must remain as they are. Obviously, the very essence of human affairs is change; and if it is not peaceful change, it will be violent change." [32] This offered the Germans a program; and one with an implied threat.

On March 7, the German Government stated officially that it hoped that "in the course of a reasonable period" the question of "colonial equality of rights . . . may be clarified through friendly negotiations." [33] Here was the moderate and sensible request the British wanted. Hitler made no hysterical demands. Doubtless, within the staid framework of gentlemanly diplomacy, a solution could be reached which would satisfy German colonial ambitions and show Germany that Britain was anxious to turn aside from the unjust restrictions of Versailles. On April 6, Chamberlain told the Commons that "mandated territories are not colonies." The Mandates were only a part of the British Empire "in what I may call the colloquial sense." It was a remark, wrote Amery, "which could not but encourage German hopes." [34]

Here was a hint of a new policy. Two days later the French proposed a change in the colonial position "from the point of view of economic rights and the co-operation of credit between European states." [35] This was something like Hoare's Geneva proposal of the previous September. But the British had progressed beyond considerations of *economic* equalities. During April the ever-alert Amery discovered that "the Cabinet generally and Neville Chamberlain in particular" were bent on offering Tanganyika to Germany.[36] Imperialists were outraged at the thought of a loss of Empire. On April 21, a colonial debate in the Commons showed the Government something of the strength of the opposition to any return of colonies. A. R. Wise maintained that no German concessions would justify our handing over people to a Government "which we know is unlikely to live up to the standard which these people have been enjoying." Hitler's own writings gave no cause for optimism. For the Imperialists the greatest justification of Imperial rule was the paternal attitude: raising the natives to a higher standard rather than depressing them. Hitler had written:

> One hears from time to time that a negro has become a lawyer, teacher, tenor or the like. This is a sin against all reason; it is criminal lunacy to train a born semi-ape to become a lawyer. It is a sin against the Eternal Creator to train Hottentots and Kaffirs to intellectual professions.[37]

Wise insisted: "we are still an Imperial race." Under pressure the Government repeated its previous assurance. It declared that "we are not considering" the question of a return of colonies. But it added a rider which, for the defenders of the integrity of the Empire, was sinister. If the colonial question was raised "by any other people it will be our duty to consider the circumstances again." There, for the Imperialists, was an admission that the Government had not abandoned the idea of concessions. A Parliamentary Group was formed to "watch over the situation." Duncan Sandys was Secretary. A deputation to Baldwin in May "met with evasion." [38]

On July 22, Sandys raised a further alarm. One hundred and eighteen MPs signed his Parliamentary protest.* Eden, by way of allaying fears that colonial changes were imminent, told the Commons that any transfer of territory would raise "grave difficulties, moral, political and legal, of which His Majesty's Government must frankly say they had been unable to find any solution." [39] A solution had, so Eden implied, been sought. What was there to suggest, let alone to guarantee, that within six months the Government might not have more success? Within the next two months a discussion of Germany's right to colonies was taken up in the correspondence columns of *The Times*. As a reaction against the pro-transfer trend of popular opinion Duncan Sandys and Page Croft brought forward a resolution at the Conservative Party Conference declaring that the question of the transfer of Mandates was "not discussible." The resolution was passed. Hoare tried to defeat it. But his appeal for "Conservative unity" was ignored.

The colonial question became a major one. Throughout 1936, Kirkpatrick wrote, "the colonial problem was always cropping up at parties." [40] In September, at the Nazi Party Congress, Hitler gave public prominence to colonial claims for the first time. The influence of Schacht, who strongly advocated a German Empire in Africa, had been effective. Hitler said a return of colonies

---

* Including Page Croft, Austen Chamberlain, Churchill, Amery, Harold Nicolson, Wise, Brendan Bracken, and Roger Keyes.

would give Germany both economic advantage and "justice." The appeal for justice was effective. Those Englishmen who traced all contemporary problems to the evils of Versailles agreed with Hitler. German propagandists sensed that the time had come to press the German claims. Two of them published articles, in English, in the January numbers of English journals. Ritter von Epp, Director of the Colonial League, explained in a special supplement to the *Journal of the Royal African Society* that colonies would provide Germany "with food and work." As for raw materials, "we are neither willing nor able to accept a position of inferiority." Here was an implied threat. Schacht in *Foreign Affairs* threatened more directly. The colonial problem, he wrote, was "not a mere problem of prestige. It is simply and solely a problem of economic existence . . . There will be no peace in Europe until this problem is solved. No great nation willingly allows its standard of life and culture to be lowered; and no great nation accepts the risk that it will go hungry."

The economic expert had explained his case. On January 20, 1937, Hitler gave the colonial demand further support when he told the Reichstag, "Our demand for colonies . . . will be put forward again and again." At the Leipzig Fair in March, Ribbentrop spoke of Germany's "small territory . . . on the poor soil of Northern Europe." [41] On May 4, Lothian had a long conversation with Hitler, in the course of which Hitler raised the colonial issue:

> England says: America needs a large vast area to feed its people. Absolutely correct.
> Russia needs a vast area to feed its people. Correct.
> France needs her colonies for the same purpose. Absolutely right.
> England needs her Empire to feed her population. Good. Quite right.
> Belgium needs her colonies for the same purpose. Good. Quite right.
> Portugal needs her colonies to feed her people. Good. *Selbstverständlich.*
> But Germany, say the English, in no circumstances needs colonies

to feed her people. This is absolutely intolerable. Such a view shows neither statesmanship, nor common sense, nor a trace of political instinct . . .[42]

Hitler wanted English friendship. "For me it was doubly difficult to be faced with such an attitude. I have always been pro-English. Long before I became Chancellor, in my writing days, I advocated co-operation with England."

Lothian told Hitler that "it was not right to assume that England took the view that Germany should have no colonies; colonial adjustment, though not on a large scale, was not impossible." [43] However impressed Lothian may have been by Hitler's reasoning, Göring's remarks to him on the same day must have made him wonder just how serious the colonial demand was. Göring maintained that Germany's "legitimate influence on the Continent" was "as important, if not more important." Lothian left Berlin feeling that "the situation was both more dangerous and more soluble" than he had supposed.[44] The nature of the solution was still in doubt. It was discussed unofficially throughout the summer. Smuts wrote to Lothian in April: "we do not mean to stick to *all* the ex-German colonies." [45]

In October, *The Times*, which until then had been unwilling to commit itself either for or against colonial concessions, clarified its views. In a leading article headed *The Claim to Colonies*, Dawson wrote:

The truth is that British public opinion is probably far ahead of the Government in its conviction that a clear understanding with Germany will have consequences more profound and more conducive to a stable peace than any other single object of our foreign policy. There is little sympathy here with the view, which has sometimes seemed to prevail on the Continent, that the proper way to treat Germany is to ring her about with vigilant allied states, sometimes masquerading as the League of Nations, like trained elephants round a tiger in the jungle, to prevent her ex-

pansion in any direction beyond the limits imposed twenty years
ago.[46]

The old limits ought to be removed. Versailles must go.

By October, the British Government had made up its mind to
make a definite offer to Germany. On September 20, Eden told
the League: "we have always been ready, and still are ready, to
discuss with any country any proposal which that country thinks
likely to be of mutual benefit." [47] On October 28, Nevile Henderson told Dalton that "the right thing" for Britain to do was
to give Germany "two substantial tracts" of British territory on
either side of the Congo. Britain should "open the subscription
lists generously." France and Belgium would then also contribute. The effect of such an offer "would be tremendous," as
Germany was "anxious to be friends with us; Hitler in particular." [48] Eden, hearing of this conversation, was understandably vexed. He said of Henderson: "I wish he would not go on
like this to everybody he meets." [49]

A British plan was being prepared. The Germans were not
certain how they should respond. The idea of a colonial Empire
had figured large in German public speeches. But it served so
fine a propaganda purpose that, once colonies were returned, all
the bitterness Hitler created around the "lost and stolen" colonies would disappear. The colonies were more useful as a
grievance to shout about than as areas to be marked German on
the map. Schacht was the leading politician in favor of an overseas Empire. Hitler was less certain about its value. On November 5, Hitler explained to a small circle which included Schacht
why Germany must avoid the British ratio of nine colored subjects for every white. It would be wrong to allow "the foundation constituted by the numerical strength of our own people to
become too weak." Britain offered colonies at a time when she
was strong. Hitler thought it more profitable to wait until
"Britain was in difficulties." [50] Hitler was unenthusiastic about
taking advantage of the British mood. Weizsäcker thought

otherwise. For him the fact of an impending British offer made it necessary for Germany to evolve a more positive policy. On the day Hitler told Schacht there was no hurry, Weizsäcker suggested a German-British Commission which should be set up to examine German claims. "What we want from England we cannot obtain by force but must obtain by negotiations." [51] The British willingness to negotiate should not be neglected.

On November 13, the *Illustrated London News* printed a map of the former German colonies and advocated a negotiated settlement. On November 17, the German Minister in Dublin was told by Walshe, the Irish Foreign Secretary, that "Germany's demand for the return of her colonies (German East Africa, South-West Africa, Samoa) definitely had prospects of success today." Walshe was right on the mood, wrong on the map. But as the German Minister noted, "Mr. Walshe is obviously well-informed" about Halifax, "with whom he is acquainted." [52] On November 18, Bullitt, the U.S. Ambassador in Paris, told Neurath that if the British wanted they were "quite at liberty" to "make a deal" with Portugal or Belgium in order to give Germany Portuguese or Belgian territory instead of British. [53] This would be necessary if the British were unwilling to give up Tanganyika, or if South Africa refused to surrender South-West Africa.

The Germans had no need to reply to diplomatic gossip, any more than to private visitors or press enthusiasms. But on November 19, the colonial question was broached by a more serious person. Lord Halifax was neither a diplomat nor Foreign Secretary, but Lord Privy Seal. His visit was, officially, entirely unofficial: nothing more than a hunting trip. But the Germans were well aware of the seriousness and stature of their visitor. When Halifax told Hitler that "today he could speak" of colonies, Hitler knew that he was no longer dealing with propagandists or apologists. Here was the German chance to put their plans forward with maximum effect; that is, if they had plans.

Hitler told Halifax that "certain nations did not have sufficient space on which to live." There was also the question of trade. Hitler knew "trade followed the flag." The absence of German flags in Africa meant no trade. It was a pity that the Conservative party had adopted "absolutely negative resolutions." The colonial question was the "only direct issue" between Britain and Germany. There were "no other difficulties" in the relationship between the two countries. But there was no question of a German threat. If the question remained unsolved, all Hitler would do was "note it, and regret it." [54]

Halifax had come to sound Hitler out, not to make positive proposals. He asked Hitler for details of the German demands. Hitler was surprised. He had prepared no "details" in advance. "It was not for Germany to state her wishes," he replied weakly. But who else could state them? Pressed, Hitler said Germany wanted "her former properties." England could, of course, propose substitute areas, if she did not wish to give up territory of strategic importance. But Hitler had no ideas on where the substitute areas should be. All he could tell Halifax was where it was that he wanted *no* colonies. The Sahara and the Mediterranean would only be a "source of trouble." The Far East held no attractions as it was an area "where the guns were already going off." Halifax suggested that a "general settlement by means of which quiet and security might be established in Europe" ought to accompany any colonial settlement. [55] Hitler was unenthusiastic.

Hitler failed to take advantage of Halifax's probe. General Blomberg went so far as to tell Halifax it was Central Europe, not overseas territory, which was of "vital importance" to Germany. [56] Only Schacht took advantage of such a prominent visitor in order to press what, for him, were real colonial ambitions. The Cameroons and Togoland "could, and should, be returned" he told Halifax. Germany should also receive a block made up of "parts of Belgian Congo and Angola, under something like a Mandate." [57] Schacht recognized the "difficulties" for Britain of giving up Tanganyika. On November 26, Chamberlain noted: "They do not insist on Tanganyika, if they can be given some reasonably equivalent territory on the west coast." [58] "They" was Schacht alone. But the British were so eager to reach agreement with Germany that they exaggerated the importance of his imaginative brain. Schacht had grandiose plans. Hitler was unwilling to back them.

The British had shown that they seriously considered colonial concessions. The Germans had mentioned, though with less unanimity or enthusiasm than might have been expected, certain areas in which they were interested. Here was a basis for agreement. The appeasement press continued to urge a settlement. On November 28, Hugh Dalton noted that *The Observer* "carries the usual Garvin slobber, including proposals for a wholesale return of colonies." [59]

On November 29, the French Government challenged colonial appeasement. Halifax met Chautemps in London and discussed the German proposals (that is, Schacht's suggestions). Chautemps "made it clear" to Halifax that he did not believe in "throwing the hungry tiger a large tender-loin in order to improve the condition of his stomach." As for the British idea that Germany should accept parts of Portuguese or Belgian territory, Chautemps was disgusted. He claimed to have "stopped all suggestions" for such a deal.[60] He was wise to oppose so curious and immoral a plan; less wise to imagine his opposition would influence the British. Unwilling to give up Tanganyika, the British Government believed that Belgium or Portugal, or both, should make concessions. The only result of French opposition was that the French ceased to be informed of further developments.

Anglo-German discussions continued. As Eden told Ribbentrop it would be "best if England could also speak for France." [61] Hitler hoped, if negotiations *were* to begin, to have a French as well as British negotiator. The British knew that this would be impossible. British eagerness grew as obstacles increased. Eden continued to impress on Ribbentrop Britain's "earnest desire" to make concessions. Surely Ribbentrop would recognize the progress that had been made? The colonial question was being treated by the Government "as a problem that was acute and had to be solved." It was even intended to establish a "Cabinet Committee" to discuss details of the settlement. There were, of course, difficulties. "A month or more" ought to pass, in Eden's opinion, before "certain clarifications" would be reached. Perhaps colonial Governments were being consulted — Eden did not say. What he did suggest was the need for a *quid pro quo* agreement. Germany would gain colonies; Britain and Germany "a greater feeling of security." The nation of shopkeepers, said Eden, could not be blamed for wanting "compensation." [62] If the Germans would offer an agreement on arms limitation, it would be easier for Britain to return the former colonies without undue public outcry, or Parliamentary pressure.

About December 10, Halifax had explained to Ribbentrop that Britain was "urgently trying to make concessions." Despite opposition in Britain, Chamberlain "was determined that something should be done." Halifax himself, however, was "sceptical." [63] Here was conflict: the desires of the Government opposed the mood of the country. Chamberlain wanted a colonial settlement to stand on its own, as an example of British generosity and friendship. But men of influence grew wary of German intentions. The more arrogant Hitler's speeches became, the more sinister Germany's rapidly increasing armament seemed. Many who regarded Germany's colonial claim as justified wanted to link a colonial settlement with an agreement on arms limitation. Chamberlain hoped Parliament would support a colonial offer without conditions. Ribbentrop even reported that Chamberlain had told him of "a remarkable change" in Parliamentary opinion. February or March would be a good time for serious discussions.[64] But Ribbentrop soon learned, if he had not known already, that it was not so simple an affair.

On December 6, Lord Londonderry, who sympathized with German colonial claims, explained to a friend that even appeasement could be realistic when it cared to be.

I am very anxious lest by our conciliatory attitude and our desire to see justice done to Germany all the German desires will take the form of grievances which, when the Germans are strong enough, they will seek to enforce by force of arms . . . It appears to me that by the shilly-shallying policy of the Government we are slowly but surely drifting towards this position. I should like to see our Government undertaking a bold policy based on limitation of armaments and the according to Germany of the position . . . she should occupy in international affairs.[65]

The German Foreign Ministry received a copy of this letter on January 19, 1938. No evidence of a "bold policy" was forthcoming, however, and on January 26, the "shilly-shallying" was resumed. Henderson told Neurath that Chamberlain's task would be made "much easier" if, during colonial negotiations, he could "point to the prospect" of a *quid pro quo* on armaments.[66] Here was weak language indeed. Far from demanding a *quid pro quo*, Chamberlain excused himself for suggesting it. Neurath could have assumed only that the armaments agreement was far from essential; but the mere mention that one was contemplated would enable Chamberlain to bypass his opponents. Certainly Chamberlain was finding support for the colonial deal *without* compensation hard to obtain. On January 25, Dawson noted how Chamberlain "stood pat on appeasement with Germany — not, he said, getting much constructive help from the FO." [67] Eden was insisting on a *quid pro quo*.[68]

Academics came to the rescue where diplomats failed. R. W. Seton-Watson wrote in February "that the convenient thesis of Germany's unfitness to administer colonies is as untrue as it is insulting, and should be recanted." [69] Chamberlain was trying his utmost to recant. In February, he called Henderson to London and gave him instructions to make a specific colonial offer to Hitler on his return to Berlin.

Rumor spread. On February 11, the Germans learned of a supposed British offer, the basis of which was a return of the Mandates. Portuguese territory, however, "would be offered in place of" Tanganyika. Chamberlain, said the informant, was himself unwilling to use the colonial offer as a "trade horse" by linking any armament agreement with it. But to "justify" the offer to the British public, Germany should offer something "towards safeguarding the peace of Europe." Chamberlain had mentioned, said the informant, not a broad limitation of armaments, but an agreement on aerial bombing.[70] One facet of disarmament would be enough.

On February 20, Eden resigned. On March 1, Chamberlain dropped all pretense that a *quid pro quo* was needed. Henderson told Ribbentrop a colonial settlement could be negotiated on its own. It would not be used as a bargaining point for other issues.[71] Eden's resignation had led to the abandonment of a *quid pro quo*. Appeasement had no need of security or justification.

On March 3, Henderson met Hitler and put forward the British colonial offer.[72] Henderson explained the offer "on a map" which he had brought with him. In Africa, between five degrees of latitude and the Zambesi, the colonies would be "redistributed." It was essential, said Henderson, that no information of this plan reach the French, "much less" the Belgians or Portuguese. Halifax had drawn up a formula to which it was hoped Hitler would agree. It was to the effect that Portugal and Belgium would "merely be informed" that conversations took place which dealt with questions "concerning Germany and England." Hitler agreed that no more than this should be made public. But he was puzzled by the proposals themselves. They seemed to him "new and complicated." What he had hoped for was the "simplest solution" of a return of Germany's former colonies. He had never wanted other people's colonies.

Henderson had to explain to Hitler what Hitler certainly knew — Britain wished to keep Tanganyika. Nor could South Africa be persuaded to part with South-West Africa. If Hitler was to be satisfied, and it was the British desire that he should be, he must accept Portuguese and Belgian territory. Henderson explained the territorial scheme to Hitler again, this time "on the globe" in Hitler's room.* Hitler protested that Germany did not want to "burden" other countries. Perhaps Portugal and Belgium "would not agree" to the British plan. Henderson tried to convince Hitler that not only Portugal and Belgium but "presumably" France "would in the end co-operate in the settlement."

The British were in a dangerous position. They had abandoned the essential precaution of a *quid pro quo*. They were promising to influence three imperial powers to accept a drastic re-arrangement, and loss, of territory, agreed upon by none of them. Fortunately, Hitler saved them from much future embarrassment. Colonies, he said, could only burden him. He had no use for them. It was a strange admission after so much shouting and propaganda. It upset the appeasers' efforts to satisfy him with colonial territory.

Hitler told Henderson that "the colonial question could wait for four, six, eight or even ten years." Henderson pressed for something more definite. Hitler promised a written reply. As Henderson wrote: "I left Berlin a year and a half later without having received it." The British offer had failed.† But Chamberlain still hoped something might come of it. On March 10, Ribbentrop told Halifax that Hitler would give a written reply to the British offer. Ribbentrop hoped a "final and lasting understanding . . . would be entirely possible." Halifax replied with some equally encouraging news. He had not been idle since Henderson's meeting with Hitler a week earlier. He had met "about eighty" press representatives to whom he had "earnestly emphasized" the importance of press influence over foreign policy. Although "England was not prepared even to consider

* Henderson wrote of "the globe of the world which always stands in Hitler's room wherever he is, a practice I would strongly recommend to all politicians and diplomatists." (Henderson: *Failure of a Mission*.)

† At the end of the interview, wrote Henderson, "I produced from my pocket an extremely good drawing of the Chancellor which a lady from New Zealand had sent me, with the request that I might get it autographed." Hitler signed. (Henderson: *Failure of a Mission*.)

control measures similar to the ones employed by Germany" Halifax was nevertheless pleased to say that "measures taken" by the BBC would ensure that programs "eliminated discussion regarding colonies." [73] That same day Wilson told a friend of his at the German Embassy that Halifax had "taken special pains" with the press, and "hoped that he had been successful." [74]

March 10 found the British still scheming, despite Hitler's rebuff. The German occupation of Austria, on March 12, ended their plans. Chamberlain was asked in the Commons whether the *Anschluss* "would prejudice the coming discussions of colonial questions." He answered: "It is obvious that in the present circumstances nothing further can be done in that direction." [75]

Some cynics thought that "present circumstances" would change soon enough. For the next seven months Lloyds quoted as insurance *against* Tanganyika being handed over "to a foreign power" the pessimistic rate of £36 15s. per cent! [76]

In November, 1938, Oswald Pirow, the South African politician, visited London. He wished to make clear to the British and German Governments a "fundamental attitude" of his party in South Africa. If this attitude found official support in Europe, it would be more likely to become official policy in South Africa. Pirow wanted "recognition in principal of a German colonial claim to South-West Africa which must be satisfied as far as possible by other means, in which connection the payment of a sum of money plays a part." [77]

We do not know how the British Government responded. The Germans revealed that the lack of interest which they had shown the previous March had been no chance occurrence. Ribbentrop wrote: "On the subject of the colonial question, I merely said (to Pirow) that the matter did not seem to be acute at present but that it could be discussed in a few years — five or six." [78]

It was the Germans who, to use a phrase of Henderson's, had "missed the market."

PART TWO

Today was a beautiful day, the sky was a brilliant
   Blue for the first time for weeks and weeks
But posters flapping on the railings tell the fluttered
   World that Hitler speaks, that Hitler speaks
And we cannot take it in and we go to our daily
   Jobs to the dull refrain of the caption "War"
Buzzing around us as from hidden insects
   And we think "This must be wrong, it has happened
      before,
Just like this before, we must be dreaming;
   It was long ago these flies
Buzzed like this, so why are they still bombarding
   The ears if not the eyes?"
And we laugh it off and go around town in the evening
   And this, we say, is on me;
Something out of the usual, a Pimm's Number One, a
      Picon —
   But did you see
The latest? You mean whether Cobb has bust the record
   Or do you mean the Australians have lost their last by ten
Wickets or do you mean that the autumn fashions —
   No, we don't mean anything like that again.
No, what we mean is Hodza, Henlein, Hitler,
   The Maginot Line,
The heavy panic that cramps the lungs and presses
   The collar down the spine.

              — LOUIS MACNEICE
              Autumn Journal: 1938

CHAPTER 5

"A Far-Away Country"

Bohemia wants to reconstruct Mitteleuropa on a new basis
which is neither German nor Russian. She therefore bases her
claims not so much on national as on international justifica-
tions. For her, although National Unity comes first, and national prosperity second, the ultimate aim is the stability of
Central Europe.
— Harold Nicolson, *Peacemaking* 1919

BRITISH statesmen knew that Czechoslovakia was a "problem"
State. Long before the Czech problem disturbed Europe, they
knew of the dangers that beset it. It contained a large German-
speaking minority difficult to incorporate in a harmonious body-
politic. Yet, alone of the Succession States, Czechoslovakia had
retained the liberal-democratic flavor with which it had been
endowed. It was linked in traditional friendship with England.
The tradition was artificial, the friendship real. Sir Samuel
Hoare, for example, had taken a close interest in the Czechoslovak movement that led to the recognition of Czechoslovakia
and had "followed with sincere admiration the fortunes of the
new State." [1]

The public had no such personal interest, but they recognized
the problems of the country long before the crisis of Autumn,
1938, became acute. The German Minister in Prague could
write at the beginning of 1938 that "Czechoslovakia, whose
name was formerly almost unknown in Great Britain, . . . today commands a solid block of supporters in the newspaper
world, the Liberal and Socialist parties and their MPs, as well as
in financial circles of the City of London." [2]

In 1937, Henlein, leader of those Sudeten Germans who disliked Czech rule, addressed the Royal Institute for International

Affairs. What he suggested then, and earlier in talks with R. W. Seton-Watson in 1935 and 1936, promised a reasonable solution for reasonable men. He accepted the indivisibility of the Bohemian lands, and the possibility of a settlement for the Sudeten Germans within the framework of the Czechoslovak constitution.[3]

English friendship towards Czechoslovakia was tempered by criticism of the position of the German minority. Henlein had been listened to in London. English attitudes were divided.

Amery "had long been familiar with the difficult internal and external problems of that artificially compacted State." [4] Forty years before he had studied the racial conflicts of the Austro-Hungarian Empire; Czechoslovakia, with its disgruntled minorities of Germans, Poles, Ruthenians, and Magyars, seemed to reflect in microcosm the difficulties of that earlier "ramshackle" state. Nevile Henderson, who referred to the Czechs as "those blasted Czechs," had spoken to people in England, so he maintained, who regarded Czechoslovakia as a new variety of interesting flower.[5] A colleague of his, he later recorded, had begun a dispatch to London: "There is no such thing as Czechoslovakia." Henderson thought this "largely true." [6]

The French, bound in a military alliance with Czechoslovakia since 1925, could not afford to be so critical. Daladier believed Czechoslovakia "had done more for the minorities than any other European State." [7] He had been there several times, and in the Sudeten districts "everywhere he had seen German schools and German officials." There was none of the open discrimination against minorities practised in other East European States.

British policy was set forth in a letter from Eden to Basil Newton, Minister in Prague, in March, 1937. England was not prepared to offer either advice or mediation to Czechoslovakia. But she urged the Czech Government to realize the importance of a "far-reaching settlement" with the Sudeten Germans, "for its own sake,"[8] and not because it might facilitate a British agreement with Germany on more general issues.*

In the autumn of 1937, the Czechs believed Germany intended to stage a rising on the Spanish pattern among the Sudeten Germans. This it was thought would lead to "voluntary" union of the Sudeten German territory with Germany.[9] Léon Blum, the French Prime Minister, was asked on September 21 whether France would regard such a move as a *casus foederis*. He answered that this was his personal conviction, but that he could not commit the French Government.[10] At the end of October, Delbos, the French Foreign Minister, emphasized that France would fulfill her obligations "whatever the form of the aggression, if the aggression is certain."[11] Henlein was in London on October 10. Vansittart told him Britain would work with Czechoslovakia to secure the most far-reaching autonomy for the Sudeten Germans. But "if the Germans marched into Czechoslovakia,"[12] Britain would be found at the side of France. As a result of his visit, Henlein announced that "no serious intervention in favour of the Czechs was to be feared from England or probably from France."[13] His remark was certainly designed for home consumption but it also reflected a basic lack of firmness in Anglo-French policy. Vansittart had spent some time during Henlein's visits to London "trying to frighten him and keep him from contact with British appeasers."[14] Vansittart had failed.

Henlein had interpreted the English atmosphere correctly. Chamberlain wrote on November 26 that he wanted to tell the Germans:

> Give us satisfactory assurance that you won't use force to deal with the Austrians and Czechoslovakians and we will give you similar assurance that we won't use force to prevent the changes you want, if you can get them by peaceful means.[15]

* Eden told Newton that the British Government was "not prepared to take the responsibility for counselling Dr. Beneš to negotiate a settlement of whose terms they are quite unaware, and which might, indeed, entail dangerous or humiliating concessions." Lord Avon, *Facing the Dictators*, p. 503.

But were there no strategic arguments? Once Austria and Czechoslovakia had been brought within the German system, however peacefully, what was to prevent Hitler using force to secure further gains? Once the first barrier had crumbled, what sanctions could Britain employ to prevent further aggrandizement? Policy was decided before its implications had been considered.

At the end of November, Chautemps, Delbos and Léger met Chamberlain, Eden and Halifax in London. Chamberlain asked Delbos to urge Beneš to agree to further concessions to the German minority.[16] Eden later told Grandi that the British and French Governments "were prepared to support a solution in conformity with German wishes, namely on the basis of autonomy." [17]

There was already a marked difference between Czechoslovakia and her friends. Hodza, the Czechoslovak Prime Minister, said autonomy was "tantamount to suicide" for the State.[18] Beneš added that Czechoslovakia would not tolerate British and French interference in their internal affairs. "They were too far away to understand these things." [19] Beneš knew that distance led to ignorance. But those who wished to meddle were undeterred.

Chamberlain, anxious to come to a general settlement with Germany, could not allow Czech intransigence to endanger his plans. The British pressed the Czechs to accept Henlein's demands. German autonomy *within* the Czech state was no crime.

Hitler annexed Austria on March 12, 1938. That evening a press photographer asked Hore-Belisha, the War Minister, to smile as he left 10 Downing Street. "Why should I smile?" he answered.[20] Some people might see the *Anschluss* as part of a healthy process of German growth. Others feared that Germany, having tasted Vienna, would hunger for Prague.

Göring told the Czechs they were in no danger. Krofta, the Czech Foreign Secretary, was not assured. He told his ambassadors "to avoid all unnecessary criticism, and to make every effort to avoid being involved." [21] Jan Masaryk, in London, was therefore "a good deal disturbed" by a proposal made at a meeting in Trafalgar Square on March 13, that a sympathetic demonstration should take place outside his house in Grosvenor Place.[22]

Lord Cecil and Churchill suggested that the matter should be taken before the League of Nations. They were treated cavalierly by Halifax. Halifax told Phipps that "such procedure would be of no practical advantage in redressing the present situation." [23] The League would be exposed to "open humiliation" which would "inevitably prejudice its reconstruction." It was unlikely, after his speech in February attacking the League, that Chamberlain would advocate its use.

"There was no point in bringing the Austrian question before the League of Nations," Halifax told the Lords on March 16. "Only a war could bring about a change in the situation thus produced. Members of the League of Nations were, however, not prepared for this." This was true. Nobody was prepared to fight for Austria. The British avoided referring the question to Geneva, not because they feared a League war against Germany, but because they knew that League interference, however ineffective, would endanger the cherished Anglo-German *rapprochement*.

On March 13, Paul-Boncour succeeded Delbos at the Quai d'Orsay. Blum, who had fallen some months earlier, became Prime Minister for a second time. The new Popular Front Government made concerted Anglo-French action improbable. It was a Government, wrote Chamberlain on March 20, "in which one cannot have the slightest confidence and which I suspect to be in closish touch with our Opposition." [24] Cadogan told Masaryk that Paul-Boncour "was not a Foreign Minister who at so serious a moment could be a worthy partner in a discussion of the European crisis." [25]

The two Governments had conflicting ideas on the solution of the Czech problem. The first person Paul-Boncour saw on entering office was Osusky, the Czechoslovak Minister in Paris. Blum was also present. They discussed the form French military assistance might take. They thought Chamberlain would make an explicit statement on the British attitude if Germany attacked Czechoslovakia. They were disillusioned. There was no question of an Anglo-French warning to Germany. "Quite frankly," wrote Halifax, "the moment is unfavourable, and our plans, both for offence and defence, are not sufficiently advanced." [26] British policy favored German co-operation over Czechoslovakia: "I should like to make it quite clear," wrote Halifax, "that if a settlement is to be reached of the problem of the German minority in Czechoslovakia, it will be necessary to bring the German Government into the negotiations." [27]

Paul-Boncour disagreed. Though he was prepared for England and France to give "counsels of moderation" to Prague, he did not want it done in public. This would only encourage Hitler to raise his demands. He told Phipps he objected to France and England approaching Germany "even later on regarding minorities in Czechoslovakia." [28] This would be a "terribly dangerous precedent" for all countries with German minorities, and would be resented by the Czechs.

The British refused to co-operate with the French. They also rejected Russian proposals. On March 17, Litvinov made a statement to the press, which he later issued as an appeal to Governments. The Soviet Government, he said,

> is ready as before to participate in collective actions, which would be decided upon jointly with it and which would aim at checking the further development of aggression and at eliminating the increased danger of a new world massacre. It is prepared immediately to take up in the League of Nations or outside of it the discussions with other Powers of the practical measures which the circumstances demand.[29]

The British wanted to solve the Czech problem in collaboration with the Germans, not with the League. The colonial offer had failed to attract German interest. Now a new problem thrust forward to absorb the energies and idealism of the appeasers. Halifax replied to Litvinov's appeal on March 24. The British, he said, would welcome a conference of all European States. But since this was unlikely to materialize,

> a conference only attended by some European Powers, and designed less to secure the settlement of outstanding problems than to organise concerted action against aggression, would not necessarily . . . have such a favourable effect upon the prospects of European peace.[30]

The appeasers refused to co-operate with the Franco-Russian alliance. France and Russia were bad enough alone. It would be disastrous to work with them together. Britain wished to work with Germany.

The "mistaken" policies of 1904 and 1907 which led to German "encirclement" were not to be repeated. Britain could now afford an independent policy. She had no obligations to Czechoslovakia. Since 1918 British opinion had refused to countenance entanglements in Eastern Europe. Chamberlain's hostility to the League was well known. It was unlikely that Britain would help Czechoslovakia through the League.

On the other hand France and Russia were bound by treaty to protect Czechoslovakia. Russia was pledged to move only if France moved first. Britain's lack of involvement might have led to a negative policy. But Samuel Hoare and Basil Newton thought otherwise.

"If I am right in thinking," reported Newton from Prague on March 13, "that Czechoslovakia's present political position is not permanently tenable, it will be no kindness in the long run to try to maintain her in it." [31] Newton wanted France and Czechoslovakia to be warned of this. If France thought it "worthwhile to try to perpetuate the *status quo* in her own interests," she should do so unaided. Newton reported a few days later that examination of the Sudeten German press indicated that Henlein's party was moving away from thoughts of "mere autonomy" towards actual "incorporation in the Reich." [32] Newton, British representative in Prague, showed little sympathy for the Czechs. He continually supported German claims.

If the present position of Czechoslovakia was "fundamentally unsound," there could be no choice except to avoid war by forcing the Czechs to make concessions to Germany. It would be foolish to threaten war if you did not believe in your own cause. Such was the logic of British policy after the *Anschluss*. Masaryk wrote to Hoare on March 14, and asked for "direct, blunt, concrete, advice," [33] Hoare discussed what to suggest with Chamberlain and Vansittart. On March 25, at lunch with Masaryk, he suggested that the Czechs ask the French and British Governments to help make "a really satisfactory arrangement for the Sudeten Germans."

"Admirable advice," wrote Halifax.

The British Government suggested that the Czechs negotiate. But it did not "possess enough knowledge of the complexities of the Sudeten German problem . . . to adjudicate on the merits of any solution that the Czechoslovak Government" might propose.[34]

The British refused to combine their good offices with the French. The latter must shed their Left-Wing Government. Blum and Paul-Boncour were doing their best to find out the attitude of the Polish and Rumanian Governments towards the passage of Russian troops through their territory. The British disliked such inquiries. Chamberlain wrote on March 20, "I have abandoned any idea of giving guarantees to Czechoslovakia, or the French in connection with her obligations to that country." [35]

Chamberlain's pessimism was widespread. Amery wrote that he was "still very uncertain whether we could do anything for Czechoslovakia, and whether we might not have to resign ourselves to falling back with Italian support, on holding Yugoslavia and the Balkans." [36]

Dalton saw Kingsley Martin, editor of the *New Statesman*, who "felt that things had gone so far that to plan armed resistance to the dictators was now useless. If there was a war we should lose it. We should, therefore, seek the most peaceful way of letting them gradually get all they wanted." [37]

On March 22, the Cabinet discussed a note to be sent to the French, and the statement to be made by the Prime Minister in the House of Commons. The note to the French was a "cold refusal to give any support to France if she went to war on account of Czechoslovakia." The statement for Parliament "read like a declaration of isolation." [38]

Duff Cooper fought hard to get both changed. Though not in favor of guaranteeing Czechoslovakia, he wished to make a "more friendly gesture to France." He insisted that when France fought Germany, "we should have to fight too, whether we like it or not, so that we might as well say so." [39]

After some argument, the Cabinet decided that "the two statements should be redrafted but that the policy should remain." Duff Cooper had lost his battle.

On March 24, Chamberlain issued a warning statement in the House of Commons. It was referred to constantly throughout the summer.

> Where peace and war are concerned, legal obligations are not alone involved, and if war broke out, it would be unlikely to be confined to those who have assumed such obligations. It would be quite impossible to say where it might not end and what Governments might not become involved.

In this atmosphere of uncertainty and indecision the views and actions of Basil Newton became all-important. Blum's Government fell in the middle of April. His successors, Daladier and Bonnet, visited London at the end of the month. It was Newton's ideas that Halifax expounded to them. The Czechs had produced proposals for solving the minorities problem. Newton was sceptical, and warned that a settlement of the minority problem "would not in itself and directly settle the German-Czech problem." Again, it was the German view. Newton accepted it uncritically. He saw Beneš on April 22. Beneš was unwilling to discuss recent German proposals for a Czech-German compromise, which were unfavorable to the Czechs. Despite this Newton introduced his ideas on the subject. Bearing in mind the "ideals of union and partnership," he suggested that the smaller national elements might be treated not as "minorities" but as "constituent races in a State of composite nationalities." He went on to discuss the possibility of a "United States of Bohemia and Slovakia." [40] Benes replied politely that he "personally agreed" with Newton's remarks, and that Czechoslovakia "could not be a national State." [41] Beneš saw no sense in offending the British. He failed to realize that his casual words would be taken so seriously.

Newton told Halifax of the discussion. Halifax then saw Daladier and Bonnet, and said that "Beneš appeared now to be thinking in terms of a State composed of different nationalities rather than a single State, including certain minorities." [42] The subtle transference of view from Newton to Beneš had been effortlessly accomplished. Views were attributed to Beneš which he had never held. Newton's hostility to Czechs and Germans living together in the same state dominated British policy. He was listened to as the man on the spot. His bias, and his limitations, were overlooked.

The Anglo-French meeting of April 28-29 followed Henlein's Karlsbad Program. This eight-point program, where it was intelligible, was partially acceptable to the Czechs. But Krofta regarded the eighth point, that the Sudetens should have "full liberty to profess the German nationality, and the German political philosophy," as "far-reaching and dangerous." [43] He saw that it could be used to restrict equality of freedom for other minority groups, including the Jews. He passed on his fears to Newton. At an early stage, therefore, the British were aware of the implications of concessions to Henlein. But they ignored them.

Daladier and Bonnet arrived in London on April 27. At last France had a Government favorable to British wishes. But the two Ministers proved unaccommodating. They sought two things: to persuade the British to bring pressure on Prague, and to obtain a British guarantee of support should the Germans reject the Czech proposal. "Fortunately," wrote Chamberlain on May 1, "the papers have had no hint of how near we came to a break over Czechoslovakia." [44]

Both Governments agreed that pressure should be brought to bear in Prague. But the British, said Halifax, would have difficulty in ascertaining the merits of any Czech scheme. They would like "the settlement value of the scheme" to be considered.[45] British policy had gone beyond Eden's remarks of the previous year, maintaining that an agreement should be made "for its own sake." Daladier proposed a British guarantee for Czechoslovakia because he believed Hitler's real object was the "destruction of the present Czechoslovakian State." His proposal was firmly rejected by Chamberlain and Halifax. They said public opinion and the Dominions would not permit it. Neither the public nor the Dominions had been consulted. This was the excuse which became more and more common as others became less and less easy to find.

After the meeting Halifax saw the German Ambassador and resurrected Joseph Chamberlain's idea of the Anglo-Saxon alliance: "doubtless the best thing would be if the three kindred nations, Germany, Britain and the United States, could unite in joint work for peace." [46]

Bonnet told Welczeck, the German Ambassador in Paris, that France and Britain were at German disposal to act as mediators. They would "exert their utmost influence to induce the Prague Government to adopt an accommodating attitude." "Any arrangement," said Bonnet, was better than world war in which "both victor and vanquished would fall victims to world communism." [47]

Bonnet understood the British desire to be on good terms with Germany. He had none of Daladier's firmness, none of Daladier's hostility to appeasement. Where Britain led, France should follow. Bonnet told Welczeck,

> People in France and Great Britain saw in this very crisis an opportunity of reaching an understanding with Germany which would finally assure the peace of Europe. It was already hoped that conversations would be opened with [Germany] on this matter in the immediate future.[47]

It was not surprising that the Russian Government was not told of the results of the Anglo-French meeting until a week later. It was not desirable for the representatives of world communism to assist the democracies to reach an understanding with fascism.

Britain and France decided to put pressure on Prague. Neither knew how much pressure would be necessary. But the problem was one to be solved by the Czechs and the Sudeten Germans, not by outsiders. Halifax told Dirksen: "we did not desire to take part in these negotiations, and we must refuse a guarantee of their outcome." [48] But England would like to know Germany's view: "The Reich's Government could perhaps make a contribution to the solution of the question by formulating in writing their desires in this respect." [48]

The Germans also wanted the problem to be solved by the Czechs and the Sudeten Germans. They had no desire to interfere with or without British help. They knew the problem had no diplomatic solution. The demarcation of frontiers did not affect the ideologies behind them.

On May 7, the British and French Ministers in Prague made their formal *démarche*. They asked the Czechoslovak Government to make a "supreme effort to reach a . . . comprehensive and lasting settlement" with the Sudeten Germans.[49]

Dirksen reported that the British Government considered the military situation "unfavorable." The French were more optimistic about the prospects of fighting.[50] The Germans learned of this discord when Kirkpatrick lunched with Prince Bismarck, a grandson of the Iron Chancellor, in Berlin. Kirkpatrick said that the British had decided to make a *démarche* in Prague, "principally because they were strongly impressed by the firm determination of the French Ministers . . . to intervene in the event of an armed German-Czechoslovak crisis." [51] French firmness made the British weak and frightened. It was Daladier, not Hitler, who would provoke war.

Henderson discussed the British *démarche* with Woermann in Berlin. "The purpose of the *démarche* was not to achieve a solution of individual problems still pending, but a general settlement based, not on a Czechoslovak National State, but a State of Nationalities." [52] He added, as his personal view, that

> France was acting for the Czechs, and Germany for the Sudeten Germans. Britain was supporting Germany in this case and he urgently hoped that Germany would not refuse some kind of co-operation with Britain in this matter, which might then, perhaps, lead to co-operation in other questions also.

Woermann sensibly refused to commit himself, but Ribbentrop saw Henderson a few days later and told him that "after a solution of the Sudeten German question Germany was to be regarded as saturated. There then still remained only a solution of the colonial question, so as to reach a lasting understanding on a wide basis." [53] Henderson replied in an *aide-memoire* that if the Germans proposed suggestions for a settlement which they considered satisfactory to the Sudeten Germans, "His Majesty's Government would consider how far they could recommend acceptance by the Czechoslovak Government."

Kirkpatrick had more specific proposals. At his lunch with Prince Bismarck on May 10, the Prince reported him as saying:·

> If the German Government would advise the British Government confidentially what solution of the Sudeten German question they were striving after . . . the British Government would bring such

pressure to bear in Prague that the Czechoslovak Government would be compelled to accede to the German wishes.[54]

On May 6, the day before the British *démarche* in Prague, the *Daily Mail* printed an article by Lord Rothermere entitled *Czechs Not Our Business*. He wrote: "Czechoslovakia is not of the remotest concern to us. If France likes to burn her fingers there, that is a matter for France." A. L. Cranfield, the Editor of the *Daily Mail*, ensured that the proofs of the article were in the hands of the German Ambassador before publication.[55] From all sides the Germans learned that Britain was no friend to the Czechs.

CHAPTER 6

Sudeten Crisis

THE GERMANS scarcely believed Kirkpatrick's remarks to Bismarck. It seemed impossible to them that Britain would favor Germany at the expense of Czechoslovakia. The information Kirkpatrick gave was soon reinforced by articles in the *New York Times* and the *Montreal Star*. On May 14, "Augur," a former diplomatic correspondent of *The Times*, wrote in the *New York Times* that "Mr. Chamberlain today . . . certainly favors a more drastic measure—namely, separation of the German districts from the body of the Czechoslovak Republic and the annexation of them to Germany." On the same day Joseph Driscoll wrote in the *Montreal Star* that "nothing seems clearer than that the British do not expect to fight for Czechoslovakia . . . That being so, then the Czechs must accede to the German demands, if reasonable." [1]

Such articles might be dismissed as flights of the imagination. But on May 10, Lady Astor had given a luncheon party attended by a dozen American journalists and the Prime Minister. Chamberlain was alleged to have told them of his plans for a four-power pact. When questioned about this in the Commons, he replied, "The Hon. Member is trying to fish around and get some information out of which he can extract some mischief, and in my opinion it is not desirable that these matters should be discussed on a fishing enquiry of this kind." The "enquiry" continued in the Commons throughout the summer. The evasions of the Prime Minister and Lady Astor served only to reveal the truth by constant denial. For some days Lady Astor succeeded in giving the impression that Chamberlain had never even been entertained to lunch on the vital day.

Unfortunately for Chamberlain his plans suffered a serious setback in the middle of May. Without warning, Czech reservists were recalled on May 20. The Czechs feared a sudden German attack. This seemed plausible. German troop movements had been reported in the frontier areas. The crisis was aggravated by the fact that Henderson in Berlin had ordered a special train in order to take members of his staff and their families on routine leave.* Disraeli's deliberate threat in 1878 to leave Berlin sprang to mind. This unfortunate coincidence fanned the flames of rumor. Although it was quickly established that Germany had had no intention of moving against Czechoslovakia, the damage had been done. The British Foreign Office remained convinced throughout the summer that disaster had only been averted by British firmness. The anti-German section of the press and public had their prejudices confirmed. Yet this crisis had arisen only because, in a highly militarized country like Germany, it was impossible to move troops around without giving someone the impression that an attack was imminent somewhere.

Undeterred by public firmness, Henderson continued to pursue Chamberlain's policy. Ribbentrop recorded on May 21 that the British Ambassador had told him: "We should only have patience, and he was certain that all would end well and that Germany would win all along the line. If only this Sudeten German problem were shifted out of the way, conversations would then be continued on all subjects." [2]

Halifax was more open to pressure than Henderson. His permanent officials at the Foreign Office pressed him to take a firm line. But his natural desire for friendship with Germany asserted itself. On May 21, Henderson called on Ribbentrop for the second time in the day, bringing him a telegram from Halifax concerning the supposed imminent invasion of Czechoslovakia. "On the score of Anglo-German relations, which Lord Halifax had so much at heart, such a step by Germany was only to be viewed with most profound regret." [3]

---

* Henderson was so shocked by the suggestion that he was being firm, that he ordered the families to remain in Berlin. (Grant Duff, *Europe and the Czechs*.)

Henderson brought Ribbentrop another message from Halifax on May 22. "Halifax considered the situation to be very grave, but earnestly hoped that we, the parties concerned, might all be stronger than fate. We should not let it get out of hand, *for then the only ones to profit would be the communists.*" [4]

Some thought that British firmness during the crisis had prevented war. They were wrong. Not only was the crisis unreal. The firmness of the British leaders was equally non-existent.

The threads of the old policy were picked up at once. Britain still wanted to solve the Czech problem with German help. Henderson saw Weizsäcker on May 23, and told him that the British Government had thought of sending an observer to the Sudeten areas. "Before sending instructions to our Minister at Prague in this sense," Lord Halifax asked Henderson to inquire of Ribbentrop "whether he would regard such a step as helpful." [5] Because the British wanted to use the Czech crisis to improve their relations with Germany, they were committed to asking German approval whenever some new step was contemplated. The Germans were only embarrassed by these confidences. If observers "could contribute to remedying grievances," Weizsäcker replied, the German Government "had no objections." They had no enthusiasm either.

At the end of May, Strang was sent to Prague and Berlin for an "on-the-spot" assessment of the situation in the two capitals. Because of the apparent British firmness during the recent crisis the Czechs felt greatly indebted to Britain. The British therefore thought their pressure on the Czechs would be more successful than before. Strang reported that Newton "takes the view that in the present situation it is better for us to go on doing something than to do nothing. If we try first one thing, then another, some solution may emerge." [6] This admirable advice was followed throughout the summer. If the solution failed to emerge it was not for want of trying.

On May 26, Noel-Baker asked Chamberlain in the Commons

if the Government would propose to send an impartial international commission to the Czech-German frontier area. It should investigate the alleged violations of the frontier, and other incidents which might arise. Butler replied that the Government would consider the suggestion.

On May 28, Henderson saw Weizsäcker and told him of Noel-Baker's suggestion. Weizsäcker noted that the British Government "had no precise views on the plan itself, the method of setting up the commission, its terms of reference, or the areas in which it would eventually operate. Neither did they wish to come forward with any plan which was not approved by the Germans." [7]

German permission was again felt necessary before any definite plan could be proposed. Weizsäcker replied that Noel-Baker's suggestion was "not quite reasonable." Henderson told him that "his Government would certainly not pursue the matter further." This initiative had failed. The British were forced back to their old policy of trying to discover what the Germans would accept. "What a good thing it would be," said Henderson, "if the German Government spoke more freely and made known the Prague concessions which, in their opinion, were not only necessary but adequate also." Weizsäcker noted that Henderson "evaded with the usual arguments this attempt to commit us to more responsibility than we had hitherto accepted." [8] The Germans were not drawn. Such open snubs, however, did not damp the ardor of the British Ambassador.

The British had not exhausted the weapons in their diplomatic armory. As early as April 30, someone in the Foreign Office suggested that an unofficial British intermediary be sent privately to Prague: a man who would perhaps enjoy the confidence of both Hodza and Henlein.[9] On May 8, Halifax wrote that "the idea of a mediator" was worth considering. The mediator "would not be an easy person to find." There the matter rested until May 30. Halifax then wrote to Phipps to say that in the event of a breakdown of negotiations between the Czechs and the Sudeten Germans,

The British and French Governments ought to be ready with immediate proposals for bringing two parties together again, without
if possible having to mediate themselves. For this purpose it occurs
to me that the two Governments might at the appropriate moment
propose to the Czechoslovak Government [that] an international
commission should investigate the cause of the deadlock and devise means for overcoming it.[10]

This suggestion was unconnected with Noel-Baker's idea, which
was concerned solely with frontier incidents. The revived plan
for a mediator came from Halifax alone.

On May 8, Dirksen analyzed the effects of the happenings of
the past month.[11] The German Government, he wrote, had
agreed completely with the British *démarche* at Prague on May
7. He referred to Anglo-German relations, and to "these hopeful beginnings." It was "well within the bounds of possibility
that the British Government's wish, that Anglo-German co-
operation in solving satisfactorily the Sudeten German demands
might lead to mutual co-operation on a broader basis, would be
no utopian dream." These hopeful beginnings had been
thwarted by the *Anschluss*, and by the May "crisis." Nevertheless, wrote Dirksen, "even Churchill's adherents do not shrink
from the idea of an incorporation of the Sudeten German part
of Czechoslovakia into Germany." Boothby wrote an article to
this effect in the *Daily Telegraph*. More serious than this was
The Times' leading article of June 3.

Independent criticism does little harm, but *The Times* could
never escape the stigma of officialdom. This article discussed the
wisdom of allowing "the Germans of Czechoslovakia — by
plebiscite or otherwise — to decide their own future, even if it
should mean secession to the Reich." It also advocated applying the same policy to the other minorities inside Czechoslovakia
as "a drastic remedy for the present unrest, but something drastic
may be needed." Drastic measures were indeed necessary, and
were eventually taken. But to suggest that they might indicate
a remedy or prove a solution was merely to introduce the ideals

of the nineteenth century into a situation which merited no such rational treatment.

Fritz Hesse was not idle in his interviews with the British press. The diplomatic correspondent of the *Daily Mail* told him of his "impression that the Prime Minister was ready to come to an understanding on both the Czech and the Colonial questions and to make far-reaching concessions in either case." [12] This correspondent refused to answer Hesse's direct question about Chamberlain's views on the Czech problem. But when asked whether he thought Chamberlain would agree to a "territorial re-arrangement" he replied, "Of course, I am quite certain of that." The diplomatic correspondent of the *Sunday Times* said that "he could not understand why we only demanded autonomy for the Sudeten Germans since it was obvious that, in virtue of the principle of nationality, a revision of the frontiers was required." "He was convinced," wrote Hesse, "that Chamberlain would be prepared to make very extensive concessions even in the territorial sphere, if we would only say clearly and exactly what we wanted." Once again the plea was heard for a clearer understanding of German aims, in order to satisfy them.

Halifax realized that the Germans were not being as cooperative as in his dreams of Anglo-German friendship they so clearly appeared to be. "In view of the probable German objections and other difficulties," he wrote to Newton on June 18, "I'm thinking of sounding the Czech Government as to whether in the event of a breakdown in their negotiations with Henlein, they would be ready to accept the services of an independent British expert who would try and reconcile the two parties." [13] Halifax had in mind someone with "practical experience of administration and of minority problems, such as an ex-Governor of an Indian Province." Halifax had been Viceroy of India. He doubtless envisaged certain former acquaintances as suitable candidates. Lord Willingdon and Sir John Anderson would have qualified. Newton replied that it would be better not to an-

nounce the suggestion of a mediator until the present negotiations had shown definite signs of failure.[14] Any attempt by
the British to anticipate future developments would only play
into the hands of the Sudeten Germans. "I think it would be
better," he added, "to avoid choosing anyone whose experience
is limited to India or the Colonial Empire, since, however fool-
ishly, the connexion might be considered derogatory by both
sides."

The British were in a quandary. They knew what to do if the
current Czech-Sudeten negotiations should fail, but until they
failed their policy was bound to remain unconstructive.

On June 9, Dirksen described how Halifax repeatedly

> stressed the British Government's desire for an improvement in
> Anglo-German relations and a settlement of outstanding questions.
> From his words there was clearly discernible the intention of mak-
> ing an approach to the German Government again, with a view to
> resuming within measurable time the interrupted negotiations.[15]

Henderson stayed with Göring at Karinhall on June 22.
"Driving round the woods to inspect his young elk and having
tea with Frau Göring, [we] discussed a great variety of subjects
from Austrian debts to the latest persecution of the Jews." [16]
Henderson suggested that if the Czech-Sudeten negotiations
failed, "Germany should show the utmost moderation and wisdom to help us . . . to find an outlet to any deadlock which
might ensue."

At the end of June, Henderson visited Ribbentrop. In the
latter's words: "Sir Nevile then asked me how we envisaged the
solution of the Sudeten German question. Could such a solution be found in autonomy for the Sudeten Germans, or was our
view that an *Anschluss* with the German-inhabited areas should
take place?" [17] Here was the key question again. How could the
British act without knowing what the Germans would approve?
Plans for plebiscites, autonomy, or secession were useless if they
could not be used as bargaining counters for German good will.

Ribbentrop replied that he "could give him no answer to this question."

Chamberlain could not advance too rapidly. There was much public pressure on the Government to inquire into conditions in Austria after the *Anschluss*. To unite with Germany may have been the wish of the majority of the population, but the anti-Nazi Austrians still had rights in the eyes of the world. When Henderson asked Ribbentrop about the fate of a number of Austrian nationals who had been arrested, he voiced the fears which were severely troubling the British Government. Public distaste for the internal conditions of Germany stood as a bar to genuine Anglo-German co-operation. Ribbentrop replied to the British Ambassador:

> I had already received from Lady Londonderry a list of such arrested persons in whom apparently Lady Chamberlain and Lady Halifax were also interested. To me such interest was incomprehensible. The British Government had never lifted a finger for the victims of the Schuschnigg régime.[18]

This was true, but the people who had really suffered under the Dollfuss and Schuschnigg régimes were not the National-Socialists to whom Ribbentrop went on to refer, but the Socialists and trade-unionists. The crushing of socialism in Austria in 1934 had caused little concern in Britain; it had caused rejoicing in Berlin.

Ribbentrop could perhaps be excused in his questioning of British sincerity. The double game played by the British of protesting in public and condoning in private did not encourage frank co-operation.

Those who wanted to protest found it awkward to do so. Immediately after Hitler moved into Austria Lord Woolton decided to make "the small effort of protest that a private citizen could make." [19] He was then in charge of Lewis's, a chain of Midland stores. He decided to boycott German goods, and cabled his buyers in Germany "to close their books, honourably

to fulfil all their contracts, and to return home." He defended
his action in a speech at Leicester. Lewis's, he said, would not
trade with a Government that "for no other reason than that
of their faith persecuted one of the oldest races in the world."
The boycott was popular. "It was what the public wanted someone to say: it gave the individual citizens something to do — a
means of expressing their emotion." Woolton's gesture was not
appreciated by the Government. He was called to No. 10
Downing Street, and was interviewed by Sir Horace Wilson.
Wilson told him that Chamberlain "strongly disapproved" of
his action and that he had "no right to interfere in this manner
in the foreign policy of the country." [19]

In June, Wohltat, Göring's Commissioner for the German Four-
Year Plan, was in London for the International Whaling Conference. He interviewed several prominent politicians, bankers,
and industrialists. Wilson asked him "whether the Führer
wanted to bring the non-German element under German sovereignty. Where were the future frontiers of Germany?" [20]
Wohltat gave him a short lecture on Greater Germany.

> The question of uniting the Germans, who lived in a solid settle-
> ment area in the middle of Europe, would be regarded by people
> who had spent many years of their youth in Austria and by the
> British people in a different way.

From Wilson's own remarks, Wohltat gathered that if the German Government would state the limits to "the expansion of
German sovereignty," the British Government would recognize
Germany's position in Central Europe. It would also favor German annexation of the Sudetenland. Once again the British
asked the Germans to state their claims in order to underwrite
them. Once again the Germans showed no interest. But as
Chamberlain would not give up his idea of solving Germany's
problems for her, his representatives could hardly give up trying
to discover what those problems were. According to Wohltat,

R. A. Butler was also "well-disposed towards Germany." Butler had said that "on the British side the wish exists to learn the extent of the German claims." In order to preserve general peace, said Butler, Great Britain "is ready to treat the Sudeten German question, too, in accordance with German wishes."

Henderson also had ideas on how to solve current problems. He told Weizsäcker on July 19 that if he could see Hitler he could induce him "to take a more favourable view of British policy." [21] He added that he had found this type of interview satisfactory when dealing with King Alexander in Belgrade.

> He believed that the positive desire to settle the present Czech crisis by peaceful means, and by building upon this to effect a comprehensive improvement in Anglo-German relations, would certainly be in accordance with the Führer's intentions also.

The exploitation of the Czech crisis was justifiable because it provided a means of improving Anglo-German relations. The British should coerce the Czechs into playing the British game. But the Germans wanted the Sudetenland, not a hypothetical agreement with Britain.

Many people had curious ideas in July. Captain Wiedemann's visit to London aroused much speculation. He asked the British to refrain from issuing stern warning. Hitler, he said, did not want to be rebuked. Wiedemann wrote of his interview with Halifax:

> We took leave with marked cordiality, Lord Halifax asking me to tell him that he [Halifax], before his death, would like to see, as the culmination of his work, the Führer entering London, at the side of the English King, amid the acclamation of the English people.[22]

Halifax's wish was never fulfilled.

From July 19 to 22, the King and Queen visited Paris. Ostensibly it was one of those occasional attempts to reintroduce a certain measure of cordiality into the Anglo-French Entente. Under a glamorous façade it provided an opportunity for Halifax to discuss the latest British scheme with the French. Halifax had already told Newton on July 16 that Lord Runciman would act as the mediator whom the British had been considering for the past months.[23] Hoare wrote that the idea of the Runciman Mission was first discussed by himself and Chamberlain on one of their morning walks round St. James's Park, "not as a debatable possibility, but as a logical incident in his plan." [24] In view of their previous policy, it was strange that the British forgot to tell the Germans of their decision to send Runciman until after it had been announced in the press.

Chamberlain *did* see Dirksen on July 22, but only to tell him that "the British Government had already prepared for the possibility of the failure of talks, and had contemplated measures to persuade the Czech Government to overcome this deadlock." [25] Dirksen gathered that these measures included "increased pressure on Prague" and "positive proposals." Dirksen had not even come to see Chamberlain. He came to Downing Street to bid farewell to Wilson before going on holiday. Wilson suggested his twenty-minute interview with Chamberlain.[26] The Germans were annoyed because press comments about this visit suggested the initiative came from Dirksen. Dirksen telephoned Wilson to correct these reports. The Germans neither took the initiative, nor sought to do so.

On July 25, Henderson gave Weizsäcker Britain's "positive proposals." The British Government "intended to send Lord Runciman to Czechoslovakia as an unofficial mediator between Sudeten Germans and Czechs." [27] From this interview Weizsäcker gathered that the British Government "now think that they can no longer withhold their influence in shaping the matter, even in minute details, and that they hope to find in Runciman a pliable go-between, in order not to have to bear the responsibility which, hitherto, they have always declined."

Since the news of the Runciman Mission had already appeared in the press, the British, usually so anxious to inform the Germans of their decisions before making those decisions public, were severely rebuked. "These were methods which we did not like," [28] Weizsäcker told Henderson. Halifax wrote hastily to Ribbentrop to apologize for the premature leak of the news, and expressed dismay that Germany treated the matter as a purely British concern. "We both desire to see the relations between Great Britain and Germany established on a basis of mutual confidence and co-operation, and the present situation seems to me to give a great opportunity for doing something to realize the hope that we both entertain." [29] For Halifax the solution of the Czech crisis was not an end in itself but the means to an end.

On July 26, Chamberlain told the Commons about the impending visit of Runciman to Czechoslovakia. He would act on his own responsibility, "not in any sense as an arbitrator, but as an investigator and mediator, and not under instructions from His Majesty's or any other Government." [30]

Runciman left without understanding the implications in R. W. Seton-Watson's *Czechoslovak Broadsheet* for July. Czechoslovakia, wrote Seton-Watson, "is the strategic key to hegemony in Europe, quite apart from any sympathies or antipathies which you may have for the only State in Eastern Europe which has been able to maintain a system of free democratic and representative government." [31]

Runciman's efforts in Czechoslovakia have been maligned. It is easy to criticize him; his impartiality seemed always a sham. He spent the weekends with German princes in the Sudetenland; he tended to listen to Czechs with Nazi leanings; even the children made fun of him:

> *Was brauchen wir 'nen Weihnachtsmann,*
> *Wir haben unser'n Runciman.*[32]

Runciman sought an honest compromise. He had many gifts and was well liked. He was less fortunate in some of his entourage. In one set of discussions with the Sudeten Germans, Geoffrey Peto, his secretary, was felt by the Germans to show "great understanding for the Sudeten German party's attitude to dislike for the Jews in Czechoslovakia, whom he described as not comparable with British Jews." [33] At a dinner at the British Legation which included the German Minister, Lady Runciman revealed "remarkable understanding for the Sudeten Germans and spoke of Bolshevik influence in Czechoslovakia." [34]

Runciman's Mission was outmoded before it began. However pro-German he might choose to be, his visit failed because the Germans were not interested in it.

The British too had other plans. Chamberlain did not want Runciman to reach a compromise solution. He did not see the value in giving way to Czech fears. He wanted to work out a solution with the Germans, which he could then urge the Czechs to accept. While Runciman listened to Czechs as well as to Germans, Chamberlain was prepared to listen to Germans alone. On August 12, Friedrich Bürger met Lord Allen of Hurtwood in Prague and wrote,

> One might almost get the impression that he was the second envoy sent by the British Government who, now that Lord Runciman's Mission is regarded in London with the greatest pessimism and scepticism, had been sent here to prepare, even now, *the next step*, namely, the four-power conference.[35]

Runciman had proved unsatisfactory. He was no magician who could provide a solution to an impossible problem. He could sympathize with the Germans, and advise the Czechs; he could not coerce them. For that task four-power co-operation was necessary. Britain was willing to take the lead.

CHAPTER 7

Coercing the Czechs

ON AUGUST 16, Crolla, Counsellor of the Italian Embassy in London, told Baron Hahn, diplomatic correspondent of the *Deutsche Nachrichten Büro*, that "Great Britain was prepared for any solution [to the Czech problem] by peaceful methods." [1] This was British policy long before the September crisis brought Europe to the verge of war. Chamberlain maintained it throughout August and September. Events had not caught him unaware. Wilson met Theo Kordt, of the German Embassy, at Conwell-Evans' house on August 23. Wilson said "he would see to it that the British Government was prepared for the time when Runciman's Mission might fail." [2] It was. Long before the Sudeten Germans turned down the Czech proposals in the middle of September, the plan which was to discredit the end of the month had been quietly considered.

Wilson asked Kordt if Hitler would regard a peaceful solution of the Czech problem "as the beginning of further negotiations on a larger scale." [2] Hitler had once told Halifax that "European culture rested on two pillars which must be linked by a powerful arch: Great Britain and Germany." Wilson thought it would be the height of folly if the "two leading white races" exterminated each other in war. Only Bolshevism would profit. He believed that with the Czech problem out of the way, the Germans could "exercise large-scale policy in the South-East." In the Balkans Germany would find her natural markets and her natural sources of raw materials. Wilson saw "no sense in sending a turkey from Budapest to London instead of to Berlin." [2] This particular policy continued through September and reappeared in the Anglo-German declaration signed the day after

Munich. Even then it was not finished. Anglo-German cooperation was the basis of appeasement.

At the end of August, Weizsäcker said there could be "no question of a more comprehensive discussion without a settlement of the more urgent Czech situation." [3] For some weeks before the Runciman Mission failed, Chamberlain showed "an intense desire to start conversations on the Czech question between Germany and Great Britain as soon as it was conceivably possible." [4] When he saw Kordt, Wilson "mentioned the possibility that a special envoy of the British Government might transmit to the Führer a proposal for a peaceful and generous settlement." [5] The special envoy was Runciman, who refused to go. From these beginnings grew the idea that Chamberlain himself might visit Hitler. George Steward, Chamberlain's Press Attaché, told Hahn that if these proposed Anglo-German conversations showed signs of success "then France could participate on the side of Great Britain and Italy on that of Germany." [6] Neither Steward nor Hahn suggested that Czechoslovakia should be represented. They anticipated the four-power conference at Munich. Chamberlain's larger scheme was beginning to materialize.

Wilson was satisfied with his discussion with Kordt, and had been "visibly moved." A new vista opened in the European perspective. Some might see snags. But, said Wilson, "if we two, Great Britain and Germany, can come to agreement regarding the settlement of the Czech problem, we shall simply brush aside the resistance that France or Czechoslovakia herself may offer to the decision." [7] Kordt told Wilson that Germany "would not agree to a solution which left the [Czechoslovak] State intact in its present extent."

Such were the ideas in the minds of unofficial negotiators. They were taken up by the Foreign Office. Halifax approved Ashton-Gwatkin's suggestion "that we should take advantage of Henlein's offer to go to Germany and persuade Hitler and others not only to support these new negotiations but also to seek a basis of a general settlement with Great Britain." [8] Ashton-Gwatkin, the Foreign Office economic expert, later wrote that it was the Runciman Mission, with Foreign Office assent, which urged Henlein "to go to Hitler and explain that he was now getting everything he wanted, so let there be peace." [9]

On August 24, Ashton-Gwatkin had flown to London from Prague, where he was with Runciman. He talked with Halifax and Chamberlain. Shortly after his return it was announced in Prague that Henlein would go to Berchtesgaden to see Hitler. This caused some concern. Runciman had been sent as an independent mediator. He had turned down the suggestion that he himself should visit Hitler, on the grounds that this would exceed his stated brief. For him to recommend Henlein to see Hitler was equally incorrect. But Henlein went to Berchtesgaden on September 1. He told Hitler that there were two choices: autonomy within the Czechoslovak State, or a plebiscite which would mean *Anschluss* with Germany. Hitler was noncommittal. He remarked that he wanted a swift solution: he said nothing about what solution he favored.

The visit caused a minor crisis in the British Foreign Office. On September 2, when the official communiqué was transmitted through Reuter, there was no one in the building to give it official sanction. According to Reuter, Henlein had called on Hitler "under instructions of Lord Runciman." [10] Some senior officials were presumably taking a long weekend. The communiqué could not be issued to the evening papers, as those left in the Foreign Office did not know if it was a secret which could be divulged.

The Cabinet met on August 30. Nevile Henderson was present. The Cabinet decided that the Czech proposals, which Beneš had recently produced, were sufficiently similar to Henlein's Karlsbad demands to constitute "a basis for promising negotiations." [11] This meeting lasted two and three-quarter hours. Only four Ministers were absent. Henderson tried to argue that Germany had no intention of using force. Certain Ministers did not believe him.

When Churchill suggested to Halifax the possibility of concentrating the Fleet in the North Sea, and of partial mobilization, Halifax replied that "the British Government did not intend from now onward to open personal discussions with prominent members of the House of Commons." [12] Churchill also suggested that warnings should be made in Berlin against settling matters by force. But Hore-Belisha had already opposed this idea in the Cabinet "unless there was an overwhelming public demand first." "On the facts," he said, there was no such demand, nor would the Dominions come in.[13] The day after the Cabinet meeting Henderson told Ribbentrop that "the Sudeten Germans and the Czechs were a matter of complete indifference to Great Britain. Great Britain was only concerned with the attitude of France." In a letter to Halifax, Henderson went as far as to describe the Czechs as "a pigheaded race." Beneš, he added, was "the most pigheaded of the lot." [14]

The ingredients for the Munich conference had thus been assembled by the beginning of September. There was, however, one country whose intervention could have proved tiresome: Russia. The four-power conference which Steward had suggested, and which had long been a British aim, did not mention her. Yet she bore responsibilities towards Czechoslovakia. And she was advocating a firm line. Bonnet attempted to conceal just how firm it was. It mattered little. The British did not have ears to hear.

On September 2, Litvinov proposed "immediate staff talks between the Soviet, French, and Czech experts," when he spoke to the French Chargé d'Affaires in Moscow.[15] He also suggested that the Russians "should raise at Geneva, under Article 11, the German threat to Czechoslovakia." "An immediate joint note" should be sent to Berlin by Britain, France, and the Soviet Union, warning Hitler not to resort to force. Bonnet suppressed this information. On September 6, he told Phipps misleading stories about Rumania not permitting Soviet airplanes to fly to Czechoslovakia's assistance over Rumanian territory. Two days earlier Léger had told Phipps that permission *would* be granted.

On September 11, Litvinov told Bonnet "that he would like to get the Czech question discussed by an *ad hoc* committee." This would involve Russian, and perhaps Czech, participation. "Let us hope no more will come of this idea," said R. A. Butler.[16]

Should Russian intervention prove serious, Henderson advocated that the British Government press for a revision of Versailles. "The advantage of the proposal was that it would exclude Russia, as not being a signatory of Versailles."[17] Strang replied to this by telling Henderson that "keeping Russia out of Europe altogether" was "not an aspect of German policy which we wish to encourage."[18] Strang spoke alone.

The stage was set for subsequent action. But nothing could be done until the Runciman Mission had failed. At the beginning of September it showed dangerous signs of succeeding. Runciman and his colleagues, officially impartial, saw their goal in sight. They worked hard and travelled far. Ashton-Gwatkin's expertise compensated for the weakness of the others. There was little time for relaxation. "I have not been able to take a day off for their wonderful partridge shooting, alas," wrote Runciman to Halifax on August 30.[19] The Sudeten leaders seemed reasonable men with genuine grievances. By exerting considerable pressure on Beneš, Runciman had secured a workable plan. Hodza announced it on September 6. According to Ashton-Gwatkin it was "very favourable to the Sudetens." It amounted to virtual acceptance of the Karlsbad program. But it proved too favorable for the Sudeten extremists, who did not want to be deprived of an excuse for further agitation. A series of border incidents gave the Sudetens an excuse to break off negotiations. The outbreaks of violence were suppressed by the Czech Government on September 13. Henlein fled to Germany. Though Beneš had been forced to compromise, he considered that even these proposals "amounted to capitulation, and would in future years be regretted by Great Britain and France."[20]

On September 6, Henderson wrote to Cadogan: "I do wish

it might be possible to get at any rate *The Times,* Camrose, Beaverbrook Press etc., to write up Hitler as the apostle of Peace. It will be terribly shortsighted if this is not done." [21] Given Henderson's brief — preparing the way for an Anglo-German *détente* — this was sound advice. "If our object is to achieve results that is the only line to take." Unfortunately for Henderson, the very next day *The Times* came out with another illjudged leader. The leader, which caused great consternation in Europe, was not officially inspired, though it was in line with Chamberlain's policy.

> It might be worthwhile for the Czechoslovak Government to consider whether they should exclude altogether the project, which has found favour in some quarters, of making Czechoslovakia a more homogeneous State by the secession of that fringe of alien populations who are contiguous to the nation with which they are united by race . . . The advantages to Czechoslovakia of becoming a homogeneous State might conceivably outweigh the obvious disadvantage of losing the Sudeten German district of the borderland.

Such "objective" remarks caused a furore. Masaryk twice hurried to the Foreign Office to secure an official denial. It was announced that the suggestion put forward in *The Times* "in no way represents the views of His Majesty's Government."

This was the story of the leader. On the afternoon of September 6, Dawson returned late after the weekend to Printing House Square. He found an uncompleted draft of a leader on the Czech problem awaiting him. He read it, deleted a passage, ordered it to be rewritten, and left for dinner. At 11:45 P.M. he was assailed with misgivings. He sent a proof of the entire article to Casey, a Francophil and the only senior member of the editorial staff in the building. Casey did not like it, and "particularly disliked the hints with which it closed." Dawson disregarded his comments, and at 12:05 sent down alterations including the phrase: "the project, which has found favour in some quarters." This remark did not appear in the first edition, hence the importance attached to it. One explanation was:

"Dawson's absence at the weekend and his late return may have given him insufficient time, before or after dinner, in which to bestow on such an article the consideration or correction it needed in the actual circumstances." [22]

On September 8, at Blackpool, the National Executive of the Labour party and the TUC produced a joint declaration to the effect that "the British Government must leave no doubt in the mind of the German Government that they will unite with the French and Soviet Governments to resist any attack on Czechoslovakia." Given this statement, it is strange that Halifax told Corbin, the French Ambassador, that he "did not think that British opinion would be prepared, any more than I thought His Majesty's Government would be prepared, to enter upon hostilities with Germany, on account of aggression by Germany or Czechoslovakia." [23]

While damping down the French — only too successfully as events proved — Halifax was quite prepared to issue a stern "warning" to the Germans. Halifax sent the British warning to Henderson. But Henderson failed to pass it on to Hitler. He thought it might provoke Hitler into doing something rash. He had thus taken policy into his own hands, wildly exceeding his ambassadorial powers. Had he known the origin of the warning, he might not have refused to deliver it. But Henderson was at the Nuremberg rally. He stayed there for five days, living in a train, without his cyphers. Halifax was unable to explain the reason for the warning *en clair*, for it had a curious history.

At the beginning of September, Weizsäcker had told Karl Burckhardt, in Berlin, that Hitler planned to overrun Czechoslovakia within six weeks. Certain Germans, he said, had come to the conclusion "that the only method" of bringing Hitler to call off his action "would be a personal letter from the Prime Minister showing that if an attack were made by Germany on Czechoslovakia, a war would start in which Great Britain would inevitably be on the opposite side to Germany." [24] This was part of a move by the German opposition to Hitler to stiffen British resolve. The move was repeated in London. On August

23, Kordt told Wilson that he and his friends thought Hitler was driving toward war. Wilson should tell Chamberlain that "the German people abhorred war, and that a steady policy on the part of the British Government could alone make him desist." Wilson asked Kordt if he would draft a letter which Chamberlain could send Hitler "making clear the situation beyond all doubt." The letter was to be "appropriate, in the view of the German Opposition, to open the eyes of the German people." Meanwhile Weizsäcker asked Burckhardt to act as his intermediary. Burckhardt promptly drove to Berne in one day (nine hundred kilometers) and saw George Warner, the British Minister, the one man in the British diplomatic service he knew well and in whom he could confide. He told Warner of Weizsäcker's idea for a personal letter.

On the evening of September 5, Warner telegraphed Halifax and transmitted Weizsäcker's message.[25] Kordt told Wilson and Halifax, in Wilson's room at No. 10, that "extraordinary times demand extraordinary means. Today I come to you not as German Chargé d'Affaires, but as spokesman of political and military circles in Berlin, who desire by every means to prevent war." [26] Kordt and his friends wanted a firm declaration from Britain that she would fight. "The declaration we suggest cannot be too unequivocal and firm enough for the purpose in question . . . German patriots see no other way out of the dilemma except in close co-operation with the British Government in order to prevent the great crime of a war." Halifax promised to inform the Prime Minister and "one or two of his colleagues in the Cabinet" and assured Kordt that "the matter would be carefully examined and treated as secret."

Halifax did as Weizsäcker asked. A strongly worded warning was sent to Henderson, to be handed to Hitler. If Germany used force, Halifax wrote,

a situation would arise leading directly to a request from the Czechoslovak Government for assistance. In such circumstances His Majesty's Government are convinced that the French Government would consider themselves bound to discharge their Treaty obligations to Czechoslovakia. France having thus become involved it seems to His Majesty's Government inevitable that the sequence of events must result in a general conflict from which Great Britain could not stand aside.[27]

Henderson never knew that the idea of this stiff note had come from Weizsäcker, and had the serious backing of Wilson and the British Foreign Office. Henderson refused to deliver it, thinking that it could only serve to anger Hitler. Isolated at Nuremberg, it was difficult for further instructions to reach him. Kordt said he thought that if Henderson had known that the message came from Weizsäcker, he might have delivered it.[28]

On the morning of September 12, Duff Cooper returned to London after a weekend in the country. He found

> a series of messages from Henderson which seemed to me almost hysterical, imploring the Government not to insist upon his carrying out [his] instructions, which he was sure would have the opposite effect to that desired. And the Government had given way.[29]

At the Cabinet meeting that day, "Simon, Hoare and Kingsley Wood were against war in any circumstances." [30] Duff Cooper opposed them. He stated that Britain was being advised on all sides "to make plain to Germany that we would fight." [31] This advice came "even from the Vatican." Yet, he lamented, the Government were prepared to listen to the "counter-advice of one man, the hysterical Henderson."

Chamberlain replied "rather tartly" that "it wasn't one man, but the results of that one man's contacts with many others. He was on the spot and must know more about it than the Vatican." Chamberlain argued that as Hitler was making an important speech that evening it was vital that Britain should not upset him. He might be driven "into making a violent speech instead of a conciliatory one." By holding his Cabinet meeting — the first since the end of August — a few hours before Hitler would end his speech at Nuremberg, Chamberlain forced his Ministers to fall in with his wishes. Duff Cooper believed: "The Cabinet was called at the worst possible moment — too late to take any action before Hitler's speech, too soon to consider the new situation which that speech might create."

Four days previously de la Warr told Duff Cooper that he thought the Government was not "taking a sufficiently decided line." He too thought a Cabinet meeting should have been held earlier. Before September 12, however, he had been sent off to lead the British delegation at Geneva. Halifax, who was to have gone, remained behind. Chamberlain gained a man who would vote for him in the Cabinet — Halifax — and lost one who well might not have done — de la Warr. But Cabinet decisions, even when manipulated, were largely irrelevant. The Prime Minister was already involved in more deep-laid plans.

That same day Antony Winn, *The Times'* Lobby Correspondent, told Duff Cooper and Oliver Stanley that *The Times* intended to start "a correspondence on the desirability of the Czechs handing over the whole of the Sudeten territories to Germany." [32] When Halifax heard of this, he rapidly contacted Dawson, who promised to do his best to "bottle up" the correspondence.[33]

Other plans were being mooted. Wilson wanted Chamberlain to pay a personal visit to Hitler. Henderson agreed.[34] Halifax thought the idea "unconventional and daring." [35] On September 13, Chamberlain informed Hitler: "In view of increasingly critical situation I propose to come over at once to see you with a view to trying to find a peaceful solution." [36]

Until that afternoon, Chamberlain believed his plan might be put into effect about September 17.[37] The date was altered. Riots in the Sudeten areas, touched off by Hitler's violent Nuremberg speech, broke Daladier's firmness. Bonnet had already lost his nerve. Léger told Phipps on September 11 that

Bonnet would probably be prepared for France to summon a
four-power conference. But he doubted "whether he could
persuade M. Daladier, who would probably fear strong opposition on the Left." [38] But if the plan was put forward by the
British, the French could accept it. Daladier was not helped by
Roosevelt's reference on September 9 to Press speculation that
the United States was aligning itself with Britain and France
in a "stop Hitler" bloc. Roosevelt said this was "a hundred
per cent wrong." [39]

Phipps revealed the dramatic nature of Bonnet's collapse on
September 13. "M. Bonnet feels that the whole question of
peace or war may be only a matter of minutes instead of days."
(Arrived at 1:25 P.M.) [40] "His Excellency seems completely to
have lost his nerve and to be ready for any solution to avoid
war." (Arrived 6:15 P.M.) [41] "M. Bonnet's collapse seems to me
so sudden and so extraordinary that I am asking for an interview with M. Daladier." (Arrived 7:10 P.M.) [42]

Phipps saw Daladier and reported his conclusions in a message
that arrived in London at 8:30 P.M. "I fear French have been
bluffing . . . Rather than give in to it, which would mean
actual suicide, he [Daladier] *would in the last resort prefer
war*." [43] Later that evening Daladier sent a message to Chamberlain, suggesting

> an immediate proposal to Hitler for a meeting of the Three Powers,
> viz: Germany for Sudetens, France for the Czechs, and Great
> Britain for Lord Runciman, with a view to obtaining that pacific
> settlement advocated in his speech last night. [44]

This telegram arrived at 10:10 P.M. Riots in the Sudetenland
seemed about to provoke a German invasion of Czechoslovakia.
The situation seemed "to be developing so fast" that by 11 P.M.
Chamberlain's plan for a personal visit was put in motion. [45]
Chamberlain would fly to see Hitler. Daladier "did not look
very pleased" when he heard. He had hoped for a conversation
à trois. [46]

The Cabinet met on the morning of September 14. Though their approval was "unanimous and enthusiastic" [47] there was no doubt that they were being told of the decision, not being consulted about it. Duff Cooper had asked for a Cabinet meeting on the evening of September 13. Chamberlain refused. He would not allow the Cabinet to hold up his peace initiative.

On September 15, Chamberlain flew to meet Hitler at Berchtesgaden, accompanied by Wilson and Strang. As the plane took off, Halifax took Kordt aside. Referring to the idea of a personal letter which had been mooted by the "German Opposition" earlier in the month, he said, "We have in the meantime decided otherwise, and think a personal interview the better plan." [48] Chamberlain wished to deal directly with Hitler; he would not be deflected by dissidents in the dictator's camp. During the flight, to improve morale, Wilson read out a selection from the laudatory letters and telegrams which had arrived at No. 10 that morning.[49] The flight was the first Chamberlain had ever made.

CHAPTER 8

Berchtesgaden

CHAMBERLAIN arrived at Munich airport. He was greeted by Nevile Henderson, who, bearing in mind that the Prime Minister was sixty-nine and had never flown before, made some appropriate comment. "I'm tough and wiry," came the reply.[1]

"There was a somewhat macabre tea-party," wrote Strang, "at a round table in the room with the great window looking out towards Austria. The small-talk of statesmen whose only point of contact is an international emergency cynically created by the one and stoically grappled with by the other is best left in oblivion." [2] Chamberlain himself seemed to think that it was worthy of record. He was sitting beneath a large Italian nude which may have distracted him.

Chamberlain: I have often heard of this room but it's much larger than I expected.
Hitler: It is you who have the big rooms in England.
Chamberlain: You must come and see them sometime.
Hitler: I should be received with demonstrations of disapproval.
Chamberlain: Well, perhaps it would be wise to choose the moment.[3]

They talked alone except for the German interpreter. Chamberlain saw no need for a second Englishman to be present. The others sat downstairs. The Germans employed the time telling Wilson the exact military and political weaknesses of France.

There was, Hitler told Chamberlain, "a situation which demanded instant solution." The Sudetens must be separated from the rest of Czechoslovakia. Chamberlain said that he agreed "in principle." But, he added, he could do nothing without the assent of his Ministers.[4] Chamberlain's agreement was crucial. Hitler could assume ministerial assent. Chamberlain controlled his Ministers, and their views were marginal. Chamberlain's agreement "in principle" was an agreement in fact: Germans in Czechoslovakia would be joined to Germany. Two weeks before "Munich" the breakup of Czechoslovakia was assured.

If the Sudeten Germans came into the Reich, Hitler went on, then the Hungarian minority would secede, as would the Polish and Slovak minorities; what was left would be so small he would not bother his head about it. Hitler had stated his interest. At 1 P.M. the same day, Henlein broadcast from Germany to the Sudeten Germans, "*Wir wollen heim ins Reich.*" Chamberlain, determined, unsympathetic to the Czechs, alone, gave Henlein his opportunity.

The next morning Wilson went to Munich with Dirksen. He told Dirksen that "although we should go into action as soon as we got home . . . there were a good many things to be done — in England, in Paris, and at Prague." [5]

In England, Leo Amery walked to the Foreign Office "and had a short talk with Edward Halifax." [6] Amery suggested that Czechoslovakia declare itself neutral and be guaranteed. He believed a plebiscite "is quite unworkable," but that it might be possible "to make a definite cession of the North-West corner which Masaryk had wanted to give up in 1919." Halifax "rather boggled at the idea of a British guarantee but otherwise was inclined to agree."

In Paris there was "considerable heart-burning." [7] By midday on September 17, neither Daladier nor Bonnet had received any information about the Berchtesgaden meeting. Halifax invited them to London. Chamberlain returned from Germany. The same day, Citrine, Herbert Morrison, and Dalton, on behalf of the National Council of Labour, spent an hour and a half with Chamberlain, Halifax and Wilson. Chamberlain described his interview with Hitler to them. He omitted to say that he had agreed "in principle" to the cession of the Sudetenland. He also repeated a story put out by Bonnet that Litvinov, in the event of a Franco-German conflict over Czechoslovakia, intended to take the matter to the League rather than fight. Dalton denied the authenticity of this story.[8] There is no evidence for it. But Bonnet knew it would please the British to hear that Czechoslovakia's *second* ally was ratting. It would enable Chamberlain to ignore Russia without qualms of conscience.

The Cabinet met that day. Lord Runciman was brought in. He had finally decided that it would be sensible to cede the Sudetenland to Germany. He described his experiences in Czechoslovakia. Duff Cooper noted that they were "interesting, of course, but unhelpful." Runciman had no constructive suggestions. Chamberlain gave an account of his visit to Hitler, whom he described as "the commonest little dog." He was, however, pleased at reports that Hitler had been impressed by him. He assumed that the Cabinet would accept the principle of self-determination, and was surprised to find that many of them refused to do so without further discussion.[9]

In Prague, Hodza admitted to Newton that "it might in the last resort be feasible to surrender Egerland."[10] But he thought that only a new Government could do it. Beneš had also considered the idea, and had rejected it. The exclusion of Egerland, said Hodza, "would of course be no adequate solution and would in any case be impossible in the present circumstances as such a precedent could not be admitted."[11] But the views of the Czechs were of no importance. Henderson, realistic as ever, revealed how the situation had changed: "In any case the *method* of solution can now only be settled with the German Government."[12]

On the morning of September 18, Bonnet, Daladier and Léger met the "Big Four" — Chamberlain, Halifax, Simon, Hoare — together with Vansittart, Wilson, Cadogan, Edward Bridges (Secretary to the Cabinet), Strang, and Frank Roberts, a junior in the Foreign Office.[18] They discussed the question posed by Chamberlain as to "whether or not to accept the principle of self-determination." On the British side no one spoke except Chamberlain and Halifax. Daladier explained that "a plebiscite seemed a weapon with which the German Government could keep Central Europe in a constant state of alarm and suspense." But the French were prepared to consider the cession of territory. Their greatest concern was to secure a British guarantee for the truncated Czechoslovakia. Daladier made it clear that he believed Hitler was planning further incursions into Central Europe. If France were to lose Czechoslovakia, Britain must share responsibility for the future of those areas beyond. Chamberlain's policy was to allow Germany a free hand in Eastern Europe. By giving a guarantee for the integrity of Czechoslovakia, which had little prospect of remaining a viable state once its frontier areas had been taken away, this policy would receive a severe setback. Chamberlain therefore did his best to avoid the guarantee. Britain was unwilling to defend Czechoslovakia.

Halifax explained that "the value of our guarantee would be purely deterrent." He added that he would like to see associated with the guarantee

> some undertaking on the part of the Czech Government that in issues involving peace and war they should accept the advice of His Majesty's Government, and that if they did not accept it His Majesty's Government would then be automatically absolved of their guarantee.[13]

The meeting adjourned while the British Ministers considered the problem of the guarantee. After two and a half hours' discussion they agreed to accept it. The meeting ended at 12:15 A.M., when proposals to be put to the Czech Government were completed. No official communiqué was issued that night. But French papers carried details of the meeting the following morning.[14] At about 11 A.M. the French Ministerial Council agreed to the proposals. At 2 P.M. they were submitted to the Czech Government in Prague. Beneš "felt guarantees which he already possessed had proved valueless." [15] What use would new ones be?

The Anglo-French Proposals to the Czechs
September 18/19, 1938

1) We are both convinced that, after recent events, the point has now been reached where the further maintenance within the boundaries of the Czechoslovak State of the districts mainly inhabited by Sudeten-Deutsch cannot in fact continue any longer without imperilling the interests of Czechoslovakia herself and of European peace. In the light of these considerations both Governments have been compelled to the conclusion that the maintenance of peace and the safety of Czechoslovakia's vital interests cannot effectively be assured unless these areas are now transferred to the Reich.

2) This could be done either by direct transfer or as the result of a plebiscite . . . We anticipate in the absence of indication to the contrary that you may prefer to deal with the Sudeten-Deutsch problem by the method of direct transfer, and as a case by itself.

3) The areas for transfer would probably have to include areas with over 50% of German inhabitants, but we should hope to arrange by negotiations provisions for adjustment of frontiers, where circumstances render it necessary, by some international body including a Czech representative. We are satisfied that the transfer of smaller areas based on a higher percentage would not meet the case.

4) . . . His Majesty's Government in the United Kingdom would be prepared, as a contribution to the pacification of Europe, to join in an international guarantee of the new boundaries of the Czechoslovak State against unprovoked aggression. One of the Principal conditions of such a guarantee would be the safeguarding of the independence of Czechoslovakia by the substitution of a general guarantee against unprovoked aggression in place of existing treaties which involve reciprocal obligations of a military character.

The Cabinet met on September 19, to discuss the outcome of the French visit. Chamberlain apologized for the speed at which it had been necessary to take the various decisions. With Halifax, Simon, and Hoare, he "had decided in favour of a guarantee . . . There wasn't time to call the Cabinet." [16] Most of the Cabinet disliked the Anglo-French plan. They agreed to it only because of the time factor, and the need to keep in with the French. Their views were unimportant. The plan was no longer in their hands. Hore-Belisha criticized the guarantee:

> I pointed out that Czechoslovakia would be an unstable State economically after the Sudeten-German areas had been transferred. It was difficult to see how it could survive. Czechoslovakia would be strategically unsound and there was no means by which we could implement the guarantee. How could we fight the Poles or the Hungarians if they attacked Czechoslovakia? I was afraid that the solution proposed was no real solution. It might only be a postponement of the evil day.

The Czech Government spent Tuesday, September 20, discussing the proposals. As *The Times* put it, the proposals "could not in the nature of things, be expected to make a strong *prima facie* appeal to the Czech Government, and least of all to President Beneš." [17]

Chamberlain was scheduled to go to Germany again on Wednesday. The Czechs took so long making up their minds that Ribbentrop instructed Weizsäcker to suggest postponing the meeting until Thursday.[18] Newton, in Prague, had been told that to help the Czech Government make up its mind, the British "strongly and definitely" advise immediate acceptance.[19] Phipps, in Paris, suggested to Bonnet that they inform Beneš that "unless his reply was an acceptance pure and simple, France and Great Britain would wash their hands of Czechoslovakia in the event of a German attack." [20] Before this could be done the Czechs issued their reply. They felt unable to decide on a question of frontiers without consulting Parliament, and the "question of peace would not be solved because (a) minority problems would again arise, (b) the balance of power would be destroyed." [21]

Newton, ever inventive, thought of a way to break Czech resistance: "If I can deliver a kind of ultimatum to President Beneš, Wednesday, he and his Government will feel able to bow to *force majeure*." [22]

Shortly after midnight, Halifax received a message from Phipps that de Lacroix, the French Minister in Prague, was "to make immediate representations to M. Beneš as to vital necessity for his acceptance of the Franco-British proposal." [23] At 12:40, Halifax wired back urging de Lacroix to "join with his British colleague in these representations. Please act immediately on receipt at whatever hour." [24]

At 2 A.M. Newton and de Lacroix issued their "Dawn *Démarche*" to Beneš. They argued with him for an hour and a quarter. Although there is no detailed account of what they said in the British documents, R. W. Seton-Watson issued a pamphlet shortly after the event in which the main proposals were outlined. The details were confirmed when the full text was published in Prague in 1958:[25]

1) That which has been proposed by England and France is the only means of averting war and the invasion of Czechoslovakia.

2) Should the Czechoslovak Republic reply in the negative, she would bear the responsibility for the war.

3) This would destroy Franco-British solidarity, since England would not march.

4) If under these circumstances the war starts, France will not take part, i.e. she will not fulfil her treaty obligations.

Dalton quoted these four points in his speech in the House of Commons on October 3. Hoare said "it was in almost every respect a totally inaccurate description of the representations that we made to the Czechoslovak Government." [26] Parliament could be deceived as easily as the Cabinet could be ignored.

At 6:30 A.M. Hodza's private secretary telephoned Newton and informed him that the Czech Government agreed to the Anglo-French proposals. It was Hodza's last act as Prime Minister, for his Government fell, and he was succeeded the next day by General Syrovy.

During the evening of September 21, Wenzel Jaksch, the leader of the German Social Democrats in Czechoslovakia, told Troutbeck, the First Secretary of the British Embassy, that his followers were lost.

> There was no place for them in the Czech districts as the Czechs themselves would have an insoluble problem with their own refugees from the mixed areas . . . They must now lay the lives of their 400,000 adherents in the hands of the British and French Governments and ask for advice as to what was to be done for them.[27]

No advice was forthcoming. Germans who hated Nazism were forced to remain in the areas the Nazis were about to enter. Many of those who fled and sought visas for England had their requests denied. The British, though claiming the power to guarantee the truncated state, could offer its threatened inhabitants neither refuge nor security.

CHAPTER 9

Godesberg

THE CABINET met on Wednesday, September 21. Chamberlain thought Hitler would want to march his troops into the Sudetenland at once, and occupy the districts where there was an overwhelming German majority. Duff Cooper and others felt the limit had been reached. They said further concessions could come only from the German side.[1]

On Thursday morning, September 22, Chamberlain said goodbye to Geoffrey Dawson at the airport, and entered the airplane which took him to Germany for the second time. He was accompanied by Wilson and Strang. He also took Sir William Malkin, the head of the drafting and legal department of the Foreign Office.

On arrival in Germany the British party went to the Petersberg Hotel at Godesberg. Magnificent rooms had been reserved overlooking the Rhine. Kirkpatrick noted that, "Fruit, cigars and cigarettes were laid out on every table and the proprietor (the owner of the famous Eau de Cologne) had provided no fewer than fifteen samples of his products: hair lotion, shaving-cream, soap, bath salts, pomades and so on." [2] Kirkpatrick removed some of the latter for his wife.

The Godesberg meetings were held in the Hotel Dreesen. Kirkpatrick was present to take notes for Chamberlain.[3] After Chamberlain had outlined the Anglo-French proposals, Hitler thanked him. Then he announced: *"Es tut mir furchtbar leid, aber das geht nicht mehr."* He could no longer accept them. He mentioned the problem of the Hungarian and Polish minorities in Czechoslovakia. It was "his duty to say that demands were being made by others which had his full sympathy, and peace could not be firmly established until these claims had been settled."

The Prime Minister said that he did not wish to dissent. He, the Führer, had said that the Sudeten question was of the utmost urgency and that was why he had addressed himself to this particular problem. The others had not the same urgency. Hitler retorted that, of course, for him as a German this problem was most urgent. But a Pole or a Hungarian would, of course, have maintained that theirs was the most urgent question.

In any case "the problem must be settled definitely and completely by the 1st October at the latest." Hitler threw out a backhanded compliment: he "never believed himself that a peaceful solution could be reached, and he admitted that he never thought that the Prime Minister could have achieved what he had." Chamberlain said he "had actually been booed on his departure today." Hitler interjected that "he had only been booed by the Left." Chamberlain replied that he "did not mind what the Left thought, but that his serious difficulties came from the people in his own party, some of whom had actually written to protest to him against his policy." [3]

In London and Paris, at 5:15 P.M., no news had arrived concerning the progress of the Godesberg talks. There *were* reports of incursions by German troops into the Egerland. Halifax felt an "entirely new situation" had arisen. [4] Previously the British and French had advised the Czechs not to mobilize. Now Léger agreed with Halifax that they should perhaps withdraw this advice. Newton was instructed to tell the Czechs *after* nine o'clock that they could mobilize. [5] If the Czechs failed to mobilize in time, and the Germans attacked, the British and French would be held responsible for having forbidden Czech mobilization in the first place. If held responsible they could hardly fail to go to war. On the other hand, premature mobilization might prejudice Chamberlain's chances of success at Godesberg.

At 9:10 P.M. Phipps was telephoned and told that Newton's instructions allowing the Czechs to mobilize had been suspended "in the light of a message from Sir Horace Wilson at Godesberg." [6] The responsibility was removed from Halifax's shoulders. Chamberlain wired from Godesberg at 2 A.M. that "we think suspension must be maintained pending tomorrow morning's conversations." [7]

The conversations at Godesberg on September 22 ended in deadlock. A further meeting was arranged for 11:30 on the morning of September 23. But instead of a further meeting, Chamberlain decided to write a letter to Hitler incorporating the substance of his remarks of the previous day.

Halifax, left alone in London for a second day, saw war as an immediate prospect. Away from the influence of Chamberlain he did not envisage further appeasement. He sought to determine the strength of possible allies. At 1:15 P.M. he telegraphed R. A. Butler at Geneva: "It would be useful if you would have a conversation with M. Litvinov on the present situation, and endeavour to elicit from him anything concerning the views and intentions of his Government." [8]

Tension mounted so swiftly that Halifax was prepared to take Russian intentions into consideration.

At 1:40 P.M. Halifax, still firm, telegraphed the Godesberg delegation that "we propose" to permit Czech mobilization at 3 P.M.[9] Henderson immediately wired back, "wait a little longer." [10] But Daladier felt that Czech mobilization should not be delayed.[11] At 4 P.M., permission was granted.[12] The Czechs decided to mobilize immediately. The British had allowed the French to take the initiative.

Butler and de la Warr, meanwhile, had been interviewing Litvinov and Maisky at Geneva.

"The Czechoslovak-Soviet Pact would come into force," said Litvinov. He welcomed the fact that we had asked him to talk to us. He had for long been hoping for conversations between Great Britain, France, and Russia, and he would like to suggest to us . . . a meeting of the three Powers mentioned, together with

Roumania and any other small Power who could be regarded as reliable. In this way we might "show the Germans that we mean business." [13]

Halifax did not receive this message from Butler until the morning of September 24. On the evening of September 23, he asked Phipps for information on the possibility of Soviet assistance, on public opinion, and on the views of French political circles. Halifax was now acting as the spokesman of a small group of politicians who were frightened by the thought of what Chamberlain might be doing at Godesberg. This group had assembled at the bidding of Simon. They prevailed upon Halifax to allow Czech mobilization despite Chamberlain's protests. At 4 P.M. Simon summoned Duff Cooper, who found Walter Elliott and Kingsley Wood awaiting him when he arrived. They were later joined by Oliver Stanley and Hailsham.

Simon said, "How is the Prime Minister going to react to this? If the worst comes to the worst, will he be ready to go to war?" Kingsley Wood, "who knows the PM better than most of us," said it was his impression that "before the PM left for Germany he thought that it was all UP." [14]

Simon then left to take his wife out to dinner, for it was her birthday.

At 10 P.M., Halifax telephoned Chamberlain. He passed on the views of his Cabinet colleagues.

> While mistrustful of our plan but prepared perhaps to accept it with reluctance as alternative to war, great mass of public opinion [in Britain] seems to be hardening in sense of feeling that we have gone to limit of concession and that it is up to the Chancellor to make some contribution. We, of course, can imagine immense difficulties with which you are confronted but from point of view of your own position, that of Government, and of the country, it seems to your colleagues of vital importance that you should not leave without making it plain to Chancellor if possible by special

interview that, after great concessions made by Czechoslovak Government, for him to reject opportunity of peaceful solution in favour of one that must involve war would be an unpardonable crime against humanity.[15]

Few Foreign Secretaries can have spoken so firmly to their chief. Halifax had seen the folly of endless, unqualified appeasement.

At Godesberg the British party waited for Hitler's reply to Chamberlain's letter. They had "a rather grim lunch" at their hotel. Chamberlain "discussed the theatre and spoke of his early days in Birmingham." [16]

At 3:25 P.M. Hitler replied, stating his own proposals in general terms. Chamberlain promptly asked for a "memorandum which sets out these proposals, together with a map showing the area proposed to be transferred." [17] This he undertook to forward to Prague. At 11 P.M. he had a final interview with Hitler to discuss the German memorandum, which was, said Chamberlain, "an ultimatum and not a negotiation." [18] "*Diktat*," interjected Henderson.[19] "It bore the word Memorandum at the top," came Hitler's reply. They discussed various modifications, prefaced by the Prime Minister's remark that "if it proved possible to achieve this peaceful solution — even if it were not agreeable to sections of British public opinion — he was hopeful that the agreement we reached might . . . be a turning point in Anglo-German relations."

Towards the end of the meeting, and perhaps conscious of the consequences of his actions, Chamberlain asked what would happen to those in the Sudetenland who disliked an *Anschluss*. "As regards communists," said Hitler, "it was high treason to indulge in communist activities in Germany, and this would apply to the Sudeten territory; but he did not mind and never minded what a communist had been before, provided that he abandoned his communist activities."

The meeting finished at 1:45 A.M. Hitler said that "Germany would of course bring up the colonial problem." Chamberlain replied that in the questions to be discussed after the solution of the Czech crisis he had in mind further and greater problems. He took his leave with "a hearty *Auf Wiedersehen.*" [20]

Hitler's Memorandum for the Czechs
September 23, 1938

Reports which are increasing in number from hour to hour regarding incidents in the Sudetenland show that the situation has become completely intolerable for the Sudeten German people and, in consequence, a danger to the peace of Europe. It is therefore essential that the separation of the Sudetenland agreed to by Czechoslovakia should be effected without any further delay. On the attached map the Sudeten German area which is to be ceded is shaded red. The areas in which over and above the areas which are to occupied a plebiscite is also to be held, are drawn in and shaded green.

1) Withdrawal of the whole Czech armed forces, the police, the *gendarmerie*, the customs officials and the frontier guards from the area to be evacuated as designated on the attached map, this area to be handed over to Germany on October 1st.

2) The evacuated territory is to be handed over in its present condition.

3) The Czech Government discharges at once all Sudeten Germans serving in the military forces or the police anywhere in Czech State territory and permits them to return home.

4) The Czech Government liberates all political prisoners of German race.

5) The German Government agrees to permit a plebiscite to take place in those areas, which will be more definitely defined, before at latest the 25th November. Alterations to the new frontier arising out of the plebiscite will be settled by a German-Czech or an international commission. The plebiscite itself will be carried out under the control of an international commission. All persons who were residing in the areas in question on the 28th of October 1918,

or who were born in those areas prior to this date will be eligible
to vote . . .

6) The German Government proposes that an authoritative
German-Czech commission should be set up to settle all further
details.

Appendix. The evacuated Sudeten German area is to be handed
over without destroying or rendering unusable in any way military,
economic or traffic establishments (plants). These include the
ground organisation of the air service and all wireless stations.

Considering the importance of Hitler's memorandum it is interesting to follow its journey, via the British Foreign Office, into
the hands of those who would most wish to see it. At 6 P.M. on
September 24, Newton gave Krofta an English translation.[21]
The vital date mentioned in clause 1 as October 1, was given to
the Czechs (by mistake) as October 13, thus allowing them an
extra twelve days before the German occupation of the area.
This error in the English version was not corrected until 9:45
P.M. the *following* day. Colonel Mason-Macfarlane left Berlin
at 3 P.M. on September 24, and made his way towards Prague
with the correct German text and the maps.

It had meant Mason-Macfarlane's flying back to Berlin, motoring
to the Czech frontier, and then walking ten kilometres in the dark
through Czech barbed-wire and other entanglements, at the
constant risk of being shot at as a raider by either Germans or
Czechs.[22]

He arrived in Prague at 11:15 P.M. on September 24. The
Czechs at once realized the evacuation was scheduled for October 1. Although the German text gave the correct date, the
uncertainty remained until the following evening,* when the
error in the English version was corrected.

* Newton telegraphed, "In English translation as telegraphed . . . crucial date
is given as October 13. German text brought to me by Colonel Mason-
Macfarlane says October 1. Which is correct?" (Newton to Halifax, September 25. Brit. Docs. 3, vol. II, No. 1088.)

The French were kept similarly ill-informed. Although Phipps had sent a copy of the Memorandum to one of Bonnet's secretaries at 10:20 P.M. on September 24, nobody else in Paris seems to have seen it until 11:30 A.M. the next day.

Chamberlain flew back from Godesberg on Saturday, September 24, and arranged for Daladier and Bonnet to come to England on Sunday. Henderson and Kirkpatrick made their way back to Berlin, pausing for a time in Cologne Cathedral while waiting for their train. Henderson, depressed, "knelt in the nave and prayed for peace." [23]

The Foreign Office was in a state of uproar when Phipps answered Halifax's request for information on the state of French opinion. Phipps wrote: "His Majesty's Government should realize extreme danger of even appearing to encourage small, but noisy and corrupt war group here. All that is best in France is against war, *almost* at any price." [24]

Strang saw the folly of what Phipps had written:

> In the Foreign Office this telegram struck us with a sense of outrage. What shocked us was that the Ambassador should hold that those who thought like Georges Bonnet were the best of France, and that those who thought like Georges Mandel were to be stigmatised as belonging to a corrupt war group.[25]

By "war group," Cadogan wrote back angrily to Phipps, "you surely do not include all those who feel that France must carry out her treaty obligations to Czechoslovakia." * "I meant," replied Phipps, "the communists who are paid by Moscow and have been working for war for months." [26]

The Cabinet met that evening. Chamberlain spoke for over an hour about his Godesberg visit and the German terms. He concluded "that we should accept those terms and that we should

---

* This rebuke was drafted by Sir Orme Sargent.

advise the Czechs to do so." [27] He also suggested that the Cabinet should adjourn till the morning. Duff Cooper protested:

> Hitherto we had been faced with the unpleasant alternatives of peace with dishonour or war. I now saw a third possibility, namely war with dishonour, by which I meant being kicked into war by the boot of public opinion when those for whom we were fighting had already been defeated.[28]

This final possibility was reserved for September 3, 1939.

On Sunday, September 25, the Cabinet met three times to discuss the crisis. Henderson sent a message to London summing up the situation with great accuracy:

> Anglo-French and individual intervention with a view to solving Sudeten problem in an orderly and deliberate fashion has failed. It will equally have failed to solve the problem without war if Czechoslovak Government reject plan . . . It can be taken for granted that the only hope of preventing or at least localising war is for His Majesty's Government . . . to make it absolutely clear at Prague that they must accept German plan or forfeit claim to further support from Western Powers.[29]

Duff Cooper could not accept this. But Chamberlain had been mulling over further schemes. At midday he told Kordt that Hitler should give an audience to Lieutenant-General Sir Frederick Maurice, President of the British Legion, who would be arriving at Tempelhof that evening. The suggestion was "to send immediately ten thousand members of the British Ex-Servicemen's Association to the areas to be occupied by Germany. The British ex-servicemen would merely exercise the function of 'neutral witnesses' during the handing over of the territory to Germany." [30] Hitler saw Maurice and politely but firmly rejected the proposal. By an oversight the Ex-Servicemen embarked at Tilbury, not knowing that Hitler had no use for them.

That afternoon Jan Masaryk, Czechoslovak Minister in London, rejected the German Memorandum.

It is a *de facto* ultimatum of the sort usually presented to a vanquished nation and not a proposition to a sovereign state which has shown the greatest readiness to make sacrifices for the appeasement of Europe . . . The nation of St. Wenceslas, John Hus and Thomas Masaryk will not be a nation of slaves.[31]

The Foreign Office found his reply premature. Strang telephoned Troutbeck in Prague to stop "the immediate publication of M. Masaryk's letter." This could "destroy all hope of negotiation, of which even now we do not despair." Troutbeck was "surprised" to hear that Masaryk had sent a reply. The Ministry of Foreign Affairs had told him the Czech reply would not be ready till the following morning.[32]

At 9:25 P.M. the British and French Ministers met in Downing Street.[33] Chamberlain's aim was to destroy any French desire to wage an offensive war. Daladier and Bonnet were subjected to relentless interrogation and cross-questioning from Chamberlain and his advocates. Chamberlain wished to know what the French would do if Hitler marched into Czechoslovakia.

M. Daladier replied that Herr Hitler would then have brought about a situation in which aggression would have been provoked by him.
Mr. Chamberlain asked what then.
M. Daladier thought each of us would do what was incumbent upon him.
Mr. Chamberlain asked whether we were to understand from that that France would declare war on Germany.
M. Daladier said that the matter was very clear.

Simon tried to discover if the French intended actually to attack Germany. At the back of Simon's mind was the idea, later to be further developed, that the French could *declare* war, and thus remain true to their obligations in one sense, but not actually take the offensive. Simon asked:

161

When the French troops had been called up to do their duty, was that duty just to man the Maginot line and remain there without any declaration of war, or was it the intention of the French Government to declare war and take active measures with their land forces?

M. Daladier said that would depend on many things.

. . . The second question he would like to put was to ask whether the head of the French Government could say if the use of the French Air Force over German territory was contemplated. This would necessarily involve entering into active hostilities with Germany.

M. Daladier said he had certainly considered the possibility of air attack. In all countries where fighting had taken place recently there had been air attacks . . .

Sir John Simon said he would repeat his question again as it seemed to have been misunderstood . . .

M. Daladier . . . said he would consider it ridiculous to mobilise French land forces only to leave them under arms doing nothing in their fortifications. It would be equally ridiculous to do nothing in the air. He thought that, in spite of Herr Hitler's recent declarations, the German system of fortifications was much less solid than Herr Hitler had indicated. It would be several months before the Siegfried Line would be really strong. He thought, therefore, that, after French troops had been concentrated, an offensive should be attempted by land against Germany. As regards the air, it would be possible to attack certain important German military and industrial centres, which could easily be reached, in spite of certain legends which had been spread abroad.

Daladier had made the military position clear. But he had not finished. He intended to discuss the "moral" angle, one distasteful to the British.

"Like a barbarian," said M. Daladier, "he had been ready to cut up this country without even consulting her and handing over three and a half millions of her population to Herr Hitler. It had not been an agreeable task for him. It had been hard, perhaps a little dishonouring; but he had felt this was better rather than to begin what we had seen twenty years ago."

Chamberlain tried to frighten Daladier with a picture of a "rain of bombs" on Paris and other French military and industrial centers. Hoare asked, "What steps could be taken to prevent Czechoslovakia being overrun?" Daladier would not be drawn. He emphasized Hitler's plans for aggrandizement. He might become "Master of Europe." Daladier was "ready to agree to certain measures of conciliation which were in accordance with moral sentiments, but a moment came to call a halt and that moment had in his opinion come. The French Government had been unanimous on this point."

The meeting adjourned at half-past midnight. On the advice of the Cabinet, Chamberlain asked for General Gamelin to be sent over the next morning.

Next morning Chamberlain saw Daladier and Gamelin alone.[34] He informed them that Wilson would fly to Germany that day on a further visit to Hitler. He also told them what message Wilson would take, and the warning he would give Hitler. Chamberlain appealed to Hitler to allow details of the transfer of territory to be settled by an international body of Germans, Czechs and English. If Hitler refused, Wilson would tell him that France and Britain would both fight for Czechoslovakia. Wilson flew to Germany.* Meanwhile, at 11:20 A.M. the Anglo-French talks were resumed.[35] Chamberlain said "there were many doubts in Germany itself as to whether the game was worth the candle." For the first time Chamberlain indicated that he realized there was opposition to Hitler in Germany. But he did not take the advice given him by various unofficial contacts. They had wanted the British and French to stand firm. Churchill, Eden, Vansittart and Conwell-Evans passed on messages from German anti-Nazis, and urged Chamberlain to heed them. The opposition could then tell Hitler, "Thus far and no further." We shall never know what they would have done had Anglo-French firmness been maintained.

* Duff Cooper wanted to mobilize the fleet during Wilson's visit to impress Hitler that Britain was in earnest. Chamberlain refused, claiming that mobilization would "ruin" any chance of Wilson's warning being accepted.

At first, it seemed the British *would* be firm. That afternoon, Reginald Leeper, a senior Foreign Office official, drafted a communiqué and issued it to the press. The French and Russians did not know of it. The communiqué read: "If in spite of all efforts made by the British Prime Minister a German attack is made upon Czechoslovakia the immediate result must be that France will be bound to come to her assistance, and Great Britain and Russia will certainly stand by France." [36]

As a result of this communiqué, Halifax wired Berlin at 4:10 P.M. with a message for Wilson, who had not yet seen Hitler. The message was from Chamberlain. "Since you left, French have definitely stated their intention of supporting Czechoslovakia by offensive measures if attacked. This would bring us in: and it should be made plain to Chancellor that this is inevitable alternative to a peaceful solution." [37]

Wilson was thus instructed to deliver a further message of warning to Hitler.

In Paris, however, Bonnet told journalists that he had had no confirmation of the communiqué. He added that it was clearly the work of Vansittart, who was no longer of any importance in the conduct of British foreign policy. It had been endorsed by an "obscure underling." But Vansittart had never seen the communiqué. Nor was Leeper "obscure." He was head of the Foreign Office News Department; a close friend of Sargent; a constant and stern critic of appeasement.

His communiqué was to have been broadcast in German by the BBC that night. For "technical reasons" this did not take place.[38] The new firmness had appeared in the press. Leeper had seen to that. But the public would hear no more of it. Rothermere wrote to Ribbentrop, "I do urge your Excellency to use your influence to postpone the decisive moment of October 1st to a later date." [39] To plead, not to warn, was the British method. Those, like Leeper, who advocated firmness, were ignored. But pleading was futile. Hitler did not intend to postpone the date. He advanced it.

Wilson, Henderson and Kirkpatrick saw Hitler at 5 P.M. They gave him Chamberlain's first message, which asked for a meeting between Czech and German representatives. Chamberlain was "willing to arrange for the representation of the British Government." Hitler agreed to a meeting, on the condition that the Czechs accept the Memorandum and the October 1 date.[40] He said:

> Whether by negotiation or whether by the exercise of force, the territory would be free on the 1st October; and if he did not know for certain that the Czechs accepted in the course of the next two or three days the territory might well be cleared of Czechs before the 1st October. On reflection he must have an affirmative reply within two days, that was to say by Wednesday. [September 28]

Wilson asked Hitler, "What time Wednesday?"

Henderson: Midnight, Wednesday?
Hitler: No, by two p.m.

Wilson described it as a "very violent hour." Hitler shrieked a great deal.* Wilson and Henderson told Hitler they "still hoped to move the Czechs in the direction of a settlement."[41] The meeting was adjourned until the following day. Wilson had been upset by Hitler's "intense emotion." He decided not to deliver the special warning concerning British and French firmness which Chamberlain had sent.[41] It was a serious mistake. Wilson thought Hitler's ravings to be the result of the strain of the moment. If tempers cooled, Hitler would become reasonable.

That night, in a broadcast, Hitler made such a violent attack on Beneš that Chamberlain lost hope of persuading the Czechs to make a fresh offer. As a result he issued fresh proposals himself which were published in Tuesday's papers and sent to Wilson in Berlin.

---

* "The epithets applied to Mr. Chamberlain and Sir Horace Wilson could not be repeated in a drawing room." (Note of Conversation. Brit. Docs. 3, Vol. II, No. 1118.)

Speaking for the British Government we regard ourselves as morally responsible for seeing that the promises [made by Czechoslovakia] are carried out fairly and fully and we are prepared to undertake that they shall be so carried out with all reasonable promptitude, provided that the German Government will agree to the settlement of terms and conditions of transfer by discussion and not by force.[42]

The next morning, Tuesday, September 27, Lord Perth, British Ambassador in Rome, asked Halifax if it would

be helpful if I were authorised to convey officially and immediately to Count Ciano the Prime Minister's declaration and to express on behalf of His Majesty's Government the hope that Signor Mussolini would use his influence to induce Hitler to accept proposals contained therein.[43]

Some sought to influence and to mediate. Others strengthened the spirit of resolution at home. That day Queen Elizabeth launched the new Cunarder that bore her name. At the ceremony she read a message from the King:

He bids the people of this country to be of good cheer . . . He knows . . . they will place entire confidence in their leaders, who, under God's providence, are striving their utmost to find a just and peaceful solution of the grave problems which confront them.

At 12:15 P.M. a representative of these "leaders" was closeted with Hitler in a final interview. The representative was Wilson. He was accompanied by Henderson and Kirkpatrick. Hitler told Wilson that he had read Chamberlain's statement. There was nothing more to say.[44] The two men talked on nevertheless.

Meanwhile at the British Embassy in Berlin a telegram had arrived which appeared to be (but was not) of more than usual importance. Con O'Neill, a junior member of the Embassy, was asked to take it to the Chancellery to show it to Henderson or Kirkpatrick. Walking past rows of SS men he arrived outside the inner sanctum. High-ranking officials — including Neurath — stood up at his entrance and bowed. Kirkpatrick came out of the meeting to see him, agitated because Hitler was behaving wildly. Wilson had refused to give way. At last the appeasers were being firm. Kirkpatrick crumpled the telegram into his pocket without reading it, and hissed in O'Neill's ear, "It's war." Kirkpatrick thought Hitler had lost all reason, and was convinced that Wilson would not retreat or compromise. O'Neill returned to the Embassy, certain that the British would at last stand firm behind the Czechs.

They did nothing of the kind. The firmness was an illusion. Hitler screamed about injustice to Germans. Wilson told Hitler that he "understood the position perfectly." Wilson said he had

> one more thing to say and he would try to say it in the tone which the Prime Minister would have used had he been himself present. Many Englishmen thought with him [Wilson] that there were many things which ought to be discussed between England and Germany to the great advantage of both countries. He would not waste time by enumerating these matters, but they included arrangements for improving the economic position all round. He himself, and many other Englishmen, would like to reach an agreement with Germany on these lines. He had been much struck, as had many others in England, by a speech in which Herr Hitler had said that he regarded England and Germany as bulwarks against disruption, particularly from the East.[45]

Hitler said that what he most resented was that Czechoslovakia seemed to be more important in English eyes than Germany. Wilson wished to continue the conversation. But Henderson advised against doing so. Just before he left, however, and alone with Hitler for a moment, Wilson said "I will still try to make those Czechos sensible." * [45]

---

* The German report of what Wilson said is slightly inaccurate. Wilson had heard Hitler shout about the wicked "Tschechen" (the German for "Czechs"). Wilson replied: "I will still try to make those Tschechen sensible." The interpreter misheard him.

Wilson took Hitler's final concession to England. It was a letter to Chamberlain offering a formal guarantee from Germany for the remainder of Czechoslovakia.

At 6:45 P.M. the British Government produced new proposals. They realized Hitler was concerned with the timing of the Czech operation, and therefore drafted a plan with a built-in timetable which they hoped both Germans and Czechs would accept.

The British Plan
September 27, 1938

1) German troops would occupy the territories of Egerland and Asch outside the Czech fortified line on October 1.

2) Meeting of German and Czech plenipotentiaries with a British representative at some town in the Sudetenland on October 3 . . . On the same date meeting of International Boundary Commission consisting of German, Czech and British members. On the same date, if possible, arrival of observers and again, if possible, British Legion . . .

Duties:

(a) to arrange for the immediate withdrawal of Czech troops and State police. (b) to lay down the broad line for safeguarding minorities in the ceded territories and for defining their rights to opt and to withdraw their property, similar arrangements being made for the German minority in the new Czechoslovakia. (c) to determine the actual instructions, based on the Anglo-French plan, to be given to the International Boundary Commission for the delimitation of the new frontier with the utmost speed.

3) October 10, entry of German troops into the zone in which the plenipotentiaries shall have indicated that their arrangements are complete . . .

4) The meeting of plenipotentiaries will have to consider whether further arrangements should be made for improving the frontier delimited by the Boundary Commission in October in order better

to meet local geographical and economic requirements in the various localities. It would be for consideration whether local plebiscites would be necessary or desirable for this purpose.

5) As soon as possible negotiations to be started between Germany, Great Britain, France and Czechoslovakia, for the purpose (a) of arranging for joint measures for demobilisation or withdrawal of troops, and (b) of revising Czechoslovakia's present treaty relationships and instituting a system jointly guaranteeing the new Czechoslovakia.

It was possible that war would intervene before there was a chance of putting the new plan into operation. To prevent war, Halifax contacted Phipps at 8:30 P.M. It would be necessary, he said, to concert the actions of England and France,

> especially as regards measures likely immediately and automatically to start a world war without unhappily having any effect on Czechoslovakia. We should be glad to know that French Government agree that any action of an offensive character taken by either of us henceforward . . . shall only be taken after previous consultation and agreement.[46]

Later that evening Bonnet agreed. He felt "more and more that it behooves us both to be extremely prudent and to count our probable and even possible enemies before embarking on any offensive act whatever." [47]

Hitler had assured Wilson that morning that he did not intend to launch a war against the West unless the West attacked him first. The danger of an Anglo-German war starting on German initiative was thus averted. Oliver Stanley told Duff Cooper that "the plot now is to frighten the French into ratting, and then to get out on their shoulders." [48]

The British Plan was sent to Newton, who announced that Krofta's "first impression seemed favourable." [49] But the French doubted if the proposals were far-reaching enough to satisfy the Germans. If the British démarche were unsuccessful, the French suggested "a further *démarche* by M. François-Poncet proposing a rather more extended German occupation." [50]

That evening, Tuesday, September 27, Chamberlain broadcast to the nation: "How horrible, fantastic, incredible, it is that we should be digging trenches and trying on gas masks here because of a quarrel in a far-away country between people of whom we know nothing."

Hoare wrote that in France "there were no gas masks." [51] Josiah Wedgwood thought,

> Gas masks and ARP were solely invented by the Government in order to terrify the old women of this country into welcoming our strong silent Prime Minister on his return from supping with the Devil. [52]

Many Englishmen knew little of Czechoslovakia. Chamberlain should not have been one of them. Czechoslovakia was a nation whose territorial integrity during the past months he had actively and industriously sought to undermine.

At 8 P.M., Duff Cooper gave the order for the mobilization of the fleet. He reported this to the Cabinet at 9:30 P.M., after Chamberlain's broadcast. Chamberlain, unwillingly at first, endorsed the order. Then he agreed that full publicity be given to it the next day.

At the Cabinet, Wilson spoke of his mission to Germany. In his opinion, "the only thing to do now was to advise the Czechs to evacuate the territory. He had drawn up a draft telegram containing this advice." [53]

At 11 P.M. Henderson saw Weizsäcker and gave him the British plan. Weizsäcker "did not believe the Chancellor would or could take it into consideration." [54] Before Henderson left he

> threw on the table a copy of the Anglo-French plan, allegedly from Sir Horace Wilson's papers. The Ambassador said that, though the paper was secret, he was giving it to me personally. I did not read the paper in the Ambassador's presence. [55]

This seems to have been a personal attempt by Henderson to indicate how far Britain had moved the Czechs from their original position.

At 11 P.M. Perth was given permission to see Ciano. Earlier, at 10 P.M., Roosevelt had proposed a conference of "nations directly interested in the present controversy." It should be held immediately in some "neutral spot in Europe." It never took place. Other conferences were being arranged.

People stirred early on the morning of Wednesday, September 28. Hitler's ultimatum to the Czechs would expire at 2 P.M. At 4 A.M. François-Poncet received his expected instructions to issue an additional *démarche*. At 8 A.M. he telephoned Henderson, who was convinced that Chamberlain would accept this "modification." At 8:30 A.M. he telephoned Weizsäcker and told him the French Plan:

> The occupation of all four sides of the Bohemian quadrilateral by German troops; districts comprising Czech fortifications were also to be occupied . . . The new element in this plan was not only that it went further than anything so far proposed to us, but also the fact that the plan was not yet known to the Czechs.[56]

The Germans were being consulted first. If they agreed, "the French Government would demand acceptance from the Czech Government. If Czechoslovakia refused, conclusions could be drawn which he did not need to define more closely."

François-Poncet asked for an interview with Hitler to present this plan. At 10 A.M. he telephoned Henderson and said he had had no reply to his request. At 10:15 A.M., Henderson telephoned Göring to tell him of this. "You need not say a word more," said Göring. "I am going immediately to see the Führer." [57] At 10:30 A.M. Henderson arrived at the French Embassy to confer with François-Poncet.

In Rome, Perth had arrived at his office at 9:30 A.M. He found a message from the previous night authorizing him to speak with Ciano about the possibility of Italian intervention. He telephoned Ciano and secured an interview. Unaware that the German ultimatum was to expire at 2 P.M., he walked leisurely to the Palazzo Chigi. He arrived at 10:20 A.M. He told Ciano that Mussolini was the only man who could induce Hitler to accept a peaceful solution. Ciano was surprised to hear that Britain and France intended to fight. "But you do not intend to fight in alliance with Russia." Perth told Ciano the *démarche* was an official step by the British Government to ask Mussolini to try to persuade Hitler to accept Chamberlain's proposals. Ciano said, "There is no time to be lost; it is a question of hours, not days." He hurried to the Palazzo Venezia, and saw Mussolini.[58]

Fifteen minutes later Ciano returned. He told Perth that Mussolini had arranged for Attolico, the Italian Ambassador in Berlin, to ask Hitler to postpone, for twenty-four hours, the action he was planning. In Berlin Attolico telephoned the German Foreign Minister and said, in English, "I must see the Führer at once, very urgent, quick, quick." [59]

About the same time, in London, Wilson saw Hesse and said that if Germany was prepared to give way "on the form," the British Government "would be prepared to push through all [their] demands with the Czechs and French." [60] Hesse suggested that a "new mediator" was needed. Mussolini was "most anxious to avert a war in which he had not the slightest interest." Wilson agreed. His own attempt to influence Hitler had failed to procure a solution. Mussolini's appearance might be more effective. Helped by Wilson, Chamberlain drafted messages for Hitler and Mussolini. He wrote to Hitler:

> I am ready to come to Berlin myself at once to discuss arrangements for transfer with you and representatives of the Czechoslovak Government together with representatives of France and Italy, if you desire. I feel convinced we could reach agreement in a week.[61]

He wrote to Mussolini:

I trust your Excellency will inform the German Chancellor that you are willing to be represented and urge him to agree to my proposal which will keep all our peoples out of war.[62]

Hitler agreed to see Chamberlain again. Mussolini replied that he was "willing to be present."

At 3:15 P.M. Henderson telephoned Cadogan and said that Hitler had invited Chamberlain to a meeting at Munich. It could begin the following morning. Mussolini and Daladier had also been invited. The news that Hitler was willing to see Chamberlain for the third time had to be given to Chamberlain. He was speaking in the Commons.

Halifax was listening to the debate from the gallery. The House and gallery were crowded to capacity.[63] Arnold Wilson arrived late for the debate, and finding the Chamber full, had to be content with a gallery seat. There he saw Queen Mary, the Duke and Duchess of Kent; the Ambassadors of America, France, Italy and Czechoslovakia. He noted the absence of Dirksen and Maisky. Wheeler-Bennett thought they were both there. He also thought that when the Prime Minister came in, "there was subdued applause for the moment was too poignant for lively demonstration." Arnold Wilson's impression was that the Prime Minister "entered amidst heartier applause than any heard since Armistice." He also thought Chamberlain's speech was relayed to the Library of the Upper House. But Wheeler-Bennett stated that although a microphone had been installed on the table of the House of Commons, "it was not used."

Chamberlain was in the middle of his speech when a messenger entered the gallery. He brought a note from Cadogan and gave it to Halifax. Halifax showed it to Baldwin, who was sitting next to him. Moments later, Lord Dunglass, Chamberlain's Parliamentary Private Secretary, appeared in the Commons, slipping in behind the Speaker's chair. He gave Hoare two sheets of paper with a few lines typed on each. Hoare handed them to Simon without looking at them. Simon read them immediately, and showed them to Inskip. Simon then stood up and put the sheets in front of Chamberlain, who did not notice them. When he did, he pushed them impatiently aside. Not until Simon himself "pushed the note into his hand did he pause for a moment in his speech to read the contents." [63]

"Shall I tell now?" he whispered to Simon. The question was heard by attentive listeners over the "dead" microphone in the Upper Library. Then Chamberlain announced that he would accept Hitler's invitation, and go to Munich.

"Thank God for the Prime Minister," cried a nameless member. Not only Hansard, but few other people were in a position to observe the ensuing pandemonium clearly.

"The whole house stood throwing its Order Papers in the air." [63]

"The House, including the Left Wing, cheered the Prime Minister enthusiastically." [63]

Churchill, Eden and Amery remained seated. Churchill later rose to wish Chamberlain good luck. Eden left the Chamber — uncertain, perhaps, as to whether he should sit silent, or stand and cheer. Only Harold Nicolson kept his seat. Almost no one had moved, at first, on the Liberal and Labour benches. They did not remain seated long. As Duff Cooper recorded:

> The scene was remarkable, all Government supporters rising and cheering, while the Opposition sat glum and silent. And then when Attlee gave the plan his blessing our side all rose again and cheered *him*, cheers in which the Opposition had to join, though looking a little foolish. [63]

An American journalist, Helen Kirkpatrick, wondered whether the element of surprise was genuine.

> Some time later, when Members of the House of Commons were reviewing the situation, they began to wonder why it had not struck them at the time as curious that the Note containing the German Chancellor's invitation had reached Lord Halifax in the Peer's Gallery, had subsequently been passed down to the Government

Benches and had been read by all the Members on the Front Bench. They later said that a note of such urgency would ordinarily have been placed in the Prime Minister's hands before anyone else was allowed to see it. . . . American correspondents . . . discovered that Hitler's invitation to the Conference which had been suggested by Chamberlain had in fact been received in London at the German Embassy at twelve o'clock. They had promptly decoded the message and had sent it instantly to No. 10 Downing Street . . . Chamberlain . . . had thus known, late in the morning, that Hitler's acceptance was virtually assured.[64]

But the interruption was not planned. Quite by the accident of the Commons' hysteria, Chamberlain had successfully avoided being challenged on the subject of the Anglo-French plan. The plan never received Parliamentary approval. Neither the Cabinet nor Parliament were asked to initiate policy. Chamberlain reserved that task for himself and Wilson. Even Halifax's doubts were overruled.

All that remained was to secure Czech acceptance. "It is essential," Halifax telegraphed Newton at 8 P.M., "that Czechoslovak Government should at once indicate their acceptance in principle of our plan and timetable. Please endeavour to obtain this without delay." At 10:40 P.M. Beneš accepted in principle. But he refused to accept those points which did not conform with the Anglo-French proposals. He begged Chamberlain not to put Czechoslovakia in a worse situation than before. The Polish Government had started to threaten the Czechs, and gave "a kind of ultimatum to take effect by next Friday." [65] They too wanted territory if Czechoslovakia was to be partitioned. Newton received the full Czech reply at 3:45 A.M. on the morning of September 29. It was transmitted to the Foreign Office an hour later. At 1:40 P.M. Halifax expressed strong hope that the Czechs "will not render more difficult the Prime Minister's already delicate task by formulating and insisting on objections to the timetable before that has been discussed at Munich." [66]

Newton replied,

You instructed me to express the hope that Czechoslovak Government will not formulate objections to timetable "*before* it is under discussion at Munich." In making my representations to Dr. Krofta, I will omit these words lest he should take them to imply that it would be open to Czechoslovak Government to formulate objections *afterwards*.[67]

Such were the methods of diplomacy.

CHAPTER 10

Munich

ON THURSDAY, September 29, the Prime Minister left for Munich. The entire Cabinet had come to the airport, on Simon's suggestion, as a "pleasant surprise." [1] Chamberlain took with him Lord Dunglass, Wilson, Ashton-Gwatkin and Strang.

On arrival at Munich airfield at noon, Chamberlain and Wilson were "rushed off" to the *Führerhaus*. The conference began at 12:30 P.M. There was no arrangement for taking notes. Chamberlain and Daladier were accompanied at the actual conference only by Wilson and Léger. Hitler and Mussolini had their Foreign Ministers present. They discussed a memorandum ostensibly put forward by Mussolini. In fact it had been drawn up by Weizsäcker, Neurath and Göring, accepted by Hitler, and telephoned to Mussolini, the previous night. [2] Chamberlain made a weak attempt to get permission for the Czechs to be present. Hitler refused. Chamberlain said no more. One of the most remarkable aspects of the conference, the absence of the Czechs, was thus decided upon without argument. Newton was not alone in realizing that the Czechs would object to the terms if anyone let them.

At 3:15 P.M. the conference adjourned for lunch. Chamberlain asked the French delegation to come to the British hotel for a short discussion before the conference reassembled. The French, unwilling or embarrassed, failed to arrive. The British and French lunched and dined at their separate hotels. Hitler entertained Mussolini.

During the dinner interval, Wilson felt he should inform the two Czech representatives of what had occurred. He saw Mastny and Hubert Masarik. But there was no question of inviting them to attend the final meetings of the conference at which the fate of their country would be decided. They remained outside.

The conference continued throughout the evening. Shortly before 2 A.M., in the early hours of September 30, the Munich Agreement was signed. The Germans were given new territory — almost all they had demanded — in the strategic center of Europe. Hitler had gained, by anger and negotiation, what he might never have won by force. Hitler's enemies in Germany were unable to call him a warmonger, and seek to overthrow him; his friends in Britain were delighted to have taken the initiative in doing "justice" to Nazi claims. The proceedings were concluded with brief expressions of satisfaction. Only François-Poncet had a moment of shame. *"Voila comme la France traite les seuls alliés qui lui étaient restés fidèles."* [3]

"What to do about the Czechs?" asked Wilson.[4] Someone said Daladier should take the agreement to Prague. Daladier refused to submit to this indignity. It was 2:15 A.M. Chamberlain and Daladier decided to go together to see the Czech representatives, who had been waiting at the British hotel. Mastny "was given a pretty broad hint that — having regard to the seriousness of the alternative — the best course was for his Government to accept what was clearly a considerable improvement upon the German memorandum." According to Mastny, Chamberlain "yawned continuously, without making any attempt to conceal his yawns, or his weariness." [5]

Ashton-Gwatkin was sent to Prague with Mastny and Masarik to take instructions to Newton, and to add the "necessary background."

Later that morning Strang was woken by a message from Chamberlain.[6] He was asked to draft a statement on the future of Anglo-German relations to which Hitler might agree. Chamberlain altered Strang's draft. Strang objected to the alteration, and said "the Anglo-German Naval Agreement, to which [Chamberlain] introduced a reference, was not a thing to be proud of." Chamberlain replied: "On the contrary, it was the type of agreement which we should now try to reach with Germany." Strang urged Chamberlain to show Daladier the proposed statement. Chamberlain replied "he saw no reason whatever for saying anything to the French."

Chamberlain saw Hitler for the last time.[7] It was not known whether the Czechs would accept the Munich terms. It was quite conceivable that they would refuse. Chamberlain realized this. He also knew that a Czech refusal would invite a German attack. He had no intention of preventing it. He reminded Hitler that it was possible that the Czechs would be "mad enough to refuse the terms." They might even "attempt resistance." If so, he realized that Hitler would have to invade. He hoped there would be no bombardment of Prague "or killing of women and children by attacks from the air." He made no mention of other forms of warfare. Hitler could only assume that if his land forces moved into Prague, Chamberlain would not be so perturbed. He matched Chamberlain's hypocrisy with hypocrisy of his own: "he would always try to spare the civilian population and to confine himself to military objectives. He hated the thought of little babies being killed by gas bombs." Chamberlain seemed content. The two leaders discussed Germany's economic problems. Then they signed a joint declaration which included the phrases Strang had disliked. "We regard the agreement signed last night and the Anglo-German Naval Agreement as symbolic of the desire of our two peoples never to go to war with one another."

Chamberlain had the pledge he had hoped for. In the Commons Harold Nicolson denounced it:

The impression created abroad by that bit of paper was that for the first time in two hundred and fifty years Britain had abandoned her policy of preventing by every means in her power the dominance of Europe by a single Power.

The democrats returned home. Chamberlain was elated for a while; Daladier was depressed. Daladier later told Amery that he turned up his coat collar to protect his face from rotten eggs when he arrived in Paris.[8] His precaution was unnecessary. No one in the crowds that welcomed the leaders home from Munich was angry enough to throw eggs, or abuse. Crowds cheered in Downing Street while Chamberlain stood at an upstairs window of No. 10 waving his "bit of paper." For Kordt the scene was "very impressive." [9] Orme Sargent watched from the Foreign Office. He was disgusted, and said bitterly: "For all the fun and cheers you might think that they were celebrating a major victory over an enemy instead of merely a betrayal of a minor ally." [10]

In Paris Daladier stood on the airport steps acknowledging the cheers. Then, turning to Léger, he whispered, "the bloody fools." [11]

These were the mechanics of Munich. The moral lies elsewhere. On the day of the conference Harold Nicolson wrote to H. A. L. Fisher:

I have a nasty feeling that I shall not approve of the results of the Munich conference. People seem unable to differentiate between physical relief and moral satisfaction. Naturally we were all overjoyed yesterday to have removed from us the actual physical fear which was hanging over us. My moral anxiety remains. The Prime Minister has not really got much understanding of dictatorial mentality, although he seems to have a marked sympathy for it. It was only under very great pressure from the Cabinet that he was induced to mobilize the Fleet and I gather that even now he does not understand that it was this action which frightened Mussolini. He imagines that Mussolini acted out of loyalty and friendship to the brother of his old friend Austen. Nor does he quite see that the other thing that frightened the dictators was our proclaimed union with France and Russia. He flung Russia over yesterday without a word of thanks or apology and I fear that the two dictators will exploit this error on his part and drive a hard bargain at Munich.[12]

For Gilbert Murray Munich was a betrayal: one from which he expected only misfortunes to follow. On October 29, he wrote to Margot Asquith:

Perhaps we have now to recognise that Great Britain is beaten and must submit. As far as I can see it, it seems clear that we are to form close co-operation with Hitler and Mussolini, make Franco master of Spain, put in a puppet government in France, either Fascist or pro-Fascist . . . worst of all we are to purge the League of Nations of all officials who are not agreeable to Germany . . . I believe that [the small nations of Europe] would still stand together to prevent German aggression if England and France would give them the lead: but of course they won't. People talk about help from the USA, but they will give us the same help as we gave to Czechoslovakia.

On September 30, fifty letters arrived at Printing House Square demanding a National Fund in Chamberlain's honor.[13] *Paris-Soir* offered him "a corner of French soil" where he might fish. The editor thought "there could be no more fruitful image of peace."[14]

On October 5, Beneš was no longer President of Czechoslovakia. Together with the external frontiers, internal democracy had disappeared. At 7 P.M. he addressed the nation which he had helped to found:

I remain what I have always been, a convinced democrat, and therefore I am leaving the field. I feel it is for the best not to disturb the new European constellation which is arising. We did our utmost to reach understanding with other nationalities, and we went to the extreme limit of possible concessions. Do not expect from me a single word of recrimination. But this I will say, that the sacrifices demanded from us were immeasurably great and immeasurably unjust. This the nation will never forget, even though they have borne these sacrifices quietly.[15]

There was a suggestion that Beneš should be succeeded as President by Jaroslav Preis, head of the Czech Zivnostvenska Bank. "An objective Czech," one English diplomat called him. He was to be appointed, according to suppressed newspaper reports, "in view of the necessity of selecting a man who enjoys the confidence of Germany."[16] On the day Beneš resigned, Preis had been in Berlin talking to Göring. Not for nothing had his bank, in July, bought up the Brüx-Dux coalfields. They were the largest in Czechoslovakia. Now they were in Germany. With the capital acquired from the former owners, Jews, Preis indeed proved "an objective Czech." He was not alone in his objectivity. The Sudeten areas were overrun by Germany. More humiliating, Czechoslovakia was overrun by her own people, and controlled by the anti-democrats.

Many Englishmen and Frenchmen had done their "duty." They had drafted the dispatches, prepared the briefs, carried the messages and given instructions. Civil servants cannot protest. It is not *their* policy they carry out. Orders come from above.

To whom, then, do the laurels go?

Not to the thousand British legionaries who marched onto their ship at Tilbury, and then marched off. They were not needed during that plebiscite which never took place. Not to the Lord Mayor of London who set up a fund for refugees. His action was generous enough. But the refugees needed visas, not money. They faced concentration camps and death.

Not to Cadogan or Kirkpatrick. Not to Butler. Not to Dunglass. They did their duty as they saw it. Hardly a murmur arose from that contented band. In later life they graced the top ranks of the professions they served. Two were heads of the Foreign Office. Butler became Home Secretary. Dunglass, when Lord Home, Foreign Minister. An impressive list.

The laurels go elsewhere.

Duff Cooper resigned from the Cabinet. "Munich" sickened and angered him. Chamberlain, he wrote, "was as glad to be rid of me as I was determined to go." [17] The Aga Khan, a well-known appeaser, argued with Duff Cooper until the early hours of the morning. "Why did you do it, dear boy, why did you do it?" [18] Others saw more clearly that Duff Cooper's resignation was not only understandable: it was a moral triumph. A. J. P. Taylor wrote to Duff Cooper on October 1: "May I express my appreciation that in this hour of national humiliation there has still been found one Englishman not faithless to honour and principle and to the tradition of our once great name? If England is in future to have a history, your name will be mentioned with respect and admiration." Josiah Wedgwood wrote to him: "Love and admiration more than you have dreamt of will I hope compensate for loss of office and salary. Anyhow this old colleague from better days is proud of you. Also I think it is a good spot on a bad page of English history. I do dislike belonging to a race of clucking old hens and damned cowards." [19] In the course of his resignation speech Duff Cooper said:

> The Prime Minister has believed in addressing Herr Hitler through the language of sweet reasonableness. I have believed that he was more open to the language of the mailed fist. . . .

> We have taken away the defences of Czechoslovakia in the same breath as we have guaranteed them, as though you were to deal a man a mortal blow and at the same time insure his life. . . .

> I remember when we were discussing the Godesberg ultimatum that I said that if I were a party to persuading, or even to suggesting to the Czechoslovak Government that they should accept that ultimatum, I should never be able to hold up my head again. I have forfeited a great deal. I have given up an office that I loved, work in which I was deeply interested, and a staff of which any man might be proud. I have given up associations in that work with my colleagues with whom I have maintained for many years the most harmonious relations, not only as colleagues but as friends. I have given up the privilege of serving as lieutenant to a leader whom I still regard with the deepest admiration and affection. I have ruined, perhaps, my political career. But that is a little matter; I have retained something which is to me of great value. I can still walk about the world with my head erect.

Antony Winn reported Duff Cooper's resignation speech for *The Times*. He said it had been well-received. Dawson suppressed his article and inserted "a concoction of his own" in which Duff Cooper's speech was described as "a damp squib." The article was headed "From our lobby correspondent," though Winn had never seen it. Winn resigned. As he put it, *The Times* was a paper "which was the first responsible advocate of secession and still has hopes of a genuine friendship with the Nazi régime." Dawson disagreed, maintaining that *The Times* "far from envisaging genuine friendship with the Nazi régime . . . aimed at genuine friendship with the German people." [20]

In the Foreign Office, Orme Sargent, William Strang and Reginald Leeper had tried their utmost to stiffen British resolve. They had wanted an honorable solution, but in vain. Their protests were ignored; their attempts to strengthen notes and dispatches were unsuccessful.

Con O'Neill, who had been less than a year in the Berlin Embassy, resigned from the Foreign Office. It was a brave man who sacrificed undoubted prospects for the wilderness of principles. He was later criticized by Wilson for being a civil servant who "expressed opinions as to policy." [21] Kirkpatrick, his senior in Berlin, was equally critical. He saw O'Neill's action as that of an angry Irishman, rather than of a diplomat trained to accept the vagaries of policy.

Paul Reynaud and Georges Mandel resigned from the French Cabinet. Churchill had dissuaded them from doing so when the British and French were forcing the Czechs to accept their plan. After Munich they could not bear to remain. Another Frenchman, General Fauchet, had been training Czech troops. He was so ashamed of Munich that he resigned, not only his post, but his French nationality. He asked to be enrolled as a Czech citizen.[22]

Wenzel Jaksch flew to London. He begged for visas for the Sudeten Social Democrats. Few visas were forthcoming. He

visited Lord Runciman, and reminded him of how he had come
to Prague as "the friend of all and the enemy of none." He had
befriended the Henleinists. How was he going to help the German democrats? Jaksch asked for visas. Runciman replied: "I
believe that the Lord Mayor is opening a fund for you all, and
if so, you will certainly find my name on the list of contribu-
tors." [23]

The necessary visas were never granted. Many of Jaksch's
associates perished in German concentration camps. Though
they fled to Prague, they were sent back to Germany. The agreement that bound them over was signed two weeks after Munich,
but was made retrospective to the day of Munich.[24] To such
cruelties the British meekly and unwisely agreed. The German
author of the plan was Dr. Hans Globke; he too has received the
reward of competence and service.*

> But once again
>   The crisis is put off and things look better
> And we feel negotiation is not in vain—
>   Save my skin and damn my conscience.
> And negotiation wins,
>   If you can call it winning,
> And here we are—just as before—safe in our skins;
>   Glory to God for Munich.
> And stocks go up and wrecks
>   Are salved and politicians' reputations
> Go up like Jack-on-the-Beanstalk; only the Czechs
>   Go down and without fighting.
> —LOUIS MacNEICE
> Autumn Journal: 1938

* Globke wrote the "commentary" for the racist Nuremberg Laws in 1935 which
made Jews second class citizens. He drew up many Nazi laws and decrees.
After the war he became the trusted adviser of the West German Chancellor,
Konrad Adenauer. In 1962 he was a Secretary of State in the Federal Republic.

PART THREE

It was not a disturbance of the understanding: the events themselves were not surprising. Nor, as became increasingly evident, was our distress due merely to disagreement with the policy and behaviour of the moment. The feeling which was new and unexpected was a feeling of humiliation, which demanded an act of personal contrition, of humility, repentance and amendment; what was happening was something in which one was deeply implicated and responsible . . .

Was our society, which had always been so assured of its humility and rectitude, so confident of its unexamined premises, assembled round any thing more permanent than a congeries of banks, insurance companies and industries, and had it any beliefs more essential than a belief in compound interest and the maintenance of dividends?

T. S. Eliot
The Idea of a Christian Society

CHAPTER 11

Economic Appeasement

To THOSE for whom political appeasement was the redress of
legitimate grievances, economic appeasement appeared even
more justifiable. British help to Germany in the economic
sphere would solve not only Germany's economic problems, but
also those of the rest of the world, dragged down by Germany's
inability to pay her way. It would lead, said Chamberlain, "to
a relaxation of the economic pressure under which many countries are suffering today." [1] Germany's economic difficulties under the Weimar Republic have been well documented — reparations and inflation. After 1933, the problems were as acute.
Because Hitler inaugurated a great public works program and
solved the unemployment problem attention was diverted from
the very real crises which Germany had to face, notably in the
field of foreign exchange.

In May, 1933, Germany's foreign creditors were told that all
external debt payments were suspended. They were asked to go
to Berlin to negotiate with the Reichsbank. On May 29, the
representatives of the short-term banking creditors arrived in
Berlin. Their chief object was to secure preferential treatment
from Schacht to the detriment of the long-term creditors. In
this they were successful. R. H. Brand and F. C. Tiarks, the
British banking delegates, had lunch with Schacht and found
his attitude "wholly satisfactory from the point of view of the
short-term creditors." [2] Schacht treated them with courtesy and
addressed them as "colleagues." By playing off Germany's various creditors against each other, Schacht succeeded in satisfying
none of them. They were not wise enough to unite against him.

Germany did more trade with Great Britain and the British

Empire than with any single other group. Germany's surplus was completely absorbed by her financial obligations under, among others, the Dawes and Young loans. There was also a heavy deficit in trade with the British Empire (161 million RM). Paul Einzig, a contemporary commentator who disliked Germany's eastward economic expansion, pointed out that Germany's large export surplus on her British trade provided the much needed sterling with which to finance imports for the purpose of rearmament. "Part of the sterling proceeds of German exports might easily have been seized for the benefit of British creditors." [3]

British bankers neither claimed their debts nor liquidated them, as did other bankers. In September, 1939, the City was caught with some £36 million in German commitments.[4]

In 1936, I. G. Farben, manufacturers, among many other things, of poison gas, had received new credits from at least two London banking houses.[5] When questioned about this in the Commons, W. S. Morrison said that the Treasury had nothing against the credits. After persistent parliamentary and press criticism, the Bank of England sent out a circular in spring, 1937, to all banks, at the Treasury's request, asking them not to grant new credits to Germany.

In July, 1936, one of the London private banking houses had produced a memorandum on Anglo-German relations which reached the German Foreign Ministry.[6] What was to be the attitude of the other big European Powers towards Germany? One alternative was to fight Germany: "the other alternative is to try to come to an understanding and to co-operate with those Germans who wish to have and are capable to work for such an understanding."

The Germans referred to were called "Nazi Moderates."

Most of these Germans will agree that free trade, general disarmament, an all round political understanding are the ideals. Not one believes that these aims can be reached at once by general conference or by the drafting of new covenants.

The method they believe in is different. This method might be right or wrong. But it must be realized that, for the time being, this is the only method upon which any foreign individual, group or nation who has any dealings with Germany can hope to further any schemes in co-operation with Germans.

This method is to build up slowly and progressively; to start with nothing but piecemeal work; to find out in which points the avowed selfish requirements of the two partners are better served by co-operation than by competition; not to start with an attempt for everlasting agreements, as the rigidity of such an agreement might produce new frictions; not to believe nor to allow their partners to believe that co-operation allows either partner to relax in his efforts to maintain his strength and efficiency; to start with bilateral agreements and if they work well to try and extend them to the third parties. . . . They think that if a certain amount of co-operation can be reached in the economic sphere, then a subsequent political understanding is bound to be easy.

This was to be the method by which Germany and England could eventually become united to each other. Formulated in 1936, it was not until the year before the war that it began to be put seriously into effect.

After Munich the policy of appeasement reached its apogee. Every day in October *The Times* offered its readers photographs on fine art paper of Mr. and Mrs. Chamberlain standing beside the King and Queen at Buckingham Palace. Every day there were photographs of the triumphant German troops marching into the Sudetenland, yesterday into Eger, today into Mahrisch-Ostrau: names that made headlines in September, but in October were forgotten or uneasily remembered. In the photographs the joyful welcome accorded to the German soldiers bore witness to the apparent justice of the Munich settlement. Photographs of refugees *had* reached *The Times*. Dawson refused to print them. An account of fête and fiesta only revealed a partial truth. The rise in the suicide rate could be depicted on a graph. The ill-treatment of those who did not sympathize with the "Nazi philosophy" could not be caught by the camera.

The feeling of relief at the prospect of peace did not last. Dirksen reported on October 7, 1938, that Halifax hoped "a further extension of the basis for Anglo-German relations found in the Munich conference between the Führer and Chamberlain would shortly be made possible." [7] But there were assertions in the press, he added, about the ill-treatment of Sudetens; "he would be grateful if by means of relevant German reports he might be able to combat such assertions, the spreading of which might in fact hamper the advocates of friendly Anglo-German relations in the realisation of their aspirations."

Prompted by this appeal, Hitler replied to it very briefly in a speech he made two days later at Saarbrücken: "We cannot tolerate any longer the tutelage of governesses! Inquiries of British politicians concerning the fate of Germans within the frontiers of the Reich — or of others belonging to the Reich — are not in place."

Such language was anathema to the Foreign Office. That they were basically anti-German was well known. Chamberlain intended to take precautions to ensure that they did not obstruct his plans. On October 11, Fritz Hesse wrote a memorandum in which he stated he had seen Steward, Chamberlain's press secretary, "a few days ago." Steward had told him that

in all future moves it was important that all major questions should be dealt with direct, thus by-passing the Foreign Office and also Sir Nevile Henderson, since it had unfortunately become apparent that the latter was not completely reliable when forwarding communications. Furthermore, the Foreign Office would always be brought in by Henderson, and thus there was the risk of causing all kinds of obstruction and undesirable publicity.[8]

That Chamberlain was still thinking in terms of colonial appeasement is clear from Steward's remark that he

further recommended that restraint should be exercised in the colonial question, and above all that German colonial demands should not be put forward publicly, because this would make it impossible for the Prime Minister to win over the Dominions for the German demands. Any raising of the colonial question publicly would let loose propaganda by all our opponents in the Dominions and thus commit the Dominions before the Government in Great Britain found any opportunity to discuss the matters objectively.

But the Germans were unwilling to be objective. Weizsäcker refused to forward Hesse's memorandum to Ribbentrop, and wrote, "I wonder whether the arguments of Dr. Hesse do not tend too strongly in a direction which, as things are now, is not the same as that taken here." [9] He told Dirksen that policy in Berlin was "moving rapidly but not in the direction of a German-British *rapprochement* at present." [10]

At such an unfavorable moment the appeasers tried a new approach. One of the arguments for returning the colonies to Germany was that her economic position would be strengthened. As Germany was uninterested in colonies, there were other ways of helping her economy. Successful economic appeasement would save both Britain and Germany the need for massive rearmament. "I suspect," wrote Jones on October 30, "that both Chamberlain and Simon are against thorough-going rearmament because of its effect on foreign trade." [11]

Once a full-scale rearmament program was in motion the British economy would lose that flexibility necessary if it were to be able to co-operate with the Germans.

October brought speeches by Chamberlain, Hoare and Simon, with direct or indirect requests that Germany should make her demands known so that negotiations might start. In private conversations, wrote Dirksen, "a delimitation of economic spheres of interest was mentioned as a point of the programme." [12]

On October 18, a German delegation, led by Rüter, on their way to Dublin, was at the Board of Trade. It had confidential and unofficial talks to explore the possibility of increasing German exports to the British colonies. Considering, as Rüter wrote, "that the Board of Trade was particularly insistent that nothing about these talks should become known to the press or the public," the suggestions made by Sir Frederick Leith-Ross must have seemed a trifle premature.[13] Sir Frederick, who was the Government's chief economic adviser, told the Germans that "the British Government would very much like to know the attitude of the German Government toward the question of co-operation in the economic field between the Four Powers, Germany, Great Britain, France and Italy."[14] He suggested that representatives of the Four Powers "should meet in the very near future for a completely unfettered discussion."

Germany needed further foreign exchange. Leith-Ross asked Rüter "whether it might not be possible for Great Britain, France and Holland to allocate to Germany a larger total of foreign currency." He mentioned a figure of twenty-five per cent more. Leith-Ross believed that "the foreign currency thus made available could then be used by Germany to pay for her imports from the Balkan countries. These countries would then in turn be in a position to buy colonial produce, and world trade would thus receive a stimulus."

Rüter was clearly interested in the proposals. He informed Berlin of their importance.

If these suggestions are taken in conjunction with Chamberlain's plans aimed at the same objective, which are mentioned in the press, their genuineness and importance ought not to be underrated in Berlin either. I think I am right also in saying that the Ministry of Economics has waited eagerly for such a suggestion, and I am therefore very impatient to know how it will be received.[15]

Berlin was less enthusiastic. In a memorandum of October 24, Clodius pointed out that, while the attitude of Sir Frederick Leith-Ross toward closer economic co-operation between the four great Powers in Europe might be regarded as a friendly gesture on the part of England, his statements were too indefinite to be acted upon by the Foreign Ministry.[16] The Economic Minister, Funk, was opposed in principle to breaking off the discussions. But he could see no possibility of comprehensive four-power economic discussions until political problems had been settled.[17] On November 3, it was announced that no decision had yet been taken about the attitude Germany would adopt towards Leith-Ross's proposals.[18]

Although the Germans had shown no desire to deal with these economic problems, Samuel Hoare still thought a solution lay within the realms of practical politics. At the end of October, Dirksen spent the weekend with Hoare at Petworth.[19] Hoare told him that for Chamberlain "the objective of an Anglo-German *rapprochement* was simultaneously dictated by the head and the heart." Hoare added that, "after a further *rapprochement* between the four European Great Powers, the acceptance of certain defence obligations, or even a guarantee by them against Soviet Russia, was conceivable in the event of an attack by Soviet Russia."

Following up Leith-Ross's initiative, Ashton-Gwatkin suggested on November 6, "that Germany should not procure her imports from the British and French colonies by barter arrangements . . . but should once again pay for them in foreign currency. If so, both British and French Governments were prepared to grant Germany a twenty-five per cent higher allocation of free foreign currency." [20] In order to meet the German objection that they could not accept the allocation unless payment of interest would be guaranteed to her by means of exports, Ashton-Gwatkin added that "this could be arranged by British pressure on the United States." He suggested that he might himself come to Berlin to discuss mutual problems.

Two days later, Ashton-Gwatkin met Prince Hohenlohe and informed him that he intended to come to Berlin. He asked if "there might be a possibility of a conversation with Field-Marshal Göring on the Four-Year Plan." [21] Dirksen believed Ashton-Gwatkin's journey would take place with the knowledge of Halifax, and possibly of Chamberlain. Gladwyn Jebb, Cadogan's Private Secretary, told a member of the German Embassy that Ashton-Gwatkin would have interesting news to give the Germans. Hohenlohe advised Ashton-Gwatkin to "have a talk" with Göring, as Göring was "impressed by the difficulties of autarchy and feeling his way towards a freer policy." [22] Woermann minuted: for this task Ashton-Gwatkin was "too small." [23]

Economic appeasement was not a policy for economic experts alone. On November 1, Halifax wrote to Phipps, "Henceforward we must count German predominance in Central Europe. Incidentally I have always felt myself that, once Germany recovered her normal strength, this predominance was inevitable for obvious geographical and economic reasons." [24]

This was a view well-canvassed by Dawson, Hoare and Londonderry. German predominance might well be "inevitable." But events in Germany after November 7 ensured that the British were no longer so eager to hasten Germany upon the road they had chosen for her.

On that day Herschell Grynszpan, a young Polish Jew, was admitted to the German Embassy in Paris. He fired a revolver at the first member of the staff whom he chanced to meet, a secretary named Herr von Rath. On arrest, Grynszpan justified his deed as an act of revenge for the cruel treatment meted out by Germany to his own parents and to the Jews in general. On November 8, von Rath died of his wounds. His death was the excuse and opportunity for an unprecedented outbreak of anti-semitism in Germany.

Leith-Ross toned down his enthusiasm. On November 10, he told Rüter that "official conferences on economic pacification could not stand on their own but must be included in the larger framework of a general political pacification." [25]

British reserve was not wholly due to the anti-Jewish outbreaks in Germany. It was occasioned chiefly through lack of any kind of reciprocity on the part of the Germans. After conversations with Hoare, Astor, Runciman and others, Hohenlohe reported that British opinion was "regretting" the German failure to respond.[26] Those who sought economic appeasement were also restrained by public opinion. Rüter alleged on November 20, that economic negotiations were being kept secret as a result of a British request.[27] Public opinion might not tolerate them.

But Dirksen was enthusiastic about economic co-operation. In the middle of December he began to stress in his talks with influential Englishmen the idea that "the way to relieve the tension must be sought in the economic field." Runciman, who had now been specially commissioned by Chamberlain "to occupy himself with German affairs," was kept informed of such ideas. He and Dirksen spent a weekend together at Brocket Hall.[28]

After Munich it was generally and publicly conceded that Germany should be allowed an economic free hand in South-East Europe. It was believed that as a result of the Ottawa Agreement Germany was compelled to seek control over South-East Europe since she was excluded from the British Empire. There were only elements of truth in this belief. Germany enjoyed good trade relations with, among others, South Africa and Australia. But a book produced by Chatham House stressed the need for and advantages of German trade in the Balkans.

Oliver Stanley launched a counter-offensive against German economic penetration in the Balkans, supported by Paul Einzig in the *Financial News*. Before Munich they seemed to have secured the support of Chamberlain, but not of Simon, for their policy. A policy of British assistance to South-East Europe was considered by the Treasury. An attempt was made to secure a credit and trade agreement with Turkey. It was delayed, however, as the Turkish delegates found Leith-Ross "very difficult to deal with." [29]

At the end of November, 1938, R. S. Hudson, Parliamentary Secretary of the Department of Overseas Trade, made a speech in the Commons condemning German trading methods. "Unless Germany was prepared to modify her trading methods and refrain from unfair competition Great Britain would beat her at her own game." Stanley supported Hudson's statement. Dirksen complained at once to Horace Wilson. Before long, both Hudson and Stanley were toeing the orthodox line of economic appeasement. Before they did so, they had succeeded for a while in overcoming Simon's opposition to their positive policy. A bill was introduced providing for export credit facilities and for a special fighting fund of £10 million which the Board of Trade was authorized to use in the national interest independently of commercial considerations.[30] There was now some chance of Eastern Europe being attended to. A gesture had been made, however small. But Hudson, in his enthusiasm for firmer measures, had overstepped the mark. He wished to halt Germany's eastward economic expansion. He also sought to hasten the rearmament program at home. Misguidedly he chose as his target the one man in the Cabinet who was pressing ahead unreservedly with reform and reorganization — the War Minister, Hore-Belisha. Gathering two dissident Junior Ministers to his side, Dufferin and Strathcona, Hudson told Chamberlain at the beginning of December that Hore-Belisha was "incompetent" and that because of him "the plans for rearmament were ineffective." [31] Unless Hore-Belisha, Inskip, and Winterton resigned, Hudson and his friends felt they could no longer serve under Chamberlain.

The revolt was mistimed and misplaced, and prematurely publicized by Randolph Churchill in the *Evening Standard*. Hudson's support melted away. Chamberlain saw Hore-Belisha on December 12, and told him that "he had not seen Hudson again, and he was now the only one left in the revolt. Hudson . . . was reported to be going round the lobby saying that either Hore-Belisha must go or he would. The PM said, 'So we shall now see who will go.' " [32]

Nobody went except Strathcona. But words whispered in Hudson's ear by Chamberlain were carefully noted. Never again did he try to thwart the policy of the appeasers. Rarely was a conversion so quickly accomplished.

CHAPTER 12

Search for Agreement

IN mid-December Schacht came to London as the guest of Montague Norman, Governor of the Bank of England. He had conversations with Stanley, Leith-Ross, and leading City financiers on questions "of general significance interesting to both parties, in particular the possibility of extending international trade, the restoration of the freedom of foreign exchange, and the conditions necessary to bring these about." [1] Schacht had a lengthy conversation with Chamberlain who showed "interest in economic questions and showed that he was well-informed." He had been Chancellor of the Exchequer and knew about economics.

Schacht thought Stanley would be prepared, "if need be," to come to Berlin for an exchange of views. Dirksen wrote to Wiehl that Schacht's visit had been a great success. In a memorandum of January 11, 1939, Wiehl recommended that Stanley's proposed visit to Berlin should be encouraged.

In an interview with Halifax on December 14, Dirksen thought "various points of contact existed in the economic field which might lead to agreements, directly fruitful and positive for economic life and thus indirectly for political relations as well." Later he told Weizsäcker that Ashton-Gwatkin was to be "only a forerunner and herald for Lord Runciman, whom the Government would like to send to Germany in order to put the final touch to the economic agreements which Ashton-Gwatkin is to initiate." [2]

Dirksen was concerned about a report he had received from Germany that the Italian Government had offered its services "as mediator to improve Anglo-German relations." Dirksen felt such mediation would be unnecessary: "When it suits our purpose to achieve a *détente* with Great Britain, we shall not need an Italian advocate to help us."

Despite the pogroms, and despite the rudeness of Hitler's speeches, Dirksen believed that Germany had only to speak, and the British and Germans would live in lasting friendship. The evidence was not lacking. Colonial appeasement had made an unpleasant stir in Britain. The attempt to ingratiate them-selves with Germany at the expense of the Czechs had lost the appeasers many supporters. But in the economic field agreement could be sought without undue publicity. To some it seemed unimportant or irrelevant: the meaningless mechanics of a capitalist system. To the appeasers it was the vital catalyst that would shape the future. As Dirksen saw, Chamberlain remained "committed to the idea of European settlement with all the obstinacy which is characteristic of his family." [3]

A program for Anglo-German co-operation was being discussed. When Rüter called on Leith-Ross on November 10, the Board of Trade proposed that to assist expansion of Anglo-German trade German and British industry should start negotiations with the object of reaching a comprehensive agreement on prices and markets. On December 21 and 22, preparatory discussions were held between the British and German Federations of Industry. [4] Koppen and Hipp appeared on behalf of the Reich Federation of Industry. Hipp thought the British Federation were "afraid of being led into a position of economic and therefore political dependence on the United States of America. We confirmed the Federation in this opinion," continued Hipp, "pointing out that Great Britain was part of Europe and that the goal which must be aimed at was the creation of a strong economic unit comprising Germany, Great Britain, France and Italy." It was proposed that the first meeting between the industrialists should take place in Germany in February.

Both Hipp and Koppen were invited to London for the annual dinner of the Chamber of Commerce on January 23. Hipp returned to Berlin on January 27. He told Rüter that he thought the Federation of British Industries "less enthusiastic than before about the continuation of the conversations and the start of official negotiations." [5] But Hudson had said in a speech at the dinner that "it would be a great achievement if in the near future some ten agreements could be concluded between the German and British industries taking part." The chief meeting was scheduled for March 15, in Düsseldorf. The German delegation was to be led by Herr von Poensgen of I. G. Farben; the British by Sir William Larke, Director of the British Iron and Steel Federation.[6] Government pressure had overcome the reticence of industry.

Since Chamberlain had openly expressed his desire to use channels other than the Foreign Office for making contact with those similarly inclined in Germany, it is not surprising to find unofficial meetings scantily documented. One such unofficial visit was that of Henry Drummond-Wolff and his wife to Berlin at the beginning of January, 1939. On January 5, Selzam told Wiehl that Drummond-Wolff was a former MP who had given up politics for politico-economic studies. His wife was an American who, Selzam thought, might be known to Wiehl from his time in Washington. Selzam had interviewed Drummond-Wolff before his departure: "The journey is of a completely private nature, although he was authorized to tell me that one of the Prime Minister's 'principal advisers' had approved it. He insisted that I should mention no names, although I know that the man in question is one of the Prime Minister's closest colleagues." [7] It was not difficult to recognize Horace Wilson from this description.

In his annual report for 1938, Dirksen wrote:

Under the pressure of natural developments, the question whether a continuation of the policy of co-operation inaugurated at Munich or individual action of the Four Powers should decide the destiny of Europe receded at first into the background. Even Chamberlain, the strongest supporter of European "Quadruple Directorate" policy, has been forced to realize this during the last three months.[8]

But if there was little chance of four-power co-operation, there were many fields which the British and Germans alone could plow. Once it was agreed that Germany had a predominant interest in the East, the British saw that they themselves could depend on the self-sufficiency of the Empire. As one British newspaper put it, "Let us forget the bulging granaries of the Ukraine and think rather of those in Canada."

Dirksen saw Ribbentrop in Berlin. "Ribbentrop betrayed a lively interest in more actively promoting Anglo-German relations in the economic sphere."[9] Dirksen continued:

I was confirmed in this impression by the fact that shortly after my return to London our Press Counsellor, Dr. Hesse, was summoned to Berlin by [Ribbentrop] and confidentially instructed to establish contact with the British Government through Chamberlain's press agent, Steward, with whom Hesse was well acquainted, with a view to a general *rapprochement*. The conclusion of a treaty of non-aggression was also to be suggested, for the signing of which [Ribbentrop] had expressed his readiness to come to London. When Hesse made these overtures, Steward declared that the matter was so important that it must be submitted to responsible political quarters. After this Dr. Hesse was invited for a talk with Sir Horace Wilson, who played the part of the listener.

Hesse told Wilson about his conversations with Ribbentrop. Wilson thought Ribbentrop had "talked sensibly" and said he would "discuss the matter in the Cabinet."[10]

At the dinner of the German Chamber of Commerce, both Hudson and Leith-Ross said that a visit to London by Funk "would certainly be well-timed for extending the informal economic conversations started in October."[11] On January 28, the Anglo-German Coal Agreement was signed, the first of many, it was hoped. Leith-Ross told Dirksen that the British Government had asked the Mines Department of the Board of Trade

> to give a dinner to celebrate the successful conclusion of the Anglo-German coal negotiations to which Funk . . . is to be invited as guest of honour from Germany, and Oliver Stanley, President of the Board of Trade, to represent Great Britain. As the President of the Board of Trade wishes to visit Germany, the British Government would be glad if Germany could reciprocate the British invitation by inviting Mr. Oliver Stanley to a dinner in Berlin.[12]

Leith-Ross also told Dirksen that "in the view of Government circles here, the Führer's speech had laid the foundation for the contemplated exchange of visits between the two Ministers of Economics and for a further active development of economic questions between Germany and Great Britain." [13] On January 30, Hitler had spoken in the Reichstag:

> In what way . . . do the interests of Great Britain and Germany clash? I have stated often enough that there is no German and above all no National Socialist, who even in his most secret thoughts has the intention of causing the British Empire any kind of difficulties. From Great Britain too are heard the voices of men who think reasonably and calmly, expressing a similar attitude with regard to Germany. It would be a blessing for the whole world if mutual confidence and co-operation could be established between the two peoples.

Dirksen wanted Funk to visit Britain. Wiehl replied that Funk had "so many engagements as a result of assuming office as President of the Reichsbank that he is quite unable to find time for a visit to London in the near future." [14] But the Germans did not object to Stanley coming to Berlin. They suggested "the middle of March" for his visit.[15]

On February 15, Henderson saw Ribbentrop. "We agreed," wrote Henderson, "that neither of us knew very clearly what line any economic discussions would take but that the first aim was

to discover where co-operation could most usefully be sought." [16]
But it hardly needed top-level meetings between economists to
arrive at Henderson's next conclusion, which he put forward in
a letter to Chamberlain on February 19. "If all went well we
should have so improved the atmosphere that we might begin to
think of colonial discussions." [17]

Halifax replied "I do not myself feel there is any hope of
making sense of colonial discussions." [18] Three days later Henderson changed his mind: "I agree with you entirely in wishing
to keep the colonial question at a long arm's length at present." [19] That day he wrote to Chamberlain again to keep him
abreast of the new development. "I should keep away from the
colonial question. I think Hitler . . . fully realizes that that
question must wait a long time yet and that economics and
disarmament must come first and create that greater confidence
which can alone give Hitler the hope of a satisfactory colonial
solution." [20]

Despite Halifax's coolness Dirksen was later told by Wohltat
that at the end of February, "the British Cabinet had decided
to restore Germany's colonies." [21]

Appeasement was sincere and underhand; it was also muddled
and uncertain. The muddle came from a sense of guilt; the
uncertainty from the need to work in the dark. A policy which
could not be discussed openly and critically could not be coherent.

Ashton-Gwatkin visited Berlin between February 19 and 26.[22]
His talks were only exploratory. He brought "no new proposals" [23] and Ribbentrop had given instructions that any further
talks with Ashton-Gwatkin were to be confined to economic
questions only and were "not to lead up to questions of foreign
policy." [24] But Ashton-Gwatkin suggested that Ribbentrop
"should invite Sir Horace Wilson to Germany." [25] According to
Hohenlohe this suggestion was a "special point in his programme." [26]

Ashton-Gwatkin saw Ribbentrop, Göring, Funk, Wiehl, and

Wohltat. It was not surprising that he failed to get a coherent picture of German economic plans. He wrote that Göring had wanted Anglo-German economic co-operation to begin "at once" and that this would lead on "to political agreements." But Wohltat emphasized that "political confidence must precede economic co-operation." He thought that "some kind of pact between the United Kingdom and Germany (and others perhaps) guaranteeing peace in Europe would be a necessary prelude to economic co-operation on any wider scale."

G. H. S. Pinsent, the Financial Attaché in Berlin, commented on Ashton-Gwatkin's conversations. He noted that although both Funk and Göring had spoken of their desire to remove the German exchange control, they "would not, in fact, be prepared to do any of the things which we hope to secure by a removal or relaxation of [it]. In actual fact, whatever Funk and Göring may say, I believe that exchange control is such a fundamental condition of the whole German economic régime that there is no prospect of its removal until that régime entirely changes its colour." Pinsent's concluding remarks were not promising:

> Altogether these conversations hold out, in my opinion, little hope of progress in economic co-operation. The things which we want — particularly arms limitation and, to some extent, freeing of the exchange — are not in reality practical politics. But the German mouth is wide open for concessions on debts, trade etc., which would in reality merely serve to strengthen their rearmament position. There may perhaps somewhere be scope for an understanding; but we have listened *ad nauseam* to what the Germans want, and it is perhaps time that we told them again in plain terms what *we* want.

Rüter had seen representatives of the Board of Trade and the Colonial Ministry. They told him that broad economic negotiations should be delayed until the results of the meeting of the industrial associations at Düsseldorf, scheduled for March

15.[27] Dirksen saw that "the English side attached greater importance to this meeting than was warranted by its rather moderate agenda; the opportunity was to be used to establish personal contacts, with a view to a general understanding between the industries of the two countries." [28]

Henderson had been away from Berlin recovering from an operation. He met Hitler at a diplomatic reception on March 1, and told him that Chamberlain and Halifax "were still thinking on the lines of Munich." [29] He asked Hitler whether he wished to hear his "general views on the situation in England." Hitler "did not give the impression that he welcomed the idea."

Henderson was now plunged into the arrangements for the visit of Stanley and Hudson, and the coming trade negotiations at Düsseldorf. Later he wrote,

> Behind the façade of privacy, the real intention of the visit was patent, and though the primary object was a modest one, it was legitimate to hope that it might lead to more general and concrete trade discussions. From economics to politics was no great step.[30]

There were two possibilities as Henderson saw it,

> (a) Whether on the economic side His Majesty's Government should refuse to go further in the direction of co-operation with Germany, so long as she pursues her present course of senseless rearmament, on the ground that any assistance would simply be employed for strengthening still further her military position; or
> (b) Whether economic co-operation should be pursued in the hope that the political atmosphere may be improved thereby and Germany may be finally induced to refrain from any political adventures which she might contemplate, and even desist up to a certain point from the present armaments race.[31]

Henderson did not doubt which was the correct choice.

> I was always disinclined to accept the over-simplified theory that Hitler would necessarily be obliged to seek further adventure in

order to avoid economic collapse. Moreover, a prosperous and peaceful Germany was a British interest and . . . the outside world, and Britain in particular, was prepared to help her overcome her financial and economic difficulties.[32]

Colonel Mason-Macfarlane was not so sure. He wrote that,

> There are naturally weighty, financial, political and (although hardly applicable to dealings with Nazi Germany) ethical arguments in favour of lending Germany a hand in her trade difficulties. From a military point of view . . . there are practically none.[33]

On March 15, Hitler occupied Prague. The Cabinet was unprepared for this. On March 10, Chamberlain had told a group of journalists that the prospects of war were diminishing. A new era of concord was being ushered in. His hopes were rudely shattered.

On March 15, the day of the occupation of Prague, Halifax informed Dirksen that it was now impossible to go forward "for the time being" with Stanley's visit to Berlin, or to achieve a settlement of general economic questions. "In Anglo-German relations the clocks had been put back considerably." [34] There was no connection, replied Dirksen, between events in Czechoslovakia and Anglo-German economic relations.

At Birmingham on March 17, Chamberlain warned Hitler that if his latest step was one in the direction of an attempt to dominate the world by force, Britain would take part "in resisting the challenge to the utmost of her power." The unspoken assumption remained that if it could be proved that the invasion of Prague was not a step towards world domination, Britain would act as a spectator.

Although the visit of Stanley and Hudson had been postponed, the meeting of the German and British industrialists went ahead as planned at Düsseldorf. They met on March 15, and signed a preliminary agreement. One clause of this stated that one of the objects of the agreement was to enable Germany to increase her foreign exchange resources. Great indignation was aroused in England when this news was known. It meant that as German troops were marching across Bohemia, Britain was planning to help the German armament program by giving them additional foreign exchange. Chamberlain, Wilson and the economists were anxious that Anglo-German economic co-operation should not end. They therefore avoided any extreme measure against Germany.

For a month there was little economic activity; but the attraction of economic appeasement soon reasserted itself. The disillusionment of March and April gave way to increased activity in May.

CHAPTER 13

Czech Gold

THE OCCUPATION of Prague ended the idyll of Munich; an idyll marked more by apathy than by constructive developments in Anglo-German relations. The appeasers, slow to exploit the spirit of Munich, now wondered how genuine that spirit had been. The public were alarmed, and began to think of the need to resist German expansion. But the Government were unable to abandon economic appeasement. It was too attractive to be cut short by Prague.

In one respect it seemed that the Treasury had learnt its lesson. To avoid giving the Germans the quantities of foreign assets which they had gained as the result of the Anschluss,* it blocked all official and private Czech assets in England. Prague was not to be the goldmine Vienna had been.

On March 15, Müller, of the German Reichsbank, arrived at the Czechoslovak National Bank in Prague. He ordered the management to surrender their gold to the German Bank. But there was very little gold actually in the bank. Their reserves were kept in London, partly in the name of the bank itself, and partly under the name of the Bank of International Settlements.[1] Müller ordered the Czech bank to instruct the Bank of England to transfer the Czech gold to the Reichsbank. By various means the executive of the Czech bank succeeded in postponing the issue of this order until March 19. Then they were forced to do it under duress. By this time the British Treasury had decided to block all Czech assets in Britain. The Bank of England refused to part with the gold.

---

* After the Anschluss, Austria's gold and foreign assets were handed over to Germany. Britain, having recognized the Anschluss, had no legal right to retain the gold.

£6 million of the gold, however, was not under the control of the Bank of England, but under that of the Bank for International Settlements. This bank decided that the Czech gold which they held should be transferred to the Reichsbank. The responsibility for this decision rested with the head of the executive of the Bank, Dr. Beyen. Beyen telephoned Fournier, the Governor of the Bank of France, to ask whether the French and British Directors of the Bank for International Settlements would allow him to effect the transfer immediately, or whether the matter should be held up until the next board meeting. Fournier counselled delay, as did Paul Reynaud, the French Finance Minister. The British, however, refused to co-operate. Neither Otto Niemeyer nor Montague Norman, the British Directors of the Bank for International Settlements, exerted their influence to prevent the gold being transferred to Germany. They would not intervene. Paul Einzig, who was conducting a single-handed campaign against economic appeasement, was later told that Norman *did* in fact consult the Treasury before taking the decision not to intervene.[2] Simon, the Chancellor of the Exchequer, denied that he had ever been consulted. It seems possible that Norman contacted Leith-Ross, or some other permanent official at the Treasury, and not the Minister himself.

Rüter came to London in May to discuss the question of the blocked Czech assets. Despite the secrecy that surrounded his visit, rumors were soon rife. Duncan Sandys, that inveterate searcher-out of unpleasant facts, put down a question in the Commons for May 18, asking whether it was true that negotiations were being concluded for the release of the Czech gold. He was asked to withdraw his question. But the news could not long remain secret. On May 19, news of the imminent return of the Czech gold to Germany was published in the *Daily Telegraph* and in Einzig's paper, the *Financial News*. Lloyd George quoted these reports in the Commons. He was told by Chamberlain that the whole affair was a "mare's nest." Such denials were not effective. Einzig was still behind the scenes. With Brendan Bracken and Robert Boothby at Einzig's elbow, Chamberlain's evasion came to nought.

The subject of the Czech gold was debated in the Commons on Friday, May 26.[3] Only with difficulty were speakers to be found on the Government side. The Tory Opposition was in full tongue. Einzig briefed them well. Bracken said,

> We at the present time, in London, are actively helping the German rearmament programme, and our Treasury officials are sitting round a table talking to people about stolen goods or about how much of these stolen goods should be given back to Germany in order to facilitate her rearmament programme.
>
> Really, this is the most squalid form of appeasement. Political appeasement is, of course, out of the question. The by-elections and the various political developments in the last few months show that that policy at any rate is dead and damned, but some form of appeasement is still, apparently, dear to the heart of the Government, so they go in for financial appeasement. But it is a very squalid form of financial appeasement, because they are appeasing the Germans with the money of the unfortunate Czechs.

Winston Churchill attacked from another angle. The Government were pursuing a dual policy; and it was a fraud.

> Here we are going about urging people to enlist, urging them to accept new forms of military compulsion; here we are paying taxes on a gigantic scale in order to protect ourselves. If at the same time our mechanism of Government is so butterfingered that this £6 million of gold can be transferred to the Nazi Government of Germany, which only wishes to use it, and is only using it, as it does all its foreign exchange, for the purpose of increasing its armaments . . . it stultifies altogether the efforts our people are making in every class and in every party to secure National Defence and rally the whole forces of the country.

Many months were to pass before unity was achieved, or before the Government wholly abandoned its appeasement policy.

Simon said in debate that he was not sure if he was *entitled* to ask the Bank of England for information about the Czech gold. He repeated this claim to Bracken at tea. Later that evening, however, Simon saw Norman, who told him that the method of accountancy of gold deposits in the Bank of England had just been changed. Whereas previously the deposit of each Central Bank held in London in the name of the Bank for International Settlements was in a separate dossier, now all gold deposits were to be pooled together in a single account. To an inquiring eye it would be impossible to tell to whom the gold belonged. If the Czech gold were to be transferred to Germany, its removal would not be noticed.

The next morning Simon disclosed this information to Sir Henry Strakosch, while playing golf with him on Walton Heath. Three days later Strakosch told Einzig that the Bank of England was not in a position to know whether the Czech gold had been handed over to the Germans or not. Einzig, with this inside information, was able to piece together a meaningful article in his newspaper on May 31.[4] Bank and Treasury officials were appalled. They could not guess how the story had leaked out. They had not reckoned on tee-side indiscretions.

Einzig's revelations may have been crucial in preventing the gold from leaving England. The Germans never claimed the gold. It stayed in England. Was this a simple mistake, or did they hope to avoid embarrassing appeasement-minded circles in London? In Einzig's opinion, undue publicity for the physical transfer of the £6 million would have made it difficult for Simon to make *further* concessions by releasing the blocked privately-owned Czech assets in Britain. Perhaps the Germans still hoped for wider agreements and further offers. They were not disappointed. They had lost the Czech gold, but their English friends remained.

CHAPTER 14

Wilson and Wohltat

IN THE EARLY summer of 1939, some appeasers suggested a meeting between Hitler and "a leading English public figure." Those visits which were a noted feature of the early years of Hitler's rule were seldom repeated in 1939. Dirksen made inquiries. He had heard that Hitler had said: "in a direct conversation conducted in German with a decent and straightforward Englishman, he would have no great difficulty in finding a satisfactory settlement for existing issues." The people Dirksen thought possible were Butler, Burgin, Ironside, Addison, and Chatfield. Wilson thought "an outstanding person" in the British business world was "had in mind." But the projected visit was never arranged. According to Dirksen, "the matter took a different turn and ended in the conversations which Staatstrat Wohltat and I had with Sir Horace Wilson." [1]

On May 10, Henry Drummond-Wolff left London by air for Berlin. This, his second visit that year, was a "purely private one." Like his first visit, it was undertaken with the knowledge of "the Prime Minister's closest economic advisers." [2] Shortly before he left he had a long talk with Wilson. He told Selzam that Britain had intended to bring up, during the abortive visit of Stanley to Berlin in March, "the question of a partial renunciation by Britain of the most-favoured-nation rights in the Balkans in favour of Germany."

Drummond-Wolff invited Rüter to his hotel for lunch on May 14.[3] He told Rüter that

Internationally the right of the most-favoured-nation treatment must form the basis of economic relations, but in the particular *national* interest exceptions must be admitted. *Internationally-minded* Jewry was the greatest opponent of any relaxation of the right to most-favoured-nation treatment.

Drummond-Wolff asked what size loan would be necessary to help Germany resolve her existing foreign exchange difficulties. This was the type of question Britain had asked when she wanted to solve Germany's colonial problem for her. Rüter gave the usual diplomatic reply. Germany "did not want to incur a new foreign debt," and in any case, "since our productive capacity was rising higher and higher, and given the tasks before us, the amount of foreign exchange we need for raw materials and food has really no upper limit."

At no point was the futility of economic appeasement more clearly revealed. Far from being "practical politics" it was a "pie in the sky."

Drummond-Wolff inquired about a possible resumption of the Anglo-German economic negotiations which had been broken off in March. These had taken two forms:

(a) the discussions between the *industrial* associations on cartel and price matters, and
(b) the official *Government* discussions on the increase in German exports to Great Britain and . . . to the British colonies to be achieved by tariff reductions and Government contracts.

Rüter thought Government discussions could not begin until those of the industrialists had shown "tangible results." The industrialists planned to continue their discussions in June.

The only political question Drummond-Wolff asked Rüter was when Germany "would make a claim for the *return of the colonies* and which colonies it would include." "I gave the usual answer," wrote Rüter, "that we claim all colonies which belong to us; that we shall raise the claim in due course; and that it will be a matter of negotiation *which* colonial territories we receive."

Halifax made it clear that Drummond-Wolff's visit was unofficial in the sense that it did not involve the British Foreign
Office. He discussed with Dirksen on May 18:

> the matter of industrial and trade exchanges, in regard to which
> the Ambassador told me that he understood German industrialists
> to be coming over to this country in June for some further dis-
> cussions with British industrial representatives. It was, I think, in
> the Ambassador's mind that out of these unofficial contacts some-
> thing more valuable might grow, but he invited no expression of
> opinion from me, and I gave none.[4]

On May 24, a document arrived in London from the Berlin Embassy: the Annual Economic and Financial Report on Germany
for 1938. It showed the impracticability of further economic
appeasement. Henderson commented,

> The Report shows Germany heading with a kind of demoniac
> persistence for her autarchic goal, but — what is much graver —
> it shows her to be so far embarked along her chosen course that
> retreat is scarcely conceivable. Whatever the roseate figments of
> Dr. Schacht's, or for that matter Dr. Funk's, imagination, an easy
> or speedy return by Germany to free currency and economic co-
> operation seems now to have receded out of the domain of practical
> politics.[5]

Henderson did not take the advice implicit in his words. He
still thought that, though beyond the range of practical politics,
economic co-operation was certainly a subject for speculation.
He told Göring on May 27, that one of the errors of the Prague
coup had been "the fact that it prevented the visit of Oliver
Stanley and Hudson which might have led to better things." [6]

To help Germany in her economic difficulties still seemed an
excellent idea to Henderson. He asked Halifax to consider asking Funk to London. "I might give the German Government
a hint that a visit to England by Funk would be acceptable to
us," he wrote on May 30.[7] Halifax did not agree. The discus-

sions with industrialists, regarded as an essential prerequisite of further co-operation, were called off. Sir William Larke had the difficult task of informing Dr. Poensgen that further discussions would be unwelcome. He wrote on June 1,

> The members of the British Delegation have a very lively and happy recollection of the great kindness which we received from you and your colleagues at Düsseldorf, which they would be delighted to have an opportunity of reciprocating in a *purely social manner* this month, if this were acceptable to you. We therefore extend to you and the members of your Delegation a cordial invitation to visit London during Wimbledon Week, when we hope to make arrangements to visit the Tournament.[8]

The prospects for a European Common Market were exchanged for tickets for tennis. Did the British Federation of Industries know that it was Göring's favorite game?

Negotiations were officially at an end. But many appeasers could not take "no" for an answer. Wohltat was in London on June 6 and 7. He met Wilson and Sir Joseph Ball at the Duke of Westminster's house. Although there is no record of their conversation, we know from later references that they discussed Anglo-German relations within a certain "framework." On June 7, Wohltat had lunch with Ashton-Gwatkin.[9]

Wohltat's idea was for Great Britain to "recognize Germany's sphere of economic interest in South-East and Eastern Europe." Halifax had earlier recognized Germany's interest in *Central* Europe. South-East Europe was the same as Central Europe for most Englishmen.

Wohltat had in mind

> a return of Germany to a liberal, or more liberal, currency policy with free, or freer, exchanges (at any rate for commercial transactions though probably not for movements of capital), and equalisation of the mark at a new parity with the pound and dollar, and an adjustment of internal prices.

Ashton-Gwatkin no longer believed in easy solutions. Though a strong advocate of economic appeasement — one of its originators in fact — he saw that Nazism had gone beyond the bounds of reason. He replied:

> The dilemma seemed to me that England would not consider economic settlement with a Germany that was continuing to arm, whereas Germany seemed to think that any measure of disarmament would weaken her position in coming to negotiations . . . I said that if we were looking for a symbol of peace I thought that it would be more effective if Herr Hitler were to remodel his Cabinet and give to certain of his advisers that opportunity for leisure which their services had so amply deserved.

Adam von Trott zu Solz, a former Rhodes scholar and a friend of the Astors, had been invited for a weekend at Cliveden at the beginning of June. He wrote a memorandum on his visit for Counsellor Hewel.[10] His most interesting interview was with Lothian, whom he sat next to at dinner, and with whom he later had a long private conversation. Lothian wanted Hitler to give the Czechs back their independence. Von Trott reported Lothian's views:

> If recognition of the national identity of the small Czech people, surrounded by Germany, could actually be made an indisputable and demonstrable reality, it would seemingly guarantee in European politics the possibility of reconciling the expansion of German power with the continued existence of the individuality of other nations. On this assumption he was firmly convinced that nothing any longer would stand in the way of the splendid rise of Germany in the world . . . England-America (which Lothian naturally likes to regard as one!) and Germany, as the only real Great Power could then jointly shape and guarantee the future of world politics.

Von Trott replied that of course Prague was "an old German city."

Von Trott also spoke to Chamberlain and Dunglass. They discussed Germany's dislike of the British "encirclement policy." Dunglass promised to do his best with Stanley. He was successful — "Stanley . . . spoke in Parliament in favour of a more practically accommodating attitude towards Germany." [10] Dunglass, though "only on the fringe of affairs," [11] had influenced affairs directly.

The idea of a European four-power pact, linked both economically and politically, had receded from view. It remained possible only in few minds. Given a certain willingness on the German side, the appeasers were ready for a *rapprochement*. But the Jewish pogroms and the seizure of Prague had greatly increased the numbers for whom a *rapprochement* with Germany was unthinkable. A mood originally confined to Vansittart, and criticized as hysterical, began to envelop the nation. Small islands of pro-Germanism remained: the anterooms of 10 Downing Street, the Treasury, Henderson.

On June 13, Henderson saw Weizsäcker, and gave the impression that he spoke with official backing. He told Weizsäcker that "the ending of the armaments race and the revival of economic relations could be the subject of discussions between London and Berlin. The colonial question could also be discussed." [12] Coulondre, the French Ambassador in Berlin, reinforced the point: "once the Anglo-Franco-Russian pact was concluded, diplomatic conversations between the Axis and the Western Powers could take place more easily than at present." [13] On June 24, Dirksen noted, "it has been possible to observe for some weeks now in conversation with leading British personalities that they were tending towards a discussion with Germany on burning problems." [14]

Negotiations were possible, but Henderson knew that official policy firmly rejected any major concessions. He told Weizsäcker on June 27, that "he wished that the Labour Party were at the helm and not the Conservatives, for in reality Chamberlain was now obliged to pursue Labour's foreign policy and also to bear the odium for its setbacks." [15]

The Germans remained uninterested. Referring to this meeting, and to the one on June 13, Weizsäcker told Dirksen, "the concrete suggestions which Henderson advances can still hardly be regarded as constructive." [16]

British policy hardened after Prague. But in a report of July 10, Dirksen thought that a change was beginning.

> Within the Cabinet, and in a small but influential group of politicians, efforts are being made to replace the negative policy of an encirclement front by a constructive policy towards Germany . . . Though . . . there are strong forces at work to stifle this tender plant . . . Chamberlain's personality gives a certain guarantee that British policy will not be delivered into the hands of unscrupulous adventurers. [17]

Henderson had ideas on how the tender plant might best be cosseted. On July 9, he suggested the draft of a letter which Chamberlain might write to Hitler.

> It is quite clear that confidence and tranquillity can only be restored in Europe by means of Anglo-German co-operation. To this end His Majesty's Government . . . will be ready . . . to discuss with the German Government all such problems as limitation of armaments, trade barriers, raw materials, "Lebensraum," and eventually Colonies, provided you, Herr Reichskanzler, are willing on your part definitely to reassure me as to your pacific intentions. [18]

After four weeks in Spain Wohltat came to London again. He led the German delegation at a Whaling Conference held at the Ministry of Agriculture and Fisheries on July 17. But there were greater problems to discuss than whales. Hudson told the Norwegian member of the Whaling Commission, Professor Bergersen, that he would like to talk with Wohltat. A meeting was arranged for the evening of July 20. On July 18, Wohltat saw Wilson for an hour and a quarter. They went over the ground covered at their meeting in June. Wilson maintained that "there was still an opportunity for co-operating . . . so soon as conditions had been created that would make that co-operation feasible." [19] At this stage, according to the German report, Wilson's secretary brought in a memorandum.* Wohltat was given to understand that it had Chamberlain's approval.[20] It suggested secret negotiations. "At present only Britain and Germany should negotiate; France and Italy should only be brought in later." The British were once again offering bilateral negotiations.

The *Wilson Memorandum*, as it appears in the German documents, was put in its final form by Wohltat for Göring's benefit. The proposals made by Wilson are joined to those of Hudson two days later. Wilson's proposals were reported as follows:

1) A joint German-British declaration that forcible aggression will not be employed by either country as an instrument of international policy. ("Joint Anglo-German declaration not to use aggression.") This should not take the form of a non-aggression pact between the two countries but of a general declaration on a political principle whereby both countries renounced the use of forcible aggression as an instrument of policy. Here Sir Horace takes the view that such a declaration would make Britain's guarantee to Poland and Roumania superfluous, since, as a result of such a declaration, Germany would not attack these States and they could not therefore feel that their national existence was threatened by Germany.

2) Mutual declarations of non-interference ("non-interference") by Germany in respect of the British Commonwealth of Nations and by Great Britain in respect of Greater Germany. I drew attention to the fact that it was not only a question of the frontiers of States and possessions, but also of territories of special interest and

* Wilson cannot remember giving Wohltat a memorandum on July 18. He in fact gave Wohltat a copy of a speech Halifax had made a few days earlier. In this speech Halifax said that, while German aggression could not be tolerated, Britain still wanted agreement with Germany on outstanding issues, and that, as in the matter of colonies, Britain would be prepared to make concessions. Wilson considered that Wohltat "would have found there and in current speeches by Mr. Chamberlain references to all the points I had discussed with him and there is nothing novel in the details set out in his 'record.' "

of economic influence. For Germany this would apply especially to East and South-East Europe. Sir Horace replied that this point needed especially careful political wording and that the political definition would probably best result from an examination of Germany's economic interests. Britain was only interested in keeping her share of European trade.

Note. By the declarations of principle in respect of (1) and (2) the British apparently wish to establish a new platform for dealing with the questions between Germany and Poland. The Danzig Question after a broad German-British agreement would play a minor part for Britain.

3) The colonial and/or mandates question. A German-British declaration on a fundamental revision of the relevant provisions of the Versailles Treaty.

As other States besides Great Britain administer mandates, amongst which are former German colonial territories, the position adopted by the British would be the starting-point for opening up the colonial question as a whole. As to the practical solution of the colonial question, members of the Cabinet have from time to time discussed plans.

Military Questions

A German-British declaration on the limitation of armaments and common policy towards third countries.

1) Naval agreement.

2) Air agreement.

3) Army agreement.

The naval agreement would be suitably modelled on the experience of the previous agreement.

The air agreement and the army agreement should take into account the special strategic and military conditions of the British Empire and of the Greater German Reich in Central Europe. The German-British agreements would have to be brought into relation with existing agreements, and agreements newly to be concluded with third countries.

On July 20, Hudson met Wohltat for an hour. According to Hudson's account of the meeting,[21] he himself thought it possible to work out some form of collaboration between England, Germany and the United States. Wohltat objected that as far as Germany was concerned the greatest difficulty was her debt, and "the problem of remitting the annual payments for interest and amortisation abroad." Could Britain and America help "on the capital side?" Hudson had discussed this with friends in America in May. He told Wohltat: "I thought we could look with some confidence to American help, and as far as this country was concerned I had little doubt."

They also discussed the colonial problem. Hudson regretfully announced that "British public opinion would never agree to the physical return of ex-German colonies to German sovereignty." But he felt that Africa was a continent which afforded European industrial countries great openings "for industrial development of a capital goods nature." Given good will on both sides, this might well lead to "some form of agreement in which Africa would be administered jointly by European Powers in trusts."

In the account Wohltat gave Göring of the meeting, Hudson's proposals were as follows:[22]

Economic Questions

1) A German-British declaration on a common policy for the supply of raw materials and food to both countries and an agreement on the export of German and British industrial products to the principal markets.

Note. Should German-British co-operation in all fields be desired, I consider it possible, from my knowledge of the views of leading British politicians, to ensure the long-term co-operation of the two greatest industrial nations. By directing the great national economic forces, which could be expanded in Europe and the world under the leadership of Germany and Britain through the co-operation of their Governments, an unprecedented economic boom could be achieved and a further raising of the peoples' standards of living, which would be a determining factor for an industrial epoch. Systematic German-British co-operation would, above all, extend to the economic development of three great markets:

The British Empire (especially India, South Africa, Canada, Australia).

China (in co-operation with Japan).

Russia (assuming that Stalin's policy develops accordingly).

German-British co-operation, which would secure peace for a foreseeable period, opens up unlimited new possibilities for all the forces of labour and capital in view of modern industrial equipment. The dangers of unemployment during the changeover of industrial production from armaments to the production of capital and consumer goods could be avoided in conjunction with these plans. It would be possible within the framework of German-British co-operation to finance the reorganisation of British and German industry. Large scale economic planning by Britain and Germany would make possible the long-term financing of the latest raw material and industrial projects in other continents.

2) *Colonial Questions*

In connection with German-British economic co-operation, Mr. Hudson discussed the plan for a "colonial condominium" in Africa. Underlying this plan is the idea of a common opening up of Africa by the European colonial powers. It would be a question of a large integrated territory, which would embrace the greater part of tropical and sub-tropical Africa. Togoland, Nigeria, the Cameroons, the Congo, Kenya, Tanganyika (German East Africa), Portuguese and Spanish West and East Africa and Northern Rhodesia might be included. In this territory the production of raw material and food, the investment of capital goods, foreign trade and currency, transport administration, police and military control could be uniformly organized.

Mr. Hudson said he was not allowed to speak officially of an understanding between British and German industry; but he supported any practical arrangement which came to his knowledge. Naturally, Britain wanted to win the next war; but he would

consider himself more than foolish if he did not try to speak to
me now instead of at the next Peace Conference. After a war the
present problems would be distinctly more difficult for all partici-
pants than they are now.

3) A joint German-English declaration on the relation of both
countries' currencies to each other, on the basis of an international
debt settlement for Germany. Loans for the German Reichsbank.
Restoration of the link between the European capital markets.
Settlement of South-East Europe's currency and debt question led
by the Berlin market. Adjustment of the most-favoured-nation
clause to the special conditions of production of the European
agricultural nations.

German-British agreement on the British share in the markets
within the special economic spheres of interest of the Greater
German Reich in Eastern and South-East Europe.

Hudson also mentioned the possibility of a conference to discuss Germany's exchange problem. There is no evidence as to
the size of the loan Hudson contemplated in the phrase "loans
to the Reichsbank." In the Press it appeared that he had offered
the Germans £1,000 million. Wilson later told Dirksen that
"it had often been discussed how the financial and economic
difficulties which it was to be feared might attend armament
limitation could be overcome. Hudson had perhaps seized upon
this idea and enlarged upon it." [23]

After his discussion with Hudson, Wohltat saw Sir Joseph
Ball. Ball told him that the General Election was scheduled for
November 14. If there were to be Anglo-German negotiations,
said Ball, they would have to start soon. Chamberlain must decide whether to fight the election on a slogan of peace or war
with Germany. Ball believed the Conservatives would win in
any case. The Government considered a German-British settlement to be an effective election slogan — "Safeguarding World
Peace with Chamberlain." But the Whips, as Dirksen realized,
were more than ever convinced that the election "could just as
surely be won on the opposite slogan of 'Preparedness for the

Coming War,' should there be no prospect of a settlement with Germany." [24]

On July 25, Daladier asked Chamberlain not to announce the date of the election before the end of August. Bonnet thought the British Government should consider postponing the holding of elections. The French had decided to prorogue parliament for a year. They feared that British elections would spoil their case for not having them in France.[25] Whereas the Germans were told the date of the British General Election, the French were not.

Wohltat spent a final half-hour with Wilson on July 21. Wilson told him that Hudson's proposals had been discussed by influential members of the Cabinet, but "without a final decision having been taken at this stage."[26] He also said that if Hitler would agree to conversations, this would be regarded as a sign of returning confidence. Would the British Government agree, Wohltat asked, to the Germans "putting other questions, besides those enumerated, on the agenda?" Wilson said yes. He told Wohltat that "the Führer had only to take a sheet of paper and jot down his points; the British Government would be prepared to discuss them." *

Wohltat gave a report of his discussions to Dirksen, and returned to Berlin.

On July 22, the papers carried stories of Wohltat's visit. They gave a garbled account of the proposals made, including that of the £1,000 million loan. How the press learned the story is not clear. Fritz Hesse wrote on July 24, that he was "reliably assured . . . that the responsibility for the indiscretion must be

* The meeting on July 18 had been less formal than Wohltat's record suggests; that of July 21 does not seem to have taken place at all. Wilson's appointment book shows seven appointments for that day, and there is no mention of Wohltat, nor can Wilson remember a second meeting. It seems probable that Hudson, not Wilson, took the initiative in putting "proposals" before Wohltat. Wohltat muddles his accounts of the various meetings that took place. He may well have thought that Wilson's name carried more weight at Berlin than Hudson's, and tried to give the impression that Wilson had been his chief contact, so that Berlin would take the plans more seriously.

laid at the door of the French Embassy, which learned of the talk on Friday and immediately sounded the alarm." [27]

Even if it was the French who did this, it would be interesting to know how they learned the story. Dirksen denied that the leakage came from Wohltat or from the German Embassy. Yet it is difficult to believe that Hudson or Wilson were intentionally responsible, since, once made public, the object of the talks was destroyed. Only the Russians took advantage of the publicity, and used it as an excuse for their *rapprochement* with Hitler the following month.

The storm did not burst properly until July 24. Duff Cooper proposed in the press that "a sort of parliamentary supervisory council, consisting chiefly of opponents of adjustment, should be set up to prevent Chamberlain from reverting to the policy of appeasement."

Dirksen telephoned Orme Sargent at the Foreign Office and complained that the story Wohltat told him was not the same as that which had appeared in the press, particularly with regard to the "story about the fantastic loan." [28] He also asked Wilson to deny Hudson's press statements. "Sir Horace Wilson . . . made no reply." [29] In the House of Lords, Lord Snell asked Halifax "how this presumably confidential conversation between a member of His Majesty's Government and a representative of another power gets into the press. I should also like to ask whether any Civil Servant was in any way connected with the enquiries or discussions that have taken place." "The answer," said Halifax, "so far as I am aware, is in the negative."

On July 22, Birger Dahlerus, a Swedish businessman, had seen Göring who "touched on the recent peace proposals that Wohltat had brought him and he regarded same as perfectly absurd — in fact, he did not treat them as serious suggestions." [30]

Although Dirksen wrote two brief reports on Wohltat's visit, neither of them reached Ribbentrop. Ribbentrop saw Wohltat's memorandum only at the end of the month. He immediately telegraphed Dirksen, asking for additional information. He also sought further details from his contact in London, Fritz Hesse. Hesse was asked to return to Berlin.

On July 29, Kordt saw Charles Roden Buxton, the Labour Party's expert on foreign affairs. Buxton told him that "he was speaking neither on behalf of the Labour Party nor on behalf of the Government." It was, he felt, necessary to return to secret diplomacy. He produced the following plan.[31]

1) Germany promises not to interfere in British Empire affairs.

2) Great Britain promises fully to respect the German sphere of interest in Eastern and South-Eastern Europe. A consequence of this would be that Great Britain would renounce the guarantee she gave to certain States in the German sphere of interest.

Great Britain further promises to influence France to break her alliance with the Soviet Union and to give up her ties in South-East Europe.

3) Great Britain promises to give up the present negotiations for a pact with the Soviet Union.

In return for this, Germany was to promise:

1) To proclaim her readiness for European co-operation (four-power pact).

2) To grant at a later stage some kind of autonomy to Bohemia and Moravia.

3) To agree to a general reduction of armaments.

Kordt thought Buxton had his plan from Wilson. To negotiate with the Germans through the Opposition foreign affairs expert was a stroke of genius. Sir Joseph Ball had tried to convince Wohltat that the Conservatives would win the next election. In Buxton's plan was evidence that Britain would continue to follow the same foreign policy, even if the Labour Party won in November. Germany could rely on them to advocate Chamberlain's favorite policy of the four-power pact. Whichever party was in power in November, the *Wilson Memorandum* or the *Buxton Plan* would be its blueprint.

On August 2, Kordt saw R. A. Butler. He wanted to see an authoritative person before returning to Germany.[32] Butler consulted Chamberlain. It was arranged for Kordt to see Wilson. Halifax was informed. According to Dirksen, "it was ascertained in Herr Kordt's conversation with Mr. Butler that Sir Horace Wilson in supplement to his conversation with Herr Wohltat would very much like to have a talk with me." [33]

Thus Dirksen, not Kordt, went to Wilson's house on August 3. For two hours they discussed the program which Wilson had laid before Wohltat. Wilson elaborated on this program, stressing the economic elements:[34]

1) The conclusion of a treaty of non-aggression.

2) An Anglo-German declaration to the effect that both Powers wanted to ease (improve) the political situation.

3) Negotiations with a view to increasing foreign trade.

4) Negotiations regarding Germany's economic interests in the South-East.

5) Negotiations regarding raw materials.

6) A non-intervention agreement.

7) Armaments.

Wilson asked Dirksen to consider, "what instructions has the Führer given as to the follow-up of Wohltat's report? What are the next steps which the German Government think should be taken?" [35]

No reply ever came.

On August 9, Halifax told Dirksen that

a period of calm making for the pacification of public opinion would create an entirely different picture, and then it would undoubtedly be possible to discuss appeasement questions. The British Government keenly desired that this should come about, and then it would be prepared to go very far for the achievement of this aim.[36]

Three days later Leslie Runciman, the son of Lord Runciman, was entertained for the weekend by the Prince Max von Hohenlohe. It was arranged that he should meet Göring, a meeting apparently desired by Wohltat.[37] Göring saw him and spoke "of a settlement of the Danzig question being a prelude to a general settlement in Europe in terms which made Mr. Runciman think that Mr. Hudson's remarks to Dr. Wohltat had produced a strong reaction at any rate in the Field Marshal's entourage." Hohenlohe gave one reason: "they can smell money and it attracts them." [38] But whatever the reason, favorable reaction of individual Germans had no practical result. The political crisis was becoming acute. Economic appeasement, however strongly favored by economists and businessmen, could only really be pursued in an atmosphere of political calm. Such calm did not return to Western Europe until after 1945.

PART FOUR

The Greatest enemy of mankind today is *Hate*, and I think it is the height of disloyalty to make foreigners think that there is a Party here who is against the Gvts. Peace policy.

— Margot Asquith to Gilbert Murray,
March 4, 1939

Whether Neville's actual policy was right or wrong, he has somehow failed to explain himself, and that is a very dangerous position when national unity is so important.

— Gilbert Murray to Margot Asquith,
March 7, 1939

CHAPTER 15

Tilea's Indiscretion

ON MARCH 15, 1939, German troops entered Prague. Germany proclaimed a protectorate over "Czechia." As Hitler had promised Chamberlain less than five months earlier, there was no bombing of Prague from the air. Hitler had no need of violence. The Prague Government had asked its people not to resist German occupation.[1] Czechoslovakia, stripped of its defenses the previous October, and abandoned by its Western allies long before March, lay naked in Central Europe. Its nakedness was Hitler's invitation. Facing the inevitable, Prague was calm. Newton reported that the crowds, "who seemed to be taken by surprise," had "behaved well." Prague itself "seems quiet." [2] After an evening of violence which the Germans were thought to have provoked, loudspeakers were put up in the main streets "to counsel the people to remain calm." The anonymous voice was obeyed.[3]

Whatever Hitler's motives in annexing new territory, and however quickly and calmly the annexations took place, Englishmen were outraged. Hitler had broken his Munich promise. He had struck out once more across Europe. In the Commons Simon maintained that all was well. He deprecated mutual security agreements, which Eden suggested and Dalton advocated.[4]

But the "give them Bournemouth" school of appeasement could not survive the occupation of Prague. Before March 15, appeasement had been triumphant. Anglo-German trade talks were about to begin. Prague broke the illusion. Calm and optimism were equally endangered. Chamberlain was forced to ask: "Was this the end of an old adventure, or the beginning of a new?" [5]

For most men the answer was simple. Hitler had only begun to show his true colors. Until March 15, only Germans had been brought into Germany. This was a reasonable return of natives to the homeland, even if accomplished by threats and violent language. On March 15, aliens were joined to Germany. They were Slavs, whose "race" made them abhorrent to Nazism. Vienna had cheered when Hitler arrived; the Sudetenland had been less enthusiastic, though some rejoiced. In Prague there were tears. The occupation was the first move in a new imperialism. On March 18, Coulondre and Henderson delivered the protests of their respective Governments against what was described as a "denial of the spirit" of Munich.[6]

Many expected further German aggression in a matter of days. Hitler did indeed move. Memel was annexed. But Memel, like Vienna, was a German city. The Memel Germans were even closer to Berlin in spirit than the Viennese. Memel's "return" to Germany was part of the old, respectable process. Something more wicked was anticipated: something in keeping with the occupation of Prague.

Prague had not been defended by Czechoslovakia's allies. Though guaranteed, it had fallen undefended. Once it had gone, the guarantees given it were forgotten. Chamberlain, Halifax and Simon made it clear that these guarantees had never been taken seriously. "The condition of affairs," said Chamberlain, "which was always regarded by us as being only of a transitory nature has now ceased to exist, and His Majesty's Government cannot accordingly hold themselves any longer bound by this obligation."[7]

But men assumed that further German aggression would be opposed by force. An old ally having been effortlessly abandoned, it was hoped that new alliances would be built up which would prove binding. Hitler's next potential victim should be discovered, and guaranteed.

It was not difficult to see where Hitler would turn next. The statesmen glanced at the map. Bonnet was convinced Hitler would turn against Rumania. Rumania controlled the Danube mouth, and was rich in oil. Even without a common German-Rumanian frontier Hitler was in a position to move against Rumania, as Hungary, the neighbor of both, was hostile to Rumania and would further Hitler's plans. Phipps asked Bonnet if he thought Rumania would be "the next course of the Nazi menu?" Bonnet replied that he thought it "very likely." [8] Henderson too saw the sequel to Prague as "domination by force of the whole of the Danube basin." [9]

Where else, other than towards Rumania, could Hitler turn? Corbin told Halifax that not Hitler at all, but Mussolini, would move next. He would "try to get something to redress the balance" between Italy and Germany. But Halifax had been well informed of Italian intentions by Lord Perth, and assured Corbin that "there were no preparations of a warlike kind" in Italy.[10] Burckhardt, the League High Commissioner in Danzig, feared Danzig would be the next trouble spot in Europe. "Extremely grave developments," he forecast, would take place "in the immediate future." German troops might even occupy Danzig "during the coming weekend." [11] But such an alarmist view was "definitely" discounted by the Polish Commissioner in Danzig,[12] while Dirksen told Halifax that the German Government would seek a solution for Danzig, not by threats or violence, but "in consultation with the Polish Government." [13]

British doubts were quickly dispelled. Confronted with so many conflicting rumors, men sought certainty, and grasped at rumors to have it. On March 16, the Rumanian Minister in London, Virgil Tilea, confirmed Western fears that Rumania was next for destruction. He hurried to the Foreign Office and told Orme Sargent that the Rumanian Government had "good reason to believe" that within the next few months the Germans "would reduce Hungary to vassalage and then proceed to disintegrate Rumania." The German aim would be a Protectorate, as over Czechoslovakia. Tilea asked Sargent how far Rumania "could count upon Great Britain." [14] When no reply had come to his request by the following morning, Tilea, in even greater alarm, asked to see Lord Halifax. The matter was urgent. It might be a question of war within weeks, even days. Halifax agreed to hear what Tilea had to say.

The meeting between Halifax and Tilea ranks as one of the most important political events of the inter-war years. England burned with anxiety. Frightened men talked of the need to resist Hitler wherever he might strike. Obstinacy replaced pessimism. Fascism was no longer "inevitable": it could be fought, and defeated. If Hitler's next victim could be found in advance, help should be offered at once: not sympathy or fine phrases, but concrete pledges that would be honored. On March 17, the victim presented himself at the Foreign Office. Facing him was not the Halifax who talked of politics "with a certain impersonal interest," [15] but the representative of the new determination. Halifax, like the British people, seemed to clench his fist in readiness to use it.

Tilea told Halifax that:

During the last few days the Roumanian Government had received a request from the German Government to grant them a monopoly of Roumanian exports, and to adopt certain measures of restriction of Roumanian industrial production in German interests. If these conditions were accepted, Germany would guarantee the Roumanian frontiers. This seemed to the Roumanian Government something very much like an ultimatum . . . In the view of his Government it was of the utmost importance that His Majesty's Government should consider with all urgency whether they could give a precise indication of the action they would take in the event of Roumania being the victim of German aggression. If it was possible to construct a solid block of Great Britain and France, it was to be expected that the situation might be saved . . . In the view of his Government, these matters might possibly be a matter of days.[16]

Halifax listened. He was perturbed. He promised to give Tilea's information to Chamberlain "with all urgency." [17] A British guarantee to defend so distant a nation would indeed put appeasement in its grave. It seemed Tilea and Lord Halifax were to be its gravediggers.

At ten that evening Halifax passed Tilea's warning to the British Ambassadors at Warsaw, Ankara, Athens and Belgrade. They were to ask the Governments to which they were accredited what their respective attitudes would be in the "circumstances foreshadowed." [18] France also insisted on knowing "exactly what resistance" these other powers would make "before we promise help to Roumania." [19] Halifax had instructed the British Ambassador in Moscow to ask whether Russia would give active help to Rumania. [20]

Halifax was in a difficult position. However strongly he might want to give Rumania assistance, he knew there were few means of doing so. Britain had no common frontier with Rumania. Contact by sea depended upon access to the Black Sea, which Germany could easily prevent. It was necessary to find Rumania a second ally: one, if possible, with a common land frontier. An ally was needed which was strong and reliable, and in no danger itself. Tilea suggested who the second ally should be. He asked Halifax if it would "make it easier" for Britain if Rumania reached an agreement with Poland about a joint treaty against Germany. [21] Here was an attractive plan. Poland could be the second ally.

There was a common Rumanian-Polish frontier. Poland, according to British intelligence, was in a strong position with regard to Germany. Poland and Germany had worked closely together since 1935. The Polish Foreign Minister, Colonel Beck, seemed determined to maintain a high level of German-Polish understanding. The two nations had much in common. Both hated Bolshevism. Both ill-treated Jews. Both disliked the Czechs. Poland had seized Czech territory when Germany annexed Sudeten areas. Poland and Germany seemed agreed on many things. If Poland could be trusted she would make an excellent ally for Rumania; she might even be able to put pressure in Berlin to make the Germans abandon their hostile attitude.

The French doubted Beck's honesty. Léger told Phipps it was unwise to trust him, as he "had betrayed Rumania or was in the process of doing so." Beck wanted to deflect the Germans southwards, to save his own skin: he was "entirely cynical and false." [22] If this were true, Britain would have to help Rumania alone; there was no question of abandoning her. Even America was anxious for Britain to show herself willing to oppose aggression. Kennedy, the American Ambassador, told Halifax that if Britain fought when Rumania was attacked, America would be "more readily moved" to support her than if she gave Rumania no help at all. If, having abandoned Rumania, Britain then decided to defend other countries, say Greece or Turkey, America might not come to her aid.[23] One ally had already been abandoned. A second betrayal would alienate American opinion altogether.

America wanted Britain to be bold. But on March 18, a curious fact came to light, which might have led Halifax to lose all interest in helping Rumania. Gafencu, the Rumanian Foreign Minister, informed him that Tilea had "misrepresented the situation." There was no threat to Rumania at all. German-Rumanian trade negotiations were "on completely normal lines as between equals." Gafencu had given Tilea "a tremendous head washing." [24] Such news ought to have stopped the panic. It failed to do so. Tilea's timely indiscretion was allowed to determine British policy. It was the driving force behind the frantic and unprecedented search for an Eastern European commitment. Prince Paul of Yugoslavia said to Halifax: "You ask me what I am prepared to do but I should like to know what you are prepared to do." [25] The burden of responsibility could no longer be avoided.

Halifax asked for Polish help in protecting Rumania. He urged Beck to agree to a four-power declaration which would act as "a plain signal of danger" to Germany. The four Powers would be Britain, France, Poland and Russia. United, explained Halifax, they would serve as a "rallying point and vitalising force" for the smaller states of Eastern Europe.[26] The Poles were unwilling to make so firm a commitment. Beck said it would alienate Germany, by giving the impression that Poland was moving away into the anti-German orbit: worse, into the Soviet orbit. Sir Howard Kennard, the British Ambassador in Warsaw, begged Beck to "ponder over" the question of a four-power declaration.[27] Britain understood Polish fears. But Rumania, she still asserted, was in great and immediate danger. National dislikes should be put aside in order to help her. The French had made it clear that they considered Rumania the "last obstacle to the triumph of German imperialism."[28]

On March 21, Halifax and Bonnet met in London. Bonnet revealed that France had also asked Beck if he would help Rumania. Beck had said that he would consider the idea. But he had one condition. Russia must be left out of the proposed guarantee. Beck insisted that if Russia came in the Germans would instigate "immediate action" in both Hungary and Rumania. The French feared that a declaration without Russia would hardly be "adequate." But a declaration without Poland would be worse. For this reason, Bonnet told Halifax, "the strongest pressure must . . . be put to bear" on Poland to commit herself. The French could stop a German advance, he said, through Switzerland. Only Poland or Russia could help Rumania. Poland was preferable, if both could not accept. If the Germans invaded Rumania and Poland gave no assistance, "France would be in a bad position."[29] France needed Poland as her eastern ally. And so did Britain.

Beck considered that the proposed declaration would provoke Germany. He told Kennard that he would not be rushed into a commitment. If Russia came in it would "definitely place Poland in the Soviet camp." This would provoke a "serious" reaction from Germany.[30] Poland was not alone in wishing to avoid being linked with Russia. On March 22, Bonnet explained to Chamberlain that Rumania doubted the need for Soviet help. "Some of the upper class preferred Hitler to Stalin."[31]

Bonnet insisted that Poland should not be given "a pretext for running out" because of Russian inclusion.[32] Chamberlain understood Polish fears. "I must confess," he wrote on March 26, "to the most profound distrust of Russia. I have no belief in her ability to maintain an effective offensive even if she wanted to. And I distrust her motives." [33] Hostility to Russia was decisive. Halifax and Bonnet agreed that the main problem was how "to persuade Poland to commit herself to support Roumania." [34]

Halifax had the answer. It was a triumph of ingenuity. Britain and France should offer Poland the same type of guarantee that they wanted Poland to offer Rumania. Poland must be wooed to the West by an offer of support for which she had made no request. She must be protected from a danger no one believed her to be in. Beck might then agree to guarantee Rumania.

Chamberlain agreed that they should "try the new procedure." [35] As at Munich, important decisions were taken by a handful of men, without full Cabinet consultations. Not a word was said in Parliament. Abrupt changes of policy were made on inspiration. The policy makers failed to ask themselves what a guarantee for Poland would involve, should Poland herself be threatened by Germany. Perhaps they believed that she never would be. The wily Beck would never allow the Germans to threaten him. He was too shrewd for that.

Halifax explained to Beck that Rumania was a "vital interest" for Poland.[36] But Beck was in no hurry to help his neighbor. Critics suspected him of being pro-German. "Nothing could be more false," wrote Vansittart, "he doubted Western resolve." [37] Beck's doubts were passed to London. Prince Paul had heard that the Polish Government "will in no circumstances commit themselves in advance to fight against Germany in hypothetical cases." [38] But within an hour of hearing Prince Paul's story, the British were saved. Beck accepted a British guarantee to Poland. Although a Polish guarantee for Rumania was not yet secured, the Halifax plan was under way. Beck had allowed Britain to guarantee his frontiers.[39] The guarantee was to be secret. He did not even want it communicated to France. He refused to sign a four-power declaration, and repeated that if Poland was associated with Russia it would provoke "immediate hostile re-action" from Germany. The British allowed their four-power plan to lapse.

The British offer of a guarantee to Poland was made on the assumption that Poland was in no danger. The Poles encouraged this view. They realized that the British would withdraw their offer if they believed Poland was threatened by Germany. Count Edward Raczynski, the Polish Ambassador in London, assured Halifax that Beck would "go a long way" to avoid trouble with Germany.[40] The only question at issue between the two countries was the problem of Danzig. Danzig was a free City attached to Poland by economic ties, but almost entirely German in population. Raczynski said Danzig was no danger-spot. Beck told Halifax that Poland and Germany would soon negotiate over Danzig.[41] Beck intended to make a "magnani-mous" offer to the Germans.[42]

Chamberlain and Halifax offered Beck a guarantee, believing him to be in no danger. At the end of March it seemed that Germany was about to invade Poland. This view was sup-ported by Ian Colvin, the Berlin correspondent of the *News Chronicle*. Colvin hurried to London, and told Halifax and Chamberlain of Hitler's supposed plan. Chamberlain decided to publicize his offer to Beck. In this way domestic opinion would be satisfied, and Beck, having received an *open* pledge, would feel bound to reciprocate by giving his own pledge to Rumania.

On March 31, Kennard was asked to obtain Beck's acceptance of the British pledge. Chamberlain himself drafted the declara-tion. If Poland were attacked, Britain "would at once lend [Poland] all the support in their power."[43] Halifax sent off the request at 4:20 P.M. At 7:50 P.M. he learned that Beck had agreed to it "without hesitation"[44] — between "two flicks" of his cigarette. Chamberlain had an assurance that would satisfy those who demanded an end to appeasement. Poland had an ally.

The British made sure that Poland was in no danger. Beck told Halifax the Poles would do "nothing provocative" against Germany.[45] Raczynski told him there were "no important questions" in dispute between Poland and Germany.[46] The British therefore began to plan for pressure to be brought on Beck for the Rumanian guarantee. It was a difficult task. Britain's pledge to Rumania, if it was to have any value, *must* be linked with Poland's. But Beck had still to be persuaded. He was due in London on April 4. Chamberlain and Halifax, while awaiting his arrival, prepared their briefs.

Beck and Halifax met for the first time on April 4.[47] Beck asked for the British guarantee to Poland to be reciprocal. This was "the only basis that any self-respecting country would accept." Halifax agreed. He did not ask himself what reciprocity involved. He told Beck that he was aware of "the position Poland occupied in the world." Halifax still worried about the obligations Beck's pledge might involve. Did Beck feel that a German attack on Poland was at all likely, he asked? Beck said he "had not noticed any signs of dangerous military action" on the German side. As for Danzig, it was "their own local . . . affair." Halifax did not argue, even though Kennard had told him that Beck was liable to make "evasive" replies.[48]

Halifax had other questions. Would Beck agree to a four-power declaration, with Russia? Beck would not. Poland "was ready to improve her relations with Soviet Russia, but would not extend them." It would be futile, perhaps fatal, for Poland to be associated with Russia. Such an association, Beck told Eden that night, would provoke Germany to "instant aggressive action." Halifax argued that Russia's military strength would be an asset against Germany. Beck disagreed. He "had not a very high opinion" of the Russian army. Halifax, weakly, agreed. He undermined his own argument. He admitted that although the

Russian army was adequate as a defensive force, it could not take the offensive. He told Beck that "one of the difficulties" with which he was faced was pressure from "some members" of the Labour Party. They wanted Russia and Britain to "join hands." Halifax, doubtful about the effectiveness of Russia as an ally, appreciated Polish fears. He agreed they were "not unnatural." He later wrote, "An intelligent rabbit would hardly be expected to welcome the protection of an animal ten times its own size, whom it credited with the habits of a boa constrictor." [49]

Halifax asked Beck what help Poland would be willing to give Rumania. It was the vital question. Beck refused to commit himself. Any specific Polish commitment, he said, would throw Hungary "automatically" into the German camp. It would be wrong to increase tension in Eastern Europe. Halifax urged the danger of "no concerted plans." Beck claimed an equal danger in "rigid political systems." Deadlock was reached on the critical issue. The meeting ended.

Chamberlain joined Halifax in the evening. He tried to draw Beck into commitments where Halifax had failed. But Beck was too clever for both of them. He alone was the professional. Vansittart wrote of Chamberlain: "An earnest opinionated provincial was bound to err if he plunged into diplomacy." [50] Beck might well have said of Chamberlain as he said of another politician whom he outwitted: "*Ce n'est pas le Colonel Beck.*"

Chamberlain feared German aggression against Poland which would involve Britain. He asked Beck to say where Hitler would move next. Beck sarcastically remarked that if German statements were taken seriously "the gravest question was on the colonial question." He said no word about Danzig. Chamberlain asked about Russia. Beck answered that "any association between Poland and Russia" would push Germany into war with Poland. If Britain and Russia wanted to talk they could. Poland "would keep clear." She was determined to be dependent on neither Russia nor Germany. If Britain wanted her, she must have her alone. Chamberlain was alarmed. Poland *alone* was not enough. Rumania must come in or the Polish guarantee would have been wasted.

Chamberlain told Beck that Rumania was "a vital spot." Beck repeated his dislike of "too rigid a system." Rumania should be left out "until the Danubian problem had cleared itself a little." Poland could not afford to alienate Hungary. Chamberlain listened without comment. But he was a stubborn man, unwilling to admit failure. He tried to frighten Beck. He pointed out that if Germany occupied Rumania "Poland would have a longer frontier with Germany." Beck knew his geography too well to be fooled. "The additional frontier," he said, "would be quite short." And it would be in the mountains, capable of being held "with quite a small force."

Chamberlain tried another approach. Surely Beck could not afford to treat the Rumanian pledge lightly? German-Polish relations were themselves so bad. Was Danzig not a cause of German-Polish friction? Beck lied effectively. Not only had Germany "never contested" Polish rights in Danzig, he said, but she had "recently confirmed them." It was doubtful whether Germany would "risk a conflict" with Poland over "local matters" of this kind. The Danzig question was "not in itself a grave one."

Beck "did not propose to trouble" Chamberlain with a detailed analysis of the Danzig problem. Had he done so he could have explained that a week earlier Ribbentrop had demanded Danzig, a road across the Polish Corridor, and Polish adherence to the anti-Comintern pact. Lipski, the Polish Ambassador in Berlin, reported how Ribbentrop had "maintained an appearance of politeness, but at bottom his manner was violent." Lubienski, Beck's *Chef de Cabinet*, considered it possible that the Germans might send an *ultimatum* demanding Danzig's incorporation in Germany.[51] Beck told none of this to Chamberlain. The second meeting ended. Britain was ignorant of the true state of Polish-German relations. Beck was free from any Russian or Rumanian commitment. Only one more meeting remained.

From the British point of view the third meeting was a failure. Chamberlain told Beck that the Anglo-Polish conversations were "tending towards a different result" from what was expected. "What was hoped for," he explained to Beck, was an arrangement by which "a number of states" would "band themselves round Great Britain, France and Poland." Instead they were producing a "bilateral Anglo-Polish agreement." Beck wanted no more than this. He said it was "against the tradition" of Polish policy to "express definite opinions about third countries without directly consulting them." Britain must accept a bilateral agreement, or nothing. The latter course was impossible. Chamberlain could not tell the public that the pledge to Poland of March 31 was to be revoked. The public demanded firmness. Chamberlain could not destroy the mood of Prague.

Chamberlain refused to give up easily, and tried a new method to frighten Beck. Would Beck not agree that Germany had aggressive plans? Beck would not. He doubted whether there was "any serious danger" of German aggression. Chamberlain suggested that Poland was militarily weak, as a result of Germany having taken the Czech munition factories. Beck informed him — it was a conscious lie — that Poland was "not at all" dependent on Czech munitions. She was "largely self-supporting." Poland, Beck claimed, was an exporter of guns. Chamberlain might like to know that the Poles "even supplied guns to Great Britain." That was enough for Chamberlain. Ill-prepared for such arguments, unused to so rigorous an opponent (even Hitler was not so consistent), he gave way. Britain agreed to change the "temporary unilateral assurance" to Poland into a "permanent and reciprocal agreement." The agreement would cover "mutual assistance in the event of any threat, direct or indirect, to the independence of either."

Chamberlain had wanted a Rumanian guarantee "to be part of the formal agreement." This was abandoned. Later Poland and Rumania agreed to ignore British pressure altogether. On April 17, Beck and Gafencu decided that no "immediate action" was needed to reach agreement on what to do if Germany attacked. It would be "undesirable," they said, to make any open declaration of what they intended.[52] No declaration was made.

The Anglo-Polish agreement surprised no one more than the British themselves. Duff Cooper realized its full implications when he wrote, "never before in our history have we left in the hands of one of the smaller powers the decision whether or not Great Britain goes to war." [53] The agreement gave Beck the power to decide whether a particular German move was aggressive or not. Should he decide that it was, Britain would have to support him and join in war against Germany. Gafencu saw the extent of Britain's commitment: Poland was the least "moral" country Britain could have chosen to defend; the sternest critic of collective security. She had annexed Russian territory in 1921 and Czech territory in 1938; she persecuted minorities; she imprisoned political opponents of the régime. Gafencu knew the Poles. The English puzzled him more. How could they, who had been till then so prudent, have "touched upon the most dangerous spot in the world." They were allied, "not to peace, but to continental war." [54] The British, Daladier told his Cabinet, were prepared to consider their frontier, as not the Rhine, but the Vistula.[55] At the mouth of the Vistula was Danzig.

The position of Danzig was laid down by the Treaty of Versailles.

Article 100 "Germany renounces . . . all rights and titles over Danzig.

Article 102 Danzig is "under the protection of the League of Nations."

Article 103 Danzig's constitution "shall be placed under the guarantee of the League of Nations."

Article 104 The Treaty ensures (1) the inclusion of the Free City "within the Polish customs frontier." (2) Poland to have "without any restriction the free use and service of all waterways, docks, basins, wharves . . . necessary for Polish imports and exports." (3) Poland to administer Danzig's railway system in relation to external traffic.

Article 105   "On the coming into force of the present Treaty German nationals ordinarily resident in the territory . . . will, *ipso facto*, lose their German nationality in order to become nationals of the Free City of Danzig."

Article 106   "German nationals over the age of eighteen ordinarily resident in the territory . . . will have the right to opt for German nationality . . . All persons who exercise the right of option must, during the ensuing twelve months, transfer their place of residence to Germany."

CHAPTER 16

Danzig Dilemma

DESPITE Beck's assurance, Danzig became the focal point of European tensions during the summer. On April 14, Halifax heard a rumor that the German Government planned the return of Danzig to Germany on Hitler's birthday six days later.[1] The Anglo-Polish Declaration of March 31, while committing Britain to support Poland, gave no clue as to Polish policy. Beck's visit had been equally uninformative. The Foreign Office wanted to know how Poland would react if the Germans "staged an internal revolt" in Danzig and then tried to occupy the city. Halifax could not tell them. He asked Kennard to clarify the situation which he himself found "by no means clear."[2] Halifax realized that Beck's protestations that all was well had been false. At the same time he had no profound objection to the German city returning to its compatriots. He suggested that if the Poles were "prepared to treat" with Germany, "would it not be well . . . to cut the ground from under the feet of the German Government by showing their disposition to negotiate?"[3] Beck replied that he "did not feel that it was opportune" for Poland to offer to negotiate with the Germans.[4] Germany must state her claims. The nation that wanted to alter the *status quo* must take the initiative.

The new appeasement had begun. Britain had promised to defend a city for whose status she had little concern. Danzig's return to Germany would cause little alarm. For four months the appeasers struggled in an unequal battle. They pressed Beck to negotiate with Germany over Danzig, and assumed that it would ultimately return to Germany. He, cleverer if not wiser than they, refused to consider a change in the city's status. It must remain a Free City. To give it to Germany, no matter under what safeguards, would invite further German claims: to the Corridor, to Silesia, to the Poznan province. The Germans would interpret Danzig's return as a sign of weakness. Beck clung to the creation of Versailles. The Germans called the Treaty a cruel imposition. The British, with less justification than the circumstances warranted, took the German view. While prepared to defend the city by declarations alone, they were unwilling to consider the possibility of an Anglo-German war arising out of their commitments.

Given their promise to Poland, the British were unable to declare outright that they would consider it reasonable if Danzig returned to Germany. Instead, they hinted here and there at the need for Polish-German negotiations. The Poles resented such hints. Strang visited Warsaw at the beginning of June. He was asked by Kennard to tell Halifax that the Polish Government "are becoming a little restive under our repeated questions to them about their attitude towards various hypothetical developments in Danzig." Britain had failed to follow up what appeared to be a declaration of joint purpose and solidarity by deeds to match the words.

"If we are not careful," said Strang, "they may come to think that we have cold feet, and that we are trying to wriggle out of our obligation." Lubienski spoke to him "quite frankly." Poland was "a little uneasy" at Britain's repeated suggestions that she must consider a compromise solution for Danzig. He explained to Strang that the Germans would construe such suggestions as a sign of British weakness. Britain's enthusiasm for negotiations "tended to create an element of doubt as to the fixity of our purpose." Poland could not forget Munich. Lubienski reminded Strang that Munich was "not a good precedent." [5] Strang reported these doubts to London.

Towards the end of June, another rumor suggested that a German coup in Danzig was about to take place. Abetz, a member of Ribbentrop's Bureau, was in Paris, telephoning to various people "announcing a coup in Danzig for the weekend." [6] The Germans, like the Poles, doubted whether Britain would fight if Danzig were annexed. Weizsäcker told Coulondre on June 30, that "we know you would fight [i.e. France], but we are not sure about England." [7] Halifax appeared calm in the face of impending German action. Daladier was alarmed. He told Phipps that "only a declaration couched in very energetic and precise terms by France and Great Britain will stop the Danzig coup." Daladier wanted an announcement that night. The Polish Ambassador in Paris was asked to telephone news of French determination to Warsaw. "If the Germans tap the wire, so much the better." [8] But Anglo-French solidarity was essential: Daladier had no doubt of that. Lubienski told Clifford Norton, Chargé d'Affaires in Warsaw while Kennard was on a month's leave, that if Britain and France remained "unshaken" a Danzig coup would be averted. [9]

This advice reached the Foreign Office at the same moment as a dispatch from the Consul-General in Danzig, Gerald Shepherd. He reported that the Germans in Danzig were saying Britain and France "will leave Poland in the lurch by not fighting on account of Danzig." Shepherd urged firmness. He deprecated any suggestion that Danzig should be returned to Germany. If this happened, he said, it would "unquestionably be followed by . . . absorption of most, if not all, of the remainder of Poland." [10] Britain ought not to panic. Large scale military operations could not be begun before August. But knowledge that such operations might take place should strengthen Britain in her resolve to oppose them. [11] As a Consul-General, Shepherd should only have reported what he saw, not commented upon it. His determination to say what ought to be said led to his immediate recall. Halifax was unwilling to contemplate a war for Danzig. He did not want to be told that Britain was obliged in such a matter. Throughout the summer, the British press played down the importance of Danzig. Shepherd's recall passed unnoticed: he was replaced by a man of the same surname — F. M. Shepherd.

The French made their declaration. Bonnet sent it to Ribbentrop on July 1. It was forthright and unequivocal.

Any action, whatever its form, which would tend to modify the *status quo* in Danzig, and so provoke armed resistance by Poland, would bring the Franco-Polish agreement into play and oblige France to give immediate assistance to Poland.

Bonnet asked Halifax to see the German Ambassador "at an early date" and to "speak to him more or less in the same general sense." [12] Halifax refused. He issued no similar declaration. The French, having decided to act, had to act alone.

Nevile Henderson firmly opposed a strong stand over Danzig, such as the French had taken. He regarded German activity in the Free City as justifiable. Military preparations, he said, were defensive as well as offensive. Some Germans, he told Halifax, "seriously believed in the possibility of a Polish coup in Danzig." It was the Poles who would force the issue. Henderson did not disagree with his informants.[13] He thought their views were common in Germany. Yet even in Germany men realized that Poland would not be so rash as to provoke war. Göring had told a number of Englishmen that "he was convinced" that Poland would "do nothing." [14]

Henderson opposed any British commitment to Poland. He told Cadogan in June: "Heaven knows what Poland is going to cost us." He thought that the Poles should "talk a little less" about their bravery, and think "a little more" about the "realities" of their geographic position.[15] If Danzig announced its re-attachment to Germany "I find it hard to believe that it would be in Poland's real interests to commence the forcible occupation of that city." [16] Beck, wrote Henderson, was a "prisoner of his Polish chauvinists." Some form of outside pressure would help the Poles to negotiate over Danzig. Henderson thought the Pope might be asked to put pressure on Warsaw, "behind the scenes." [17]

Henderson distrusted the Poles, and feared provocative action

on their part. Clifford Norton thought these fears entirely un-
justified, and tried to give a more pro-Polish turn to policy
throughout the summer. In frequent letters to Cadogan and
Sargent he put the case for greater British trust in Beck. He
knew that Beck's reputation was one of trickery and deception.
Those diplomats who did not hate Beck despised him. In his
shifty manners and circumspect statements they thought they
recognized a villain.

Norton thought otherwise. His former chief, Vansittart, wrote
of Beck: "I had some liking for Beck despite his faults. He just
meant to keep both his neighbours out of his country." [18] Norton agreed, and was on friendly enough terms with Beck to wine
and dine with him unofficially and to meet him during hunting
trips in the east of Poland. Norton told Halifax that Beck and
Field-Marshal Smigly-Rydz were "extremely prudent and moderate men." Norton knew that Halifax feared a Polish move into
Danzig. Henderson encouraged Halifax to believe that such "a
sudden decision" would be made. Norton knew this was unlikely. "They are not going to be easily provoked into minor
follies," he wrote.[19]

Norton's conviction found few supporters in London. Henderson's insistence that the British guarantee gave Poland an
excuse to act wildly was listened to and accepted. Henderson
told Cadogan that Britain had "led [Poland] far up the garden
path" by her promises.[20] Norton described such a view as "rub-
bish." [21] He told Cadogan that Beck and Smigly-Rydz had both
"reached the same conclusion, i.e. not to adopt a forward military policy regarding Danzig." It was stupid of Britain to show
herself suspicious of Polish intentions. "The Poles feel that they
are really our allies, and we shall get the best out of them by
treating them as if we felt it too." Norton disliked the way in
which Henderson wrote of the Poles as rash men, about to break
the bounds of level-headedness. Norton knew that Britain's own
performance in the past was not likely to win the trust of others.
"May I whisper to you that from the Polish point of view our

record in protecting victims of aggression has not recently been impressive. We, too, have a record to live down." [22]

Poland and Britain had both acted unwisely during the Czech crisis; the one too aggressive, the other too weak. But mutual recrimination was useless. It could only encourage the Germans. Norton insisted that "Polish and British mutual and moral support should be used *everywhere and in every problem* to sap the morale of the aggressors." [23] Halifax and Chamberlain seemed to listen. A statement was drawn up which Chamberlain proposed to read in the Commons. It said that a coup in Danzig "would involve a menace to Poland's independence which we have undertaken to defend." [24] There was, however, a hint of future negotiations, which "ought to be possible . . . as the atmosphere cools." [25]

Norton showed Beck the proposed statement. Beck was afraid this suggestion would be used by Germany as an excuse "for spreading the idea that there were doubts and hesitations in Great Britain." [26] Norton knew that Beck himself doubted British resolve. He wanted Halifax to allow Beck to alter the statement if he thought it necessary. This would enable him to "retain the fullest confidence in our collaboration." [27] Halifax agreed. Beck asked Halifax to omit the compromising phrase in which he said that the Polish Government "would approach such conversations [with Germany] objectively but with goodwill." [28] The phrase was omitted when Chamberlain spoke in the Commons on July 10. But the cutting away of compromising phrases involved no change in British policy. Norton's energy and skill, not Halifax's wisdom, prevented a finger from being pulled out of the dike wall.*

Chamberlain had spoken firmly. But appeasement continued. It was not without reason that people in Warsaw said to each

* Norton was supported in Warsaw by Frank Savery, the Consul-General. Savery had been in Poland since 1919, and fully appreciated Polish fears. As Raczynski wrote to the authors: "Savery was certainly for years the trusted adviser on Poland of British Ambassadors in Warsaw . . . he was always discreet and friendly. He certainly understood our problems."

other in the streets: "Remember Munich." Norton told Halifax that "the only way we shall defeat this propaganda and diminish the risk of hanging separately seems to me to be by hanging together." He recognized the "very helpful modifications" that had been made in Chamberlain's speech. But he warned Cadogan that Anglo-Polish collaboration "is bound to be a slow growth." [29] Norton sought to encourage such collaboration, others to destroy it. The strength of such men was shown during the Anglo-Polish financial negotiations begun in June. It was unfortunate for the Poles that the Englishman with whom they had primarily to deal was Sir Frederick Leith-Ross.

Poland wanted a cash loan. But Britain proved slow in recognizing her need. The negotiations dragged on slowly, with little understanding on the British side, and growing resentment on the Polish side. The Polish financial commission, led by Colonel Adam Koc,* arrived in London on June 14. Two weeks later Raczynski told Halifax that he was "worried about the lack of progress." So was Norton.

Only one meeting had been held between Koc and Leith-Ross in the previous ten days, and that a "purely nominal" one. The British had promised a "general decision on principle" a week earlier. None had been reached. Raczynski feared "that Poland might not after all be granted the assistance necessary for perfecting her defences." [30] The fear was justified by events. On July 1, the Treasury offered Poland eight million pounds. It was a much smaller sum than Poland wanted. It was offered only on certain stringent conditions, which Koc felt unable to accept. He left London for Warsaw "in a state of depression and alarm." The British conditions had given him the impression that Britain "did not regard the question as one of any great urgency." Raczynski told Halifax that considering "the present

---

* Koc was a leading member of the Polish ruling class, and Head of the Security Services under Pilsudski. An *éminence grise* during the Colonel's government, he was in London when war broke out, and emigrated to New York. He is Major Pyc in J. Bandrowski's novel, *General Barcz*, an allegorical story about Pilsudski.

times of anxiety" the offer was "indeed, a modest one." Koc
would have a difficult time in Warsaw "trying to explain why so
little had been granted and why so much time had been required
to offer so modest a sum." [31]

Norton was "rather disturbed" when he read that the main
condition imposed upon Poland *before* a loan could be given
was the "fundamental readjustment of Polish economic and
financial conditions" involving a devaluation of the zloty. He
thought that if the conditions were made public, it would "have
the worst possible effect" on Anglo-Polish co-operation. It was
just such an "over-bearing insistence on all manner of conditions" that had alienated Poland from France. The Poles would
regard the devaluation demand as nothing but interference. It
might "easily provoke a collapse in public morale." [32]

Norton was no economist. The powers of the Treasury were
great for this very reason. Economics was a sphere in which diplomats could hardly be experts. But Norton refused to be bullied
by Leith-Ross's expertise. Although the Treasury could produce
"good arguments" in support of the conditions it was imposing
on Poland, Norton knew "that is not the way the Poles see
things." It would be absolutely wrong, he told Sargent on July 5,
"to force our view through by using Poland's dire necessity as an
argument." Polish sensitivity, he insisted, should not be ignored.[33]

Halifax rallied for a while to Norton's view. General Sir Edmund Ironside was sent to Warsaw as a special envoy to enquire
into how Britain and Poland could best co-operate. He spent
four days in Poland, and assured the Polish Government of
Britain's "absolute determination" to fulfill the terms of the
British guarantee. But words were not enough. Beck and Smigly-
Rydz "spoke very strongly" about the financial impasse.[34] Ironside was unable to convince them that Britain had realized the
"urgent necessity" of financial collaboration.[35] He could only
tell them he was personally opposed to the attitude adopted by
the Treasury. To emphasize this, he telephoned London "a

number of times" from Warsaw to protest about the manner in which the negotiations were taking place.[36]

After two weeks of discussion the Poles decided, with "great reluctance," that they could not accept the British terms.[37] The Treasury moved slowly and unwillingly. Leith-Ross agreed that Koc and Hudson should negotiate an Anglo-Polish coal agreement. But the discussion had not even started when war broke out.[38] The other financial problems dragged on dismally. Raczynski was "distressed to the point of incoherence" by Leith-Ross's unwillingness to abandon the stern conditions upon which he insisted.[39] Norton knew there was "no time to lose" if Poland was to be given money in time to use it effectively. He considered the Treasury were foolish in thinking that the Poles would mis-spend the loan, and told Halifax that it was "definitely" for military purposes. If it were withheld on account of impossible conditions, it would seriously affect Poland's military potential.[40]

Koc asked for a loan that would be convertible into dollars to enable Poland to buy arms from America. Simon told him that "this would seriously affect our own financial position." The British Government "could not agree."[41] The loan was refused. The refusal and the excuse were both shabby, some said despicable. While Simon produced economic vetoes on Poland, Treasury officials were offering the Germans widespread economic advantages in return for an Anglo-German non-aggression pact.[42] Orme Sargent saw that it was madness for the Poles to be "roughly handled"[43] while the Germans were treated in so privileged a way. Yet this was done, and done on purpose. Anglo-German economic co-operation was a dream the appeasers were loath to abandon. Poland's needs could not be allowed to stand in the way of its fulfillment. Wohltat was told that, given a non-aggression pact and close Anglo-German economic co-operation, the question of Danzig would play a "minor part" in British policy. Wilson even suggested that given such co-operation between Britain and Germany, the

Anglo-Polish pact would become "superfluous." This information was not passed to Warsaw. Norton never knew of it.

Danzig was a German city organized by a local German leader. It was legislated for by a German senate and separated from East Prussia by a river. The abuse cried out for remedy. The appeasers saw the return of Danzig to Germany as a necessary revision of the Versailles Treaty. It would ensure justice even at an hour when Germany's own record was far from conducive to talk of fair dealing. But the public were anxious to stand by Poland. For many the betrayal of Czechoslovakia had been an act of shame whose repetition would be intolerable. Chamberlain was worried about the growing public firmness. He "exhorted" his Cabinet to be "as economical as possible in their references to foreign affairs." [44] He looked to negotiations, not to firm commitments, for the path to peace. On July 13, he told Daladier that he would like to see an Italian-French *rapprochement*. Mussolini's disposition to exercise a restraining influence over Danzig would help Britain. "Mussolini," said Chamberlain, "is the one man who can influence Hitler to keep the peace." [45] He was also the man who could pass on to Hitler any British proposals for negotiations between Poland and Germany, and who could indicate to Hitler that Britain was willing to concede him Danzig.

Henderson spent most of July urging such concession. Nothing would convince him, he told Halifax, that "the Poles are not supremely foolish, if they fail to make the best bargain now with Hitler himself that they can." If Danzig were left as a "running sore" the Poles would lose the Corridor itself. "It should not really be difficult to find an equitable solution, whereby every economic and strategic necessity would be reserved to Poland, while permitting the re-inclusion of the city as a Free City in East Prussia." Henderson hoped Ironside would be instructed "to preach hard common-sense" to the Polish leaders. "Otherwise," warned Henderson, "Poland will miss the tide." Only by putting Danzig "back into its proper perspective," would there be peace. For Henderson that perspective was a Prussian one. Poland, by refusing to recognize this, and by refusing to consider Danzig's return to Germany, would be left on the beach. Henderson told Halifax: "I just hate to think of the many tides which have been missed during the past twenty years, simply from refusing to look facts in the face." [46]

The facts as Henderson saw them were not facts for everyone. Frank Roberts, in a Foreign Office memorandum, considered British firmness before July may well have influenced Hitler to refrain from violence against the Poles. A German official had said that a crisis might be avoided over Danzig "provided nothing shook Herr Hitler's new belief that the Western Powers meant business." [47] Roberts agreed. But Halifax ignored the logic of his argument, and began to consider how he could push the Poles into negotiations over Danzig.

Halifax refused to believe that Hitler had designs beyond Danzig. On July 21, he asked both Burckhardt and Beck to consider the possibility of "early and private discussions" that would promote a "good atmosphere for negotiations on concrete questions." [48] If the Danzig question could be "developed favourably" this would open the door to "other things." [49] Halifax failed to explain what these "other things" were. Wilson was less reticent. He had explained to Wohltat three days earlier that Britain and Germany could work together to evolve a joint trade policy, and to promote a condominium in Africa in which Germany would share. Here were some "other things" that could only be accomplished once Europe had achieved a more permanent state of political calm than she had that summer. If Poland were to concede Danzig, calm would return, and the appeasers' plans for an Anglo-German *rapprochement* would flourish.

Henderson was afraid that the Poles would anger the Germans, and "force" Germany into an anti-Polish move. There had been "quite a deal of Polish provocation," he wrote on July 25. Someone in the Foreign Office wrote "No" in the margin of Henderson's remark.[50] But Henderson had made up his mind. He described Hitler as the most "favourably disposed German" the Poles would ever be able to deal with; he was "Austrian and not a Prussian," and Poland held no attraction for him.[51] If he were confronted with Polish "intimidation" he might, of course, be forced to choose between loss of prestige and war. He might well choose war. What was important was for Britain to put pressure on Poland, both in the direction of "moderation," and of direct negotiations with Germany over Danzig.[52] The Foreign Office disliked Henderson's continual harping on Polish rashness. Sargent told Adrian Holman, in the Berlin Embassy, that the Poles would *not* provoke the Germans over Danzig.[53] Norton's words had been heeded.

Throughout July Norton sent strongly worded dispatches criticizing what Henderson said. He doubted "whether the present moment was a good one" for negotiations to be begun. The anti-German front was not yet very strong. Before negotiations began its strength should be "visible and apparent not only to its partners, but also to its opponents." Norton realized that negotiations would serve no useful purpose. "Even if Danzig were removed from the front of the stage . . . there is little basis for hopes that such a settlement would introduce the millennium." [54] Henderson commented that such speculations were "rather hypothetical." [55] But Norton, like Gerald Shepherd, saw the futility of piecemeal concessions. He considered the rulers of Germany to be "imbued with the desire to dominate all Eastern Europe." For as long as such a desire lasted "no difficulties . . . should be allowed to shake the firmness of the Anglo-Polish alliance." [56]

Norton thought it would be disastrous to push Poland into discussions over Danzig. He knew Henderson was wrong to write that Hitler "may consider it more prudent, having achieved so much, not to start a war for what remains." [57] Norton said

Germany would use any Polish-German discussions to weaken Anglo-Polish co-operation. That same day, July 26, Henderson told Halifax that Danzig ought to be declared a "*German* Free City and not one under a façade of League of Nations *cum* Polish control." Until this was done, and Poland persuaded that it ought to be done, "there will be no real peace" for Eastern Europe.[58]

Norton was furious at the cavalier way in which Henderson treated the Anglo-Polish commitment. But Norton's views were challenged in London. Halifax attempted to by-pass him. Norton was criticized for being pro-Polish. He replied in a letter to Orme Sargent:

Of course I am affected by the fact that I live here and that I am only in partial possession of the facts, but I start from the broad hypothesis that a strong Poland during the next few months is a major British interest and that even if the Poles behave in a proud and childish manner, it is our duty as a senior partner to guide them on the lines of discretion. In fact, as in many other cases, it is our duty from our greater wisdom to show tolerance and understanding, and help them to help themselves. That object has definitely not been achieved. It cannot be right that the major object of His Majesty's Government in a political and military sense should be frustrated by technical and theoretical difficulties put in such a way as to cause consternation and dismay amongst our allies, and "*Schadenfreude*" among our enemies, out of all proportion to the sum involved. It is not a question of whether the Poles have been stupid or not, but that our diplomacy (save the mark!) has produced a result contrary to what I conceive to be a major British interest, namely a calm and confident Poland, strong in itself and its faith in its allies.[59]

The appeasers always asked; "What else could Chamberlain have done?" In Norton's rhetorical phrases lay an adequate answer.

CHAPTER 17

Pledges to Poland

KENNARD returned to Warsaw from leave on July 30, earlier than he had intended to on account of the growing crisis. He disliked the way in which the loan had been burdened by conditions "of a rather humiliating description." [1] He hoped that a cash credit loan would still be possible, despite the Treasury's insistence that only an export credit loan could be granted.

Kennard agreed with Norton that the Polish Government was "definitely not out to provoke a war." [2] But Henderson was convinced that the Poles were about to "humiliate" Germany. He asked Halifax to put pressure on Beck to prevent a challenge to Hitler's pride.[3] Hitler would "climb down" if he were given half a chance, but the Poles would not let him. Henderson told Halifax on August 8, that the Poles would "force an issue" that year. By making use of Britain's pledge they would gain unfair advantage over Germany.[4] Kennard disagreed outright. He thought the Polish Government were "fully alive" to the need for avoiding "unduly energetic language" that might make the situation "more tense." [5] Kennard reported that Smigly-Rydz, in a recent speech, had been "not unduly provocative." The Danzig Senate had tried to stop the Polish Customs inspection guaranteed to Poland at Versailles. The Poles had forestalled the move in a "firm but studiously moderate" manner.[6] Kennard wrote: "I think these people are being prudent." [7] Halifax agreed. He told the British Consul in Danzig: "I am convinced that attitude of Polish Government will continue to be moderate if no provocation is offered." [8] Henderson feared Polish threats that might anger Germany. Halifax learned on August 11, of German threats that were far more extreme than any the Poles could ever contemplate. Hitler had spoken to Burckhardt, who was known to be extremely anti-Polish. Burckhardt thought Hitler's "boasting" was due to "fear." It was boasting of a peculiar sort. "If the slightest incident happened now, I shall crush the Poles without warning in such a way that no trace of Poland can be found afterwards. I shall strike with the full force of a mechanised army, of which the Poles have no conception." [9]

Burckhardt was not alarmed. He insisted that Hitler had not yet made up his mind to "liquidate" Poland even though he had threatened to do so. Burckhardt told Halifax that Hitler could still be satisfied and war avoided. The appeasers should be bold. It was Hitler who was afraid. To Burckhardt he had "seemed nervous, pathetic and almost shaken at times." He had spoken of his willingness to discuss matters with an Englishman.

Hitler told Burckhardt that language was the only obstacle in the way of direct conversations between him and a prominent Englishman. Hitler wanted such conversations. In a passage "not communicated to the French" by the British Foreign Office, Hitler had said, "I had a hard and difficult youth, and was not able to learn languages." He wanted to meet an Englishman who spoke fluent German. "I have great sympathy for another man, Lord Halifax. They have said much ill of him to me since, but my first sentiment prevails. I thought he was a man who saw things on a big scale and desired a peaceful solution. I hope one day to see him again." Hitler's ramblings were not in vain. Halifax, flattered perhaps by Hitler's mention, began "considering the suggestion" of sending an Englishman to talk with Hitler.[10] On August 15, Kennard was instructed to tell Beck that Poland should "make it plain" to Germany that Poland was "at all times ready to examine the possibility of negotiations over Danzig." [11] Henderson approved of Halifax's instructions. On August 16, in a letter to Strang, he described Hitler as "the most moderate as far as Danzig and the Corridor were concerned." [12]

Not everyone thought likewise. Two days earlier Ciano had gone to the seaside with the Polish Ambassador and had spoken to him "in vague terms" about the need for moderation. But Ciano knew that if Hitler meant to destroy Poland such advice was futile. The Italian Counsellor at Warsaw had told him that Poland would fight to the last man. The churches were filled with people praying and singing a hymn, "O God, help us to save our country." Ciano knew that neither negotiations such as the British favored, nor prayers, were of any use. "These people will be massacred by German steel tomorrow. They are innocent. My heart is with them!" [13]

In Moscow on August 15, the Anglo-French military talks with Russia had reached a "fundamental problem." The pact Russia envisaged included a promise that in the event of a German attack Russian troops should be allowed to cross Polish territory. Strategically it was a reasonable request. Only by an immediate incursion into Polish territory could Russian troops make the necessary contact with the German army. But the Poles were unwilling to allow a single Russian soldier to set foot on their territory, even if the Germans had already moved in the west. The danger from the east was greater. Russia was the enemy of centuries. The Poles thought that any Russian advance would lead to loss of territory. Much of the east of Poland had been taken from Russia by force in 1921. It was only to be expected that Russia would try to reverse the harsh terms of the treaty of Riga, which had concluded the Russo-Polish war.

France would have preferred a Franco-Soviet to a Franco-Polish pact, and Bonnet demanded Beck's "immediate" consent to the Russian terms. It was, he said, "unthinkable" that the Poles should refuse.[14] Beck did refuse. He told Kennard that "if Poland agreed this would lead to an immediate declaration of war on the part of Germany." [15] Germany would regard any Russo-Polish agreement as a direct and immediate threat. But Beck's fear of Russia was greater than his fear of Germany.

As Kennard told Halifax, Beck was "unable to shake his innate mistrust of Russian intrigue." [16]

Bonnet still hoped to change Beck's firmness. He thought it

would be possible to refuse to sign an Anglo-Polish Treaty until Poland agreed to the passage of Soviet troops. The British, unwilling to be committed to a Soviet alliance, would not put undue pressure on Poland. They asked Beck to agree, but it was a half-hearted request. They knew Beck was determined to prevent "admission of Soviet troops into Poland." [17] They knew why Poland feared Russia. On August 20, Kennard asked Halifax to remember:

> It is not twenty years since Russian armies were at the gates of Warsaw . . . although Russia has for centuries been a natural enemy, it must be admitted that the Polish Government are not guided solely by prejudice, and have strong internal political reasons for their attitude . . . Poles of all classes are obsessed with fear of communism [and] no Pole would ever expect to recover any territory occupied by Soviet troops.[18]

Halifax urged the Poles to change their minds, though less firmly than Bonnet had requested. Kennard saw no hope of such a change[19] and described Beck on August 21 as "absolutely obdurate." [20] The obduracy had its effect. The Polish refusal to allow Soviet troops to enter Poland destroyed any chance of Anglo-French agreement with Russia. Denied a democratic ally, Stalin accepted a totalitarian one. Halifax learned of the Russo-German non-aggression pact on August 22. Britain had lost an ally for a two-front war. Poland had lost an ally on her eastern front.

The "Nazi-Soviet" pact frightened the British public. The anti-appeasers felt they had won. Now that Poland had been abandoned by the East it was surely incumbent upon the West to honor its obligations without question. The new mood of firmness appeared to be reflected in the Foreign Office. Halifax announced that the Russo-German pact "does not modify the attitude or policy" of Britain towards Poland.[21] Chamberlain spoke in the Commons of Britain's determination to honor her agreement. Even Henderson realized that "we cannot leave Poland in the lurch."[22]

But the appeasers never remained firm for long. The essence of their craft was weakness, vacillation and uncertainty. Beneath the façade of bold words lay thoughts of compromise. Henderson told Halifax, on August 22, that the Poles ought to negotiate *at once* over Danzig. He feared two things. Britain might be too outspoken in her criticism of Germany. Poland might resist British pressure to negotiate.

Above all, Britain must not threaten Germany. "*Anything but intimidation,*" he emphasized.[23] It was not enough to be sympathetic towards Germany. Henderson had explained to Strang on August 16, that the Poles were also far from innocent.

> The ill-treatment of the German minority in Poland must be stopped . . . Warsaw with its civilised and intelligent, not to say astute clique with which one consorts there, is one thing: outside in the country the Poles are an utterly uncivilised lot . . .
> We would not say boo to Beneš last year, till we were on the abyss of war. And we can't say boo to Beck this year.[24]

Halifax was uncertain of how to say "boo." The previous year's show had been performed largely without him. He had not gone to Munich. He did his best and urged Beck to consider "some *démarche* from his side."[25] On August 23, Halifax promised Ciano that Britain would try to create "conditions" in which Polish-German negotiations would be possible. He did not disagree with Ciano when the latter described the Russo-German pact as having "made the position of Poland hopeless."[26]

The Poles did not want to negotiate. Raczynski told Halifax that he was "very sceptical" as to the value of talks while Germany was "still engaged in the technique of the nerve war." Beck was "extremely anxious" for the Anglo-Polish treaty to be signed.[27] Before it was signed, negotiations were out of the question. That very day, August 23, some thirty German divisions were moving towards the Polish frontier. As a result, Smigly-

Rydz had mobilized about two-thirds of the Polish army.[28] There would, however, be no provocation by Poland. Kennard informed Halifax that "strict orders have been given to prevent any provocative action." [29]

As tension mounted, Halifax urged negotiations. He told Lipski to speak to Hitler "tomorrow at the latest." [30] Lipski did in fact see Göring on August 25, but Göring told him that "he no longer had influence to do much in the matter." [31] Hitler was at Berchtesgaden, far from the crisis which the advance of his divisions had created. He must have known that, despite the firmness of their public utterances, the appeasers would be pushing the Poles towards surrender.

Henderson was not alone in urging Polish-German negotiations. Dahlerus, Göring's Swedish friend, hoped to influence Britain to accept the idea of Polish-German discussions. Perhaps it was Hitler who told Dahlerus to attempt to influence British policy. Dahlerus telephoned a businessman friend of his, Spencer, at the Foreign Office and asked whether there was "any chance of selling rubber in London." Spencer understood the reference and replied that although he could not speak for the "purchasers" he could tell Dahlerus "that they were ready to come to any reasonable arrangement." [32]

Who could tell Halifax what *was* reasonable? At 12:45 P.M. on August 25, Henderson again urged Lipski to see Hitler,[33] and ignored the implications of weakness that such a visit would entail. Kennard thought that such a meeting would be madness. At 2 P.M. he telegraphed: "I am extremely doubtful whether [Lipski's visit to Hitler] would really serve any useful purpose. Any such approach would be sure to be construed as a sign of weakness and it might even provoke the very ultimatum we seek to avoid." [34]

Henderson reported at 9:30 P.M. that the Poles were "too suspicious and too afraid of giving appearance of weakening." He told Halifax that Britain should put pressure on Poland to give way.[35] Halifax took Henderson's arguments seriously. He realized that even if Germany should attack Poland, there was no need for Britain to rush automatically into war. That evening he devised a formula which would enable Britain to appear to honor her pledge to Poland without involving her in hostilities with Germany. He suggested that if Germany attacked Poland, Britain should demand that German troops halt "within a fixed time limit." They should then express their "readiness to enter into negotiations." [36] Once again, Henderson had won. A German-Polish war would result in Anglo-German *conversations*.

Beck was unwilling to accept so weak a British commitment. He wanted Britain to support Poland militarily, not to offer negotiations over Poland's mutilated body. He instructed Raczynski to press for the most advantageous terms possible. He would accept nothing less than those of the British declaration of March 31. Raczynski was successful. On August 25, the Anglo-Polish Treaty was signed. Halifax abandoned his formula, which could no longer represent declared policy. Raczynski put his signature to as firm a commitment as could have been devised; one much firmer than British policy since April had suggested would be agreed upon. But the published firmness was in direct contrast to a deeper, more lasting weakness.

The Anglo-Polish Treaty of Mutual Assistance[37] was intended to give Poland an active ally in the event of a German attack. Perhaps, by its very boldness, it would act as a deterrent. Germany could see that Britain was in earnest. The published clauses were models of diplomatic clarity. Article One stated that, "Should one of the contracting parties become engaged in hostilities with a European Power in consequence of aggression by the latter . . . the other contracting party will at once give the contracting party engaged in hostilities all the support and assistance in its power."

It was not aggression alone that would bring the Treaty into operation. Article Two made it clear that the Treaty covered "any action by a European Power which clearly threatened, *directly or indirectly*, the independence of one of the contracting parties."

This promise of support in the event of an indirect threat as well as of a direct attack was indeed far-reaching. But the Treaty did not specify Danzig as coming under its provisions. This was a signal weakness. Germany had for some months been demanding the return of Danzig to Germany. Such a demand was certainly an indirect threat; and some would have said a direct one. Yet the published Treaty contained no word about Danzig. The Germans could only assume that Henderson's prayers had been heard, and that Halifax and Chamberlain had decided to admit the justice of Germany's claim.

Duff Cooper wrote in July:

> Lack of decision is the worst fault from which a policy can suffer. So soon as a decision has been taken no time should be lost in announcing it and in making it plain to the world. It is of the first importance that we should know our own minds; it is of almost equal importance that the world should make no mistake about our intentions.[38]

The British decision had not been "made plain" to the world. Under Polish pressure Halifax had agreed to give as firm a guarantee to Danzig as to Poland itself. But he was unwilling to commit himself openly. The British pledge to defend the *status quo* of Danzig was contained in a *secret* Protocol of the Treaty.[39] There, in secret, the most important commitment was made. Hitler could not know of it, and assumed that Britain would not oppose the return of Danzig to Germany. Beck knew of it, and was able to refuse to discuss the future of Danzig with Germany, knowing that a German move to seize the Free City would be followed by British action in support of Poland. Beck knew that the Secret Protocol was precise and final: "The case contemplated by Article Two of the Agreement is that of the Free City of Danzig." Thus even an indirect threat to Danzig would bring the Treaty into operation.

Beck did not know that the guarantee had not been given spontaneously. Kennard and Norton had always advocated a strong British commitment; perhaps they were at last being listened to. Yet among the plans Halifax had considered was one drawn up by Roger Makins, in which one of the "possible" settlements of the Polish-German conflict was to be: "Poland to accept principle that Free City has the right to determine its political allegiance." [40]

The Anglo-Polish Treaty was signed; hidden weakness seemed unimportant. But Halifax had no intention of allowing the Poles to think that the firmness of words represented any *real* firmness. A few minutes after Halifax and Raczynski had signed the Treaty, Halifax told the Polish Ambassador that although he "recognized how vital to Poland was the position in Danzig," he "could not feel that, if there were ever any opportunity of conversations being held about Danzig, the Polish Government would be right or wise to reject it." Furthermore, he thought that the Polish Government "would make a great mistake if they sought to adopt a position in which discussions of peaceful modifications of the status of Danzig was ruled out." [41]

Raczynski was alarmed. He explained to Halifax that "there was much to be said for maintaining a stiff attitude" to discussions with Germany. The Poles had found "no sign of any desire for compromise from the German side." Halifax disagreed. He told Raczynski that "compared with a year ago" Britain had greatly increased its strength. The difficulty of "conversations pursued from weakness was . . . happily . . . to a great extent modified." [42] Hypocrisy, not honey, was bred in the lion's side.

CHAPTER 18

Coercing the Poles

THE POLES relied implicitly on the British guarantee. The British had other plans. Under the Agreement all other plans would have to be discussed with the Poles. Article Five pledged the two Governments to "exchange complete and speedy information concerning any development which might threaten their independence, and, in particular, concerning any development which threatened to call the said undertaking into operation."

Halifax was unwilling to let Beck know what he was doing. Within a few hours of promising to exchange "complete and speedy" information, the British Government began to consider, and to put into effect, a new policy concerning Danzig, of which the Poles were told nothing. The new policy affected them directly. But in direct contravention of their new agreement the British kept silent.

The plan was this. Halifax would tell Hitler that Britain was prepared to consider negotiations over the future status of Danzig. There was no longer a question of asking the Poles to take the initiative. Hitler would be asked directly to state his demands. If he agreed to do so, the British would then put pressure on Poland to accept the German terms. It was the Czech "crisis" again. By offering Hitler a negotiated solution for Danzig, the British knew that Hitler would realize that they favored the return of Danzig to Germany. The negotiations would doubtless take every claim and criticism into account, but there could be little doubt that they would lead finally to Hitler's demand being met.

Henderson met Hitler on August 25. Their talk gave Henderson a renewed faith in Hitler's assertion that, beyond the return of Danzig, Germany had no further quarrel with Poland.

Hitler told Henderson that "he accepts the British Empire and is willing to pledge himself personally for its continued existence." Such a pledge was conditional, but the conditions were not impossible for Britain to fulfill. Britain would have to satisfy Hitler's colonial demands "which are limited, and can be negotiated by peaceful methods." Hitler would himself take the initiative, and "approach the British Government with an offer." Again, there was a condition. Hitler's offer could not be given then, but only after "the solution of the German-Polish question." And as if to show how quickly such a solution would benefit Britain, Hitler promised that his Imperial pledges and plans would come "immediately after" such a solution. The "German-Polish question" was a troublesome obstacle to closer Anglo-German co-operation. But it was an obstacle easily removed.[1]

Henderson told Halifax that Hitler had spoken "calmly and reasonably." Henderson had been "impressed with his apparent earnestness and sincerity." [2] Hitler had said he was "by nature an artist not a politician, and once the Polish question was settled he would end his life as an artist not a warmonger." [3] Hitler wanted to know the British attitude towards the German-Polish problem. Henderson returned to London to fetch the British answer. What solution of the problem would Britain accept? Would they allow him to have Danzig — and return to his painting?

Hitler did not know that Halifax had signed a pledge guaranteeing Danzig's *status quo*. Halifax himself sought to abandon that pledge, and sought to abandon it without informing the Poles. On August 25, Halifax decided to ask Mussolini to inform Hitler that Britain was willing to put pressure on Poland to negotiate over Danzig. Hitler would understand that this "suggestion" from Mussolini had a source other than Mussolini's own, albeit fertile, imagination.

On August 26, Halifax asked Mussolini to tell Hitler, without revealing that the information came direct from London, that "if the settlement [between Poland and Germany] were confined to Danzig and the Corridor, it did not seem [to Britain] impossible, within reasonable time, to find a solution without war." [4]

Mussolini, anxious to avoid war, agreed to pass on Halifax's message. At the same time, Halifax took the precaution of ensuring that the Poles would not know of Britain's intentions, despite the fact that the Agreement of August 25 pledged Britain to inform Poland of those intentions. At about 11 P.M. on August 25, Halifax informed Kennard: "You will of course understand that no sort of indication may be given [to the Poles] that we are in consultation with Mussolini, nor of the kind of procedure for negotiation that we have been turning over in our minds." [5]

In one respect Mussolini was the ideal go-between for Halifax to have chosen for so subtle a move. Mussolini had no desire to become embroiled in an Anglo-Italian war as a result of a German invasion of Poland. Yet the possibility was always there. Hitler might insist that Mussolini should act as an ally. The British would themselves honor their obligations to Poland. Mussolini had already made it clear to Hitler that he would be an unwilling, and even a dangerous ally. He told the Germans that the Italian artillery had only half the range of its French counterparts in the Alps,[6] and told Hitler, on August 25: "At our meetings war was envisaged for after 1942." [7] The Germans tried to persuade Mussolini that Britain and France would fail to fight if Poland was attacked; but Mussolini expressed his certainty that the British *would* fight. Mussolini would take no chances. On August 26, he sent Hitler a list of raw-material requirements which he wanted at once and *in toto* — a request beyond Germany's economic ability to meet. Yet with it came the ominous comment: "Unless I am certain of receiving these supplies, the sacrifices I should call upon the Italian people to make . . . could well be in vain, and could compromise your cause along with my own." [8]

Mussolini was unwilling to be drawn into a German war. Halifax asked him to pass on a British message intended to avert war altogether. As at Munich, Mussolini would have the double pleasure of being at the center of European diplomatic activity and of being there to prevent war.

As a man seeking to avoid war, Mussolini was an ideal collaborator for Halifax. But as a diplomatist he was much less capable of subtlety and persuasion. Halifax was a master of suggestive diplomatic notes. Mussolini was not. In the very same dispatch in which he passed on to Hitler Halifax's plea for a "solution without war," he also passed on another suggestion which had crossed his mind that even if Hitler *did* invade Poland, a major European war would be avoided. All Germany would have to do was to adopt, after the attack on Poland, "a purely defensive attitude" towards the West. Then "after Poland's overthrow it would be easier to find the right moment [to negotiate]." [9]

Halifax's plan for "a solution without war" had found an incompatible bedfellow in this second scheme for a "limited" war. Mussolini's two schemes were illogical. If he thought Hitler could conquer Poland and still avoid war with Britain and France, why should he suggest a negotiated solution with Danzig as Hitler's only gain? He made the solution without war sound second-rate. Halifax was unaware that the force of his message had been weakened.

On August 25, the British asked Mussolini to consider the idea of neutral observers along the German-Polish frontier.[10] On August 27, they asked him to use his influence to bring about "a lowering of temperature in the frontier area." [11] For his part Mussolini, under pressure from Ciano, stopped telling Hitler that a peaceful solution might be possible *after* a German conquest of Poland. On August 29, he informed him that in his opinion "the British proposals [for German-Polish negotiations over Danzig] contain the prerequisites . . . for reaching a solution favourable to Germany [with which] the rhythm of your splendid achievements will not be disturbed, and you will add a fresh indubitable success to those you have already obtained." [12] The flaw in Mussolini's letter was the flaw in the British case. The only solution without war was the Danzig solution, whereby Danzig would become German. But Hitler could hardly regard the return of Danzig as a "fresh indubitable success." Far more attractive to him was the idea of a victorious war against Poland followed by negotiations in which Germany would absorb and the Western Powers accept the new conquest.

If Hitler believed that the British would not honor their obligations to Poland, he need not take the offer of Danzig seriously. If he accepted it, he could hardly find another excuse for military action against Poland. If he rejected it, he could use the crisis to launch an attack. All that he needed was to convince himself that the Anglo-Polish Agreement was a bluff; a threat of firmness on Britain's part behind which lay the familiar indecisions and weakness. On August 26, he told his generals that he did not shrink "from solving the Eastern questions even at the risk of complications in the West." [13] But the West gave him little reason to think that such "complications" would arise. Hoare was said by a German informant to be of the opinion that if Germany invaded Poland, Britain "can always fulfil the letter of a declaration without going all out." [14] Such a view hardly gave Hitler the impression that he was risking very much in attacking Poland. Certainly he would not have agreed with Kirkpatrick that, as a result of the Anglo-Polish Agreement, "the German Government are wobbling. The signature of the Polish pact has fallen like a bombshell. We should be conciliatory in form; absolutely firm in substance . . . We have an unexpectedly strong hand." [15] Perhaps Kirkpatrick did not know, as Halifax knew, that the terms of the Polish pact were already being twisted by Britain in order to give Germany the advantage.

The British had approached Mussolini without consulting the French beforehand, or even informing them that it had been done. Both Britain and France were under treaty obligations to defend Poland's territorial integrity, and to maintain the status of Danzig. Britain was not alone in looking to Rome for a way out. The French too had been using Mussolini in an attempt to persuade Hitler to accept negotiations over Danzig, with the assumption that Danzig would ultimately become German. On August 25, Daladier, in a talk to the French nation, emphasized that France "was prepared to co-operate in the solution of every difference by means of negotiation." [16] A day later he wrote to Hitler that "today there is nothing that need prevent any longer the pacific solution of the international crisis with honour and dignity for all peoples." [17] The concept of honor was a curious one: Germany was to be satisfied by Danzig, Poland by accepting its loss.

The Germans had been creating incidents along the Polish frontier. Bonnet told the Italian Ambassador in Paris that France was "exerting the strongest influence *on Poland* to refrain from any provocative action against Germany." [18] No one was putting pressure on Hitler to stop frontier incidents. The British had indeed asked Mussolini to do so, but neither Britain nor France did so directly.

In secret Britain was preparing to abandon her pledges of a few days earlier. The French were more openly defeatist. De Monzie, the Minister of Public Works, suggested that "there was now nothing to be done but to allow Germany to have her way." [19] Both powers had specific obligations and both were seeking to avoid them. Yet throughout the crisis that led to war they showed a marked aversion to working together, either by informing each other of their respective moves, or working out joint moves. Whether the policy was to run away or to fight, both were determined to do it alone. A tragic comment on the Anglo-French division was Phipps's report to Halifax on August 26: "M. Bonnet told me in the strictest confidence that the French Government are in touch with Mussolini. I did not reciprocate by revealing that we also were in touch with the Duce." [20]

On August 28, the French Ambassador in Rome, François-

Poncet, told Percy Loraine, the British Ambassador, that France was thinking of making concessions to Italy to persuade her not to fight as Germany's ally, should Germany invade Poland. Among the proposed French concessions was an arrangement over Tunis, possibly the "cession of Jibuti" (the French port on the Gulf of Aden), and "certain of the Suez directorships." François-Poncet had given away secret information — it was surely Loraine's obligation to do the same. Had Britain been considering anything similar? asked the Frenchman. Loraine was discreetly silent. I had, he reported to Halifax "to put on my best pair of skates." [21] He gave François-Poncet no details. But he could hardly deny outright that the British intended to make concessions. Although Halifax had rejected the idea of offering specific pieces of territory to the Italians, he had evolved a formula which would doubtless show the Italians that Britain meant business. "His Majesty's Government would welcome consultations [with Italy in regard to] respective as well as common interests." [22] Thus Franco-Italian and Anglo-Italian interests would flourish, but any Anglo-French interests would be neglected. And Polish interests, as embodied in two solemn treaties, would be allowed to go to the wall.

The British persisted in imagining that there was no German threat to Poland, but only a German claim to Danzig. Yet the threat to Poland was real. Throughout England the sense of an impending German move was growing. Once again "British" policy was created by a handful of men and carried out by those men in utmost secrecy. The public had no idea that behind the strength of public utterances lay so strong a determination to make the Poles surrender. Even if "only" Danzig's status were to change, the "surrender" would be real, involving as it did the withdrawal, in the face of harsh and uncompromising threats, from a treaty obligation. The Treaty had been made as a result of great public pressure. It was a sham Treaty.

Henderson wanted the Poles to agree to negotiate over Danzig. The Poles refused. Such a refusal confirmed his belief that the Poles had shown wisdom only once "in the course of their history" [23]: when they elected Jan Sobieski king in the seventeenth century. The Poles were afraid of making the slightest concession to Germany. It was a fear, wrote Henderson to Halifax, for which "exaggerated prestige and *amour propre*" were responsible.[24] Perhaps it was not *amour propre*, but a shrewd assessment of German policy, that made the Poles afraid of showing the slightest sign of weakness. Henderson urged British pressure on Poland to persuade the Poles to send a diplomat to Berlin, to negotiate with the Germans. The Poles knew their recent history too well. Eastern European statesmen who arrived in Berlin intending to negotiate usually left with an ultimatum. They were then forced to surrender not mere frontier areas, but the very props of national sovereignty. Henderson thought that Hitler would be satisfied if Poland surrendered Danzig. The Poles believed that Hitler had designs on Poland itself, and that concessions over Danzig would encourage him to raise his demands.

Kirkpatrick pointed out the danger of allowing Hitler "to play his old game of securing concrete concessions in return for purely illusory promises." [25] Halifax was not always willing to listen to this view. In June and July he had crossed swords with Shepherd, the British Consul General in Danzig. Halifax had been determined to recall Shepherd as quickly as possible. He had told him to wait in Danzig "until your substitute is acquainted with local conditions. I hope that postponement will not be long." [26] Halifax's hope had been realized then.

It had been easy to remove a troublemaker in July; in August it was impossible. Many diplomats thought as Shepherd had done. When Henderson urged that the Poles go to Berlin to negotiate, Loraine said the move "would savour too much of a capitulation." [27] Kennard regarded such a visit as "too much like Canossa." [28] Whereas Henderson imagined that Hitler might go to war for Danzig were Danzig denied him, Kennard saw more clearly, as Shepherd had done, that "if Hitler decides on war, it is for the sole purpose of destroying Polish independence." [29]

On August 26 and 27, the British Government drafted its reply to Hitler's "offer" of August 25, in which Hitler had said he would "accept the British Empire" after a "solution" of the Danzig problem. Hitler's most specific demand had been that "the problem of Danzig and the Corridor must be solved." There was no indication of the type of solution Hitler had in mind. The British reply took a long time to complete. Wilson and Butler wrote the first draft on August 25, suggesting Polish concessions. Chamberlain worked on it that night. The Cabinet met to discuss it at 6:30 P.M. on August 26. Hore-Belisha wrote:

> Nevile Henderson present. I thought the draft prepared was fulsome, obsequious and deferential. I urged that our only effective reply was to show strength and determination, that in no circumstances we should give the impression that we would weaken in our undertaking to Poland. Kingsley Wood supported me.

> PM did not take our suggestions in any unfriendly spirit. Having been up most of the [previous] night drafting reply, he perhaps did not see it as objectively as those of us who came to it with a fresh mind.[30]

The reply to Hitler was not settled that evening. On August 27, it was still being discussed. The Cabinet met at 10:30 A.M. for an hour and a half. At lunch Henderson, Simon and Hore-Belisha went through the new draft. Hore-Belisha noted: "My object was to stiffen the reply." He had wanted to "clear the draft of any suggestion that we are qualifying our guarantee to the Poles or bringing pressure to bear on them, and this attitude should be rigorously maintained." [31]

That afternoon Dahlerus flew to London from Berlin and told Chamberlain, Halifax, Wilson and Cadogan that Hitler would ask for the return of Danzig and the Corridor. This was the first intimation the British had had of the nature of German demands. Chamberlain told him that "the maximum the

Poles would concede would be Danzig." [32] This was untrue. It was a statement of intention of which he had no indication from the Poles. It went directly contrary to the Anglo-Polish Treaty. Although Chamberlain considered that "the Poles would fight rather than surrender the Corridor," it seemed that the Poles were *expected* to surrender Danzig. Halifax "impressed" on Dahlerus the need for "direct discussions" between Germany and Poland. Now the British Government "knew" that Danzig was Hitler's aim, they could bring pressure to bear on Poland for the Free City's surrender.

Chamberlain and Halifax knew what Hitler wanted. They had no desire to deprive him of Danzig. Dahlerus was told to pass back such thoughts to Berlin, not as the final British answer to Hitler's offer, "but rather to prepare the way for the main communication." [33] No British reply would be sent to Hitler until Dahlerus had returned to Germany, and informed Hitler of the British position. The British hoped that Dahlerus would pass back to them the actual reply that Hitler would like to receive. Dahlerus returned to Berlin that evening. He saw Göring, but was unable to see Hitler, as "Hitler too tired." [34] Göring and Hitler discussed the matter by telephone, and Göring gave Dahlerus Hitler's reply. At 2 o'clock on the morning of August 28, Dahlerus passed on Göring's message to Ogilvie Forbes at the British Embassy in Berlin. Dahlerus continued to telephone the British Embassy during the morning of August 28, to pass on further items of interest which emerged while he talked to Göring. According to Dahlerus Hitler had said: "Great Britain must persuade Poland to negotiate with Germany immediately and it is most desirable that in reply to be brought by Sir N. Henderson this understanding to persuade Poland should be made." [35]

Dahlerus himself thought, not necessarily unprompted, that "if the [British] reply contains a statement that Great Britain has already urged Poland to open direct negotiations with Germany this would be immensely valuable."

Halifax was informed by telephone from Berlin that Dahlerus had summed up Hitler's "temperamental character." Hitler was full of "good-will." He was interested only in "saving face." Britain should not be "cold or governessy." And finally Halifax heard (it was 9:30 A.M.) that "Hitler and Göring liked Henderson." [36]

The Cabinet met at midday. As a result of what some Ministers considered the "defeatism" of the Wilson–Butler draft, a new reply had been prepared by Strang and Malkin. Hore-Belisha was "quite satisfied" with its "much stiffer" terms, and went to lunch with Churchill.[37] After the Cabinet had broken up Cadogan received a telegram from Ogilvie Forbes. Dahlerus had said: "Herr Hitler suspects that the Poles will try to avoid negotiations. Reply should therefore contain a clear statement to the effect that the Poles have been strongly advised *immediately to establish contact* with Germany and negotiate." [38]

At 2 P.M. Halifax, without recalling the Cabinet to discuss Hitler's new suggestion, incorporated that suggestion in his reply. He telegraphed Kennard: "His Majesty's Government earnestly hope that . . . Polish Government will authorize them to inform German Government that Poland is ready *to enter at once into direct discussion* with Germany. Please endeavour to see M. Beck at once and telephone reply." [39]

Halifax had turned German demands into British proposals, consciously and willingly.

Before Kennard could carry out his instructions, which went contrary to all he had been urging during the past months, Dahlerus had telephoned Ogilvie Forbes again, and suggested that "If Poles refused to approach Germans . . . help of Swedish King [should] be invoked. Mr. Wenner-Gren, Swedish chairman of Electrolux, has a yacht which might be used as a meeting place." [40]

But it was not necessary to consider a marine meeting. British pressure on Poland to accept direct negotiations with the Germans had been successful. Five days earlier Halifax had been unwilling to apply pressure himself. Wilson had seen Kennedy, the American Ambassador, who reported to Washington: "The British wanted one thing of us and one thing only, namely that we put pressure on the Poles. They felt that they could not, given their obligations, do anything of this sort but that we could." [41]

Now these obligations had been forgotten, and with success. At 4 P.M., only two hours after Halifax had called for the Poles to accept negotiations, Kennard telegraphed: "Poland is ready to enter at once into direct discussions with Germany." [42]

Henderson returned to Berlin with the British note. On the evening of August 28, fortified with "half a bottle of champagne," [43] he spoke to Hitler. Hitler read the British note. It read: "The next step should be the initiation of direct discussions between the German and Polish Governments." The British "have already received a definite assurance from the Polish Government that they are prepared to enter into discussions." The note contained a number of conditions. The discussions would have to be on a basis of safeguarding "Poland's essential interests" and also "the securing of the settlement by international guarantee." [44] These were the conditions, presumably, that Hore-Belisha had insisted upon being added. But all the strength that had been infused into these proposals was lost by the way Henderson presented them. After Hitler had read the British note Henderson told him,

> from notes which I had made in the conversations with (Chamberlain and Halifax) [that] we in England regarded it as absurd that Britain should be supposed . . . to consider the crushing of Germany as a settled policy . . . Whatever some people might say, the British people sincerely desired an understanding with Germany and no one more so than the Prime Minister.[45]

This revelation drew Ribbentrop to comment that Chamberlain had once told *him* that such an understanding was "his dearest wish." Henderson went on to tell Hitler: "Today the whole British public was behind the Prime Minister." If Hitler would co-operate, "the Prime Minister could carry through his policy of an understanding." Ribbentrop asked Henderson "whether I could guarantee that the Prime Minister could carry the country with him in a policy of friendship with Germany." Henderson replied "there was no possible doubt whatever that he could." Hitler saw a chance of raising the hardly-laid ghost of the Wilson-Wohltat plan. He asked whether Britain "would be willing to accept *an alliance* with Germany." Here was Henderson's chance to point out that circumstances had changed; that it was now a question, not of broad schemes of future policy, but of a necessary and immediate decision on a specific issue. But the appeasers never knew when to make a stand. Asked about the possibility of an alliance Henderson replied that "speaking personally I did not exclude such a possibility."

Vansittart objected, in a minute for Halifax, to Henderson's answer. It was, he wrote "very dangerous indeed":

> If the Germans were clever enough to allow it to transpire that this question had been put to the British Ambassador and that he had answered it in the terms employed, I think we should have to face a great deal of indignation and suspicion in this country, and above all there would be a great loss of confidence and suggestions of perfidy in France, Turkey, Poland, Roumania, Greece and so on. I think Sir Nevile Henderson should receive instructions to avoid this topic altogether . . . there can be no possible question of anything of this kind within visible time. An alliance means a military alliance if it means anything. And against whom should we be allying ourselves with such a gang as the present régime in Germany? The merest suggestion of it would ruin us in the United States.[46]

Halifax agreed that Henderson had gone too far, and that he ought to be shown "how boggy the ground is."

A private note was sent to Henderson,[47] but it could not eradicate the impression of weakness and indecision that Henderson gave Hitler. Hitler himself was given no indication that Henderson's attitude towards an alliance had been criticized or repudiated in London. During their talk, Hitler had emphasized Poland's guilt. Poland had refused to act moderately towards Germany. At one moment Hitler "spoke of annihilating Poland!" [48] Here was an indication that Danzig and the Corridor might not be all that he desired. It was a clue consciously ignored. Henderson could still say that the major obstacle to a settlement was Polish *"amour propre,"* not unreasonable German demands.[49] Halifax knew of Hitler's threat. It was on his instructions that it had been omitted from the text of Henderson's meeting that had been sent to Beck.[50] The Poles were not meant to know that Hitler harbored such thoughts towards them, or, rather, that Britain was aware that he harbored them. British policy was based upon their denial. In April Beck had denied the existence of threats to Danzig in order to win an Anglo-Polish alliance "on the cheap"; in August the British wished such threats into oblivion, hoping to avert an Anglo-German war by the "peaceful" transfer of the Free City. The Foreign Ministers of both nations indulged in fantasies which they knew to be false.

Halifax read of Hitler's threat to "annihilate" Poland. He could still write that he was "at a loss to know" why the Poles had taken mobilization measures.[51] Hitler had yet to reply to the "British" proposals for direct Polish-German negotiations. Henderson imagined that Hitler would accept them. He worked out in his own mind how they should be carried out. Beck, he decided, should see Hitler. In this way the Poles would "make their contribution to world peace." But what guarantee could Henderson give that Beck would be treated with greater fairness than his predecessors on that stony road? And were there no German "contributions" that might be of value? Munich had taught the British that it was easier to make the weak man submit than to put pressure on the strong.

Henderson met Hitler on August 29 to receive Hitler's answer. The interview did not go as Henderson had hoped. The Germans did not respond to British generosity in offering to put pressure on Poland. They would indeed accept a Polish negotiator. But they demanded his arrival "by Wednesday, August 30," that is within twenty-four hours. Such a demand, said Henderson, savored of an ultimatum. This was "strenuously and heatedly" denied by Hitler and Ribbentrop.[52]

Hitler had agreed, in his answer, to negotiate with Poland solely as proof of his desire to be friendly with Britain. He was angered by Henderson's suggestion that his terms were like an ultimatum; surely Henderson could see that the matter was urgent? Two mobilized armies faced each other, with "Germans being massacred in Poland." Hitler began to shout. Henderson, he maintained, "did not care how many Germans were being slaughtered in Poland." Henderson himself was provoked by "this gratuitous impugnment of the inhumanity of His Majesty's Government and of myself." He lost his temper and "proceeded to outshout Hitler. I told him that I would not listen to such language from him or anybody . . . I added a great deal more shouting at the top of my voice . . . I glared at Hitler the whole time . . . If he wanted war (I said) he would have it."[53]

Hitler was understandably surprised by this unprecedented outburst. He continued to rant. But his theme changed. He told Henderson that he had always sought to win Britain's friendship. He respected the British Empire. He liked Englishmen "generally." Henderson thought these remarks "quite honest." He considered Hitler free of "conscious hypocrisy" when he spoke of his desire for good relations with Britain. But Henderson left the meeting "filled with the gloomiest forebodings," and "depressed at my own inadequacy."[54]

Henderson was not alone in being depressed by Hitler's new anger and sense of urgency. Göring had also been frightened by Hitler's outburst, and sent Dahlerus to London to "explain this

unfortunate incident." Dahlerus left Berlin at 5 A.M. on August
30. He was well briefed. Both Ogilvie Forbes and Göring had
informed him of the Hitler-Henderson encounter. Dahlerus
saw Chamberlain and Halifax that morning. He told them that
it was "not essential" for a Polish delegate to present himself in
Berlin that same day (Wednesday), in spite of Hitler's insistence.[55] Chamberlain "felt very doubtful" about the suitability
of Berlin as the meeting place. He said that "it was only reasonable" to give the matter "a little more time." At 12:30 P.M.
Dahlerus spoke to Göring on the telephone and was told that
Hitler was anxious "to secure the friendship of Great Britain"
and to show the world "that the Germans are not so black as
they are painted."[56] Hitler was drafting proposals that, in
Göring's opinion, would contain an acceptance of the principle
of a plebiscite for the Corridor. Dahlerus hoped that Hitler's
terms would be ready that night. Göring told him: "The
Führer's on it." Dahlerus suggested the proposal should be given
to Lipski, the Polish Ambassador in Berlin, rather than to another negotiator either in Berlin as Hitler wanted, or elsewhere,
as Chamberlain preferred. It was no insult to ask the Polish
Ambassador to go to the Chancellery.

Halifax asked Dahlerus to speak to Göring again, to ask that
the proposals "should not be put forward in the form of a
'Diktat.'" Göring was telephoned, and told Dahlerus that
Hitler was "drafting his proposals in the form of a basis for
discussion"; a fact that Göring thought "miraculous." But a
Polish representative would still have to come from Warsaw.
Hitler's condition could not be cancelled. Göring repeated this
at 3 P.M.[57]

Henderson had not been idle in Berlin. His fertile imagination had been seeking some means, other than British pressure
on the Poles, which would lead to a lessening of tension, especially along the German-Polish frontier. Along this frontier
Hitler's eyes were fixed; and his emotional outbursts would only
be inflamed by further incidents, of whatever origin. At mid-

day Henderson suggested that the Pope ought to be persuaded
to put forward some "definite impartial solution." [58] Henderson
explained to the Papal Nuncio in Berlin that he envisaged something like a neutral frontier commission, composed of ecclesias-
tics. The Papal Nuncio seemed to regard laymen as more suitable.[59]

Neither Henderson nor the Nuncio realized that Papal initiative had already been taken, but of a less impartial nature. The
Pope told the Polish Government that information had reached
him that, if Poland would surrender Danzig to Germany, Hitler
would then be willing to negotiate over the Corridor and minority problems. The Pope recommended this information for the
"most careful consideration" of the Poles.[60] But the Pope had
no reason to believe that this extreme solution would satisfy
Hitler. The idea had come from Mussolini, who, acting on the
off-chance that the proposal *would* be adequate, had persuaded
the Pope to forward it. Papal patronage gave blackmail the air
of grace. But it did not make the question clearer of what it
was Hitler actually wanted, if indeed he was to be satisfied by
any Polish concessions at all. Osborne, the British representative
at the Vatican, told the Cardinal Secretary of State that "he
could not help being a little doubtful about the correctness of
the information" which the Pope had received.[61] It had been
passed on nevertheless.

On the same day that the Pope informed the Poles that Hitler
would negotiate *after* the surrender of Danzig, they learned
from Britain that they could and must negotiate with Germany,
without having committed themselves to any specific territorial
changes in advance. How were the Poles to know which of their
well-wishers gave the advice Hitler wished them to accept? The
British had been sceptical about the accuracy of the Papal
information. Yet the British advice was itself based on what
the British *thought* Hitler would demand, rather than what he
had actually demanded. The Pope said Danzig must be surrendered before negotiations began. This meant that after the

surrender of Danzig further concessions would have to be made. The British gave the impression that even the case of Danzig would stand on its merits. If this was so, surely the Poles could then make the return of Danzig to Germany a bargaining point *against* further concessions? The British did not tell the Poles that they had learned, through Dahlerus, that Hitler insisted upon the return of Danzig.

The divergence between the Papal and the British claims can easily be explained. Neither well-wisher knew what Hitler's official demands would be. Both knew he wanted to see a Polish negotiator that very day. Neither knew to what exact purpose. Both had heard rumors of demands. Neither had seen them written down.

Henderson was aware that Papal initiative on the scale discussed by him and the Nuncio would be inadequate. It was not a question of keeping tempers cool, but of persuading either the Germans to be reasonable and patient in their demands, or the Poles to submit to those demands even if the German manner was one of threats and exaggeration. Henderson decided it was necessary to force Poland to give way. Unaware that the Pope had also accepted this view, he pressed on with his own plans. He wanted a Polish surrender. A surrender it would indeed be, if a Polish negotiator went to Berlin prepared to give up, in the face of German threats and British pressure, rights guaranteed by the Treaty of Versailles, the Franco-Polish Treaty, and the Anglo-Polish Agreement.

CHAPTER 19

Henderson Versus Kennard

At 2 in the morning of August 30, Halifax told Henderson that he considered the German demand for a Polish negotiator to appear that day in Berlin "unreasonable." The Germans "must not expect this." [1] But Henderson acted before Halifax's comments reached him. As soon as his interview with Hitler on the night of August 29 had ended, he urged the French Ambassador in Berlin "strongly to recommend to French Government that they advise Polish Government to propose immediate visit of M. Beck as constituting in my opinion sole chance now of preventing war." [2] France should put pressure on Poland, since Britain had "as usual done all the spade work with the Germans." The Poles must not be allowed to "talk all the time of their *amour propre*, prestige and signs of weakening." Britain would "not be guiltless of some of the responsibility for disaster" if she allowed the Poles to do so. [3]

Henderson saw Lipski and told him that he "much doubted if Hitler wanted war." Hitler's threats had "gone so far," however, that it was necessary to give him an opportunity to "draw back." [4] Henderson therefore "implored" Lipski to persuade his Government to send a negotiator to Berlin. [5] He said all this without Halifax's knowledge or approval. At 10 A.M. on August 30, Kennard informed Halifax that he was quite opposed to applying the sort of pressure on the Poles that Henderson considered necessary.

I feel sure that it would be impossible to induce the Polish Government to send Colonel Beck or any other representative immediately to Berlin to discuss a settlement on basis proposed by Herr

Hitler. They would certainly sooner fight and perish than submit to such humiliation especially after examples of Czecho-Slovakia, Lithuania and Austria. I would suggest that if negotiations are to be between equals they should take place in some neutral country . . . World opinion is clearly in favour of direct negotiations on equal terms and is behind Poland's resistance to a dictated settlement.[6]

At 1 P.M. Henderson recommended to Halifax that "the Polish Government should swallow this eleventh hour effort to establish direct contact with Herr Hitler." [7] But he began to wonder whether or not Hitler was contemplating the use of force if he could not achieve his ends "by so-called peaceful fair means." At 6:30 P.M. Henderson again urged Halifax to put pressure on the Poles. One had to consider, he said,

> not only immediate present in which it is essential not to display any indication of yielding to Herr Hitler's threats but also future. If there is to be any genuine peace in future between Poland and her powerful neighbour grievances of latter which are not of Herr Hitler's making but national must be eliminated. In my opinion in order to achieve this end City of Danzig . . . must revert to Germany; there must be direct and extra-territorial communication between Reich and East Prussia; and German minority in Poland must be got rid of by means of some exchange of population. On no other basis can there ever be genuine and lasting peace between the two countries. No diplomatic compromise has a hope of surviving indefinitely . . .

> I can only urge once more importance of Poland accepting at once proposals for direct negotiations . . .[8]

Even if the Germans were unwilling to reach a negotiated solution Poland's acceptance would have the effect of "putting herself right in the eyes of the world."

Chamberlain, like Henderson, regarded *Polish* stubbornness as the great obstacle to peace. Kennedy told Cordell Hull:

"Frankly he is more worried about getting the Poles to be
reasonable than the Germans." [9] But during the morning of
August 30, Dahlerus had shown the British something of the
difficulty of obtaining any German withdrawal from the demand
that Danzig must be returned. Kennard's dispatch of 10 A.M.
had been forthright in opposing the German proposals. The
Cabinet met at 11:30 A.M. Hore-Belisha opposed the immediate arrival of a Polish negotiator in Berlin. He said he "thought
it was important to make it clear we were not going to yield on
this point." Someone at the meeting, with good memories of
Munich, suggested that Chamberlain "should send a personal
message to Hitler." The nature of the message was not revealed.
Some members of the Cabinet thought the Polish-German
meeting place should be Italy, and they had the support of
Kennard on this. Hore-Belisha disagreed, and told the Cabinet
that

> to present to Mussolini this opportunity of appearing as the *tertius
> gaudens* at the end of all this sorry business would be to strengthen
> fascism by increasing its prestige quite unnecessarily at a moment
> when it seems to be more than a little uncertain of itself.[10]

Hore-Belisha tried to prevent any negotiations, wherever held,
while German threats continued. That evening Chamberlain rejected the policy that Henderson had been advocating throughout the day. The Germans wanted a Polish negotiator "with full
powers" to come to Berlin; this was "understood" from a
"mutual friend" (i.e., Dahlerus). But the Cabinet had decided:
"We cannot advise Polish Government to comply with this
procedure which is wholly unreasonable." They wanted the
Germans to adopt "the normal procedure," and to hand their
proposals, when ready, to the Polish Ambassador, "for trans-
mission to Warsaw." [11] Once the normal channels were used,
the British could "be counted on to do their best in Warsaw
to facilitate negotiations." At the same time Halifax tried to
influence Beck in favor of negotiating; it was the German pro-

posal for direct discussions that was "really important." The Polish Government should "be prepared to do so without delay." [12] But they should do so in Warsaw. Hore-Belisha's pressure had been successful.

Only two problems remained for the British. The Germans would have to give up their demand that a Polish negotiator must go specially to Berlin with full powers to negotiate a settlement; and the Germans would have to state officially what their actual proposals were. Hitler, presumably, had been drafting them that afternoon, if what Göring had told Dahlerus was correct.

At 7:40 P.M. Henderson was sent a British note for immediate communication to Hitler. The British understood that Hitler would "presently" be putting forward the German proposals "in an elaborated form," and expressed the hope that these proposals "will be fully examined during the discussions." [13] At 9:05 P.M. the message was altered. It was understood that the Germans "are drawing up proposals for a solution." [14] There was to be no hint officially that the British had already received the substance of the German proposals. Yet on the basis of them they had been putting pressure on the Poles to negotiate. At midnight Henderson called on Ribbentrop. The meeting was delayed by half an hour to enable Henderson to decipher the altered note. Ribbentrop's mood, "from the outset," was of "intense hostility, which increased in violence as I made each communication in turn. He kept jumping to his feet in a state of great excitement, folding his arms across his chest, and asking if I had anything more to say. I kept replying that I had . . ." [15] Ribbentrop said that "all the provocation" had come from Poland. Henderson told him that the British had "constantly warned" the Poles against "all provocative action," as indeed they had. Ribbentrop retorted that the British advice "had had bloody little effect." "I mildly retorted that I was surprised to hear such language from a Minister for Foreign Affairs." [16] Henderson said he "would not fail to report" Ribbentrop's remarks to the British Government. Ribbentrop "calmed down a little and said they were his own." [17] The two men then discussed the problem of Polish-German negotiations.

Henderson suggested that when the German proposals were ready the Polish Ambassador should be invited to transmit them to his Government "with a view to immediate opening of negotiations." His Majesty's Government "could be counted upon to do their best in Warsaw to temporise negotiations." Ribbentrop, by way of reply, produced "a lengthy document which he read out in German aloud at top speed." [18] The document contained Hitler's proposals for a German-Polish settlement, embodied in sixteen points. They were curiously similar to the proposals which Dahlerus had brought to London the previous day. The British had been right to "understand" that Hitler would merely "elaborate" them.

Henderson told Halifax that he thought Ribbentrop would eventually hand him the paper on which the proposals were written. Because of this "I did not attempt to follow too closely the sixteen or more articles it contained." In his memoirs he described how Ribbentrop "gabbled through to me as fast as he could, in a tone of the utmost scorn and annoyance." He had been able, so he wrote, to "gather the gist" of only six or seven of the sixteen points. "But it would have been quite impossible to guarantee even the comparative accuracy of these without a careful study of the text itself." Ribbentrop never gave him the text to look at, yet he was able to send Halifax the "main points" accurately enough, and to consider them as a "not on the whole too unreasonable" basis for negotiations.

The points Henderson passed on to Halifax were these: [18]

1 Restoration of Danzig to Germany.
2 Corridor to be demarcated (details of southern line given).
3 Plebiscite in Corridor on basis of 1919 population.
4 International commission to police Corridor.
5 Gdynia to be reserved to Poland.
6 Danzig to be purely commercial city and demilitarized.

Ribbentrop said that the proposals were "now too late," as a Polish negotiator had not arrived in Berlin.[19] But he agreed that if the Polish Ambassador were to call on him he would show him the proposals. Henderson saw a last chance to put pressure on the Poles. Before he sent off his account of the proposals to Halifax, and before he could possibly know what the attitude of the British Government would be, he asked Lipski to call on him. The two men met at 2 A.M. on the morning of August 31. It was Henderson's moment of power. He alone knew of the sixteen points. Not having passed them on to Halifax, he did not know Halifax's reaction to them. Henderson told Lipski that the terms were "not unreasonable." Without mentioning Ribbentrop's mood, or his "most violent terms" in saying that he would never ask Lipski to call on him, Henderson gave Lipski the following advice, "in very strongest terms."

> He should at once ring up Minister for Foreign Affairs (Beck) and say he had heard from me that detailed proposals had been individually elaborated and that he would like to call on Herr Ribbentrop with a view to learning and communicating them to Polish Government. I suggested he should do this tonight on his responsibility.[20]

Henderson asked Lipski to tell Beck that Smigly-Rydz, the Polish Field-Marshal, should meet Göring "at once." Lipski "undertook to make this suggestion to his Government"; but he refused to telephone it that same night as Henderson had asked. Henderson told Halifax next morning: "He is so inert or so handicapped by instructions of his Government that I cannot rely on his action being effectively palliative." [21]

Henderson tried to contact Lipski again before 9 A.M., but without success. Lipski was "out for a walk." [22] Lipski had not obtained a negotiator, nor was he willing to do so. At 10:15 A.M. Henderson told Weizsäcker that on his own personal initiative he was urging the Poles to negotiate.[23] Wishing to show the Poles the sixteen points, and possibly even to examine them for the first time himself, he contacted Dahlerus. At last he was shown "full notes" of the German proposals. Henderson does not appear to have asked himself why it was necessary to use both himself and Dahlerus as go-betweens. Could not the German Government contact the Poles direct? Hitler had told Henderson it took only ninety minutes to fly from Warsaw to Berlin. It took even less time to telephone. If the Germans wanted the Poles to take their sixteen points seriously, there was an easy method by which they could be given directly to Beck. But Hitler was not interested in a solution. As he later told his interpreter; "I needed an alibi, especially with the German people, to show them that I had done everything possible to maintain peace. That explains my generous offer." [24]

For Henderson, German generosity was genuine. He told Halifax how Göring had described the sixteen points "as very moderate and which in fact appeared so to me though I was not given the opportunity of studying them." [25] With the arrival of Dahlerus and his notes Henderson was able to see the proposals. They impressed him as sound. Even before seeing them he had telephoned Halifax, at 11:33 A.M., urging that the Poles should avoid "raising the question of procedure." Lipski should receive instructions "on British responsibility" telling him "immediately to ask for interview." [26] Henderson wanted Halifax to give instructions to Lipski. He tried to telephone Lipski himself, but Lipski was telephoning Warsaw. At 12:20 P.M. he telephoned Halifax again to say that as Dahlerus had brought the proposals in note form he had already sent Dahlerus, together with Ogilvie Forbes, to see Lipski.[27] Ogilvie Forbes introduced Dahlerus to Lipski as a "neutral intermediary in the confidence of the Cabinet, of the Embassy, and of the German Government." [28] Dahlerus then read Lipski the German proposals, and "emphasized their reasonableness and moderation as a basis for a settlement honourable to both sides." Beck, or "some other suitable representative," should come to Berlin "today." If this was impossible, Lipski should himself seek an interview with Hitler.

Lipski was "showing signs of strain." Dahlerus left the room "to have the proposals put in writing." While he was out of the room Lipski told Ogilvie Forbes:

> that this plan was a breach of Polish sovereignty and was quite out of the question . . . It would be fatal for M. Beck or a Polish representative to come to Berlin. We must for heaven's sake stand firm and show a united front, and Poland if deserted by her allies was prepared to fight and die alone. The German offer was a trap. It was also a sign of weakness on the part of the Germans.[28]

Ogilvie Forbes's reaction was not recorded. He returned to the Embassy with Dahlerus, their mission a failure. On arrival at the Embassy Dahlerus went to Henderson's room. At 12:30 P.M. he telephoned 10 Downing Street. The telephone was answered by Wilson. Dahlerus told Wilson that "he had spent the night with Göring," and that the German proposals were "extremely liberal." Hitler had put them forward "with the sole intention" of showing Britain how much he wanted a "friendly settlement" with her. Dahlerus began to tell Wilson of his meeting with Lipski. Wilson told him to give his information to Henderson. Dahlerus went on. He complained that it was "obvious to us" that the Poles were "obstructing" the possibility of a negotiation."[29] Wilson could well understand why Henderson, Ogilvie Forbes and Dahlerus were annoyed by Polish obstruction. But such "obstruction" was understandable. Poland had lost confidence in Britain.

Wilson did not wait for Dahlerus to explain why he and his British friends considered the Poles obstructive. "I again told Dahlerus to shut up, but as he did not do so I put down the receiver." Half an hour later Halifax warned Henderson: "You really must be careful of use of telephone. Dahlerus's conversation at midday from Embassy was most indiscreet."[30] Dahlerus had been indiscreet, not wrong. Halifax held no brief for the Poles. Kennard had explained the Polish case clearly enough. So had Norton. But Halifax wanted a Polish surrender. Dahlerus was indiscreet because he revealed that British pressure was *already* being applied. Officially, Hitler's demands were unknown.

At 12:30 P.M. Henderson telegraphed Halifax. The German terms "sound moderate to me and are certainly only so in view of German desire for good relations with Britain." Henderson had accepted Hitler's plea. "This is no Munich," he claimed, "since we are behind Poland who will never get such good terms again guaranteed as they will be internationally." [31] The Polish Government should "be insistently told" to give Lipski "immediate instructions." The Polish Government was unwilling to be forced into negotiations without having seen the German terms in advance. Dahlerus's production of his notes could hardly be regarded as an official German communication.

Halifax asked Beck to instruct Lipski to ask "immediately" for the German proposals. Lipski should be ready to transmit them to Warsaw, so that the Poles "may at once consider them and make suggestions for early discussions." [32] Halifax and Henderson had gone too far. Even Chamberlain was alarmed. The Foreign Office resented Henderson's influence, and hated his anti-Polish bias. Henderson was warned that the British Government "does not share view expressed [in telephone conversation of Dahlerus] as to obstructive attitude of Polish Government." [33] Chamberlain himself had come to realize that the fault did not lie entirely with the Poles. He insisted that "it would be impossible to ask Poland to give up her rights on Danzig in advance of negotiation." [34]

At 12:50 P.M. Ciano telephoned Halifax with a personal message from Mussolini. The Italians proposed a conference for September 5 to revise Versailles. The Italians had not yet asked the Germans. But would the British be willing to support such a conference? Halifax consulted Chamberlain. Once again Chamberlain stood firm. There could be no value, he stressed, in a conference held "under the threat of mobilized armies." [35]

Unknown to the British, Hitler decided, that afternoon, to abandon all thought of gains through negotiation. He gave orders for the invasion of Poland to be begun early next morning, September 1. The sixteen proposals were of no further use. The Italians, equally unaware that Hitler had made up his mind for war, asked Hitler to receive Lipski. Attolico saw Hitler at 7 P.M., and urged him to accept Italian mediation. Hitler refused. Was "everything now at an end?" asked Attolico. Yes, said Hitler.[36] The Italians were thus the first to know that Hitler had decided to invade Poland.

Attolico at once contacted Ciano, and told him war was imminent. Ciano called for Loraine. "I propose," wrote Ciano "that I commit an indiscretion. If a scandal comes of it I am willing to be sacrificed, but the situation will be saved. The Duce approves." Ciano told Loraine that Italy would "never start a war against you and the French." Percy Loraine was "moved. He is on the verge of tears. He takes my two hands in his and says: 'I have known this for fifteen days.'"[37]

Loraine had long known that Italy intended to be neutral. But for Ciano to tell him so in such clear terms was an admission that war was near, and that the Italians had some intimation of it. Halifax received this news from Loraine at 11 P.M.[38] In front of him lay a telegram from Kennard, received half an hour earlier.

His Majesty's Ambassador at Berlin appears to consider German terms reasonable. I fear that I cannot agree with him from point of view of Warsaw. While to the uninitiated they may seem plausible the Polish Government will certainly regard them as an attempt to strangle her under the cloak of legality . . .

If Poland submits to peremptory and humiliating [demands] she will have surrendered the principle that discussions must be on a free and equal basis and in no sense under menace or pressure. This is a vital aspect of Polish independence which His Majesty's Government are pledged to sustain . . .

As to terms themselves . . . they are when stripped of legalistic language clearly calculated to undermine the existence of the Polish State . . .

Any suspicion that her allies could possibly wish such terms to be taken as basis for negotiation might even drive Polish to offer resistance singlehanded to provocations they have for so long endured with fortitude and prudence.[39]

Kennard's argument went unheard. Shortly after midnight Henderson telegraphed: the "Polish Government should be urged in unmistakable language" to send a negotiator to Berlin. "The German proposals," he wrote, "certainly do not endanger the independence of Poland . . . from the long point of view the Poles will miss their market if they do not discuss." [40] Halifax agreed. Twenty minutes after receiving Henderson's suggestion he telegraphed Kennard: "I do not see why the Polish Government should feel difficulty about authorizing Polish Ambassador to accept a document from the German Government." As for a plenipotentiary, "the suggestion that a demand for [his] presence amounted to an ultimatum was vigorously repudiated by Herr Ribbentrop." The British Government still had a part to play. "If negotiations are initiated," continued Halifax, "His Majesty's Government will at all times be ready, if desired, to lend any assistance in their power to achieve a just settlement." [41]

But Hitler wanted neither a Pole to appear in Berlin, nor an Englishman to assist him. At 4 A.M. on September 1, German "mechanized troops" crossed the Polish frontier.[42]

PART FIVE

I sit in one of the dives
On Fifty-second Street
Uncertain and afraid
As the clever hopes expire
Of a low dishonest decade. . . .

Faces along the bar
Cling to their average day:
The lights must never go out,
The music must always play,
All the conventions conspire
To make this fort assume
The furniture of home;
Lest we should see where we are,
Lost in a haunted wood,
Children afraid of the night
Who have never been happy or good.

— W. H. AUDEN
September 1, 1939

CHAPTER 20

War Without War

Friday, September 1. At 5:30 in the morning General Gort, British C-in-C, telephoned Hore-Belisha: "Germans are through." [1] Ten minutes later Hitler spoke over Berlin radio and announced that the German Army was fighting "for honour and vital rights of reborn Germany with hard determination." Halifax received the text of this broadcast from Reuter at 7:28 A.M. [2] An hour later he heard from Kennard that Cracow and Kattowice had been bombed at 6 A.M. The Germans had crossed the Polish frontier in at least two places. [3] It was no longer a question of the status of Danzig alone, Poland's sovereignty had been violated. There had been neither a German ultimatum nor a declaration of war.

Under the terms of the Mutual Assistance Agreement of August 25, Britain was pledged to act "at once," with "all the support and assistance in its power." She did not. If Hitler calculated that it was posible once more to make gains in Eastern Europe without British interference, it was a shrewd calculation. Those who were responsible for British foreign policy *were* unwilling to honor their Polish Pact simply because Polish territory had been attacked. The desire for a negotiated solution, even in the face of overt threats, had been manifest in the days and hours before the German onslaught. With that onslaught, and with the bombing of cities and the encroachment of armies, the British willingness for negotiations remained. British policy was unable to adjust itself to the possibility of an Anglo-German war. The clear terms of a treaty signed five days earlier were ignored.

It was perhaps on Hitler's initiative that the first German

feelers were sent out to see if the British would consider negotiations in spite of the German invasion. Shortly before 10 A.M. on Friday Dahlerus telephoned the Foreign Office. He told Spencer that he was "arranging" for Henderson to see Hitler after he had addressed the Reichstag at 10 A.M. After the meeting, suggested Dahlerus, he and Ogilvie Forbes would fly to London. Spencer asked: "Could you limit the hostilities until you had been to London?" [4] With this question it was made clear to the Germans that the invasion alone was not to be considered a cause for war. Given some "limit," the British might be willing to negotiate. It was at least certain that treaty obligations were not to stand in the way of a search for terms on which negotiations would be possible.

Dahlerus suggested that negotiations should take the form of an English mediation. General Ironside and Ogilvie Forbes, "or someone else and one Frenchman," should mediate between Poland and Germany. If the Poles were to discuss a settlement with the British and French, it could then be taken "from the British and French to the Germans." [5]

It was quite clear to the Poles that by invading Poland proper, and not Danzig alone, and by invading on all fronts, the Germans aimed at the total conquest of Poland. There was therefore only one act that Britain could perform. Her treaty obligations must be carried out. Britain must declare war on Germany. At the very moment when the text of Dahlerus's plea for negotiations reached the Foreign Office, Raczynski called to see Halifax, and informed him that "it was a plain case as provided for by the Treaty." Halifax was noncommittal. There was certainly no question of Britain declaring war on Germany that morning, though Halifax had "no doubt" that, if the facts were as Raczynski claimed, Britain would "take the same view" that the Treaty was involved.[6]

Fifteen minutes later Henderson told Halifax: "Herr Hitler may ask to see me after the Reichstag as last effort to save the peace." [7] Henderson took the possibility of negotiations seriously. He considered "the only possible hope now for peace" was for the Polish Marshal, Smigly-Rydz, "to announce his readiness to come immediately to Germany to discuss as soldier and plenipotentiary the whole question with Field-Marshal Göring." [8]

Henderson had demanded a Polish visit to Berlin before Poland had been invaded, despite the fact that it would take place in an atmosphere of violent threats, and with every disadvantage for the Poles.

He still urged Polish concessions. It was difficult to see what frontier concessions the Poles could make now that the German army had pushed across the frontiers, and was heading towards the major towns. It was even more difficult to know how the commander-in-chief of the Polish army, an army locked in war, could leave his post and make the journey to his enemy's capital. It would be tantamount to surrender.

Henderson, prompted by Göring and perhaps also by Hitler, was suggesting that a Polish visit to Berlin might lead to a negotiated peace. Unwilling to declare war, Britain and France had a single expedient left to them. They could demand that the Germans withdraw from Poland.

Polish soil would have been violated, and Polish soldiers killed. But if the Germans could be persuaded to withdraw, there were many British diplomats and politicians who would be willing to overlook the brutality of the invasion, and negotiate a Polish-German peace, making the necessary concessions to Germany.

The idea of allowing the Germans to withdraw their troops from Poland, and of following this with a conference, was discussed in London and Paris during Friday morning. Cambon, the French Counsellor, called at the Foreign Office and said that if the Germans were asked to withdraw their troops, the demand "ought to be accompanied by a time limit." [9] Cambon was afraid that the Germans, if given no definite time limit within which to withdraw, would produce counter-proposals in order to postpone an Anglo-French decision to declare war. Any suggestion that it was possible to negotiate on the timing of a German withdrawal would give the Germans a chance of "generally confusing the issue."

The French were anxious for Mussolini to put forward the idea of a conference, and told the Italians that they wanted "the peaceful settlement of the conflict that has broken out between Germany and Poland."[10] In the French note there was no indication of who was responsible for the conflict. Ciano noted that the English were "more sceptical" about the chances of a conference than the French. Yet both Britain and France hoped that a negotiated solution might still be possible. The Italians, wrote Ciano, were "more sceptical still," for they knew "about the rabid determination of the Germans to fight."[11]

Yet at midday the Germans tried to give the impression that they were willing to consider negotiations and "moderation." To end British fears that they were bombing towns, Kordt telephoned Halifax from the German Embassy to say that it was "untrue" that Warsaw and other towns were being bombed.[12] An hour later Dahlerus telephoned again, and said that he had seen Göring and Hitler at midday. Hitler, according to Dahlerus, "had emphasized . . . his anxiety not to bring about a world war" and had declared that "he was not bent on a war of conquest" but wanted "to discuss matters with Great Britain."[13] It seemed that Hitler had agreed to allow Britain to mediate between Germany and Poland.

Dahlerus himself wanted to fly at once to London with Ogilvie Forbes, but Cadogan, who was speaking to him, "could not see what purpose would be achieved by that." Within an hour Dahlerus had telephoned again. This time the British were able to inform him of their policy. The Cabinet had met before lunch, and at 1:25 P.M. the position was clear. The British would not consider the fact of an invasion as a cause for war. They were willing to contemplate the settlement of the German-Polish "problem" by negotiations. There was one condition. There could be no negotiations, and no mediation, "while German troops are invading Poland." Such an idea was "quite out of the question." [14] But if Germany would suspend hostilities and withdraw her troops, a solution without war would still be possible. No time limit for the withdrawal was insisted upon.

The idea of a solution "without war" once war had begun was a strange one. Kennard told Halifax that Beck had just telephoned him, in the middle of an air-raid, and had insisted that German action "constitutes act of war." There could be only one British response. Britain should take "some action of a military character" to relieve pressure on the Polish front. A British air attack in the West would draw off some of the German planes attacking Poland. Beck made it quite clear that various "open" towns had been bombarded, with civilian casualties. Noël, the French Ambassador in Warsaw, suggested that both British and French wireless stations "should repeatedly point out" that Germany had "openly and flagrantly attacked Poland without warning." [15]

Within two hours of Kennard's telling Halifax of the nature of the German attack, Henderson, who up till midday had continued to urge the Poles to accept negotiations, changed his mind. It was a dramatic change, and a complete one. This staunch appeaser had wanted, before lunch, to see the Polish commander-in-chief leave his troops and hurry to Berlin. After lunch his appeasement ended. He told Halifax, at 3:45 P.M.:

I do not feel that I can usefully acquiesce in any further suggestions from here which would only once again be outstripped by events or lead to nothing as the result of methods followed or of considerations of honour and prestige . . .

Last hope lies in inflexible determination on our part to resist force by force.[16]

Henderson had decided that it must be war. Yet he considered responsibility for the conflict to be evenly divided. It was the "mutual distrust" of Germans and Poles that made it certain that further appeasement could only fail. There was no question of any excess of guilt on the part of the Germans. Henderson regarded the mutual distrust as "so complete" that he made no moral evaluation either way.

At 4 P.M. Kennard sent further details of German air attacks. Kattowice, Cracow and Poznan had been bombed.[17] During the afternoon the staff of the British Embassy in Berlin burnt all their ciphers and confidential documents, and left their normal residences to move to the Adlon Hotel, which was next to the Embassy. The U.S. Chargé d'Affaires was asked to take over British interests "in the event of war." [18] Perhaps it was this new firmness that encouraged Dahlerus to telephone London again. The situation, he told Spencer at the Foreign Office, was "too bad, very sad." But there was no need for despondency. Dahlerus insisted that "there will be a solution in a few days; they are most anxious over here."

Dahlerus did not reveal what solution the Germans had in mind. But in order to show that German magnanimity was not lost, he himself was ready "at any time" to fly to London.

Göring was prepared to "limit aerial attacks to aerodromes and fortifications." There would be "no attacks on civil population." The Foreign Office took note of Dahlerus's remarks, and agreed that he should telephone them again.[19]

If the British had any doubt as to whether Hitler would consider negotiations, Dahlerus's assertions must have been welcome. Halifax was preparing a note for the German Government, in place of the ultimatum which the Poles hoped he would deliver. He told Henderson that the note was "in the nature of a warning and is not to be considered as an ultimatum." [20]

The warning stated that unless the German Government

has suspended all aggressive action against Poland and are prepared promptly to withdraw their forces from Polish territory, His Majesty's Government . . . will without hesitation fulfil their obligations to Poland.[21]

The warning still contained no definite time limit. When were the Germans to withdraw their forces? Would they have to begin "promptly" upon receiving the warning? Would the withdrawal, once begun, be allowed to take twenty-four hours, or forty-eight? Would the *suspension* of hostilities be enough, with withdrawal to be negotiated later? These questions could not be answered from the text of the note. The very insistence on it being a warning rather than an ultimatum weakened the nature of its demands.

Henderson saw Ribbentrop at 9:30 that evening, and asked, as instructed, for an "immediate answer" to the British note. Ribbentrop said he would have to show the note to Hitler. Henderson said he understood: "I was at his disposal at whatever time" the reply might be ready.[22]

Ribbentrop had been "courteous and polite." Henderson thought Hitler's answer to the warning "will be an attempt to avoid war with Britain and France." But Henderson no longer believed in the chance of a solution without war. He told Halifax that he thought Hitler's reply was "not likely to be one which we can accept."[23] The British were being firm, but not firm enough. They were trying to appease once more. But their hearts were no longer in it.

Duff Cooper dined with Churchill and Sandys at the Savoy Grill. Leaving the Savoy, he met the Duke of Westminster, an appeaser and an anti-semite. The Duke began by "abusing the Jewish race" and "rejoicing that we were not yet at war." He told Duff Cooper that "Hitler knew after all that we were his best friends." Duff Cooper was outraged. "I hope," he retorted, "that by tomorrow he will know that we are his most implacable and remorseless enemies."[24] But Saturday was to come and go without war. If it came at all, Westminster asserted, the blame would go to Duff Cooper and the Jews.

CHAPTER 21

The Revolt of Conscience

Saturday, September 2. The first news to reach the Foreign Office that morning was from Kennard — a report that a total of three hundred German aircraft had flown over Poland on Friday. Seventeen German and four Polish planes had been shot down. German bombs dropped had included "250 kilogrammes HE also incendiary." [1]

The British also learned that during the night the French had asked Beck to consider an Italian proposal for a conference. Beck had replied: "It was not time to talk of conferences but of mutual aid in resistance to aggression." According to Beck, "every Pole is now asking how quickly and effectively we can implement the alliance." [2] Beck rejected the Italian proposal. Unknown to both himself and the British, it was not an Italian proposal at all, but a French one. The French, unwilling to take the initiative openly, had asked the Italians to do it for them. "Yielding to French pressure," wrote Ciano, "we suggest to Berlin the possibilities of a conference . . . contrary to what I expected, Hitler does not reject the proposal absolutely." [3]

The French were embarrassed by the nature and method of their plans. They were unwilling to inform the British for fear that the British would reject the idea of a conference.

When the British learned of the French approach to Ciano, Roger Makins noted: "His Majesty's Government were neither consulted nor informed of this *démarche*." [4] Noël told Kennard that Beck had been questioned about a conference, but added that "this was very secret." "It should not be revealed" that Noël himself had told Kennard. [5]

A conference could only involve even longer delays than the demand for withdrawal of German troops. Phipps noted that to curtail the declaration of war "unduly," as France was doing, "would be resented by public opinion and would not be in the true interests" of France, Britain, "or even Poland." [6] Public opinion was a new factor. Could Phipps seriously consider that public pressure might influence diplomacy? The public had certainly expected war to be declared, if not on Friday, then by Saturday morning. Both the fact and nature of German aggression were well known. There could be absolutely no doubt by Saturday morning that Germany had been the aggressor, and that the Germans wanted to conquer Poland.

Halifax had set no time-limit to the German reply. By not replying, the Germans gave themselves more time to attack Poland without fear of interference from Britain.

The insistence on a time-limit after which no further bargaining could be considered would force the Germans either to withdraw their troops or to accept war with Britain and France. The British and French were both unwilling to commit themselves to a timetable. The French still hoped that Ciano would persuade Hitler to accept the idea of a conference. They thought that a time-limit would exasperate Hitler, and harden his mind against the idea of a compromise. Halifax began to see the danger of setting no time-limit to the warning. He told Phipps that "delays in Paris and attitude of French Government are causing some misgiving here."

It was clear to the British Cabinet that Bonnet was eager to impose as few conditions as possible on the Germans. But the British Cabinet insisted on conditions. "We shall be grateful for anything you can do," Halifax informed Phipps, "to infuse courage and determination into M. Bonnet." [7]

Henderson reported that some people thought opposition to the Polish war was strong inside Germany. If the war were allowed to continue without Western intervention for a few days more, the anti-war group in Germany would seize power. Halifax discounted this. We must not rely, he said, on reports of "disaffection or indecision" inside Germany itself. "Firm and immediate action on our part . . . alone might yet save the day." [5] The Cabinet demanded firmness. But, though his words were bold Halifax wavered.

Bonnet hoped that the longer the ultimatum was delayed the more chance there was of Hitler's accepting a negotiated solution. He succeeded in interesting Halifax in the idea of a conference. Throughout Saturday afternoon those in favor of a conference did their utmost to bring one about. At 2 P.M. Ciano asked Loraine to see him at once. On arriving at the Italian Foreign Office Loraine found François-Poncet in the waiting-room. The French Ambassador had been "similarly summoned." [9] The two men were ushered into Ciano's room and asked to confirm that the "warning" of the previous evening had in no way been an "ultimatum." This they did. Loraine sent someone to the British Embassy for a copy of Halifax's instructions to Henderson, which were brought back to Ciano and "satisfied him on that point." While the instructions were being brought, François-Poncet and Loraine persuaded Ciano to telephone Bonnet. Bonnet willingly confirmed that the note had not been an ultimatum.[10] Ciano told Bonnet that Hitler wanted until Sunday noon "in order to work out and consider the question of an armistice and a conference." This German offer, noted Ciano, "produced lively satisfaction" in Paris.[11]

Ciano then telephoned Halifax to ask whether the British would postpone the setting of a time-limit until the Germans had accepted or rejected a conference. Halifax told Ciano that "the indispensable condition" for a conference was that the Germans should withdraw their troops from Poland. Ciano replied that he thought that the maximum to which the Germans would agree would be an armistice, with troops staying where they were, and a conference on the following day (that is, Monday).[12]

Halifax did not reject a conference. Nor was he yet prepared to set a time-limit to the British warning. But on Cabinet insistence he had made the withdrawal of troops an essential condition. The French were less ready to insist on conditions.

At 4 P.M. Halifax learned from Bonnet that the French considered that "a conference might be contemplated." The "really essential point," said Bonnet, was not the withdrawal of troops, but the representation of Poland at the conference.

Halifax promised to "reply as soon as possible" to Bonnet's further request that the Germans be allowed to delay their reply to the warning until Sunday midday. He said he would also find out "the final and definite views" of the British Government on the idea of a conference.[18]

At 4:20 P.M. Kennard emphasized the need for action rather than talk. "I earnestly hope that all possible will be done to expedite despatch of war material. This would have excellent effect from moral as well as purely military point of view." [14] Kennard did not know it was the idea of a conference, not of effective military action, that was being considered in London and Paris. As "smoke rose from Warsaw," further negotiations seemed absurd. Yet the French supported them, and Halifax was anxious to do likewise.

The British Cabinet met at 4:30 P.M. Halifax told them that *the French* were unwilling to set a limit to the previous day's warning. He added that the Germans were to be given till Sunday noon to accept or reject a conference. Halifax seemed in favor of this. Raczynski was called in. He told the Cabinet that the German attack had been "violently resumed" that morning, and spoke of "heavy bombing from the air" on towns since midday. He urged the implementation of the Anglo-Polish guarantee. His plea was listened to. Hore-Belisha told his Cabinet colleagues: "I was strongly opposed to further delay, which I thought might result in breaking the unity of the country. Public opinion was against yielding an inch." [15]

Once again public pressure was mentioned as an important factor in the crisis. Not only was the public anxious to have done with further discussion and delay, but first a diplomat, then a politician, voiced their anxiety, and considered it of importance in shaping policy.

The burden of Hore-Belisha's argument was this: as the warning to Germany had gone unanswered and unheeded, Britain should send an ultimatum to expire that night at midnight. The Cabinet discussed the proposal, and finally, after strong initial opposition, those in favor of action gained the support of the majority. The decision was reached, binding on all Ministers. Hore-Belisha wrote: *"Unanimous decision was taken that ultimatum should end at midnight."* [16]

The Cabinet were agreed. It was for Halifax to put their unanimity in formal terms and to inform the Germans that the warning was now an ultimatum, with midnight as the time of expiry. Chamberlain could announce the decision in the Commons within the hour: the House was waiting for him. At midnight Britain would be at war.

But despite the Cabinet's clear resolve, the decision never passed beyond the walls of 10 Downing Street, with the exception of a telephone call to Paris. When the Cabinet meeting ended Cadogan telephoned Bonnet and told him that unless Hitler withdrew his troops, the British would send their ultimatum. The news went no further. It was never passed to the Germans. The Commons never heard of it. Nor did Kennard. Alas, Bonnet had not yet made up his mind as to whether the withdrawal of troops *should* be an essential condition of a conference.* The French Cabinet was "going to deliberate" whether a troop withdrawal would be necessary. France would not allow an ultimatum to expire that very midnight. The French were "firmly decided that ultimatum must be of forty-eight hours." [17] The British Cabinet by insisting on midnight at the latest, and by assuming that an ultimatum would be sent by 6 P.M., allowed only six hours between the delivery of the

* Mandel told Duncan Sandys: "Votre Chamberlain, il est faible. Mais notre Bonnet, il est lâche."

312

ultimatum and its expiry. The French wanted forty-eight hours.

The British and French had taken up incompatible positions. The unanimity of the British Cabinet made it impossible for the British to delay their ultimatum whatever the French might desire. The question of public anxiety was real. Chamberlain was to speak in the Commons that afternoon. His expected appearance at 3 P.M. had already been delayed in order to find out the French position. Now that position was known. The British Cabinet had also made up its mind. It was for Chamberlain to announce their decision as soon as possible. It was 5 P.M. Chamberlain could be expected to tell the Commons that the Cabinet had decided upon an immediate ultimatum. Parliament and the nation waited for his announcement. It was hoped that Britain would fulfill her obligations to Poland with the maximum speed. The German armies pressed forward. There could be no delay. Edward Spears had never seen the Commons "so stirred, so profoundly moved, as it was that afternoon." [18]

An ultimatum would result, or so it was generally assumed, in military action on the part of Britain and France. Only such action could help Poland. Henderson told Halifax that "unexpected initial Polish resistance has upset German time programme." [19] Here was a chance for British intervention to have a salutary effect. The German armies, despite the bombing of all the major Polish cities, had not yet broken through the Polish defenses. There was still time for action on the western front to force the Germans to lessen the impetus of their eastern attack. If this could be done before German troops broke up the Polish formations, it might be some weeks before the Germans gained any real military advantage. With the approach of October, Polish territory would become less and less friendly towards an invader. Rain and mud would hinder his advance.

Kennard made it clear that German air superiority was attributed by the Poles "to our delay in declaring war." German attacks were becoming "more serious." The Poles considered that a British entry into the war "would certainly divert a great concentration which is at present on the [eastern] front." [20] But neither the logic of the military situation, nor Kennard's plea, nor the Cabinet's unanimity, could break the spell of appeasement.

Halifax, unknown to his Cabinet colleagues, hid their unanimity from the world. He still hoped that negotiations *would* be possible. Although at 6 P.M. he had asked Phipps to see if Daladier would accept a midnight ultimatum,[21] half an hour later, in a telephone conversation with Ciano, he revealed his intention of favoring a conference.[22]

Halifax told Ciano that withdrawal of troops was an "essential condition" for a conference. On this point the British were firm. Ciano did not think that Hitler would accept. Halifax urged him "to try his best." For if troops were withdrawn, all would be well. "It would be possible to get back to the original basis of negotiations" — that is, the *status quo* of "two or three days ago" followed by Polish-German discussions, based on the assumption that Danzig would go to Germany. Britain would offer her services as mediator. Halifax repeated that the British warning "was *not* an ultimatum."

The Cabinet had been betrayed. Halifax told Ciano that Chamberlain intended to "mention the fact that the Italian Government had proposed a conference" when he spoke in the Commons. Ciano hoped he would not do so. But Halifax told him that the British Government "were under an obligation to make the position quite clear to our own people." It was an obligation many times disregarded during the previous weeks. Now, with the pressure of a no longer docile public demanding the end to secret fumblings and a "second Munich," the Government could not risk too much unannounced activity. Halifax realized that he would have to make clear that a conference was still a possibility, however unpopular such clarity might be. But something of the old double-dealing remained. Although it was necessary to tell the Commons about the conference Halifax told Ciano that: "If we did so, however, it would be in a restrained way." Why the "if," and why "restrained"? The odds against honesty were still formidable. Halifax promised Ciano that "we would not say anything more" about the withdrawal condition. There was still to be no time-limit attached. He ended his con-versation by asking Ciano once more "to do his best with Berlin."

Ciano considered Halifax's proposals, and reverted to his earlier pessimism. The British insisted on a withdrawal *before* a conference. Ciano realized that it was a condition Hitler would never accept. He told Loraine that as a result of the British condition "it is rather hopeless" to ask the Germans to agree to a conference. Loraine was not put off by Italian defeat-ism. He urged Ciano to put the proposal to Berlin, "and let it take its chance." Ciano repeated that he thought "there was no chance whatever" of Hitler accepting.[23] But he promised Loraine that he would speak to Mussolini and the French.

The French also realized that Hitler would reject the with-drawal condition. At 7:30 P.M. the French Cabinet met. "When we were leaving," wrote de Monzie, "I pressed Bonnet to dis-regard the British *non possumus.*" It was "indefensible" to de-mand the withdrawal of German troops. "Could there not be a third solution . . . a symbolic withdrawal of a few miles?" [24]

Unaware that Ciano had lost faith in the idea of a conference, and the French in a withdrawal of troops, Chamberlain went to the Commons at 7:30 P.M. He must announce the British posi-tion. Spears wrote: "The benches were packed. The unbearable suspense was about to be relieved. One and all were keyed up for the announcement that war had been declared." The Cabinet knew there would be an immediate ultimatum. Others were equally certain. "Most were ready to show their intense relief that suspense was ended by cheering wildly. But as we listened, amazement turned into stupefaction, and stupefaction into ex-asperation." [25] Chamberlain still spoke of the possibility of nego-tiations.

He admitted that the Germans had not yet replied to the

Anglo-French warning. But he attributed their silence to the possibility that they were considering the Italian proposal for a conference. The Commons was outraged at the thought of further discussions. That Chamberlain should appear to favor them made him seem an abettor in the destruction of Poland. The British insisted upon the withdrawal of troops. But there was still no time-limit to their demand. Chamberlain announced: "If the German Government should agree to withdraw their forces, then His Majesty's Government would be willing to regard the position as being the same as it was before the German forces crossed the Polish frontier." Given a withdrawal of troops, "the way would be open to discussion" between Germany and Poland. Britain was willing "to be associated" in these discussions.[26]

Not war, but further negotiations. Halifax had triumphed. "The House was oozing hostility," wrote Spears. Duff Cooper had "lost all serenity." Amery wrote:

The House was aghast. For two whole days the wretched Poles had been bombed and massacred, and we were still considering within what time-limit Hitler should be invited to tell us whether he felt like relinquishing his prey! And then these sheer irrelevancies about the terms of a hypothetical agreement between Germany and Poland . . . Was all this havering the prelude to another Munich? A year before the House had risen to its feet to give Chamberlain an ovation when he announced a last-moment hope of peace. This time any similar announcement would have been met by a universal howl of execration.[27]

Two MPs were sick. Amery and Duff Cooper were "red faced and almost speechless with fury." [28] Duff Cooper "never felt so moved." [29] Chamberlain sat down "without a cheer." Dalton thought that a free vote would have overthrown Chamberlain and Simon. "There was a terrific buzz." [30] The Chief Whip, Captain Margesson, feared physical violence.

Chamberlain's statement alarmed the Cabinet. Hore-Belisha

had the impression "that we are weakening on our undertaking to Poland and that the French were ratting." In view of the Cabinet decision three hours earlier, he and his Cabinet colleagues "were completely aghast." [31] Greenwood spoke after Chamberlain. Amery, conscious of the urgency of the occasion, and fearing a "purely partisan speech" from the Labour man, called out: *"Speak for England!"* [32]

Greenwood did his best, but the emotion of the moment was too strong, and he stumbled over his words.

> Tomorrow we meet at twelve. I hope the Prime Minister then — well, he must be in a position to make some further statement — (*Hon. Members:* definite) — And I must put this point to him. Every minute's delay now means the loss of life, imperilling of our national interests —
> *Mr. Boothby:* Honour.
> *Mr. Greenwood:* Let me finish my sentence. I was about to say imperilling the very foundations of our national honour.[33]

The invocation of honor hit at appeasement where it was most weak. The appeasers claimed to have sought a sensible, rational policy. The moral problem had been too much for them. Any accusation that they were acting with dishonor was difficult to answer. It might seem sensible to refuse to go to war for Poland. It could not be honorable. The debate was a bitter one. Greenwood spoke of how "resentment, apprehension, anger reigned over our proceedings." [34] The House broke up, according to Amery, "in confusion and dismay." [35] As Spears wrote, Chamberlain "was now fully aware that the House would not accept any further procrastination." [36] *

The demands of Parliamentary opinion could not be refused. Chamberlain went to his room in the Commons, and Green-

---

* "Some said that Mr. Chamberlain was preparing to give way again . . . the atmosphere of the House of Commons was heavily charged. The Prime Minister alone preserved a detachment which to many seemed a little ill-timed . . . It would have required very little for Mr. Chamberlain to have been howled down." (Sir Charles Petrie: *Twenty Years Armistice and After*, pp. 241-242.)

wood followed him in. There were no civilities. Greenwood told Chamberlain that unless "the inevitable decision for war" had been taken before Parliament met on Sunday "it would be impossible to hold the House." [37]

When the debate had ended Simon had gone to *his* room with Hore-Belisha, Anderson, de la Warr and Elliot. After careful consideration they agreed Simon should be their spokesman and should insist on the Cabinet's earlier decision being implemented. Their minds were made up. The group went to Chamberlain's room. Greenwood had left. They entered, and Simon "put the case very forcibly" to Chamberlain that war must be declared.[38] There must be no further delay. Chamberlain must make an immediate statement about a British ultimatum. If the French would not agree to immediate action, it should be done without them.

While the Cabinet demanded that Chamberlain should stand by their collective decision a most forceful dispatch had arrived from Kennard. Beck said the Poles were hampered by German air superiority, and "very discreetly suggested that there should be some diversion as soon as possible in the west." For Beck it was essential that British aircraft "draw off a considerable proportion of German aircraft" from the eastern front. Kennard agreed with Beck. "Every effort," he said, ought to be made "to show activity on western front." But there could be no activity on a front that did not exist. Kennard urged: "*I trust I may be informed at the earliest possible moment of our declaration of war.*" [39]

Halifax ignored Kennard's request. The possibility of negotiations still attracted him. He told Henderson to give the text of Chamberlain's Commons speech "immediately to certain quarters" (i.e., Dahlerus, Göring). Halifax wanted the German Government to "have as much time as possible to consider their reply." [40] Halifax still hoped for a favorable reply. Ciano and Bonnet had both suggested that one might be forthcoming by midday Sunday. Parliament did not want to wait so long. But with the end of waiting would come the death of appeasement.

Henderson sent a copy of Chamberlain's speech to Dahlerus.[41] With the speech was Henderson's visiting card, and written across both sides of the card were Henderson's instructions: "Enclosed text of Mr. Chamberlain's speech may interest you: especially if you brought it to the knowledge of a certain quarter. N.H.2/10[sic]/39." Diplomacy still dallied with the methods of detective fiction. Dahlerus found the speech "permeated with the desire to try to prevent a catastrophe." But what could Dahlerus do that the Foreign Office, trained in crises, could not? He telephoned Göring and arranged to meet him on Sunday morning. Then he went to the British Embassy and saw Ogilvie Forbes. Ogilvie Forbes was no longer hopeful. He told Dahlerus that "he was convinced that the British Government's policy was directed against the Hitler system." The Danzig question was not the real issue. A German *démarche* now would be useless. The Germans must be shown the need to "make a radical change in their methods." There was no question of allowing Hitler to continue his "unscrupulous policy."

Halifax still hoped for delay. He thought that with further time before the ultimatum was sent, an ultimatum would prove unnecessary. Hitler might agree to withdraw his troops. But with the uproar that followed Chamberlain's speech, further delay was no longer possible.

Duff Cooper dined with his wife at the Savoy Grill. The Under-Secretary of State for Air (Harold Balfour) walked past their table. Duff Cooper asked him if he was still a member of the Government. He made a gesture "of shame and despair." [42]

The Minister of Transport (Euan Wallace) came in, but said nothing. He thought Duff Cooper would "cut" him if he tried to talk to him. But the Minister knew that the Cabinet was known to be divided. He left Duff Cooper the message that Chamberlain's announcement "had taken the whole Cabinet by surprise." They were insisting on a Cabinet meeting before midnight.

Duff Cooper went to Churchill's flat. Eden, Boothby, Brendan Bracken and Sandys were there. "We were all in a state of bewildered rage." [43] They expressed their "deep anxiety" lest Britain should fail in its obligations to Poland.[44] Boothby thought that Chamberlain could no longer survive as Prime Minister if he failed to declare war within a matter of hours. Churchill could go to the Commons next day and "break" him. The group realized that if Churchill turned against Chamberlain the Government would fall. But Churchill refused to do so. Chamberlain had offered to make him First Lord of the Admiralty. And he had accepted.

Duff Cooper realized that Churchill could either "split the country" or "bolster up Chamberlain." [45] Churchill chose the latter. He would not lead a revolt against the Prime Minister.

Raczynski telephoned. He wanted to speak to Sandys. Sandys hurried to the Polish Embassy. Raczynski was most upset that Britain was about to desert Poland. Sandys replied that whatever the Government might say, and whatever its actions might seem to imply, "the feeling in the country and Parliament will carry us into war in support of Poland, with or without Chamberlain." [46] Later that night Churchill wrote to Chamberlain: "There was a feeling tonight in the House that injury had been done to the spirit of national unity." [47] But Churchill was not to make good the injury. Duff Cooper's wife wrote: "Conspiracy was in the air . . . The heavens themselves were blazing forth the death of something, while Brutus and the rest plotted through the night." [48] But Caesar Chamberlain had a long road to travel yet, and Brutus Churchill "and the rest" were many months from power.

Chamberlain telephoned Halifax at 8:30 P.M., and told him that his statement "had gone very badly." [49] Halifax hurried to 10 Downing Street. "I had never known Chamberlain so disturbed." [49] The two men dined together. Chamberlain told Halifax that the House was "infuriated." Unless they could "clear the position" next day he did not believe that the Government "would be able to maintain itself." [49]

At about 9 P.M. Simon, Hore-Belisha, Anderson, Elliot and de la Warr met again in Simon's room "and sent PM a letter rehearsing our points." [50] At 9:30 P.M. Halifax learned that the Italians "do not feel it possible" to ask the Germans to accept a conference. The withdrawal condition had been too much. If Hitler "chooses of his own account" to withdraw his troops, said Ciano, "well and good." But the Italians "do not feel able to press him to do so." [51]

Shortly before 10 P.M. Chamberlain telephoned Daladier and told him "there had been an angry scene in the House of Commons." Chamberlain added that "his colleagues in the Cabinet were also disturbed." If the French insisted on a forty-eight hour ultimatum beginning at midday on Sunday "it would be impossible for the [British] Government to hold the situation here." [52] Chamberlain wanted France and Britain to announce together an ultimatum at 8 A.M. Sunday, which would expire at midday Sunday. Daladier wanted to wait until midday Sunday for the German reply, before even considering an ultimatum.

That evening the Germans tried to prevent a British declaration of war. Hesse and Kordt telephoned Wilson. They asked him whether, in the event of a German withdrawal, the British would be prepared to concede Germany Danzig, and a road from Danzig to Germany across the Corridor. This, they said, was a "proposal." Wilson repeated the British conditions. No negotiations could take place until a German withdrawal. But Wilson made it clear that once the Germans had withdrawn, "the British Government would be prepared to let bygones be bygones." They could start Anglo-German negotiations "immediately." [53] Thus a vicious military attack, begun without declaration of war, and continued, with the bombing of towns, for forty-two hours, could be relegated into the obscurity of a *bygone* in order to assist an Anglo-German *rapprochement*.

At 10 P.M. Raczynski saw Halifax at the Foreign Office. The center of Warsaw had been bombed that afternoon. Raczynski asked what the time-limit was to the warning of twenty-four hours earlier. "The position of Poland was getting bad with the delay." Halifax told Raczynski that he was "not in a position" to tell him of a time-limit. There *was* none as yet. But the British were "fully alive both to the cruel strain to which his country was being subjected, and to the urgent necessity of relieving it in any way that we could at the earliest possible moment." Raczynski was not reassured. Halifax told Kennard that "he could not conceal from me that the moral effect of this delay on Poland was devastating." [54]

Simon and Anderson left the Commons for No. 10. They informed Chamberlain once more that the Cabinet decision could not be shuffled away.[55] Britain must send an ultimatum at once.

The revolt of conscience destroyed appeasement. Halifax told Bonnet that a British time-limit would have to be made that evening, "*owing to the difficult position which had arisen in House of Commons.*" [56] It seemed "very doubtful" whether the Government could "hold the position" in Britain if there were further delay. The urgency of the Government's dilemma was underlined when Halifax told Bonnet that if the French wanted to deliver their ultimatum later than 8 A.M. they must do so on their own. Anglo-French solidarity, a feeble creature on any showing, had died an ignominious death.

Halifax put down the telephone. Together with Kirkpatrick he walked from the Foreign Office to 10 Downing Street. Crossing the road they met Dalton. Would Dalton say that the Labour Party would "favour our declaring war alone" now France was unwilling to act at once? Dalton did not know. Kirkpatrick, conscious of the strength of public pressure, told him, firmly, "that unless we went to war we were sunk." Public opinion was "bewildered and disturbed." [57]

At No. 10 the Chief Whip was closeted with Chamberlain. He "warned him," in no uncertain terms, "that unless we acted on the following day there would be a revolt in the House." [58]

The Cabinet met at 11 P.M. It was clear that the latest possible time for an ultimatum to expire was midday the next day, when Parliament reassembled. Without war, the Government would be overthrown. The only question that remained was to fix the precise time for the ultimatum to be sent and to expire. Hore-Belisha pressed for a 2 A.M. ultimatum to expire at 6 A.M.[59] His promptings were, for a while, successful. Halifax told Henderson at 11:50 P.M., "I may have to send you instructions tonight . . . please be ready to act." [60]

But the tactic of delay had yet to die. Despite Hore-Belisha's insistence that "the less time involved the better" before the ultimatum expired, the final decision was to send it next morning, at 9 A.M., to expire at 11 A.M. The Germans were given another night and morning to advance, undisturbed either by a British declaration of war, or by the military action that it was assumed would follow such a declaration. The unwillingness to face realities was best shown in Halifax's telegram to Kennard, sent a few moments before the Cabinet met. In it, despite what Beck, Raczynski and Kennard had made clear about German bombing, Halifax gave the Germans the benefit of the doubt. Asking Kennard for details of where bombs had been dropped, he said: "In the meantime it is accepted Germans are attacking only military objectives." [61] It had almost become a maxim of British diplomacy that the Germans could do no wrong.

Sunday, September 3. The British decision for war had been made. Kirkpatrick and Halifax walked back to the Foreign Office. Henderson was told to ask for an appointment with Ribbentrop at 9 A.M.[62] Kirkpatrick and the Foreign Secretary had nothing more to do. There was no need to send Henderson the text of the ultimatum until morning. Halifax "seemed relieved" that the decision had been made. "He called for beer, which was brought down by a sleepy resident clerk in pyjamas. We laughed and joked . . ." [63]

Halifax went to bed. While he slept the French made one last attempt to obtain a conference, and to by-pass the British insistence that German troops withdraw first. Taking up de Monzie's idea of a "limited" withdrawal, Bonnet telephoned

Ciano and asked whether a "symbolic withdrawal of German troops could be obtained." [64] Bonnet had no means of knowing the British reaction to this move. As with his previous approach to the Italians, he failed to tell the British of what was in his mind. But he should have been warned by Corbin's message of 2 A.M. that if Chamberlain and the Cabinet failed to present an ultimatum before Parliament met, "they risked overthrow." [65] The French proposal was never submitted to the Germans. Ciano himself decided that Hitler would not hear of such an idea. "Nothing can be done. I throw the proposal in the waste-paper-basket without informing the Duce." [66] The last attempt to appease the strong at the cost of harming the weak had failed.

Twice during the night Kennard telegraphed to Halifax. In the first telegram Kennard passed on the opinion of the British Consul at Kattowice, who "agrees with me that the moral effect of speedy declaration of war . . . would be very great." But there could be no going back on the Cabinet decision. Had Hore-Belisha had his way, Kennard would already have known that war was less than four hours away, and could have passed the news to Beck. Had the earlier Cabinet decision been adhered to, Britain would already have been at war for two and a half hours. The final hesitation was the most painful, morally as well as militarily. Kennard made it clear that: "Delay in implementing Anglo-Polish Treaty is difficult for Poles to understand and makes my position and that of head of Military Mission very awkward and unenviable." [67]

In his second dispatch that night Kennard told Halifax of Beck's belief that the German ability to concentrate on Poland, as a result of Britain's failure to declare war, was having "a moral effect on civilian population and rendered counter attacks by Polish armies very difficult." Beck may well have despaired of any British action whatever. He made it clear to Kennard that if Germany "was allowed to crush Poland," the sequel, a German move against Britain, "was only a question of time." Kennard could do no more than repeat the views that were also his own.[68] Halifax knew Kennard's opinion well enough. No comment of Kennard's was necessary after Beck's rebuke. The crisis of the past two days had revealed many things. Not least among them was the wisdom of Howard Kennard.

The British ultimatum was delivered at 9 A.M. It expired at 11 A.M. No attempt was made, officially, by the Germans, to reply to it before it expired, or to meet its terms. Only Dahlerus, mesmerized perhaps by the hopes which he had himself so persistently produced, sought, after 9 A.M., to avert the British decision. He was certain at 10:15 A.M. that "if there could be give and take on both sides a conference could be arranged." He told the Foreign Office by telephone from Berlin that the German side "were most anxious to try to satisfy the British Government and to give satisfactory assurances not to violate the independence of Poland." Of course, withdrawal of troops was impossible. "Never in world history had an army withdrawn before negotiations." If the British would consider negotiations, "in the light of the background of the Versailles Treaty," Dahlerus was certain that there would be "a good chance of world peace." A German reply to the ultimatum, said Dahlerus, "was on its way." [69] It never came. At 10:50 A.M. Dahlerus telephoned once more. He suggested "as a last resort" that Göring should "fly over to London to discuss matters." Halifax, wearying no doubt of the pleadings of this indefatigable optimist, replied that to Britain's "definite question" there must be a "definite answer." [70] There were ten minutes left for its arrival. At 11 A.M. Britain was at war.

At midday Dahlerus and Henderson had their last meeting. Henderson was unable to hide "his profound grief and disappointment." All that he had worked for during two years of crowded diplomatic activity was in ruins. He had sought an understanding between England and Germany, not because he was afraid of German power, but because he believed in the positive value of German friendship. United, Great Britain and Germany could stave off external pressures, and avoid internal dissension. Divided, they opened themselves, and the rest of Europe, to whatever evils might seek to impose themselves upon them. Henderson had pressed so strongly for Anglo-German unity that, as Dahlerus wrote, "certain circles in England regarded him with scepticism and considered him susceptible to Nazi influence." It was an unfair judgment. Dahlerus "never found him the dupe of German policy." [71] But he looked for a flexibility and a sanity in that policy which did not exist.

War was declared. But appeasement lived on. Public pressure had driven Britain into war. But the public had yet to be made aware that "support and assistance" was difficult to define; easy to evade.

> On a Sunday in September there were deck-chairs in the sun,
> There was argument at lunch between the father and the son
> (Smoke rose from Warsaw) for the beef was underdone
> (Nothing points to heaven now but the anti-aircraft gun) :
> > With a hey nonny nonny
> > And a hi-de-ho.
> > > —WILLIAM PLOMER
> > > Father and Son: 1939

CHAPTER 22

Leaflets Versus Bombs

ON SEPTEMBER 3, 1939, Britain and France were once again at war with Germany. Many accounts of the prewar story assume that this date marks the end of an epoch. For Henderson, 1939 had played like a Greek tragedy, grinding inexorably to its pre-destined conclusion. The historian L. B. Namier considered Henderson's classical analogy "pseudo-artistic clap-trap." [1] The book which ends, like his, in September, implies that the heroes defeated the villains on September 3. But going to war was not heroic — nor was appeasement defeated. Many people were glad that the inevitable had not been further postponed. "The long frustration was over; the power of evil had at last been challenged." [2] For Chamberlain it was a "grievous disappointment" that peace could not be saved, "but I know my persistent efforts have convinced the world that no part of the blame can lie here. That consciousness of moral right which it is impossible for the Germans to feel must be a tremendous force on our side." [3]

Others felt England had no monopoly of morality. The idealists could only grieve that the anti-fascist struggle had ended in war. Stephen Spender wrote: "The fact was that the anti-fascist battle had been lost. For it was a battle against totalitarian war, which could have made the war unnecessary." [4]

The declaration of war brought new hope to the Poles. At last Britain would fulfill her pledges. Poland would receive "all the support and assistance" in Britain's power.

The Polish Air Attaché took a message to the Air Ministry on September 5. [5] It asked for immediate action by British bombers against German airports and industrial areas within the radius of the RAF. This action would relieve German pressure on Poland. Amery saw Kingsley Wood the same day and asked if the Government was going to help the Poles. He received no answer and "went away very angry." [6] Amery mentioned the plan which was currently popular, of setting the Black Forest alight with incendiary bombs. "Oh, you can't do that," said Kingsley Wood, "that's private property. You'll be asking me to bomb the Ruhr next." [7] There was no question of bombing the Essen munition works or the German lines of communication. Since they were private property, "American opinion" would be alienated.[8] Dalton approached Kingsley Wood about this project, but was assured that it would be contrary to the Hague Convention. "They must concentrate on real military objectives." [9]

It was announced in the Commons on September 6, that the Germans were bombing only Polish military objectives. They were not attacking the civilian population as such. Yet Britain was informed on September 3 by the Polish Government that twenty-seven Polish towns had been bombed and over a thousand civilians killed.[10] After consulting Raczynski and Opposition leaders, Spears decided to raise in the Commons "the question of the lack of support we are giving the Poles." Before the question was asked, he was told that Kingsley Wood would like to see him.

"Owing," said Kingsley Wood, "to our unfortunate democratic system, questions of strategy could be discussed publicly in the House, and this was most dangerous." [11]

The matter was dropped.

Raczynski received instructions from Beck on September 9 to "put the position clearly before the British Government and ask for a more definite answer regarding war plans and help for Poland." [12]

That evening Daladier told Lukasiewicz, the Polish Ambassador in Paris, that the French had been willing to help for the past three days. But the British had refused to do anything for fear of "upsetting the Americans." Whether used by France or Britain to save face, this excuse had worn thin. Raczynski told Cadogan on September 11: "This is very unfair to us. The least that we can ask is, what are you prepared to do?" Cadogan said an answer would be forthcoming that day. But no reply was received then or later.

The same day Dalton, who had many friends in Poland, suggested to Kingsley Wood that he himself should go there as "a symbol of the reality of our Alliance against Germany." Kingsley Wood replied that he "did not like the proposal," and later, that it was "not considered advisable." [13]

On September 13, Churchill told Dalton that it was in the British interest not to make the first move in air warfare in the West. Churchill thought delay would enable the British and French armies to improve their defenses by sandbagging. More aircraft could be turned out. "In order to influence American opinion," the first women and children to be hit should be British and not Germans. The last argument failed to take account of the Poles. In addition the Germans turned out more equipment during the phoney war than the British. As for sandbags, General Alan Brooke was continually bewailing the fact that they were in plentiful supply in England, but that there were none in France where they were most needed.[14] It was a problem of transport, not production. Churchill said, "In the long run, the only way to help Poland is to win the war against Germany." This did not betoken any immediate help for Poland. "In the long run," the Poles were dead.

British treatment of the Poles was symptomatic of a deeper malaise. Many Englishmen thought Germany would never be defeated by Chamberlain's Government. Others thought she should not be.

Chamberlain had introduced Churchill into his War Cabinet and Eden into his Government. But the so-called National Government could not hope for national support. The hatred for

Chamberlain himself, his minions and his ministers, had grown too strong. Dalton explained why Labour refused to join the Government. Labour had no confidence in Chamberlain and Simon, he said. "We should want Sir Horace Wilson shifted. If we heard that he had been appointed Governor of the Windward Islands and had left England to take up this most responsible post, we should be favourably impressed." [15] Dalton told Butler on September 20, that his colleagues thought "a number of Ministers should be sacked, as incapable of running the war." In Dalton's view, Simon, the Chancellor of the Exchequer, should be shot first. Butler diplomatically observed that "in the Foreign Office, the view was held that, if any Department was losing the war, it was the Treasury." [16]

To some of the Labour leaders the appeasers appeared as little better than criminals. But much of the dissent against Chamberlain's policy and Government was caused by those whose qualifications led them to suppose they were in a position to run the war more efficiently than those actually in charge. Lloyd George had won the last war. He felt he could bring this one to an end sooner than anyone had imagined. "He hates the Government in general, and Neville in particular, and feels bitterly that he has little or no chance of altering the course of things." [17] Leo Amery was reduced to reading Proust, and felt he could be making a more constructive contribution to the war effort.

To restore the drooping spirits of anti-appeasers tours of the Maginot Line were encouraged. A group of MPs went round it at the end of October. Amery amused Daladier afterwards "by describing the whole affair as 'L'enfant prodigieux d'un mariage entre une cuirasse et une mine.' " [18] Dalton roared with laughter and Harold Nicolson quoted appropriate passages of French poetry.[19]

But the bitterness against the men in charge could not be laughed away. Chamberlain saw where the bitterness began. "The Amerys, Duff Coopers, and their lot are consciously swayed by a sense of frustration because they can only look on."

They wanted to be working to defeat Germany. They disliked those who were supposed to be doing it. Chamberlain wrote: "The personal dislike of Simon and Hoare has reached a pitch which I find it difficult to understand." [20] Others understood it more easily.

Friendship with Germany, which had been British policy for several years, and the aim of Chamberlain and his father for half a century, could not be cast off quickly. In July Britain had offered alliance. In September the two countries were at war. The habit of many years could not be abandoned in a few months. Perhaps the various peace moves which began once war broke out were nothing but routine exercises for the Foreign Office. Just as Chiefs of Staff must plan for all contingencies from defense to total war, in alliance or alone, against many or few, so the diplomats of great nations must be prepared for all eventualities. But in September, 1939, what arguments were there for peace? Hitler had attacked a non-German state. He had bombed its cities. Germany lay open to retaliation. England and France had bombers and bombs. Pacifists objected to civilian bombing, but total quiescence had never been the official policy of the British Government. The country was pledged to fight. War had not been renounced as an instrument of policy.

There were a number of peace moves.[21] However important they might have been, they were conducted with marginal men in a marginal way. A description of one will show the nature of them all. Shortly before the outbreak of war Baron William S. de Ropp, employed by the British Air Ministry, had met Rosenberg in Berlin.[22] He told him that "in the event of war, he had been selected as political adviser on Germany to the Air Ministry." De Ropp was a naturalized Englishman, and a frequent lecturer to the Anglo-German Fellowship. Rosenberg told him that "it was a question of persuading the Dominions, within the framework of the British constitutional system, to make a joint statement in London directed against the whole policy of the Churchill and Eden group." De Ropp replied that if possible "he would initiate talks along these lines." [23] He also considered it to be "in the interests of both countries if, after the disposal of Poland, which was assumed to be likely, ways and means should be found to prevent a European struggle from finally breaking out." [24]

Three weeks after the outbreak of war, Rosenberg received a postcard by a "roundabout channel" from "Squadron-Leader" de Ropp. De Ropp asked if the Germans would arrange for someone known to him personally to meet him in Switzerland at the end of the month. There would be a "private exchange of views," in which Hitler's views on England and France would be exchanged for those of the British Air Ministry. The Ministry had "now become of extreme importance as a result of the war situation."

Following de Ropp's request a member of the Nazi Party's Foreign Policy Department was sent to Montreux to invite him to Berlin. De Ropp was surprised by the idea that he should himself go to Germany. He told the emissary that "in this extraordinary situation he must first make enquiry of his own Ministry." Having contacted London, he revealed that the Air Ministry "did not believe that in the interest of the matter it ought to sponsor such a journey with the reception which would be involved."

The opportunity should "be postponed to a more suitable time." Lest the Germans should think that this was an indefinite postponement, de Ropp added on November 10, to a representative of Rosenberg, that "the British Air Ministry . . . by no means wished to be a party to the present policy of England of waging war to the finish. There were too many British Empire experts in the Ministry not to know the dangers to the Empire itself." [25]

The Air Ministry was defeatist. Considering that much of the war would be fought in the air, this was disastrous. The only Ministry which reorganized itself on a war footing, and contemplated a *real* war, was the Admiralty. Churchill's past experience and vigor burst in. The Admiralty awoke. Churchill made sure that *his* men fought the war. But he could not influence other Ministers. They continued to slumber, to vacillate and to find inadequate excuses for their inadequacy.

Air-power was vital in modern war. The air Battle of Britain was later decisive. But the treatment which the Air Ministry received from the politicians who controlled it in the prewar period is extraordinary. That the personnel were defeatist as a result is not surprising. When politicians are lifeless, civil servants can do little to arouse them.

Many myths circulated in the thirties about air-power and air superiority. "The heavy bomber will always get through," was one. A joke current in Germany at the time of the Munich crisis illustrated the problem:

> "The English," said the Berliners, "have so many aeroplanes that the sky is black with them, and the French ones are so numerous that you can't see the sun for them; but when Göring presses the button, the birds themselves have got to walk." [26]

The accuracy of figures was immaterial. When Lindbergh told everyone in September, 1938, that the German Air Force was enormous, and the Russian one useless, he was believed at once. The fear of heavy bombing lay heavy over the prewar years, and prejudiced action. A week before war began Josiah Wedgwood wagered five pounds that there would be no bombing of London for six months. It made headline news. It was unbelievable that anyone so wise could make so rash a guess.

If ever a department was dominated by those who believed in appeasement, it was the Air Ministry. Hoare, Londonderry, Swinton, Kingsley Wood, and again Hoare. If the spiritual home of the appeasers was at Cliveden, their happiest working hours were spent in the Air Ministry. From here poured forth the facts and figures that made war seem impossible; the true opiate of the appeasers.

Since the initial premise of prewar thinking was wrong — that an opponent would immediately use bombers on the outbreak of war — the policy derived from it proved equally incorrect. The execution of policy suffered as a result. It is difficult to instill a sense of responsibility into a man who thinks he will be killed in a bombing raid before his plans are put into operation.

The hypnotic effect of the threat of heavy bombing can be seen by examining the attitude of British strategists towards a European war in the years before it broke out. Their theories started from a fixed point: the heavy bombing of England by the enemy. No future war would take place without this aerial intervention, and strategic policy must be built round it. Bombing would be immediate, and effective. When in 1940, according to the Prince Hohenlohe, the late Aga Khan and others advised Hitler to send his heavy bombers over England, they were not being unusually brutal. They were merely reflecting the inadequacies of the military thinking with which they had been familiar before the war. According to the Germans the Duke of Windsor believed that "continued severe bombings would make England ready for peace." * The Aga Khan thought that the heavy bombing of England would be more successful than invasion and that soon he would be able to toast Hitler's arrival at Windsor in champagne.†

* German Minister, Lisbon (Huene) to German Foreign Ministry July 11, 1940:
"The designation of the Duke as Governor of the Bahama Islands is intended to keep him far away from England, since his return would bring with it very strong encouragement to English friends of peace, so that his arrest at the instance of his opponents would certainly have to be expected. [The Duke] is convinced that if he had remained on the throne war would have been avoided, and he characterizes himself as a firm supporter of a peaceful arrangement with Germany. The Duke believes that continued severe bombings would make England ready for peace." (*Germ. Docs.* D. X No. 152.)

† Prince Max Hohenlohe to Senior Counsellor Hewel July 25, 1940 (Schloss Rothenhaus, Sudetenland.):
"[The Aga Khan] asked me to convey to you the following with a request that you relay it to the Führer. The Khedive of Egypt, who is also there, has agreed with him that on the day when the Führer puts up for the night in Windsor, they would drink a bottle of champagne together. He

The military thinking of Chamberlain's Government directly contradicted the theory that appeasement was a policy put forward to gain time for rearmament. After the *Anschluss* the Government considered that in a war with Germany the British contribution to Allied strength should consist mainly of naval and air forces. "We should avoid sending a large army to the Continent; the role of the army should be limited to home defence and the defence of British territories overseas." [27] The declared aim was for a force of five divisions equipped for imperial defense rather than for continental warfare.

The role of the air force was to be largely defensive. It had to be strong enough to resist any attack upon England itself. There was no provision for "air participation in large scale land operations or for the despatch of large mobile air forces overseas." [28]

After Munich Chamberlain told Daladier that he was concentrating the rearmament program on anti-aircraft defense. The French Premier was not impressed. "Obviously anti-aircraft defence was important, but in his view, it was better to defend London by having bombers which might go and bomb German towns rather than by concentrating principally on anti-aircraft guns." [29] Daladier wanted Britain to send two divisions to France "at least as early as the eighth day after the outbreak of hostilities." Chamberlain refused to commit himself but agreed that further *talks* should take place.

After the occupation of Prague British policy seemed more realistic. Anglo-French staff talks were opened on March 29, 1939. They were a renewed symbol of the military nature of the

---

knew that the King of Egypt would do likewise with them, if he were present. If Germany and Italy were thinking of taking over India, he would place himself at our disposal to help in organizing the country; he was counting for that on his well-known following and on several young maharajas . . . America's material war aid should not be overestimated, since England was lacking in trained manpower for the aircraft etc. furnished. England could soon be largely cut off from vital supplies. The struggle against England was not a struggle against the English people, but against the Jews. Churchill had been for years in their pay." (Germ. Docs. D. X No. 188.)

Anglo-French alliance, though not of its effectiveness. Eden had insisted on the talks: a "posthumous" triumph. The belief that the British contribution to Allied strength could be restricted to naval and air forces was abandoned. A British army would be sent to the Continent. The decision to double the Territorial force and to introduce conscription followed logically, even though there were doubts in the Cabinet, and much unnecessary delay. Many failed to understand that Germany could not be prevented from fighting in the East by Allied *defensive* warfare in the West.

Many refused to believe that fighting would be necessary. Hoare realized that after Munich Chamberlain "undoubtedly hesitated between hope and disillusionment. The outlook was obscure, but on the whole, the forces of peace seemed to be gaining ground." [30] The mood of optimism was not destroyed in March, 1939. Hoare wrote: "Hitler's entry into Prague was not, as many declared, the end of the peace policy. Chamberlain and his colleagues never abandoned the hope of preventing a world war until it actually broke out." Once it had broken out, it was not obvious to Hoare, to Kingsley Wood, to Simon or to Chamberlain that military action would serve any immediate purpose. They were not alone in thinking that freedom from attack would enable Britain to make good her deficiency in armaments. In January, 1940, at a luncheon, an exponent of this view explained, "Time is on our side." A quiet voice answered: "Time is an unfriendly neutral on the side of the strongest." "Is that Shakespeare?" asked a female guest. "No," replied another, "it's good Sargent." It was Orme Sargent. He was right.[31] The outcome of delay would be defeat. As Harold Macmillan warned the Commons on January 17: "Time properly used is on our side, but we must not take the complacent view that the mere continuation of the war without any serious military losses to ourselves means that it will necessarily end in our favour."

When war came Britain's army was transferred to the Continent. There was no question of a bombing offensive over Germany. In reply to the bombs that fell on Warsaw, Cracow and Kattowice, England dropped leaflets. The British believed that the German people had only to be informed of the wickedness of their rulers for them to rise up as one man against them. Kingsley Wood told Dalton that these "truth raids" caused the German authorities great irritation. The Germans had seen in India, that same year, how leaflets had been dropped on a hostile tribe one day, bombs the next. It was thought that techniques used by the British in Waziristan would be used in Europe. As a result all German air-raid precautions were put into operation in the belief that bombs, and not leaflets, would be dropped once the "truth raids" had begun.[32] But many of the British aircraft were hardly in a position to drop leaflets, let alone bombs. On October 27, four aircraft dropped leaflets on Frankfurt, Munich and Stuttgart. In the first one, two members of the crew became unconscious because of the cold, both engines stopped and the plane made a crash landing. One engine failed in the second plane; the crew baled out except for the tail gunner who failed to receive the order. In the third plane, the front gunner was completely iced up in his turret. The crew of the last plane returned safely but were "incapable of coherent thought or action." [33]

To the Air Force of this period, wrote Hoare, "it was a chapter of heroic bravery, of forlorn hopes, of brilliant improvisation." [34] But this was no substitute for single-minded action and efficient planning. Kingsley Wood lacked the qualities necessary to drag the Air Ministry from defeatism. As Hoare wrote, Kingsley Wood's "ill-health and inexperience of service questions had tended to obscure the activities of the Air Force in a war that did not seem to be real war." Hoare might have added that many of the activities did not seem to be real activities.

H. G. Daniels, a former *Times* correspondent, who since the outbreak of war had been Press Attaché at the British Legation in Berne, said "the war was madness for England and had to be ended in shortest order." David Kelly, British Minister in Berne, according to a German report, supported him.[35] Pacifists thought war a disaster for mankind. Others saw the war as inflicting a mortal blow on England alone. Some saw it as the breeding-ground of emergent communism. De Ropp suggested that Germany should use the Bolshevik menace in its propaganda against England. Since England, he declared, had told the Germans that the destruction of the régime was a war aim, Germany should point out that the successor could only be communist. The successful blackmail that had been carried out by Germany since Versailles should be continued. "I took cognisance of this," wrote de Ropp's German interviewer, "without mentioning that, probably out of consideration for Russia, we could not employ such propaganda at all." [36] The pact with the Soviet Union raised some curious ethical problems.

De Ropp seemed to have achieved one thing. As a result of his inquiries the Germans discovered that "the English circles which want an early peace because of their concern for the Empire have brought it about that henceforth no official organ will proclaim the overthrow of the German régime *as a war aim*." [37]

If this was what de Ropp intended he was not to remain successful for long. On October 21, Hore-Belisha outlined British war aims over the radio:

We did not enter the fight merely to reconstitute Czechoslovakia. Nor do we fight merely to reconstitute a Polish State. Our aims are not defined by geographical frontiers. We are concerned with the frontiers of the human spirt. This is no war about a map . . . This tyranny, whose challenge we have accepted, must and will be abased . . . Only the defeat of Nazi Germany can lighten the darkness which now shrouds our cities, and lighten the horizon for all Europe and the world.[38]

A Cabinet Minister could hardly be prevented from speaking his mind. The BBC was firmer elsewhere. They refused to allow Sir Horace Rumbold to broadcast on Germany on the grounds that he was too anti-German. A similar ban was put on Harold Nicolson.[39]

Nazi Germany would be overthrown, and *a* Polish State reconstituted. There was no mention in Hore-Belisha's broadcast of *the* Polish State which had existed before September. Poland had caused Great Britain the final embarrassment of going to war. Few people felt very kindly towards her. The guarantee had never been entirely popular, nor was Poland a country to which Britain was bound by natural ties of friendship. Poland had many of the vices of a totalitarian régime, without possessing the charm and fascination of power. Perhaps because of Dalton's known friendship for Poland it was regarded as a preserve of the Labour Party; hence a word of abuse. In 1938, in the course of a debate, Commander Bower, a Tory MP, shouted across the floor at Shinwell: "Go back to Poland." [40] He was rewarded with a slap on the face. Shinwell had Polish ancestry. He was also a Jew.

Even in the Foreign Office there was little enthusiasm for Poland. Ivone Kirkpatrick, who had become Head of the Central Department, was no exception. He wrote later,

> The Poles are very charming people, but they seem to be guided in politics less by reason than by emotion. In the early days of the war they pressed us strongly to relax the rules governing our blockade of Germany in order to permit the passage of two trains of munitions from Roumania to the hard-pressed Polish Army. The trains could not have got there in time. The blockade was essential to the Allies, but the Poles brushed that sort of argument aside.[41]

The Poles had questions to raise concerning the immediate implementation of pledges. They too had their arguments brushed aside.

On September 24, Dahlerus saw Ogilvie Forbes, who had been transferred on the outbreak of war to Oslo. Dahlerus thought that after the recent speeches of Chamberlain and Churchill it was unlikely that there would be any Anglo-German negotiations for peace. Ogilvie Forbes denied this, taking the view that

the British Government could very well conduct such negotiations with Germany if only a formula were found which assured to the peoples of Europe their territorial integrity and their freedom by means of a treaty among the great European Powers. Poland was considered lost, so they took the position that it was now a matter of at least saving their own skins.[42]

The British thought that if the four-power pact which Chamberlain cherished could be put into practice, Hitler's immediate gains might be secured, and there would be peace once more.

Some Germans opposed to Hitler were thinking along the same lines. In October Erich Kordt and Hasso von Etzdorf, besides making plans for a military coup against Hitler, drew up conditions of peace which, having overthrown Hitler, they would present to the British.

A peace which would not infringe Germany's ethnic frontiers (approximately as fixed at Munich), and would establish an overland connexion between East Prussia and the Reich, and restore to Germany the Upper Silesian industrial districts. Such a solution would satisfy her real national interest. It would avoid burdening Germany with alien elements, and yet, for geographic and economic reasons, would secure for her a predominant influence over a rump-Czechia and a rump-Poland.[43]

Two days after his visit to Ogilvie Forbes, Dahlerus had an interview with Hitler and Göring. Hitler maintained that his condition for peace discussions was "an entirely free hand in Poland." He had no intention of allowing anyone to interfere in the solution of the Polish questions except perhaps the Russians. They had "a weighty word to say in the matter." Poland was of course Hitler's last demand; "beyond this he was entirely prepared to join in guaranteeing the *status quo* of the rest of Europe." [44]

Poland was not a country to fight over. Hitler was disappointed by it. He had been to the front, only to find that "the Vistula, supposed to be Poland's great river, was silted up everywhere and navigable only by rowboat."

At this interview, three weeks after war had begun, Hitler was prepared to discuss peace terms. He thought it would be best if France or a neutral country would take the first step towards peace discussions. "The Duce, for example, could take over this rôle." Dahlerus replied that the Duce was not considered sufficiently neutral by the British, but that the Queen of the Netherlands had been thought of.

The following day German troops marched into Warsaw. The *Blitzkrieg* had proved successful.

On October 6, the day after he reviewed his troops in Warsaw, Hitler made his first and only comprehensive peace appeal to the Western Powers, in the Reichstag. His speech was prepared in pamphlet form in English in order that it might be dropped by airplanes over England. To German surprise the terms of peace were so widely reported in the British newspapers that this proved unnecessary. Hitler advocated the holding of a European conference on the problems arising from the collapse of Poland, including Germany's colonial claims and the limitation of armaments.

Hoare had envisaged quite different proposals. He wrote to Lothian that he thought Hitler might have made "a very attractive peace offer, possibly going to the point of offering to retire himself in the interests of peace, with a view to enlisting the support of the neutrals and damaging morale in France and England." [45] It was remarkable that a senior member of the War Cabinet could imagine that Hitler might resign after the extremely successful operation against Poland in which his policy seemed to have been vindicated. Hoare went on to suggest that the British should discover Hitler's position "rather than to meet his speech with a curt and immediate refusal."

The terms of peace were publicly turned down by Chamberlain on October 12. The fear of air attack had died down. In rejecting Hitler's overtures, Britain's leaders had little idea of

Hitler's future plans. Churchill thought Britain's policy should be to leave Hitler "to stew in his own juice during the winter while speeding forward our armaments and weaving-up our alliances." Hitler was rapidly overcoming the opposition of two of his generals, Brauchitsch and Halder, and hoping to attack France later that autumn. The success of the *Blitzkrieg* against Poland had convinced him of the value of taking the initiative, and shown the weakness of the West. Britain and France would surely have taken advantage of his preoccupation in Poland had they wished to fight seriously. The seventy-six Anglo-French divisions faced, in September, only thirty-two German divisions behind the Siegfried line. The French made small advances into the frontier areas between the Maginot and Siegfried lines. No important military action was taken, or considered. Even if the British had wished to object to this policy, they were bound to defer to the French. Britain provided only four divisions to the French seventy-two. General Gort, the British commander-in-chief, was not even under the French commander-in-chief, General Gamelin, but subordinate to General Georges, in charge of the north-east sector of the front.

Like Britain, France was unwilling to help Poland by pursuing an active military policy. Yet France's obligations were even more specific than Britain's. Under the Franco-Polish military protocol of May 19, 1939, France was to open an offensive on the Western Front by the sixteenth day of war. She was pledged to send into action between thirty-five and thirty-eight divisions. No offensive was planned. No divisions advanced. General Jodl said at the Nuremberg Trial that "if we did not collapse in 1939, that was due only to the fact that during the Polish campaign" the seventy-six British and French divisions, which faced thirty-two German divisions, "were completely inactive." General Keitel agreed that "an attack on the part of the Western Powers would have met only a show of defence, which would certainly not have been effective."

CHAPTER 23

"Decayed Serving Men"

HITLER decided to attack France in October. The weather prevented him, or merely provided the excuse for an alteration of plan. It was as well for the Western Allies. Anglo-French relations were growing closer, but strategic co-operation was more difficult to secure. "A wasted day as far as work was concerned," recorded General Alan Brooke on October 31,

> but I hope that as a result of it our good relations with our allies were more closely knitted . . . Champagne-lunch consisting of oysters, lobsters, chicken, pâté-de-foie-gras, pheasant, cheese and fruit, coffee, liqueurs, etc. We sat down at one P.M. and got up at three P.M.[1]

Although the German attack westward had been postponed, German troops were alert throughout the winter waiting for a favorable opportunity to march. Germany's interest in peace moves was therefore small. Dahlerus sought "to ascertain from England whether the British are interested at all" in the peace appeals of the monarchs of Holland and Belgium.[2] Göring informed him by telephone on November 11, that "the German Government is no longer interested in his [Dahlerus's] sounding out England, because the official attitude of the British Government has already indicated unequivocal rejection of the German position."[3]

Hitler, on the crest of a victorious wave, dismissed the possibility of peace moves. But before his planned move against the West became known, there were many Englishmen who were prepared to compromise over the fate of Poland. Lloyd George sharply criticized Chamberlain for having rejected Hitler's peace moves. Lord Derby wrote to Lord Beaverbrook:

> I wish I knew what we are fighting for — if it is to beat Hitler to a pulp, I understand and strongly sympathise, but if it is to reconstitute Poland, I am not so enthusiastic. If it had not been for the League of Nations, which I abominate — or for Locarno, which I always thought a very much overrated treaty — we should not be fighting now for Poland.[4]

At least the aged aristocrat had firm ideas as to what he wanted done to Hitler. He shared the uncertainty of others about the future of Poland. As Dalton saw: "We were letting them down and letting them die, while we did nothing to help them." [5]

During October, R. A. Butler had talks with Maisky. The former champion of collective security was now the representative of a Power allied with the Nazis. His account reached Moscow, and then Berlin. Butler told Maisky on October 18:

> The British Government would be ready to make peace even tomorrow if it received assurance that the understanding reached would ensure peace for twenty or twenty-five years. The British Government would regard as such assurance a guarantee pronounced by all major Powers, in particular the United States and the Soviet Union. In such an event the British Government would be prepared, in the event of a lasting peace, to make important concessions to Germany even in respect to colonies.[6]

British policy, as seen, at least, by the nimble R. A. Butler, was moving away from Chamberlain's idea of a purely European pact. It sought a wider guarantee. Butler did not mention Poland to Maisky. A month later he made his view clear to Bastianini. The Italian had asked "whether the rumour circulating in London was true that evacuation of Poland by German troops was England's basic condition for any kind of agreement." Butler denied "in the most categorical manner" that this was the intention of his Government: "the absurdity of such a demand, which Germany — or any Great Power — could never accept, was obvious." [7] The reconstitution of Poland within her 1919 frontiers was no longer regarded as a desirable or feasible possibility. As for a "peaceful solution," said Butler, "neither the Foreign Office nor the Prime Minister excluded such an eventuality *a priori*."

Cadogan unwittingly had misled Bastianini when he saw him some days earlier, and stated that the restoration "of a Polish state" was "indispensable." The accent, however, was on *a* Polish state and not on "indispensable." [8]

Halifax himself seemed prepared to contemplate peace moves at the expense of those European countries already conquered. According to information received by the German Foreign Ministry, he talked with a Danish businessman, Pless-Schmidt, and showed "lively interest in an early peace and readiness to enter into negotiations." The draft proposals Halifax discussed had been put forward by the Foreign Minister of Finland:

1) Poland was to be reconstituted as an independent state, bounded on the west by the German border of 1914, and in the east by the Russian border of September, 1939.

2) Czechia was to be given a Government of her own under German suzerainty, and to remain part of Germany's military sphere of interest.

3) The colonies were to be returned.

4) An alliance between belligerent countries, plus Italy and Spain, to guarantee peace in Europe. From this alliance Russia was to be omitted. [9]

This proposal was not followed up. But in April, 1940, Halifax was making further peace moves with the unofficial German Opposition.

Von Hassel, former German Ambassador to the Holy See, received a message from Halifax stating the British conditions for peace. Halifax stipulated that if Hitler and Ribbentrop were removed Britain would be willing to co-operate with a National-Socialist Government. She would accept Göring's leadership. In addition Germany must abstain from an offensive in the West. In return Britain was prepared to recognize the *status quo* with respect to Czechoslovakia and Poland.[10] The message reached General Brauchitsch. He refused to consider it, as the invasion of Norway had just begun. He did not think it was possible to organize a successful political coup in the middle of a military campaign. Nor were the conservative, but anti-Nazi, generals interested in Göring's elevation to power. Even if Halifax had been prepared to accept a German Government under Göring's leadership, the Opposition in Germany could hardly have been expected to allow a Nazi minion to rule in Hitler's stead.

Chamberlain also considered the possibility of a negotiated peace, and of a German Government purged of the extremer Nazi elements. He wrote he had a "hunch" that the war would end in spring 1940. "It won't be by defeat in the field but by German realization that they *can't* win and that it isn't worth their while to go on getting thinner and poorer when they might have instant relief." If peace were made the Germans might "not have to give up anything they really care about." Hitler, of course, would have to go. "He must either die, or go to St. Helena, or become a real public works architect, preferably in a 'home.' His entourage must also go." But Göring might possibly stay, and take up "some ornamental position in a transitional Government." [11]

Former appeasers saw the folly, and futility, of defeatism and compromise. In 1938 Eden had described defeatism as "an ugly name for an ugly thing." Few listened to him then. But on February 11, 1940, Thomas Jones wrote that, even at Cliveden, "No one is satisfied that Neville C. is directing the war with the necessary energy and imagination. He deals with the problems in front of him but he has no prevision nor circumvision. Halifax is timid and hesitant . . . Winston has bursts of output but he is far from being the Winston of 1914-18. Simon is a Rolls-

Royce brain but cannot steer . . . Horace Wilson is envied because of his power."

In peacetime the policy of appeasement had been made possible by the removal of those in influential positions who opposed it. War brought the anti-appeasers nearer power. But the appeasers claimed one more victim. Chamberlain's declared policy as Prime Minister had been rearmament, and better relations with Germany and Italy. The second part of his policy had failed. The first had been inadequate. What improvements there were in the Services before the war were largely the work of Hore-Belisha. Appointed by Chamberlain in 1937 as his War Minister, Hore-Belisha had worked steadily through the following years implementing Chamberlain's decision to rearm and trying to make the decision firmer. His democratization of the army aroused antagonism, but few doubted that it was necessary. Chamberlain considered that he had done "more for the army than anyone since Haldane." [12] An able head of a Department, Hore-Belisha had not made trouble in the Cabinet. Although War Minister he was not a member of the Foreign Policy Committee. He appeared to have supported the Prime Minister over Munich. But after Munich his criticisms were outspoken, especially of Chamberlain's failure to take rearmament seriously. Chamberlain used Wilson more than once to bring Hore-Belisha into line. But Hore-Belisha refused to accept Wilson's pressure, and fought successfully for conscription.[13]

On the outbreak of war, as a Service Minister, he entered the War Cabinet. In November he toured the defenses in France. He made caustic comments about the general state of unpreparedness. This did not please Lord Gort. General Ironside told Hore-Belisha that "the officers were most upset" at the criticisms made about "lack of defences." [14] Gort threatened to resign for he disliked Hore-Belisha's popularity. One of Gort's ADCs saw Reith in January, 1940. "He was worried and annoyed about a news film in which Hore-Belisha and Gort had appeared." Hore-

Belisha had been applauded: Gort "received in apathetic silence." [15]

The King went to France. On his return he asked to see Hore-Belisha. But Hore-Belisha never received the message, and was thus unable to answer the criticisms the King had heard in France. On the King's instructions Chamberlain saw Ironside, presumably to pass on Gort's criticisms. Chamberlain flew to France. He saw Hore-Belisha on his return, and advised him to be "careful." On January 4, he told him that there was "prejudice" against him.[16] He was offered the Board of Trade, which he refused. He resigned the following day. Chamberlain wanted to offer him the Ministry of Information. Halifax objected that "it would have a bad effect on the neutrals both because HB was a Jew and because his methods would let down British prestige." [17]

Hore-Belisha had resigned. Chamberlain thought the ex-Minister "did not and could not see where he had gone wrong, and only thought that he had been treated with great injustice and prejudice." [18] Hore-Belisha had not been entirely mistaken. Chamberlain's protests seem those of a guilty man. The appeasers were never united in all they did. The prejudices of one were not necessarily common to all. But the bonds that held them together were stronger than any divergence of views, and the actions of one group affected the others. Nine months earlier appeasement would have gained had Hore-Belisha resigned. His resignation, or his "dismissal" as it was openly called, came too late. Of no practical value in prolonging the "phoney war" or bringing about an early peace, it was the last positive achievement of the appeasers. In a war fought against "prejudice," fought to end anti-semitism and discrimination against minorities, a champion of these aims had been sacrificed in the name of the very causes against which he was fighting.*

* Wedgwood told the Commons on January 16: "The Prime Minister denies that the Secretary of State was dismissed because he was a Jew. He cannot deny that the prejudice against him was because he was a Jew."

In the week of his resignation Hore-Belisha was fiercely libelled by the weekly journal *Truth*. A copy of its issue of January 12 was sent to every member of the Commons and the Lords. In that issue was an attack on Hore-Belisha, anti-semitic in tone, and on certain companies of which he had been either chairman or director some ten years before. The damaging and libellous material which this article contained was in the hands of MPs before Hore-Belisha made his resignation speech. He received advice from Simon "that it would not be in the public interest for him to take an action against *Truth* with all the publicity it would involve." [19] Because these articles were blatantly anti-semitic Simon feared they would give pleasure to Hitler if widely discussed.

If Hore-Belisha were to take action, it would also be asked in the courts why *Truth* had waited for ten years to launch such an attack upon him, and why it had chosen the momentous weekend before his resignation speech, when his prestige was so high, for its attempt to discredit him. Such discredit, coming shortly before he explained his resignation, made Parliament less willing to spring to his defense. Only the popular press lamented his fall. "Were Generals reprimanded?" asked the *Daily Express*, "and did they take revenge?" It was not only the Generals who had been revenged.

During a two-day debate in the Commons, on May 7 and 8, Leo Amery indicated that enough was enough. The defeatism of Chamberlain's Government must be brought to an end, or the war would be lost, by defeat, or by the humiliation of a compromise peace.

Somehow or other we must get into the Government men who can match our enemies in fighting spirit, in daring, in resolution and in thirst for victory. Some three hundred years ago, when the House found that its troops were being beaten again and again by the dash and daring of the Cavaliers, by Prince Rupert's cavalry, Oliver Cromwell spoke to John Hampden: "Your troops are most of them old, decayed serving men and tapsters and such kind of fellows . . ."

I have quoted certain words of Oliver Cromwell. I will quote certain other words. I do it with great reluctance, because I am speaking of those who are old friends and associates of mine, but they are words which, I think, are applicable to the present situation. This is what Cromwell said to the Long Parliament when he thought it was no longer fit to conduct the affairs of the nation: "You have sat too long for any good you have been doing. Depart, I say, and let us have done with you. In the name of God, go!"

Chamberlain saw no reason to go. Norway had fallen to Hitler. That was all. The war was not over, and while it lasted, Chamberlain was quite prepared to direct it. He resented Amery's challenge, and replied: "We should do better to occupy ourselves with increasing our war effort than disputing about the form of Government."

But the dispute continued. Those who opposed the Government did so, not because they disliked Chamberlain personally, but because they thought his conduct of the war inadequate. One of the dangers, Wedgwood told the Commons, was "facile optimism, that saps the morale of the whole country." Roger Keyes wore his Admiral's uniform for the debate. He emphasized, without needing to speak, that Britain was at war. More than words were needed.

Chamberlain remained optimistic. Herbert Morrison announced there would be a division. Chamberlain countered that he had "friends" in the House. Lloyd George, turning against appeasement with as much violence as he had, earlier, supported it, mocked at Chamberlain's reference to his friends, and urged Chamberlain to make one further sacrifice — himself. Lloyd George's invective was not enough. Chamberlain's following, though shaken, survived. He had a majority of eighty-one on the division. Thirty Conservatives had voted with the opposition. Over sixty had abstained. Chamberlain remained in office. Yet his opponents thought all was over. "We ought to sing something," said Harold Macmillan, and Wedgwood started on *Rule Britannia*.[20] But Chamberlain did not see why he should go. He told his sister that a number of those who had voted against him had written to say "they had nothing against me except that I had the wrong people in my team." [21]

On May 10, the Germans invaded Holland and Belgium. Chamberlain asked Attlee and Greenwood to join a coalition Government. The Labour leaders were undecided. While they deliberated at Bournemouth, Chamberlain called his Cabinet together in London. Reith, who was present, noted that "he did not refer to Amery or any of the other Conservatives who had attacked him. He was in good form; the news from the Low Countries had stimulated him." As a result of the invasions he was "ready for action if encouraged and authorised to act." [22] The meeting continued. Horace Wilson was handed a message. He passed it across the table, towards Chamberlain. Reith was the first to read it. It was a statement by Attlee and Greenwood. They were not prepared to serve under Chamberlain.

Kingsley Wood told Chamberlain that he would have to resign. The invasion of the Low Countries made a coalition necessary. If Labour would not serve under him, Chamberlain must go. Kingsley Wood was emphatic. Chamberlain had always trusted him and accepted his advice. Now there was a hint that Kingsley Wood had been plotting behind Chamberlain's back, planning his overthrow.[23] Chamberlain had expected greater loyalty from so old and proven a friend. Such loyalty was denied him. Wilson was infuriated by Kingsley Wood's betrayal, but could do nothing. Chamberlain recognized the kiss of Judas. That afternoon he called the Cabinet once more, and announced that he was no longer Prime Minister.

Under the new régime, things changed. There were new men, and a new authority.

Kingsley Wood alone of the appeasers retained the confidence of Churchill's Government. He, not Churchill, had broken Chamberlain's power. He remained in the Government after May, 1940, and became Chancellor of the Exchequer.

The decayed serving men went to serve elsewhere: Hoare as Ambassador to Spain, Halifax to follow Lothian as Ambassador to the United States, Simon to the Woolsack, Chamberlain to die.

The fate of one other man illuminates the end of a policy and of an era. In 1937 Chamberlain had installed Sir Horace Wilson in a room adjoining the Cabinet Room at No. 10, looking out over the Horse Guards Parade. On May 11, 1940, Wilson arrived as usual. As he opened the door, he saw, on the sofa confronting him, Brendan Bracken and Randolph Churchill: "They stared at Sir Horace, but no one spoke or smiled. Then he withdrew, never to return to that seat most proximate to power." [24]

Cabinet Ministers

MAY, 1937—SEPTEMBER, 1939

Prime Minister:
Chamberlain

Lord President:
Halifax
Hailsham (Feb '38)
Runciman (Oct '38)

Lord Chancellor:
Hailsham
Maugham (Feb '38)

Lord Privy Seal:
De la Warr
Anderson (Oct '38)

Exchequer:
Simon

Home Office:
Hoare

Foreign Office:
Eden
Halifax (Feb '38)

Colonies:
Ormsby-Gore
MacDonald (May '38)

Dominions:
MacDonald
Stanley (May '38)
MacDonald (Oct '38)
Inskip (Jan '39)

War:
Hore-Belisha

India:
Zetland

Air:
Swinton
Kingsley Wood (May '38)

Scotland:
Elliot
Colville (May '38)

Board of Trade:
Stanley

Admiralty:
Duff Cooper
Stanhope (Oct '38)

Health:
Kingsley Wood
Elliot (May '38)

Agriculture:
Morrison
Dorman-Smith (Jan '39)

Labour:
Brown

Co-ordination of Defence:
Inskip
Chatfield (Jan '39)

Transport:
Burgin
Wallace (April '39)

Minister without Portfolio:
Burgin (April '39)

Minister of Supply:
Burgin (July '39)

Duchy of Lancaster:
Winterton (Mar '38)
Morrison (Jan '39)

Education:
Stanhope
De la Warr (Oct '38)

Biographical Sketches

ALLEN OF HURTWOOD, Reginald Clifford, Baron. 1889-1939
Son of a draper. Educated at Berkhamstead School; University
College, Bristol; Peterhouse, Cambridge. Chairman of the "No
Conscription Fellowship," 1914-18. Its members refused military service and some, like Allen, refused "alternative service"
on conscientious grounds. He was imprisoned three times, 1916-
17, and went on hunger strike. Visited Russia in 1920 with an
ILP delegation. During the twenties, with his wife, he conducted a co-educational school on modern lines near Guildford.
He supported Ramsay MacDonald when the Labour Government dissolved in 1931, and was made a peer in 1932. He was
a firm supporter of the League and of collective security. In
1935 he met Hitler and Göring in Berlin. He advocated justice
to Germany by a revision of the Versailles Treaty. He was in
Czechoslovakia in the summer of 1938, and suffered a complete
breakdown that autumn. He died in Switzerland on March 3,
1939. His ashes were scattered in Lake Geneva.
Publications:
Preface to *Conscription and Conscience* (1922), *Putting Socialism into Practice* (1924), *Socialism and the next Labour Government* (1925), *Labour's Future at Stake* (1932), *Britain's
Political Future* (1934), *Peace in our Time* (1936).

AMERY, Leopold Stennett. 1873-1955
Born in India; son of an Indian Forest Department official.
Educated at Harrow and Balliol. First in Mods and Greats.
Fellow of All Souls' 1897 (in same year as John Simon). *Times*
editorial staff, 1899-1909. In charge of reporting the South
African War. Barrister, 1902. Unsuccessful Unionist candidate,
1906, '08, '10. MP (Unionist), 1911-45. Served in Flanders and

Near East in Great War. Assistant Secretary to the War Cabinet, 1917. On staff of War Council. Under-Secretary, Colonial Office, 1919-21. Parliamentary Secretary, Admiralty, 1921-22. First Lord of the Admiralty, 1922-24. Secretary of State, Colonies, 1924-29. Dominion Affairs, 1925-29. Without office throughout the thirties, and a constant critic of appeasement. Secretary of State for India and Burma, 1940-45.

Publications:
Times History of South African War, 7 volumes (1909), *Empire and Prosperity* (1930), *The German Colonial Claim* (1939), *My Political Life,* 3 volumes (1953-55).

ASHTON-GWATKIN, Frank Trelawney Arthur. 1889-1976
Son of a clergyman. Educated at Eton and Balliol. Won the Newdigate Prize (1909) with a poem on Michelangelo. Entered the Consular Service (Far East), 1913. In the Foreign Office after the war. Attended: Disarmament Conference at Washington, 1921-22; Imperial Economic Conference at Ottawa, 1932; Monetary and Economic Conference, London, 1933; Member of Runciman Mission to Czechoslovakia, 1938. Accompanied Chamberlain to Munich. On the outbreak of war he became Policy Adviser to the Minister of Economic Warfare. 1940, Assistant Under-Secretary and Chief Clerk at the Foreign Office. He retired in 1947 and became Associate Director of Studies at Chatham House, 1947-52.

Publications:
Novels (under the pseudonym of John Paris): *Kimono, Sayonara, Banzai, The Island beyond Japan, Matsu.* Nonfiction: *The World in March 1939* (with Arnold Toynbee) (1952), *The British Foreign Service* (1949).
In these lectures (*The British Foreign Service*), he told of the conflict between Treasury and Foreign Office caused by the successful effort of the Secretary of the Treasury, Sir Warren Fisher, to get himself recognized as "Head of the Civil Service" (1919-39). A Treasury minute to this effect was signed in 1919 by the then Chancellor of the Exchequer, Sir Austen Chamberlain, who later, as Foreign Secretary, admitted that he had not realized the implications of what he had done. This document

gave Warren Fisher the last word in the appointment of the official heads of the Government Departments, their deputies, and their Chief Establishment Officers. He extended this authority so as to interfere in the appointment of British Ambassadors and in the submission and non-submission of Foreign Office advice to the Cabinet. Ashton-Gwatkin wrote: "This nefarious system was an important contributory cause of the weakness of the Foreign Office authority in the thirties and one of the reasons Foreign Office warnings about Germany and the warnings from British representatives abroad did not reach the Cabinet in an effective form." On February 10, 1939, Sir Warren Fisher was succeeded as Head of the Civil Service by Sir Horace Wilson. There is further information on the role of Warren Fisher in Walford Selby's *Diplomatic Twilight*.

ASTOR, Nancy Whitcher (Viscountess Astor). 1879-1964
Born in Virginia, U.S.A. M.P. (Unionist) 1919-45. First woman to take her seat in Parliament. Known to be strongly anti-French. Entertained many of the appeasers at her home, Cliveden, but had relatively little influence on policy. Her son William Waldorf (educated at Eton and New College, Oxford) was Parliamentary Private Secretary to Sir Samuel Hoare, 1936-39.
Publications:
My Two Countries (1923).

ASTOR, Waldorf (Viscount Astor). 1879-1952.
Educated at Eton and New College, Oxford. Blue in polo, steeplechasing and sabres. MP (Conservative), 1910-19. Inspector of Quartermaster-General Services, 1914-17. Parliamentary Private Secretary to Lloyd George, 1918; to Minister of Health, 1919-21. Delegate to League of Nations, 1931. Chairman of Directors, *Observer*. Chairman Royal Institute of International Affairs, 1935-49. Lord Mayor of Plymouth, 1939-44.
Publications:
The Planning of Agriculture (1933), *Mixed Farming and Muddled Thinking* (1946).

BALL, Sir (George) Joseph. 1885-1961
Educated at King's School, Strand; King's College, London. Called to the Bar, Gray's Inn, 1913. Served in Great War (OBE). Director of the Conservative Research Department, 1930-39. Business interests. (1961) Chairman, Henderson's Transvaal Estates Ltd; Director, Consolidated Goldfield of South Africa Ltd.

BARRINGTON-WARD, Robert McGowan. 1891-1948
Educated at Westminster and Balliol. President of the Union. Staff of *The Times*, 1913. Assistant Editor, 1914. Active Service in Great War; MC, 1917, DSO, 1918. Assistant Editor, *Observer*, 1919. Assistant Editor, *The Times*, 1927. Deputy Editor and chief leader-writer, 1934. Supported and encouraged Dawson in devoting *The Times* to a more thorough and consistent appeasement policy than any other newspaper. Editor *The Times*, 1941.
Publications:
The Foreign Office and its Agencies (1914), *Platoon Training* (1918), *James Gow (Headmaster of Westminster: A memoir)* (1924).

BARTLETT, Vernon. 1894-1983
Educated at Blundell's School. Traveled abroad, 1911-14. *Daily Mail*, 1916. Reuters Agency, 1917. Paris Peace Conference with Reuters. Joined *The Times*, 1919. Broadcast regularly on foreign affairs, 1928-34. Joined *News Chronicle*, 1934. MP (Independent Progressive), 1938-50. After an initial flirtation with Nazism, he became a strong opponent of appeasement.

BRACKEN, Brendan (Viscount Bracken). 1901-58
Born in Ireland. Educated in Australia and at Sedbergh. MP (Unionist), 1929-45; (Conservative), 1945-51. Chairman of *Financial News*. Managing Director *Economist*. A close confidant of Churchill. He had an independent and critical mind, and caused Chamberlain's Government much embarrassment. Parliamentary Private Secretary to Churchill, 1940-41. Minister of Information, 1941-45. First Lord of Admiralty, 1945. Direc-

tor of AEI. Chairman *Financial Times*. Trustee of National
Gallery.

BUTLER, R. A. 1902–82
Born in India. Educated at Marlborough and Pembroke, Cambridge. President of the Union. First in Modern Languages and
History. Fellow of Corpus Christi, Cambridge, 1925-29. Conservative MP since 1929. Under-Secretary of State, India Office,
1932-37. On the resignation of Cranborne, February, 1938, he
became Under-Secretary of State for Foreign Affairs (1938-41)
with the responsibility of being Foreign Affairs spokesman in
the Commons. Of this period in his career, a contemporary
critic wrote; "Mr. R. A. Butler is not handicapped by genius,
originality or emotion. He is an ideally efficient Minister, indus-
trious, full of accurate information which he is too cautious to
divulge." Minister of Education, 1941-45. Minister of Labour,
June-July, 1945. Chancellor of the Exchequer, 1951-55. Lord
Privy Seal, 1955. Home Secretary, 1957. Deputy Prime Minister,
1962. Created Baron, 1965.

CADOGAN, Sir Alexander George Montagu. 1884–1968
Educated at Eton and Balliol. Diplomatic Service. Peking,
1933-36. KCMG, 1934. Deputy Under-Secretary of State, Foreign Office, 1936-37. Permanent Under-Secretary, 1938-46. Permanent Representative to the United Nations, 1946-50. Chairman BBC, 1952-57. Government Director, Suez Canal Company, from 1951. Director, National Provincial Bank. Director,
Phoenix Assurance Company.

CHAMBERLAIN, (Arthur) Neville. 1869-1940
Son of Joseph Chamberlain, and half-brother of Austen Chamberlain. Left Rugby early to study metallurgy and engineering
design at Mason Commercial College, Birmingham. Decided
not to pursue an industrial career and joined a firm of account-
ants. Abandoned accountancy and went to farm sisal in the
Bahamas on his father's estate, 1890-97. "It was a life of extreme
hardship, and all in vain; the soil was too thin for the crop."
The extreme loneliness of life intensified his natural shyness

and reserve. He returned to Birmingham and was active in local government. He became Chairman of the General Hospital; Chairman of the City Council, 1911; Chairman of the Town Planning Committee, and Lord Mayor. In 1916 he established a Municipal Savings Bank against the opposition of strong banking interests. In the same year Lloyd George asked him to become Director of the War-Time Voluntary Labour Recruitment scheme. "His efforts were fruitless," as Lloyd George developed an intense personal dislike for him and allowed him little authority. He resigned after seven months. In 1918 he became a Conservative MP; no other Prime Minister entered Parliament so late. He refused to serve in the same Cabinet as Lloyd George. He held four ministerial posts, 1922-24; Postmaster-General, Paymaster-General, Minister of Housing, and Chancellor of the Exchequer. In office for too few months to present a budget. Minister of Health, 1924-29, Chancellor of the Exchequer, 1931-37. Responsible for the Ottawa Tariff agreement. At Ottawa he was impressed by the skill of Sir Horace Wilson and continued to rely on him for advice and assistance until the end of his political career. Prime Minister, 1937-40. Held a nominal post under Churchill, 1940.

CHURCHILL, Sir Winston Leonard Spencer. 1874-1965
Educated at Harrow and Sandhurst. Entered Army, 1895. Served in India, 1896-97; Egypt and Sudan, 1898. Newspaper correspondent during Boer War. Taken prisoner by Boers, but escaped. MP (Conservative) 1900-06; (Liberal) 1906-22; (Conservative) since 1924. Under-Secretary of State for Colonies, 1906-08; President, Board of Trade, 1908-10; Home Secretary, 1910-11; First Lord of the Admiralty, 1911-15. Served in France, 1916. Minister of Munitions, 1917. Chancellor of Exchequer, 1924-29. Out of office, 1929-39, he fought many battles — to withhold self-government from India; to keep Edward VIII on the throne; and, with great vigor and determination, to destroy appeasement and all its works. He was suspect to both Labour and Conservative MPs, and even those who disliked appeasement as he did were unwilling to be associated with him. He worked largely alone, striking appeasement blow after blow

in the House of Commons. In 1939 he accepted office in Chamberlain's government, a compromise many anti-appeasers resented. But it enabled Churchill to fight the naval war from its first days. Prime Minister, 1940-45. Leader of the Opposition, 1945-51. Prime Minister, 1951-55.

CONWELL-EVANS, T. Philip. 1891-1972
Educated at Jesus College, Oxford. Ph.D. Lecturer at Königsberg University, 1932-34. He was at first a great admirer of Nazi Germany. Joint Honorary Secretary of the Anglo-German Fellowship. A close friend of Lord Lothian. Arranged Lord Lothian's visit to Hitler, and acted as interpreter. Corresponded with many appeasers and other public men, including Lloyd George and Gilbert Murray, attempting to influence them in favor of an appeasement policy. Was with Lloyd George on the latter's visit to Hitler. He saw the folly of appeasement in July, 1938, urged a firm policy during the Czech crisis. He attempted to use his knowledge of Nazism to alter Chamberlain's policy. He became a close friend of Vansittart, and acted as a go-between with the German opposition to Hitler after the outbreak of war.
Publications:
Foreign Policy from a Back Bench 1904-1918 (1932). (Based on the papers of Noel-Buxton). *The League Council in Action.*

DALTON, Hugh (Baron Dalton of Forest and Frith). 1887-1962
Son of a clergyman. Educated at Eton and King's, Cambridge; London School of Economics. Barrister, Middle Temple, 1914. Reader in Commerce, University of London, 1920-25. Reader in Economics, 1925-36. Labour MP, 1924-29; 1929-31; 1935-59. Parliamentary Under-Secretary, Foreign Office, 1929-31. A determined critic of the National Government's foreign policy throughout the thirties. Much of his information was gleaned from his friends; Jan Masaryk, the Czech Ambassador; Maisky, the Russian Ambassador; and Raczynski, the Polish Ambassador. He thus had a clearer insight into the problems of Central Europe than many of his colleagues in the Labour Party. Minister of Economic Warfare, 1940-42. President of the Board of Trade, 1942-45. Chancellor of the Exchequer, 1945-47. Duchy

of Lancaster, 1948-50. Town and Country Planning, 1950-51. Local Government and Planning, 1951. Created a life peer, 1960.

Publications:
With British Guns in Italy, Inequality of Incomes in Modern Communities, Principles of Public Finance, The Peace of Nations, Practical Socialism for Britain, Hitler's War. Memoirs: *Call Back Yesterday, The Fateful Years, 1931-45.*

DAWSON, George Geoffrey. 1874-1944
Educated at Eton and Magdalen, Oxford. Civil Service (Post Office) and All Souls', 1898. Colonial Office, 1899. Assistant Private Secretary to Joseph Chamberlain, 1901. Private Secretary to Lord Milner, 1901-05. Editor Johannesburg *Star*, 1905-10. Editor *The Times*, 1912-19 and again, 1923-41. Dawson was an intimate friend of Baldwin and "more intimate than most people with Neville Chamberlain" (DNB). Editor *Round Table*, 1914-44.

DUFF COOPER, Alfred (Viscount Norwich). 1890-1954
Son of a surgeon. Educated at Eton and New College, Oxford. Foreign Office, 1913-17. Fought in France, 1918. MP (Unionist), 1924-29; (Conservative), 1931-45. Junior Minister, War Office and Treasury, 1928-35. Secretary of State for War, 1935-37. First Lord of the Admiralty, 1937-38. Resigned after Munich, and remained a strong critic of appeasement. Minister of Information, 1940-41. For this task he proved unpopular; the instruments of his security-tightening were known as "Cooper's Snoopers." Ambassador to France, 1944-47. Viscount, 1954.

Publications:
Talleyrand (1932), *Haig* (1935-6), *The Second World War* (1939), *David* (1943), *Sergeant Shakespeare* (1949), *Operation Heartbreak* (1950), *Old Men Forget* (autobiography) (1953).

DUNGLASS, Alexander Frederick Douglas Home (later Earl of Home). 1903-95
Educated at Eton and Christ Church. MP (Unionist), 1931-45; (Conservative), 1950-51. Parliamentary Private Secretary to

Neville Chamberlain, 1937-39. Accompanied Chamberlain to Munich, 1938. Joint Under-Secretary Foreign Office, 1945. Minister of State, Scottish Office, 1951-55. Minister for Commonwealth Relations, 1955-60. Foreign Secretary, 1960. Prime Minister (as Sir Alec Douglas-Home), 1963-4.

EDEN, Anthony (Lord Avon). 1897-1977
Educated at Eton and Christ Church. First in Oriental Languages. MP (Conservative), 1923-57. Parliamentary Private Secretary to Austen Chamberlain (Foreign Secretary), 1926-29. Succeeded Dalton as Parliamentary Under-Secretary, Foreign Office, 1931-33. Lord Privy Seal, 1934-35. Minister for League Affairs, 1935. Foreign Secretary, 1935-38. Resigned in February, 1938, owing to fundamental disagreement between himself and the Prime Minister. Returned to the Government on the outbreak of war as Minister for Dominion Affairs, 1939-40. War Office, 1940. Foreign Office, 1940-45; 1951-55. Prime Minister, 1955-57. Created Earl of Avon, 1961.
Publications:
Places in the Sun, Foreign Affairs 1939, Freedom and Order (Speeches), *Days for Decision* (Speeches), *Full Circle* (Memoirs), *Facing the Dictators* (Memoirs).

HALIFAX, Edward (Edward Lindley Wood, Baron Irwin, Viscount Halifax). 1881-1959
Educated at Eton and Christ Church. Fellow of All Souls'. Unionist MP, 1910-25. Minister of Education, 1922-24. Minister of Agriculture, 1924-25. Viceroy of India, 1926-31. Minister of Education, 1932-35. Succeeded to peerage, 1934. Minister of War, 1935. Lord Privy Seal, 1935-37. Foreign Secretary, 1938-40. Possible candidate for the Premiership, May, 1940. Succeeded Lothian as Ambassador to Washington, 1941-46.
Publications:
John Keble, Indian Problems (1932), *Speeches on Foreign Policy* (1940), *Fulness of Days* (Memoirs) (1957).

HENDERSON, Sir Nevile. 1882-1942
Born at Horsham, Sussex. His father owned a merchant shipping firm, and was a director of the Bank of England. He died

when Nevile was a child. Educated at Eton and abroad. Joined the Foreign Service in 1905. Served in St. Petersburg, 1905 and 1912, Tokyo, 1909, Rome, 1914, Nish, 1914, Paris, 1916. In 1920 he was in Constantinople under Sir Horace Rumbold. Cairo, 1924-28. Minister in Belgrade, 1929-35, where he formed a close friendship with King Alexander and was known as the "uncrowned king" of Yugoslavia. Buenos Aires, 1935, Berlin, 1937-39. He returned to England on the outbreak of war. His offer to return to Belgrade as Ambassador was declined.

Publications:
Failure of a Mission (1940), *Water Under the Bridges* (1945).

HOARE, Samuel (Viscount Templewood). 1880-1959
Educated at Harrow and New College, Oxford. First in Mods and History. Assistant Private Secretary to Alfred Lyttelton (Colonial Secretary), 1905. MP (Conservative), 1910-44. Air Minister, 1922-24, 1924-29. Secretary of State for India, 1931-35 (with R. A. Butler as his Under-Secretary). Foreign Secretary, 1935. Resigned as a result of the public uproar aroused by his proposed pact with Laval which concerned a compromise with Mussolini over Abyssinia. First Lord of the Admiralty, 1936-37. Home Secretary, 1937-39. A humane Home Secretary, his broad-mindedness was unpopular. His Criminal Justice Bill, with the abolition of judicial flogging, was shelved owing to the outbreak of war. His plans were not put into effect until 1948. Lord Privy Seal, with a seat in the War Cabinet, 1939-40. Air Minister, 1940. Ambassador to Spain, 1940-44. Created Viscount Templewood, 1944.

Publications:
Ambassador on Special Mission (an account of the war years in Spain) (1946), *Crime and Punishment* (1949), *The Shadow of the Gallows* (1951), *Nine Troubled Years* (1954), *Empire of the Air* (an account of his years as Air Minister) (1957).

HORE-BELISHA, Leslie. 1894-1957
Educated at Clifton and St. John's, Oxford, Paris and Heidelberg. President of the Oxford Union. Served in France, Flanders and Salonika in the Great War (Major). Called to

the Bar, 1923. MP (Liberal-National), 1923-42; (Independent), 1942-45. Parliamentary Secretary, Board of Trade, 1931-32. Financial Secretary, Treasury, 1932-34. Minister of Transport, 1934-37. Introduced the Pedestrian Crossing and the "Belisha" beacon. Secretary of State for War, 1937-40. Opposed the slow speed of rearmament, and tried to arouse Chamberlain to the dangers that confronted the country. The only Jewish member of the Cabinet. His religion, as well as his outspokenness, led to his downfall. War.Cabinet, 1939-40. A constant critic of Churchill's conduct of the war. Minister of National Insurance, 1945. Created Baron, 1954.

HUDSON, R. S. (Viscount Hudson). 1886-1957
Educated at Eton and Magdalen, Oxford. Diplomatic Service, 1911-23. Unionist MP, 1924-45. Parliamentary Secretary, Ministry of Labour, 1931-35. Minister of Pensions, 1935-36. Secretary, Department of Overseas Trade, 1937-40. Minister of Shipping, April-May, 1940. Minister of Agriculture and Fisheries, 1940-45. Created Viscount, 1952.

INSKIP, Thomas (Viscount Caldecote). 1876-1947
Born in Bristol, the son of a solicitor. Educated at Clifton and King's, Cambridge. He addressed religious meetings in the town and had serious thoughts of becoming a missionary. Called to the Bar and practiced on the western circuit. KC, 1914. MP (Conservative), 1918-39. Solicitor-General, 1922. He was generally recognized both by his associates and by his adversaries as the main instrument in defeating the revisions of the Prayer Book in 1928. In 1936, Baldwin and Chamberlain agreed to appoint him Minister for the Co-ordination of Defence. Making his first speech in this capacity, Inskip said, "I may say, with all sincerity, that it never occurred to me that I was likely to be asked to accept these responsibilities. Nor did it ever occur to me — I can say this in all seriousness — that I would ever be able to discharge these duties even if they were offered to me . . . I do not claim to be a superman." On the outbreak of war he received a peerage and became Lord Chancellor. 1940 (May) Minister for the Dominions, (October) Lord Chief Justice.

JONES, Thomas. 1870-1955
Educated at Pengam County School, University College, Aberystwyth, Glasgow University, and London School of Economics. Investigator on Poor Law Commission, 1906-09. Professor of Economics, Queen's University, Belfast, 1909-10. Hon. Trustee, *Observer*. Deputy Secretary to the Cabinet. Secretary to the Economic Advisory Council. Secretary of Pilgrim Trust, 1930-45. Trustee, 1945-54. A leading member of the Cliveden "set," he became disillusioned with appeasement in 1938.
Publication:
Diary with Letters: 1931-50.

KENNARD, Sir Howard. 1878-1955
Educated at Eton. Diplomatic Service, 1901. Served in Rome, Teheran, Washington, Tangier, Belgrade (Minister), Stockholm, Berne. Ambassador, Warsaw, 1934-39. With Polish Government, Paris, 1939-40. Retired, 1940. "It will no doubt be astonishing to most that the Government did not retain his services longer, Kennard knew Poland and knew the Poles, and his retention as Ambassador would seem to have been the obvious course, and doubtless his knowledge would have been of great value." (*Times* obituary).

KIRKPATRICK, Sir Ivone. 1897-1964
Born in India. Educated at Downside. Diplomatic Service, 1919. Served in Rio de Janeiro, Rome, Vatican. First Secretary, Berlin, 1933-38. Assistant Under-Secretary of State, Foreign Office, 1945. Deputy Under-Secretary, 1948. Permanent Under-Secretary, Foreign Office, German section, 1949. United Kingdom High Commissioner for Germany, 1950-53. Permanent Under-Secretary of State, Foreign Office, 1953-57. Chairman of the Independent Television Authority, 1957.
Publication:
The Inner Circle (Memoirs) (1959).

LEITH-ROSS, Sir Frederick. 1887-1968
Educated at Merchant Taylors' and Balliol. First in Mods and Greats. Treasury, 1909. Asquith's Private Secretary, 1911-13.

British representative on the Finance Board of the Reparations Commission, 1920-25. Deputy Controller of Finance, Treasury, 1925-32. Chief Economic Adviser, HMG, 1932-46. Chief British Financial Expert, Hague Conferences, 1929, 1930. Chairman of the International Committee on Inter-Governmental Debts, 1931. Led British Delegation at World Economic Conference, 1933. War Debts Mission to Washington, 1933. Negotiated Financial Agreements with Germany, October, 1934. Chairman of the Economic Committee of the League, 1936-37. Director-General, Ministry of Economic Warfare, 1939-42. UN-RRA, 1944-46. Governor of the Bank of Egypt, 1946-51.

LLOYD GEORGE, David. 1863-1945
Son of a schoolmaster. Articled as a solicitor, 1884. Liberal MP, 1890. Opposed Boer War. President, Board of Trade, 1905. Chancellor of Exchequer, 1908. Minister of Munitions, 1915. Secretary of State for War, June, 1916. Prime Minister, December, 1916-22. Led British delegation to Paris Peace Congress. Brought Danzig under League of Nations. Justified German rearmament on the grounds that the Allied demands had been too harsh. Urged the abolition of reparations in 1932, when "his hostility to France and partiality to Germany became increasingly marked" (Thomas Jones, DNB). Visited Hitler, 1936. Became an opponent of appeasement after Munich, and advocated closer Anglo-Russian co-operation. Urged peace negotiations shortly after the outbreak of war. Peerage, 1945.
Publications:
The Great Crusade (1918), Is it Peace? (1923), Slings and Arrows (1929), The Truth about Reparations and War Debts (1932), War Memoirs, 6 volumes (1933-36), The Truth about the Peace Treaties (1938).

LONDONDERRY, Marquess of (Charles Stewart Henry Vane-Tempest-Stuart). 1878-1949
The eldest son of Viscount Castlereagh. Educated at Eton and Sandhurst. MP (Conservative), 1906-15. Succeeded to the peerage, 1915. Occupied in both Irish and English politics. Leader of the Senate of Northern Ireland in 1921. Secretary of

State for Air, 1931-35. Attended the disarmament conference at Geneva, often as head of the British delegation, 1932-33. He was severely attacked in England by Labour and pacifist circles for raising objections to the abolition of bombing aircraft (by international agreement). He met the Nazi leaders in 1936 and 1937. Ribbentrop came to stay with him. His daughter, Maureen, married Oliver Stanley. He died in February, 1949, as a result of a gliding accident in 1947.

Publications:

Ourselves and Germany (an account of his meetings with Nazi leaders, including an interview with Hitler) (1938), *Wings of Destiny* (a defense of his policy as Air Minister) (1943). (He later told a friend that this book had been "mutilated by the War Cabinet in 1943." Hence its inadequacies.)

LOTHIAN, Lord (Philip Henry Kerr). 1882-1940

Educated at the Oratory School, and at New College, Oxford. First in History. Abandoned Catholicism to become a Christian Scientist. Member of Milner's "Kindergarten" in South Africa. Secretary of Transvaal Indigency Commission. First Editor of *Round Table* (1910), a quarterly magazine devoted to championing the organic unity of the British Commonwealth. Private secretary to Lloyd George, 1916-21. "More responsible than anyone else" for the preface to the Versailles Treaty. Lloyd George wrote of Kerr's "priceless help" and retained his services after the war: "I could not have kept fully in touch with events abroad without Mr. Kerr's intelligent and informed vigilance." Secretary to Rhodes trustees, 1925. Succeeded to peerage, 1930. Liberal Party representative in MacDonald's Cabinet. Under-Secretary of State for India, 1931-32. Left the administration in 1932 on account of the Ottawa Agreement. Expressed his belief in an eventual universal federation of mankind in his Burge Memorial Lecture, 1935. A close friend of the Astors, Conwell-Evans, Dawson, and Thomas Jones. At his country houses, many appeasers met — as much as at Cliveden, if not more so. Saw the folly of appeasement in 1938, and admitted to Vansittart that he had been wrong in his assessment of German aims. Urged Halifax to bring Churchill into the Government and to mobilize the Fleet, in July, 1939, but in vain. Ambassador, Washington, 1939-40.

MOORE, Sir Thomas Cecil Russell. 1886-1971
Educated at Portora Royal School and Trinity College, Dublin. Regular Army, 1908. Served in France, 1914. General Staff, Ireland, 1916-18, Russia, 1918-20, and Ireland, 1920-23. MP (Unionist) since 1925. Member of Anglo-German Fellowship, a frequent visitor to Germany, 1933-38; he found much to admire in Nazism, and less to criticize than did many of his contemporaries. Since the Abolition of Judicial Flogging in 1948, he has strongly advocated its return. He is a leading figure in the movement to prevent the abolition of capital punishment. Chairman, Remainder Central Ltd.; Director, Werner Laurie Ltd., Eastwoods Ltd. and General Accident Assurance Corp., Ltd.

MURRAY, George Gilbert Aimé. 1866-1957
Son of President of New South Wales Legislative Council. Left Australia at age 11. Educated at Merchant Taylors', and St. Johns, Oxford. Fellow of New College, Oxford, 1888. Professor of Greek, Glasgow University, aged 21. Regius Professor of Greek at Oxford, 1908-36. Trustee of British Museum, 1914-48. A close friend of many Liberal leaders, he frequently drafted resolutions for the National Liberal Council. He had a deep dislike of appeasement. An academic friend wrote, when Murray became involved in prewar politics: "Once more you are forced to divide your days between the underground work in the mine of political activity and the dwelling on Olympus with the gods and heroes of Aeschylus."
Political Publications:
The Foreign Policy of Sir Edward Grey (1915), *Faith, War, and Policy* (1918), *The Problems of Foreign Policy* (1931), *Liberty and Civilisation* (1938).

NEWTON, Sir Basil Cochrane. 1889-1965
Educated at Wellington, and King's, Cambridge. Unmarried. Foreign Office, 1912. Peking, 1925-29. Counsellor, Berlin, 1930-

35. Minister, 1935-37. Minister, Prague, 1937-39. KCMG, 1939. Ambassador, Iraq, 1939-41. Retired, 1946.

NICOLSON, Sir Harold George. 1886-1968
Son of a diplomat. Born Teheran, Persia. Educated at Wellington and Balliol College, Oxford. Foreign Office, 1909; Madrid, 1910; Constantinople, 1911; Paris Peace Conference, 1919. With League of Nations, 1920. Foreign Office, 1920-29. Counsellor in Teheran and Berlin. Joined *Evening Standard*, 1930. MP (National Labour), 1935-45. A man of great intellectual and literary accomplishments, a stern critic of appeasement, a strong advocate of the Anglo-French alliance, he felt deep shame at the wild joy of the Commons when Chamberlain went to Munich. MPs resented his criticisms. He replied, on October 5, 1938: "I know that in these days of realism principles are considered as rather eccentric and ideals are identified with hysteria. I know that those of us who believe in the traditions of our policy, who believe in the precepts which we have inherited from our ancestors, who believe that one great function of this country is to maintain moral standards in Europe, to maintain a settled pattern of international relations, not to make friends with people who are demonstrably evil, not to go out of our way to make friends with them but to set up some sort of standard by which the smaller powers can test what is good in international conduct and what is not — I know that those who hold such beliefs are accused of possessing the Foreign Office mind. I thank God that I possess the Foreign Office mind."

NORTON, Sir Clifford John. 1891–1990
Educated at Rugby and Queen's College, Oxford. Active service in Great War, Gallipoli, Palestine. Political Officer, Damascus, Haifa, 1919-20. Diplomatic Service, 1921. Private Secretary to Sir Robert Vansittart, 1930-37. Counsellor, Warsaw, 1937-39. Minister Berne, 1942-46. KCMG, 1946. Ambassador Athens, 1946-51. Delegate to the United Nations, 1952-53. Of his years in Poland he wrote: "We were actors in a moving tragedy, not proud of our roles, but saying our lines with conviction. Who

wrote the lines and who allotted the parts, I do not profess to know." His own part, in those sad years, was one of honor.

OGILVIE FORBES, Sir George Arthur. 1891-1954
Educated at New College, Oxford, and Bonn University. Served in Great War; Egypt, Gallipoli. ADC to Lieut-Gen. Sir F. S. Maude, C-in-C, Mesopotamia. General Staff War Office, 1918. Diplomatic Service, 1919. Stockholm, Copenhagen, Helsingfors. First Secretary Belgrade, 1925, Mexico City, 1927-30. Chargé d'Affaires Holy See, 1930-32. Baghdad, 1932-35. Madrid, 1935-37. KCMG, 1937. Counsellor Berlin, 1937-39. Oslo, 1939. Minister, Havana, 1940-44. Ambassador Venezuela, 1944-48. Retired, 1949. Member of Council, Catholic Union of Great Britain, 1949. Member Executive Committee Scottish Council for Industry and Development, 1953.

O'NEILL, Sir Con Douglas Walter. 1912–88
Educated at Eton and Balliol College, Oxford. Fellow of All Souls, 1935-46. Called to the Bar, 1936. Diplomatic Service, 1936. Third Secretary, Berlin, 1938. He resigned in protest against the Munich agreement. Served in War of 1939-45 (Intelligence Corps). Leader writer on *The Times*, 1946-7. Returned to Foreign Office, 1947. Served in Germany, 1948-53. Counsellor, Foreign Service, 1951-3. Head of News Department, Foreign Office, 1954-5. Chargé d'Affaires, Peking, 1955-7. Ambassador to Finland, 1961. Knighted, 1962. Ambassador to the European Community at Brussels, 1963.

PHIPPS, Sir Eric Clare Edmund. 1875-1945
The son of a diplomat. Educated at King's, Cambridge. Diplomatic Service, 1889. Served in Paris, Constantinople, Rome and Paris, where he was Private Secretary to the Ambassador, Sir F. Bertie, 1909-11. First Secretary Petrograd, Madrid, Paris (1916). Secretary to the Paris Peace Congress, 1919. Counsellor, Brussels, 1920-22. Minister, Paris, 1922-28. KCMG, 1927. Minister, Vienna, 1928-33. Ambassador, Berlin, 1933-37. Paris, 1937-39. Director of the Midland Bank. Retired "at his own request," 1939. He was "Latin rather than English in appearance, a man of great charm and wit, shrewd and somewhat

cynical. In normal times there would probably have been greater scope for his special qualities than was possible when Hitler's rise to power made all compromise futile and even dangerous" (Orme Sargent, DNB).

DE ROPP, Baron William. b. 1887
The son of a Lithuanian baron. Educated in Dresden. Travelled widely throughout the British Empire, of which he was a fervent admirer. Naturalized British subject, 1915. Served in the Great War in the Wiltshire Regiment and the Royal Flying Corps. *The Times* political correspondent in Berlin in the late twenties. Export and foreign information agent for the Bristol Aeroplane Company. Employed by the Air Ministry. Close friend of many Nazis, chiefly Rosenberg. He met Hitler frequently. On the outbreak of war he moved from Berlin to Switzerland, and was employed by the British until 1944 as a go-between. His early experiences with the Nazi leaders were described in a series of unrevealing articles in the *Daily Mail* in October, 1957.

RUMBOLD, Sir Horace George Montagu. 1866-1941.
The son of a diplomat. Educated at Eton. Attaché, The Hague 1888-90. Served in Cairo, Teheran, Vienna, Cairo (1900-06), Munich, Tokyo (1909-13), Berlin (1913-14). Minister, Switzerland, 1916-19. KCMG, 1917. Minister, Poland, 1919-20. Ambassador, Constantinople, 1920-24, Madrid, 1924-28, Berlin, 1928-33. Signed Lausanne Treaty, 1923, on behalf of British Empire. He was an outspoken opponent of any form of appeasement from the beginning of the Nazi régime.
Publication:
The War Crisis in Berlin (1914).

RUNCIMAN, Walter (Lord Runciman of Doxford). 1870-1949
Born at South Shields. A Methodist. Educated at South Shields High School, privately, and at Trinity, Cambridge. Third in History. Career in shipping and politics. Defeated Churchill at Oldham in 1899 (Liberal). Financial Secretary to the Treasury, 1907. President of the Board of Education, 1908. President of the Board of Agriculture and Fisheries, 1911. President of the Board of Trade, 1914. He resigned with Asquith in 1916, and

lost his seat in 1918. Defeated in four subsequent elections. He held office in the National Government of 1931, at the Board of Trade. He remained there, unlike most Liberals, as he supported the Ottawa agreements. He resigned with Baldwin in 1937, and was made a viscount. He was sent to Czechoslovakia in the summer of 1938.

SALISBURY, 5th Marquess, Robert Arthur James Gascoyne-Cecil (Lord Cranborne). 1893-1972
Educated at Eton and Christ Church, Oxford. MP (Unionist) 1929-41. Parliamentary Under-Secretary for Foreign Affairs, 1935-38. Resigned with Anthony Eden, the Foreign Secretary, in protest against Chamberlain's appeasement policy. Paymaster General, 1940. Secretary of State for Dominion Affairs, 1940-42 and 1943-45. House of Lords, 1941. Leader of the House of Lords, 1942-45 and 1951-57. Knight of the Garter, 1946. Secretary of State, Commonwealth Relations, 1952. Lord President of Council. Resigned in 1957 because of his opposition to the release of Archbishop Makarios from detention.

SANDYS, Duncan. 1908-87
Educated at Eton and Magdalen, Oxford. Foreign Office, 1930. London and Berlin. Resigned, 1933, in protest against the Government's German policy. Married a daughter of Winston Churchill, 1935. MP (Conservative), 1935-74. An important member of the anti-appeasement groups that formed around Churchill and Eden between Munich and the fall of Chamberlain's Government. Norway Expeditionary Force, 1940. Disabled on Active Service, 1941. Financial Secretary, War Office, 1941-43. Minister of Works, 1944-45. Member of the European Consultative Assembly, Strasbourg, 1950-51. Member General Advisory Council, BBC, 1947-51. Minister of Supply, 1951-54. Minister of Housing and Local Government, 1954-57. Minister of Defence, 1957-59. Minister of Aviation, 1959-60. Secretary of State for Commonwealth Relations, 1960-4. Created Baron, 1974.

SARGENT, Sir Orme. 1884-1962
Educated at Radley. Foreign Office, 1906. At Paris Peace Conference, 1919. KCMG, 1937. The strongest opponent of ap-

peasement within the Foreign Office. He refused any compromise, however attractive superficially. For him Chamberlain's three visits to Germany were more than a single capitulation — they were "a season ticket to Canossa." Permanent Under-Secretary, Foreign Office, 1946-49. Church Commissioner. Honorary Fellow of St. Antony's College, Oxford. Known to some as "Moley" for his underground activities against appeasement; to others as "the good Sargent"; both epithets are appropriate.

SIMON, John (Viscount Simon). 1873-1954
Son of a Congregational Minister. Educated at Fettes and Wadham College, Oxford. Fellow of All Souls'. President of the Union. Called to the Bar, 1899. A brilliant lawyer, he possessed one of the finest analytic minds of his generation. KC, 1908. MP (Liberal), 1906. Solicitor-General (1910-13), Attorney-General with seat in the Cabinet, 1913-15. Home Secretary, 1915-16. Foreign Secretary, 1931-35. Home Secretary, 1935-37. Chancellor of the Exchequer, 1937-40. Supported appeasement in 1938, but opposed a "second Munich" in 1939. Lord Chancellor, 1940-45.

> *Sir John Simon*
> *Is not like Timon.*
> *Timon hated mankind.*
> *Simon doesn't mind.*

Vansittart wrote: "None, I think, ever called him Johnnie, but John longed to be liked and winced more often than he 'let on' . . . Fashion mocked John as Foreign Secretary. Others were no happier when they tried."
Publications:
Comments and Criticisms (1930), *Portrait of My Mother* (1937), *Retrospect* (Memoirs) (1952).

SPEARS, Sir Edward Louis. 1886-1974
Educated privately. Kildare Militia, 1903. Commissioned, 1906. Captain, 1914. Served in Great War. Brigadier-General. Four times wounded. MC, CB, CBE. Commander, Legion of Honour. *Croix de Guerre* with three palms. Head of British Military Mission, Paris, 1917-20. Retired, 1920. MP (National Liberal), 1922-24; (Unionist), 1931-45. Major-General, 1940.

Churchill's personal representative with the French Prime Minister, 1940. Head of British Mission to General de Gaulle, 1940. Head of Spears Mission to Syria and Lebanon, 1941. First Minister to Syria and Lebanon, 1942-44. Chairman, Anglo-Arab Association. Chairman, Ashanti Goldfields Ltd. Director, Portland Cement. President, British Bata Shoe Company.
Publications:
Lessons of the Russo-Japanese War, Cavalry Tactical Scheme, Liaison 1914 (1930), *Prelude to Victory* (1939), *Assignment to Catastrophe* (1954).

STANLEY, Oliver. 1896-1950.
Younger son of Lord Derby (1865-1948). Educated at Eton. Served in Great War. MC, *Croix de Guerre.* Called to the Bar in 1919. MP (Conservative), 1924, Parliamentary Private Secretary to the Minister of Education, 1924-29. Under-Secretary of State, Home Office, 1931-33. Minister of Transport, 1933-34. Largely responsible for the Road Traffic Act of 1934. Minister of Labour, 1934-35. President, Board of Education, 1936-37. President, Board of Trade, 1937-40. Succeeded Hore-Belisha as Secretary of State for War in January, 1940. Replaced by Eden in May. Rejoined the army. Colonial Secretary, 1942-45. He married the daughter of Lord Londonderry.

STRANG, William (1st Baron Strang of Stonesfield). 1893-1978
Son of a farmer. Educated at Palmer's School, University College, London, and the Sorbonne. Quain Essay, 1913. Served in Great War (MBE). Turned down offer of Lectureship in English at Hong Kong University, 1919. Foreign Office, 1919. Belgrade, 1919-25. Acting Counsellor, Moscow, 1930. Counsellor, 1933. Succeeded Ralph Wigram as Head of the Central Department, Foreign Office, 1937. Assistant Under-Secretary of State, 1939-43. Head of the British Mission to Moscow that sought an Anglo-Soviet agreement, 1939. Critical of Chamberlain's conduct of Foreign Affairs which he considered inadequate and naïve. UK representative, European Advisory Commission, 1943-45. Political Adviser to C-in-C British Forces of Occupation in Germany, 1945-47, Permanent Under-Secretary,

Foreign Office (German Section), 1947-49. Permanent Under-Secretary, 1949-53. Chairman, National Parks Commission. Member of the Nature Conservancy. Member of the General Advisory Council of the BBC. Chairman of the Royal Institute of International Affairs.
Publications:
The Foreign Office (1955), *Home and Abroad* (1956), *Britain in World Affairs* (1961).

VANSITTART, Robert (Lord Vansittart). 1881-1957
Educated at Eton. Entered the Diplomatic Service, 1902. Served in Paris, Teheran, Cairo, Stockholm. Curzon's secretary, 1920-24. Assistant Under-Secretary of State for Foreign Affairs, and Principal Private Secretary to the Prime Minister, 1928-30. Permanent Under-Secretary of State, Foreign Office, 1930-38. Worked incessantly to destroy the pro-German trend of British policy. Chief Diplomatic Adviser to the Foreign Secretary, 1938-41, a post without influence. Created a peer, 1941. He wrote:

> *Yet if the hands of youth should ever rake*
> *The ash of our sad time, it holds a friend*
> *Whose heart was in the cause all warmth will make*
> *Its own until the end.*

Publications:
Plays and poems. *Black Record* (a wartime indictment of the Germans, judged by their history), *Roots of the Trouble, Lessons of My Life, The Mist Procession* (Autobiography to 1936).

WILSON, Sir Horace John. 1882-1972
Educated at Kurnella School, Bournemouth, and the London School of Economics. Civil Service, 1900. Assistant Secretary, Ministry of Labour, 1919-21. Permanent Secretary, Ministry of Labour, 1921-30. Because of his agile and astute mind he was described by the Minister of Labour (J. H. Thomas) as "a ruddy wonder." Chief Industrial Adviser to the Government, 1930-39. His skill at negotiations and drafting made him invaluable at the Ottawa Conference. Seconded to the Treasury for services with the Prime Minister (Baldwin), 1935. Retained in that

position by Neville Chamberlain, 1937-40. Had a room in 10 Downing Street while Chamberlain was Prime Minister. He supported, encouraged and at times initiated Chamberlain's foreign policy. Permanent Head of the Civil Service, 1939-42. Honorary Fellow of the London School of Economics, 1960. W. J. Brown wrote of him that he

> built up for himself, during his tenure of the Secretaryship of the Treasury, a more powerful position in Britain than almost anybody since Cardinal Wolsey . . . soft-spoken, deferential, courteous, almost self-deprecating — he was in appearance the ideal Civil Servant, the antithesis of the power-making politician . . . he came to the top as a result of these qualities. He possessed first an immense industry. Nothing appeared to matter except the job. He seemed to have no vices and for that matter no human feeling. He possessed a rigid self-control proof against attack and even insults . . . tireless, caring for nothing but power, conscientious and hard-working, free from the failings of greater men, patient of rebuff, and rising again after every reverse, he rose because he had to. His influence was almost wholly bad . . . In all the critical years, when swift, bold, strong action alone could have served our need, Wilson's temporising, formula-evolving mind reinforced and emphasised the weakness of the Prime Minister.

WOOD, Sir Kingsley. 1881-1943

Born in Hull, the son of a Wesleyan Minister. Educated at the Central Foundation Boys' School, London. Articled to a solicitor. Elected to the LCC, 1911. Chairman Building Acts Committee, 1913-14. Knighted, 1918. Conservative MP, 1918. Urged immediate establishment of Ministry of Health, 1918. Introduced Early Closing Bill, 1920. Parliamentary Secretary to Neville Chamberlain, 1924-29. Civil Commissioner Northern Division, General Strike. Postmaster General, 1931-35. Given a seat in the Cabinet at Chamberlain's suggestion, 1933. Minister of Health, 1935-38. Secretary of State for Air, 1938-40. It was an unenviable post, and public attention was fixed upon it. Would the Minister achieve air parity with the Germans? As a contemporary wrote: "The House of Lords having now become a refuge for our melancholy succession of Air Ministers, Sir Kingsley may be grimly reflecting while he works, that it is 'parity or a peerage' for him." He secured neither. Although the RAF increased its fighting strength 100 per cent between March, 1939, and March, 1940, it was not enough. Kingsley Wood's defeatism was in no small way responsible for the failure. Lord Privy Seal, 1940. Urged Chamberlain to resign, May, 1940. Appointed Chancellor of Exchequer by Churchill. He had the wisdom to install Keynes in the Treasury with a room of his own.

Notes

All quotations in the Introduction to the New Edition (pages ix-xiv) are taken from Martin Gilbert, *Winston S. Churchill*, Volume Five (1922-1939), Heinemann, London, 1976.

PART ONE

CHAPTER 1

The Birth of Appeasement: 1933

1 Lloyd George, *War Memoirs*, p. 1,987.
2 Treaty of Versailles. Articles 27-8, 42-4, 99, 100-108, 119-27, 181-97, and 231-44.
3 J. M. Keynes, *The Economic Consequences of the Peace*, p. 102.
4 *ibid* pp. 51-279.
5 Hugh Dalton, *Hitler's War*, p. 20.
6 J. R. M. Butler, *Lord Lothian*, p. 217. April 6, 1937.
7 Vansittart, *The Mist Procession*, p. 46.
8 For Churchill's admiration of Mussolini, see Salvemini *Prelude to World War Two*, p. 108.
9 The philosopher was Bertrand Russell. Gilbert Murray papers.
10/11 Lothian, Appendix IV pp. 354-62. June 3, 1936.
12 Claud Cockburn, *The Week*, no. 166, June 17, 1936.
13 Brit. Docs. 2, vol. IV, no. 245, Rumbold to Simon. March 2, 1933.
14 *ibid* no. 253, Rumbold to Simon. March 2, 1933.
15 *ibid* no. 263, Rumbold to Simon. March 14, 1933.
16 Hoare, *Nine Troubled Years*, p. 299.
17 Vansittart, p. 274.
18 Brit. Docs. 2, vol IV, no. 265, Rumbold to Vansittart. March 15, 1933.
19 *ibid* para. 12.
20 *ibid* vol. V, no. 5, Rumbold to Simon. March 28, 1933.
21 *ibid* no. 21, Rumbold to Simon. April 5, 1933.
22 *ibid* no. 30, Rumbold to Simon. April 13, 1933.
23 Letter to Gilbert Murray. Murray Papers.
24 Lord Londonderry, *Ourselves and Germany*, p. 97. February 21, 1936.

25 Germ. Docs. C, vol I, no. 406, Hoesch to Foreign Ministry. August 16, 1933.
26 Murray Papers.
27 Murray Papers, October 24, 1933.
28 Brit. Docs. 2, vol. V, no. 30, Rumbold to Simon. April 13, 1933.
29 *ibid* no. 36, Rumbold to Simon, April 26, 1933, Note 5.
30 *International Affairs*, May-June 1933. The talk was at the end of March.
31 *ibid* Question of Mr. Israel Cohen.
32 Brit. Docs. 2, vol. V, no. 36, Rumbold to Simon. April 26, 1933.
33 *ibid* no. 139, Rumbold to Simon. May 11, 1933.
34 Lothian, p. 197, December 1933.
35 *ibid* p. 197, November 24, 1933.
36 Conwell-Evans to Murray. Murray papers. November 5, 1933.
37 Murray to Conwell-Evans, October 27, 1933.
38 Brit. Docs. 2, vol. V, no. 127, Cadogan to Leeper. Enclosure. May 10, 1933.
39 Vansittart, p. 478.
40 Brit. Docs. 2, vol. V, no. 179, Leeper Memo, May 29, 1933.
41 *ibid* no. 244, Simon to Rumbold. July 10, 1933.
42 *ibid* no. 2229, Rumbold to Simon. June 30, 1933.
43/44 *Dictionary of National Biography*, Sir Horace Rumbold by J. Marshall-Cornwall.
45 Private information.
46 Brit. Docs. 2, vol. V, no. 371, Vansittart Memo. August 28, 1933.
47 Fritz Hesse, *Hitler and the English*, pp. 11-12.
48 *ibid* p. 11.
49 Germ. Docs. C, vol. I, no. 86, Hoesch to Foreign Ministry. March 15, 1933.
50 *The Times*, June 26, 1933.
51 Brit. Docs. 2, vol. V, no. 324, Newton to Vansittart. August 12, 1933.
52 Thomas Jones, *Diary with Letters*, p. 129. April 28, 1934.
53 *ibid* p. 125, March 1, 1934.
54 *The Times*, September 27, 1933.
55 V. Bartlett, *Nazi Germany Explained*, pp. 242-3.
56 *ibid* p. 65, and Halifax, *Fulness of Days*, p. 188.
57 Bartlett, p. 267.
58 A. L. Kennedy, *Britain Faces Germany*, pp. 83-6.
59 Germ. Docs. C, vol. I, no. 152, Hoesch to Foreign Ministry. April 12, 1933.
60 *ibid* vol. II, no. 57, Hoesch to Foreign Ministry. November 10, 1933.
61 *ibid* vol. I, no. 237, Hoesch to Foreign Ministry. May 15, 1933.
62 *ibid* vol. II, no. 59, Hoesch to Foreign Ministry. November 11, 1933.

CHAPTER 2
Hitler's Visitors

1   Royal Archives, Windsor, 1-62, no. 113. Col. Swaine to Queen Victoria's Private Secretary. December 28, 1900.
2   Germ. Docs. C, vol. I, no. 406, Hoesch to Foreign Ministry. August 16, 1933.
3   *Hansard*, April 13, 1933.
4   Vansittart, p. 484.
5/6   Lothian Appendix IV, p. 354, Letter to Eden. June 3, 1936.
7   Germ. Docs. C, vol. I, no. 13, Hoesch to Foreign Ministry. February 6, 1933.
8   Fritz Hesse, *Hitler and the English*, p. 10.
9   P. Schwarz, *This Man Ribbentrop*, p. 189.
10   *ibid* p. 199.
11   Londonderry, pp. 110-11.
12   *Daily Telegraph*, November 4, 1936.
13   Murray Papers.
14/15   Brit. Docs. 2, vol. V, no. 495, Phipps to Simon, October 26, 1933.
16   Ciano Diary 1937-38, p. 166.
17/18   Vansittart, p. 482.
19   Jones, p. 39.
20   Murray Papers, March 4, 1939.
21   Jones, p. 129, April 28, 1934.
22   Ivan Maisky, *The Origins of the Second World War*, Broadcast Talk 1961.
23   *Sunday Dispatch*, October 22, 1933.
24   Simon Haxey, *Tory MP*, p. 196.
25   *The Times*, May 3, 1935.
26   Arnold Wilson, *Walks and Talks Abroad*, pp. 138-141.
27   *Sunday Dispatch*, October 22, 1933.
28   *Manchester Guardian*, June 11, 1938.
29   *News Chronicle*, July 20, 1938.
30   Foreign Relations of the United States 1937, vol. II, p. 376, August 5, 1937.
31   Paul Schwarz, *This Man Ribbentrop*, p. 199.
32   *ibid* p. 205.
33   *ibid* p. 208.
34   Norman Angell, *The Defence of Empire*, pp. 183-4.
35   Murray Papers.
36   *ibid* June 1938.
37   *ibid* June 1938.
38   *ibid* 1955.
39   Frank Owen, *Lloyd George*, p. 737.

40 *Daily Express*, September 16, 1936.
41 Owen, p. 737, September 27, 1937.
42 Brit. Docs. 3, vol. I, no. 218, Henderson to Halifax. May 14, 1938.
43 Foreign Relations of United States 1937, vol. I, p. 84, Bullitt to Cordell Hull. April 30, 1937.
44 *Ambassador Dodd's Diary*, p. 239. April 5, 1935.
45 Private information.
46 Schwarz, pp. 188-9.
47/48 Dalton, p. 105.
49 Jones, p. 205. May 23, 1936.
50 Lothian, p. 202. December 14, 1934.
51/52 *ibid* Appendix III, pp. 330-7, Note of interview with Hitler.
53 *The Times*, January 31, 1935.
54 Lothian, p. 206.
55 *ibid* p. 206. April 7, 1937.
56 *ibid* p. 216. December 14, 1934.
57 *ibid* Appendix 3 (b), pp. 337-45, Interview with Hitler. May 4, 1937.
58 Survey of International Affairs, 1938.
59 Lothian, Appendix 3 (b), pp. 337-45, Interview with Hitler. May 4, 1937.
60 Dodd, p. 411.
61 Jones, p. 167. February 21, 1936.
62 *ibid* pp. 179-82. March 8, 1936.
63 Versailles Treaty, Articles 42-4.
64 Jones, p. 180. March 8, 1936.
65 Claud Cockburn, *The Week*, no. 154, March 25 and no. 156, April 8, 1936.
66 Lothian, p. 213.
67 Paul-Boncour, *Souvenirs*, 3, p. 37.
68 Salvemini, *Prelude to World War Two*, p. 436.
69 Paul-Boncour, pp. 40-44.
70 Lord Avon, *Facing the Dictators*.
71 Paul-Boncour, pp. 40-44.
72 Claud Cockburn, *The Week*, no. 154, March 25 and no. 156, April 8, 1936.
73 Jones, p. 180. March 8, 1936.
74 *ibid* p. 197. May 16, 1936.
75 *ibid* pp. 198-201. May 17, 1936.
76 *ibid* pp. 205-208. May 23, 1936.
77/78 *Hansard*, April 6, 1936.
79 Ivone Kirkpatrick, *Inner Circle*, p. 71.
80 Jones, p. 208. May 23, 1936.
81 Vansittart, pp. 507-10.
82 Kirkpatrick, p. 65.

CHAPTER 3

The New Men

1 Nevile Henderson, *Failure of a Mission*, p. 79.
2 Dodd, p. 388.
3 Halifax, p. 191.
4 Henderson, p. 80.
5 *ibid* p. 97.
6 Halifax, p. 184.
7 Jones, p. 377. November 15, 1937.
8/9/10 Maisky Broadcast.
11 Jones, p. 210. May 25, 1936.
12 Maisky Broadcast.
13 Dirksen Papers, vol. I, no. 12. July 10, 1938.
14 Hoare, p. 258.
15 Jones, p. 351. June 12-14, 1937.
16 Simon, *Retrospect*, p. 227.
17 Dirksen Papers, vol. II, no. 5, Kordt to Dirksen. August 29, 1938.
18 M. Hyde, *United in Crime*, p. 60.
19/20 Jones, p. 350. May 30, 1937.
21 Duff Cooper, *Old Men Forget*, p. 209.
22 Hoare, p. 260.
23 Dirksen Papers, vol. II, no. 5, Kordt to Weizsäcker. August 23, 1938.
24 Cato, *Guilty Men*, pp. 86-90.
25 Strang, *Home and Abroad*, p. 127.
26 Woolton, *Memoirs*, p. 140.
27 J. C. W. Reith, *Into the Wind*, pp. 307-8.
28 Hoare, p. 301.
29 *ibid* p. 257.
30 Halifax, p. 216.
31 Halifax, p. 183.
32 Hoare, p. 280.
33 Halifax, p. 185.
34 J. Wedgwood, *Memoirs*, p. 225.
35 E. Kordt, *Wahn und Wirklichkeit* (Quoted by L. B. Namier, *Times Literary Supplement*. May 1, 1948).
36 Duff Cooper, p. 220.
37 Referring to the Fourteenth Century Parliament, *Mum and the Soothsegger*, Early English Text Society.
38 Jones, p. 305. January 15, 1937.
39 Jones, p. 314. February 15, 1937.
40 A. J. P. Taylor, *Origins of the Second World War*, p. 158.
41 Private information.
42 Hoare, p. 299.

43 Dalton, *The Fateful Years*, p. 105.
44 Weizsäcker, *Memoirs*, p. 134.
45 Dictionary of National Biography, *Nevile Henderson*, by Orme Sargent.
46 Brit. Docs. 3, vol. II, Appendix I, Henderson to Halifax. September 13, 1938.
47 *D. N. B. Henderson*, by Sargent.
48 *The Times*, June 2, 1937.
49 *Hansard*, June 8, 1937.
50 Dodd, p. 417. June 2, 1937.
51 *Sunday Times*, p. 425.
52 Jones, p. 298. January 3, 1937.
53 Survey of International Affairs, *Eve of War 1937*, p. 39.
54 *The Times*, June 23, 1937.
55 *ibid* February 28, 1937.
56 Londonderry, p. 116.
57 Lothian, Appendix III, pp. 337-45, Interview with Hitler. May 4, 1937.
58 *The Times*, August 7, 1937.
59 J. E. Wrench, *Geoffrey Dawson and Our Times*, p. 361. May 23, 1937.
60 *ibid* p. 360, Note 1.
61 Churchill, *The Gathering Storm*, pp. 152-3.
62 Dirksen Papers, vol. II, Appendix I, Stumm to Dirksen. May 2, 1938.
63 Germ. Docs. D, vol. I, no. 95, Selzam to Foreign Ministry. January 5, 1938.
64 *ibid* no. 101, Woermann to Foreign Ministry. January 14, 1938.
65 A. C. Johnson, *Eden*, p. 146.
66 Lord Avon, *Facing the Dictators*, pp. 447-8.
67 *ibid* p. 521.
68 *The Times*, July 9, 1937.
69 Germ. Docs. D, vol. I, no. 50, Ribbentrop to Foreign Ministry. December 2, 1937.
70 *Hansard* (House of Lords). October 21, 1937.
71 A. C. Johnson, *Eden*, p. 141.
72 A. C. Johnson, *Halifax*, p. 421.
73 Jones, p. 368. October 17, 1937.
74 *ibid* p. 370. October 24, 1937.
75 *ibid* p. 371. October 26, 1937.
76 Germ. Docs. D, vol. I, no. 13, Richthofen to Foreign Ministry. October 27, 1937.
77 Douglas Reed, *Insanity Fair*, p. 359.
78 Germ. Docs. D, vol. I, no. 24, Ribbentrop to Foreign Ministry. November 15, 1937.

79 *ibid* no. 25, Memo by Mackensen. November 15, 1937.
80 *ibid* no. 29, Selzam to Foreign Ministry. November 18, 1937.
81 Survey of International Affairs, 1937, vol. I, pp. 338-9.
82 Kirkpatrick, p. 97.
83 Jones, p. 359. July 21, 1937.
84 Germ. Docs. D, vol. I, no. 31, Memorandum enclosed in Neurath to Henderson. November 20, 1937.
85 Johnson, *Halifax*, p. 441.
86 Germ. Docs. D, vol. I, no. 75, Ribbentrop to Foreign Ministry. December 14, 1937.
87 Germ. Docs. D, vol. I, no. 78, Minute by Weizsäcker after he talked to Prentiss Gilbert, U.S. Ambassador in Berlin, who had recently spoken to Vansittart in London.
88 *The Times*, February 14, 1938.
89 Germ. Docs. D, vol. I, no. 128. Memorandum. February 25, 1938.
90 A. L. Rowse, *All Souls and Appeasement*, p. 28.

CHAPTER 4
Colonial Appeasement

1 Treaty of Versailles. Article 119.
2 F. S. Joelson, *Germany's Claim to Colonies*, p. 237. June 11, 1936.
3 *ibid* p. 243. February 24, 1931.
4 A. Hitler, *Mein Kampf*.
5 *ibid* p. 126.
6 Joelson, p. 246.
7 *Hansard*. March 24, 1933.
8 Joelson, p. 249.
9 B. Bennett, *Hitler Over Africa*, p. 167, Major Weigel to Dr Wiehl. August 8, 1933.
10 *ibid* p. 179, Dr. Jung to Major Weigel. May 31, 1933.
11 *ibid* pp. 168-9, Dr. Bohle to Major Weigel. March 10, 1934.
12 Joelson, p. 251.
13 *Daily Herald*, July 20, 1933.
14 Kirkpatrick, p. 52.
15 Murray Papers.
16 L. S. Amery, *The German Colonial Claim*, pp. 142-3.
17 *Daily Mail*, March 21, 1934.
18 *ibid* August 5, 1934. The journalist was Ward Price.
19 *Hansard*, May 3, 1935.
20 Joelson, p. 254.
21 *The Times*, March 4, 1935.
22 *The Times*, August 5, 1935.

23 *Sunday Dispatch*, August 25, 1935.
24 *Daily Herald*, September 3, 1935.
25 *The Times*, September 11, 1935.
26 *Hansard*, October 22, 1935.
27 Lothian, p. 206.
28 *The Times*, January 7, 1936.
29 Documents on International Affairs, 1937, p. 216. January 17, 1936.
30 Londonderry, pp. 72-9. January 31-February 4, 1936.
31 *Hansard*, February 12, 1936.
32 Johannsen and Kraft, *Germany's Colonial Problems*, p. 76. March 1936.
33 Documents on International Affairs, 1937, p. 219.
34 Amery, *The German Colonial Claims*, p. 124.
35 Documents on International Affairs, 1937, p. 251.
36 Amery, *My Political Life*, vol. 3, p. 248.
37 Quoted in the Commons, April 21, 1936.
38 Amery, vol. 3, p. 248.
39 *Hansard*, July 27, 1936.
40 Kirkpatrick, p. 83.
41 Documents on International Affairs, 1937, pp. 227-31.
42/43 Lothian, Appendix III, pp. 337-45. Interview with Hitler. May 4, 1937.
44 *ibid* pp. 217-20, Memo. May 11, 1937.
45 *ibid* p. 220. April 7, 1937.
46 *The Times*, October 28, 1937.
47 Documents on International Affairs, 1937, pp. 245-7.
48 Dalton, *The Fateful Years*, pp. 106-7.
49 *ibid* p. 109.
50 Germ. Docs. D, vol. 1, no. 19, Memo by Hossbach.
51 *ibid* no. 21, Memo by Weizsäcker.
52 *ibid* no. 28, Hempel to Foreign Ministry. November 17, 1937.
53 Foreign Relations of the United States, pp. 167-9, Bullitt to Cordell Hull. November 23, 1937.
54 Germ. Docs. D, vol. 1, no. 31, Neurath to Henderson.
55 Foreign Relations of the United States, pp. 198-9, Memo by Sumner Welles. December 15, 1937.
56 *ibid* pp. 183-5, Johnson to Cordell Hull. December 3, 1937.
57 *ibid* pp. 189-91, Biddle to Cordell Hull. December 8, 1937.
58 Feiling, p. 333.
59 Dalton, p. 109.
60 Foreign Relations of the United States, pp. 186-8, Bullitt to Cordell Hull. December 4, 1937.
61/62 Germ. Docs. D, vol. I, no. 50, Ribbentrop to Foreign Ministry. December 2, 1937.
63 *ibid* no. 75, Bismarck to German Embassy, Rome. November 24, 1937.

64 *ibid* no. 81, Ribbentrop to Foreign Ministry. December 17, 1937.
65 *ibid* no. 104, Memo by Mackensen, January 19, 1938. Enclosure Londonderry to Gall. December 6, 1937.
66 *ibid* no. 108, Memo by Neurath. January 26, 1938.
67 Wrench, p. 367.
68 Private information.
69 R. W. Seton-Watson, *Britain and the Dictators*, p. 77.
70 Germ. Docs. D, vol. 1, no. 112, Memo by Strempel. February 11, 1938.
71 *ibid* no. 131, Memo by Ribbentrop. March 1, 1938.
72 *ibid* no. 138, Ribbentrop to Henderson. March 4, 1938.
73 *ibid* no. 147, Memo by Ribbentrop. March 10, 1938.
74 *ibid* no. 148, Memo by Kordt. March 10, 1938.
75 *Hansard*, March 16, 1938.
76 G. Roberts, *The Nazi Claim to Colonies*, p. 21.
77 Germ. Docs. D, vol. IV, no. 268, Dirksen to Foreign Ministry. November 15, 1938.
78 *ibid* no. 270, Memo by Ribbentrop, no. 270. November 18, 1938.

PART TWO

CHAPTER 5

"A Far-Away Country"

1 Hoare, p. 285.
2 Germ. Docs. D, vol. II, no. 47, Eisenlohr to Foreign Ministry. January 12, 1938.
3 R. W. Seton-Watson, *From Munich to Danzig*, p. 56.
4 Amery, vol. 3, p. 259.
5 Germ. Docs. D, vol. II, p. 776.
6 N. Henderson, *Water Under the Bridges*, p. 219.
7 Brit. Docs. 3, vol. I, no. 164, Record of Anglo-French Conversations April 28-29, 1938.
8 *ibid* no. 140, Newton to Halifax. April 12, 1937.
9 Germ. Docs. D, vol. II, no. 10, Hencke to Foreign Ministry. October 29, 1937.
10/11 *ibid* no. 21, Forster to Foreign Ministry. November 16, 1937.
12 *ibid* no. 13, Memo by Altenburg. November 6, 1937.
13 *ibid* no. 5, Eisenlohr to Foreign Ministry. October 17, 1937.
14 Vansittart, *Bones of Contention*, p. 111.
15 K. Feiling, *Life of Neville Chamberlain*, p. 333.
16 Brit. Docs. 3, vol. I, no. 164, Record of Anglo-French Conversations. April 28-29, 1938.
17 Germ. Docs. D, vol. II, no. 33, Rintelen to Missions Abroad. December 18, 1937.

18/19   *ibid* no. 38, Eisenlohr to Foreign Ministry.   December 21, 1937.
20   G. E. R. Gedye, *Fallen Bastions*, p. 399.
21   New Documents on the History of Munich, p. 399, no. 1, Krofta to Czech Legations. March 12, 1938.
22   Brit. Docs. 3, vol. I, no. 61, Halifax to Newton. March 12, 1938.
23   *ibid* no. 57, Halifax to Phipps. March 12, 1938.
24   Feiling, p. 347.
25   Dirksen Papers, vol. I, p. 103, Masaryk to Krofta. April 4, 1938.
26/27   Brit. Docs. 3, vol. I, no. 107, Halifax to Phipps. March 23, 1938.
28   *ibid* no. 112, Phipps to Halifax. March 24, 1938.
29   *ibid* no. 90, Maisky to Halifax. March 24, 1938.
30   *ibid* no. 116, Halifax to Maisky. March 24, 1938.
31   *ibid* no. 86, Newton to Halifax. March 15, 1938.
32   *ibid* no. 98, Newton to Halifax. March 19, 1938.
33   Hoare, p. 293.
34   Brit. Docs. 3, vol. I, no. 133, Halifax to Newton. April 9, 1938.
35   Feiling, p. 347.
36   Amery, vol. III, p. 239.
37   Dalton, p. 162.
38/39   Duff Cooper, p. 218.
40   Brit. Docs. 3, vol. I, no. 150, Newton to Halifax. April 19, 1938.
41   *ibid* no. 156, Newton to Halifax. April 23, 1938.
42   *ibid* no. 164, Record of Anglo-French Conversations. April 28-29, 1938.
43   *ibid* no. 158, Newton to Halifax. April 26, 1938.
44   Feiling, p. 253.
45   Brit. Docs. 3, vol. I, no. 164, Record of Anglo-French Conversations. April 28-29, 1938.
46   Germ. Docs. D, vol. II, no. 134, Kordt to Foreign Ministry. April 29, 1938.
47   *ibid* no. 144, Welczeck to Foreign Ministry. May 1, 1938.
48   *ibid* no. 145, Dirksen to Foreign Ministry. May 3, 1938.
49   Brit. Docs. 3, vol. I, no. 171, Halifax to Newton. May 4, 1938.
50   *ibid* no. 170, Halifax to Newton. May 4, 1938.
51   Germ. Docs. D, vol. II, no. 151, Memo of Bismarck. May 10, 1938.
52   *ibid* no. 149, Woermann to German Embassy, Italy. May 7, 1938.
53   *ibid* no. 154, Memo Ribbentrop. May 11, 1938.
54   *ibid* no. 151, Memo Bismarck. May 10, 1938.
55   Dirksen Papers, vol. II, nos. 1 and 2, Cranfield to Dirksen May 5, 1938 and Dirksen to Cranfield May 6, 1938.

CHAPTER 6

Sudeten Crisis

1 G. E. R. Gedye, *Fallen Bastions*, p. 400 et seq. Following questions in the Commons, Driscoll's article was reprinted in June in the *News Chronicle*.
2 Germ. Docs. D, vol. II, no. 184, Ribbentrop Memo. May 21.
3 *ibid* no. 186, Ribbentrop Memo. May 21.
4 ibid no. 189, Weizsäcker. Minute and Enclosure. May 22.
5 *ibid* no. 197, Weizsäcker. Minute and Enclosure. May 23.
6 Brit. Docs. 3, vol. I, no. 349, Notes by Strang, Prague. May 26-27.
7 Germ. Docs. D, vol. II, no. 216, Weizsäcker Minute. May 28.
8 *ibid* no. 224, Weizsäcker Minute. May 31.
9/10 Brit. Docs. 3, vol. I, no. 347, Halifax to Phipps. Note 1. May 30.
11 Germ. Docs. D, vol. II, no. 244, Dirksen to Foreign Ministry. June 8.
12 *ibid* no. 247, Dirksen to Foreign Ministry. June 9.
13 Brit. Docs. 3, vol. I, no. 425, Halifax to Newton. June 18.
14 *ibid* no. 431, Newton to Halifax. June 21.
15 Germ. Docs. D, vol. II, no. 245, Dirksen to Foreign Ministry. June 9.
16 Brit. Docs. 3, vol. I, no. 439, Henderson to Halifax. June 23.
17/18 Germ. Docs. D, vol. II, no. 278, Ribbentrop Memo. July 3.
19 Woolton, *Memoirs*, pp. 130-2.
20 Germ. Docs. D, vol. II, no. 279, Wohltat to Weizsäcker, Enclosure. July 4.
21 *ibid* no. 302, Weizsäcker Minute. July 20.
22 *ibid* vol. VII, Appendix III. H (iii) von der Chevallerie Memo.
23 Brit. Docs., vol. I, nos. 495-8, Newton to Halifax. June 16.
24 Hoare, p. 298.
25 Germ. Docs. D, vol. II, no. 309, Dirksen to Foreign Ministry. July 22.
26 Dirksen Papers, vol. 2, no. 29.
27 Germ. Docs. D, vol. II, no. 315, Weizsäcker Minute. July 26.
28 *ibid* no. 318, Weizsäcker Minute. July 26.
29 *ibid* no. 232, Weizsäcker to Mackensen. June 1.
30 *Hansard*, July 26.
31 R. W. Seton-Watson, *Czechoslovak Broadsheet*, no. 1. July.
32 Gedye, p. 459.
33 Germ. Docs. D, vol. II, no. 339, Hencke to Foreign Ministry. August 6.
34 *ibid* no. 373, Hencke to Foreign Ministry. August 19.
35 *ibid* no. 351, Hencke to Foreign Ministry. August 13.

CHAPTER 7
Coercing the Czechs

1 Germ. Docs. D, vol. II, no. 389, Dirksen to Weizsäcker. August 24.
2 *ibid* no. 382, Kordt to Weizsäcker. August 23.
3 *ibid* no. 400, Weizsäcker to Kordt. August 27.
4 *ibid* no. 389, Dirksen to Weizsäcker. August 24.
5 ibid no. 382, Kordt to Weizsäcker. August 23.
6 *ibid* no. 389, Dirksen to Weizsäcker. August 24.
7 Dirksen Papers, vol. II, no. 7, Kordt to Dirksen. September 1.
8 Brit. Docs. 3, vol. II, no. 686, Halifax to Newton. August 25.
9 Ashton-Gwatkin to L. B. Namier, *In the Nazi Era*, p. 143.
10 Germ. Docs. D, vol. II, no. 429, Kordt to Foreign Ministry. September 3.
11 *ibid* no. 408, Kordt to Foreign Ministry. August 30.
12 *ibid* no. 418, Kordt to Weizsäcker. September 1.
13 Hore-Belisha, p. 138.
14 Germ. Docs. D, vol. II, no. 425, Ribbentrop Memo. September 3. Brit. Docs. 3, vol. II, Henderson to Halifax.
15 Dalton, p. 182.
16 Brit. Docs. 3, vol. II, no. 835, Butler to Halifax. September 11.
17 *ibid* no. 771, Henderson to Halifax. September 4.
18 L. B. Namier, *In the Nazi Era*, p. 162.
19 Brit. Docs. 3, vol. II, no. 723, Runciman to Halifax. August 30.
20 *ibid* no. 788, Newton to Halifax. September 6, Note 4 (telegram of September 7).
21 *ibid* no. 793, Henderson to Cadogan, September 6.
22 *History of the Times*, vol. IV, Part II, pp. 745-6.
23 Brit. Docs. 3, vol. II, no. 814, Halifax to Phipps. September 9.
24 *ibid* Appendix IV (iv), Skrine-Stevenson to Strang, September 8.
25 *ibid* no. 775, Warner to Halifax. September 5.
26 L. B. Namier, *In the Nazi Era*, p. 91 et seq.
27 Brit. Docs. 3, vol. II, no. 815, Halifax to Kirkpatrick. September 9.
28 Private information.
29 Duff Cooper, p. 226.
30 Jones, p. 406.
31/32/33 Duff Cooper, p. 227.
34 Brit. Docs. 3, vol. II, Appendix 1, Henderson to Wilson (2 letters) September 9.
35 Feiling, p. 357.
36 Brit. Docs. 3, vol. II, no. 862, Halifax to Henderson. September 13.
37 *ibid* Note 2.
38 ibid no. 833, Phipps to Halifax. September 11.
39 *ibid* no. 835, Butler to Halifax, note 3. September 11.
40 *ibid* no. 848, Phipps to Halifax. September 13.

41 *ibid* no. 852, Phipps to Halifax. September 13.
42 *ibid* no. 855, Phipps to Halifax. September 13.
43 *ibid* no. 857, Phipps to Halifax. September 13.
44 *ibid* no. 861, Phipps to Halifax. September 13.
45 *ibid* no. 875, Halifax to Phipps. September 14.
46 *ibid* no. 883, Phipps to Halifax. September 14.
47 Duff Cooper, p. 228.
48 E. Kordt, *Nicht Aus Den Akten*, Quoted by L. B. Namier, *In the Nazi Era*.
49 Wheeler-Bennet, *Prologue to Tragedy*, p. 108.

CHAPTER 8
Berchtesgaden

1 Henderson, p. 149.
2 Strang, *At Home and Abroad*, p. 137.
3 Feiling, p. 366.
4 Brit. Docs. 3, vol. II, no. 89, Notes by Chamberlain of his conversation with Hitler, and *ibid* no. 896, notes by Schmidt of the same conversation.
5 *ibid* no. 897, Notes by Sir Horace Wilson of conversations during visit to Berchtesgaden.
6 Amery, vol. III, p. 271.
7 Brit. Docs. 3, vol. II, no. 907, Phipps to Halifax. September 17.
8 Dalton, p. 179.
9 Duff Cooper, p. 229.
10 Brit. Docs. 3, vol. II, no. 902, Newton to Halifax. September 16.
11 *ibid* no. 888, Newton to Halifax. September 15.
12 *ibid* no. 906, Henderson to Halifax. September 17.
13 *ibid* no. 928, Record of Anglo-French Conversations, Downing Street. September 18.
14 *ibid* no. 959, note, Phipps to Halifax. September 19.
15 *ibid* no. 961, Newton to Halifax. September 19.
16 Hore-Belisha, p. 142.
17 *The Times.* September 20.
18 Brit. Docs. 3, vol. II, no. 971, Note by Cadogan. September 20.
19 *ibid* no. 964, Newton to Halifax. September 20.
20 *ibid* no. 973, Phipps to Halifax. September 20.
21 *ibid* no. 978, Newton to Halifax. September 20.
22 *ibid* no. 979, Newton to Halifax. September 20.
23 *ibid* no. 988, Phipps to Halifax. September 21.
24 *ibid* no. 989, Halifax to Phipps. September 21.

25 *New Documents on the History of Munich*, No. 42, Krofta to Masaryk.
26 *Dalton*, p. 196.
27 Brit. Docs. 3, vol. II, no. 1,008. Newton to Halifax. September 21.

CHAPTER 9
Godesberg

1 Duff Cooper, p. 231.
2 Kirkpatrick, p. 113.
3 Brit. Docs. 3, vol. II, no. 1,033.
4 *ibid* no. 1,020, Halifax to Léger. September 22.
5 *ibid* no. 1027, Halifax to Newton. September 22.
6 *ibid* no. 1030, Note 1, Halifax to Phipps. September 22.
7 *ibid* no. 1035, British Delegation, Godesberg, to Halifax. September 23.
8 *ibid* no. 1043, Halifax to Butler. September 23.
9 *ibid* no. 44, Halifax to British Delegation, Godesberg. September 23.
10 *ibid* no. 1046, Henderson to Halifax. September 23.
11 *ibid* no. 1047, Phipps to Halifax. September 23.
12 *ibid* no. 1049, Halifax to Newton. September 23.
13 *ibid* no. 1071, Butler to Halifax. September 24.
14 Duff Cooper, p. 233 and Hore-Belisha, p. 144.
15 Brit. Docs. 3, vol. II, no. 1058, Halifax to Chamberlain. September 23.
16 Kirkpatrick, p. 119.
17 Brit. Docs. 3, vol. II, no. 1057, Chamberlain to Halifax. September 24.
18 *ibid* no. 1073, Notes of a conversation between Chamberlain and Hitler at Godesberg. September 23-24.
19 Kirkpatrick, p. 220.
20 Germ. Docs. D, vol. II, no. 583, Memo by Schmidt of Hitler-Chamberlain discussion.
21 Brit. Docs. 3, vol. II, no. 1080, Newton to Halifax. September 24.
22 Henderson, p. 158.
23 Kirkpatrick, p. 122.
24 Brit. Docs. 3, vol. II, no. 1076, Phipps to Halifax. September 24.
25 Strang, *At Home and Abroad*, p. 135.
26 Brit. Docs. 3, vol. II, no. 1099, Phipps to Cadogan. September 26.
27/28 Duff Cooper, p. 234.
29 Brit. Docs. 3, vol. II, no. 1087, Henderson to Halifax. September 25.

30 Germ. Docs. D, vol. II, no. 631.
31 Brit. Docs. 3, vol. II, no. 1092, Note from Masaryk to Halifax. September 25.
32 *ibid* no. 1095, Note by Strang. September 26.
33 *ibid* no. 1093, Record of Anglo-French Conversation, Downing Street, September 25.
34 *ibid* no. 1096, Note 1 and no. 1143, Note 1.
35 *ibid* no. 1096, Record of Anglo-French Conversation, Downing Street, September 26.
36 Churchill, *The Gathering Storm*, p. 242.
37 Brit. Docs. 3, vol. II, no. 1111, Halifax to Henderson, for Wilson. September 26.
38 Wheeler-Bennett, *Prologue to Tragedy*, p. 150.
39 Germ. Docs. D, vol. II, no. 614, Rothermere to Ribbentrop. September 26.
40 Brit. Docs. 3, vol. II, no. 1118, Notes by Kirkpatrick of a conversation between Wilson and Hitler, September 26; no. 1115, Wilson to Chamberlain, September 26.
41 *ibid* no. 1116, Wilson to Chamberlain. September 26.
42 *ibid* no. 1121, Chamberlain to Wilson, 1 A.M. September 27.
43 *ibid* no. 1125, Perth to Halifax. September 27.
44 *ibid* no. 1129, Notes by Kirkpatrick of a conversation between Wilson and Hitler. September 27.
45 Germ. Docs. D, vol. II, no. 634, Memo by Schmidt on Hitler-Wilson Conversation. September 27.
46 Brit. Docs. 3, vol. II, no. 1143, Halifax to Phipps. September 27.
47 *ibid* no. 1150, Phipps to Halifax. September 27.
48 Duff Cooper, p. 240.
49 Brit. Docs. 3, vol. II, no. 1153, Newton to Halifax. September 27.
50 *ibid* no. 1151, Phipps to Halifax. September 27.
51 Hoare, p. 305.
52 Wedgwood, *Last of the Radicals*, p. 231.
53 Duff Cooper, p. 239.
54 Brit. Docs. 3, vol. II, no. 1155, Henderson to Halifax. September 28.
55 Germ. Docs. D, vol. II, no. 655, Weizsäcker Minute. September 28.
56 *ibid* no. 656, Weizsäcker Minute. September 28.
57 Henderson, p. 163.
58 Brit. Docs. 3, vol. II, no. 1231, Perth to Halifax. September 30.
59 Kordt, *Wahn und Wirklichkeit*, p. 125.
60 Hesse, *Hitler and the English*, p. 57. (Hesse gave the wrong date.)
61 Brit. Docs. 3, vol. II, no. 1158, Halifax to Henderson. 11:30 A.M. September 28.
62 *ibid* no. 1159, Halifax to Perth. September 28.
63 Described in Wheeler-Bennett, *Prologue to Tragedy*, p. 168; Arnold

Wilson, *More Thoughts and Talks*, p. 162; Duff Cooper, p. 240; Raczynski, *In Allied London*; A. J. P. Taylor, *The Troublemakers*, p. 197; Germ. Docs. D, vol. IV, no. 248, Kordt to Foreign Ministry. October 3.
64 Helen Kirkpatrick, *This Terrible Peace*, pp. 124-5.
65 Brit. Docs. 3, vol. II, no. 1194, Newton to Halifax. September 29.
66 *ibid* no. 1210, Halifax to Newton. September 29.
67 *ibid* no. 1217, Newton to Halifax. September 29.

CHAPTER 10
Munich

1 Duff Cooper, p. 241.
2 Ciano, *Diary 1937-38*, p. 167. L. B. Namier, *Europe in Decay*, pp. 124, 135.
3 Ciano, *Diary 1937-38*, p. 166.
4 Brit. Docs. 3, vol. II, no. 1227, Note by Horace Wilson.
5 Gedye, p. 483, and Ripka, *Munich Before and After*.
6 Strang, *Home and Abroad*, p. 147.
7 Brit. Docs. 3, vol. II, no. 1228, Record by Schmidt.
8 Amery, vol. III, p. 337.
9 Germ. Docs. D, vol. IV, no. 248, Kordt to Foreign Ministry. October 3.
10 Bruce Lockhart, *Friends, Foes and Foreigners*, p. 196.
11 J. P. Sartre, *The Reprieve*, p. 398.
12 H. A. L. Fisher Papers, Bodleian Library, Oxford, Box A (A-N).
13 Wrench, p. 378.
14 *The Times*, October 1, 1938.
15 Gedye, p. 488-9.
16 *ibid* p. 497.
17 Duff Cooper, p. 243.
18 Lady Diana Cooper, *The Light of Common Day*, p. 248.
19 Duff Cooper, p. 249.
20 Wrench, p. 249.
21 Rowse, p. 45.
22 Amery, vol. III, p. 253.
23 Gedye, p. 491.
24 Brit. Docs. 3, vol. III, Appendix V, Document (v) Enclosure.

PART THREE
CHAPTER 11
Economic Appeasement

1   *Hansard*, March 14.
2   Einzig, *Appeasement*, p. 72.
3   *ibid* pp. 74-5.
4   *ibid* p. 77.
5   *ibid* p. 78.
6   German Foreign Ministry Archives 5841 H.
7   Germ. Docs. D, vol. IV, no. 249, Dirksen to Foreign Ministry. October 7.
8   *ibid* no. 251, Dirksen to Weizsäcker. October 12.
9   *ibid* no. 254, Weizsäcker to Dirksen. October 17.
10 *ibid* no. 253, Weizsäcker to Dirksen. October 17.
11 Jones, p. 418. October 30.
12 Dirksen Papers, vol. II, no. 29.
13 Germ. Docs. D, vol. IV, no. 259, Rüter to Clodius. October 20.
14 *ibid* no. 257, Dirksen to Foreign Ministry, Enclosure. October 19.
15 *ibid* no. 259, Rüter to Clodius. October 20.
16 *ibid* no. 5, Memorandum by Clodius. October 24.
17 German Foreign Ministry Archives 2005/442772.
18 Germ. Docs. D, vol. IV, no. 261, Wiehl to Dirksen. November 3.
19 *ibid* no. 260, Dirksen to Foreign Ministry. October 31.
20 *ibid* no. 262, Conversation between Wienke and Ashton-Gwatkin. November 6.
21 *ibid* no. 265, Dirksen to Weizsäcker. November 9.
22 Brit. Docs. 3, vol. IV, Appendix II (ii) Note 1.
23 German Foreign Ministry Archives 2005/442785-6.
24 Brit. Docs. 3, vol. III, no. 285, Halifax to Phipps. November 1.
25 Germ. Docs. D, vol. IV, no. 267, Minute by Rüter. November 10.
26 German Foreign Ministry Archives 2005/442785-6.
27 *ibid* 2005/442787-90.
28 Dirksen Papers no. 29.
29 Einzig, *Appeasement*, pp. 93-4.
30 Einzig, *World Finance*, 1938-39, p. 204.
31 Hore-Belisha, p. 162.
32 *ibid* p. 163.

CHAPTER 12
Search for Agreement

1 Germ. Docs. D, vol. IV, no. 280, Dirksen to Foreign Ministry. December 16, 1938.
2 *ibid* no. 281, Dirksen to Weizsäcker. December 16, 1938.
3 L. B. Namier, *In the Nazi Era*, p. 159. July 5, 1938.
4 Germ. Docs. D, vol. IV, no. 289, Reich Federation of Industries to Foreign Ministry. January 4, 1939.
5 *ibid* no. 302, Memo by an Official of the Economic Policy Dept. January 27, 1939.
6 *ibid* no. 314, Memo by Hipp. February 2, 1939.
7 German Foreign Ministry Archives 2005/442811-3.
8 Germ. Docs. D, vol. IV, no. 286, Dirksen to Foreign Ministry. January 24, 1939.
9 Dirksen Papers, vol. II, no. 29, pp. 148-92.
10 Hesse, *Hitler and the English*, p. 62.
11 Germ. Docs. D, vol. IV, no. 299, Dirksen to Foreign Ministry. January 24, 1939.
12/13 *ibid* no. 305, Dirksen to Foreign Ministry. January 31, 1939.
14 *ibid* no. 308, Wiehl to Dirksen. February 6, 1939.
15 *ibid* Note 4, Dirksen to Wiehl. February 8, 1939.
16 Brit. Docs. 3, vol. IV, no. 109, Henderson to Halifax. February 16, 1939.
17 *ibid* Appendix I (iii), Chamberlain to Henderson. February 20, 1939.
18 *ibid* Appendix I (iv), Halifax to Henderson. February 20, 1939.
19 *ibid* Appendix I (vi), Henderson to Halifax. February 23, 1939.
20 *ibid* Appendix I (vii), Henderson to Chamberlain. February 23, 1939.
21 Dirksen Papers, vol. II, no. 29, pp. 148-92.
22 Brit. Docs. 3, vol. IV, Appendix II, Report on Ashton-Gwatkin's visit to Germany. February 19-26, 1936.
23 Germ. Docs. D, vol. IV, no. 316, Wiehl Memo. February 20, 1939.
24 *ibid* no. 316, Note 2, Minute 2497/518145-47.
25 *ibid* no. 317, Hewel Memo on Ashton-Gwatkin's conversation. February 20, 1939.
26 *ibid* no. 323, Wiehl Minute. February 25, 1939.
27 German Foreign Ministry Archives 2005/442831-3.
28 Dirksen Papers, vol. II, no. 29, pp. 148-92.
29 Brit. Docs. 3, vol. IV, no. 163, Henderson to Halifax. March 3, 1939.
30 Henderson, p. 185.
31 Brit. Docs. 3, vol. IV, no. 172, Henderson to Halifax. March 3, 1939.

32 Henderson, p. 198.
33 Brit. Docs. 3, vol. IV, no. 172, Henderson to Halifax. March 3, 1939.
34 Germ. Docs. D, vol. IV, no. 244, Dirksen to Foreign Ministry. March 15, 1939.

CHAPTER 13
Czech Gold

1 Einzig, *Appeasement*, p. 124.
2 Einzig, *In the Centre of Things*, Ch. 19, pp. 186-94.
3 *Hansard*, May 26, 1939.
4 Einzig, *In the Centre of Things*, Ch. 19, pp. 186-94.

CHAPTER 14
Wilson and Wohltat

1 Dirksen Papers, vol. II, no. 29.
2 Germ. Docs. D, vol. VI, no. 368, Selzam to Wiehl. May 11.
3 *ibid* no. 380, Rüter Conversation with Drummond-Wolff. May 14.
4 Brit. Docs. 3, vol. V, no. 559, Halifax to Henderson. May 19.
5 *ibid* no. 616, Henderson to Halifax. May 24 (Received June 8).
6 *ibid* no. 659, Henderson to Halifax. May 28.
7 *ibid* no. 671, Henderson to Halifax. May 30.
8 German Foreign Ministry Archives, 2791/54793.
9 Brit. Docs. 3, vol. V, no. 741, Minute by Ashton-Gwatkin. June 7.
10 Germ. Docs. D, vol. VI, no. 497, Memo by von Trott. June 1-8.
11 His own phrase, letter to the authors. January 24, 1962.
12 Germ. Docs. D, vol. VI, no. 521, Memo Weizsäcker. June 13.
13 *ibid* no. 539, Memo Weizsäcker. June 17.
14 *ibid* no. 564, Dirksen to Foreign Ministry. June 24.
15 *ibid* no. 572, Memo Weizsäcker. June 27.
16 *ibid* no. 577, Weizsäcker to Dirksen. June 28.
17 *ibid* no. 645, Dirksen to Foreign Ministry. July 10.
18 Brit. Docs. 3, vol. VI, Appendix I (ix), Henderson to Halifax. July 9.
19 Brit. Docs. 3, vol. VI, no. 354, Record by Wilson. July 19.
20 Germ. Docs. D, vol. VI, no. 716, Wohltat Memo. July 24.
21 Brit. Docs. 3, vol. VI, no. 370, Record by Hudson. July 20.
22 German Foreign Ministry Archives, 2791/547959-65.
23 Dirksen Papers, vol. II, no. 24, Minute. August 3.
24 Dirksen Papers, vol. II, no. 14, Report. July 24.

25 Brit. Docs. 3, vol. VI, no. 449 (Campbell to Halifax) and no. 46 (Phipps to Chamberlain).
26 Dirksen Papers, vol. II, no. 13, Memo by Dirksen. July 21.
27 Dirksen Papers, vol. II, no. 16, Review by Hesse. July 24.
28 Brit. Docs. 3, vol. VI, no. 467, Minute by Sargent. July 27.
29 Dirksen Papers, vol. II, no. 15, Memo by Dirksen. July 24.
30 Brit. Docs. 3, vol. VI, Appendix IV, Record of Conversation. July 22.
31 Dirksen Papers, vol. II, no. 22, Dirksen to Weizsäcker. August 1.
32 Brit. Docs. 3, vol. VI, no. 533, Note 2.
33 Dirksen Papers, vol. II, no. 24-I, Report by Dirksen. August 3.
34 *ibid* no. 24-II.
35 *ibid* no. 24-IV.
36 Dirksen Papers, vol. II, no. 25, Minute of Conversation. August 9.
37 Brit. Docs. 3, vol. VII, Appendix I (i), Minute by Ashton-Gwatkin. August 15.
38 *ibid* Annex to (i), Record by Leslie Runciman. Undated.

PART FOUR

CHAPTER 15

Tilea's Indiscretion

1   Brit. Docs. 3, vol. IV, no. 258, Henderson to Halifax. March 15.
2   *ibid* no. 282, Newton to Halifax. March 16.
3   *ibid* no. 296, Newton to Halifax. March 16.
4   *Hansard*, March 15.
5   *The Times*, March 18.
6   Brit. Docs. 3, vol. IV, no. 308, Halifax to Henderson. March 17.
7   *Hansard*, March 15.
8   Brit. Docs. 3, vol. IV, no. 270, Phipps to Halifax. March 15.
9   *ibid* no. 288, Henderson to Halifax. March 16.
10 *ibid* no. 280, Halifax to Phipps. March 15.
11 *ibid* no. 275, Shepherd to Halifax. March 15.
12 *ibid* no. 293, Shepherd to Halifax. March 16.
13 *ibid* no. 279, Halifax to Henderson. March 15.
14 *ibid* no. 298, Minute by Sargent. March 16.
15 Ciano Diary, p. 10. January 12.
16 Brit. Docs. 3, vol. IV, no. 395, Halifax to Sir R. Hoare. March 17.
17 *ibid* para. 6.
18 *ibid* no. 390, Halifax to Kennard, Knatchbull-Hugesson, Waterlow and Campbell. March 17.
19 *ibid* no. 408, Phipps to Halifax. March 18.
20 *ibid* no. 389, Halifax to Seeds. March 17.

21 *ibid* no. 395, Halifax to Sir R. Hoare. March 17.
22 *ibid* no. 405, Phipps to Halifax. March 18.
23 *ibid* no. 416, Halifax to Lindsay. March 18.
24 *ibid* no. 399, Sir R. Hoare to Halifax. March 18 and no. 431. March 19.
25 *ibid* no. 420, Campbell to Halifax. March 19.
26 *ibid* no. 433, Halifax to Seeds. March 19.
27 *ibid* no. 447, Kennard to Halifax. March 20.
28 *ibid* no. 440, Campbell to Halifax. March 20.
29 *ibid* no. 458, Record of Anglo-French Conversation. March 21.
30 *ibid* no. 479, Kennard to Halifax. March 22.
31/32 *ibid* no. 484, Record of Anglo-French Conversation. March 22.
33 Feiling, p. 403.
34/35 Brit. Docs. 3, vol. IV, no. 484, Record of Anglo-French Conversation. March 22.
36 *ibid* no. 489, Kennard to Halifax. March 22.
37 Vansittart, *Mist Procession*, p. 536.
38 Brit. Docs. 3, vol. IV, no. 511, Campbell to Halifax. March 24.
39 *ibid* no. 518, Halifax to Kennard. March 24.
40 *ibid* para. 11.
41 *ibid* no. 523, Kennard to Halifax. March 25.
42 *ibid* no. 547, Kennard to Halifax. March 28.
43 *ibid* no. 568, Halifax to Kennard. March 30.
44 *ibid* no. 573, Kennard to Halifax. March 30.
45 *ibid* no. 595, Kennard to Halifax. April 1.
46 *ibid* no. 598, Halifax to Kennard. April 1.
47 *ibid* vol. V, nos. 1, 2, 10, 11, 16, Anglo-Polish talks. April 4, 5.
48 *ibid* vol. IV, no. 605, Kennard to Halifax. April 2.
49 Halifax. *Fulness of Days*, p. 206.
50 Vansittart, p. 430.
51 Szembek, *Journal*, p. 433.
52 Brit. Docs. 3, vol. V, no. 207, Kennard to Halifax. April 18.
53 Duff Cooper, *The Second World War*, p. 320.
54 Noël, *L'Agression Allemande Contre La Pologne*, p. 325, Note 1.
55 Zay, *Carnet Secrets*, p. 54, March 29.

CHAPTER 16
Danzig Dilemma

1 Brit. Docs. 3, vol. V, no. 163, Ogilvie Forbes to Halifax. April 14.
2 *ibid* no. 197, Halifax to Kennard. April 17.
3/4 *ibid* no. 208, Kennard to Halifax. April 18.
5 *ibid* vol. VI, no. 16, Minute by Strang. June 9.

6 *ibid* no. 186, Phipps to Halifax. June 30.
7 *ibid* no. 289, Norton to Cadogan. July 10.
8 *ibid* no. 186, Phipps to Halifax. June 30.
9 *ibid* no. 188, Norton to Halifax. June 30.
10 *ibid* no. 197, Shepherd to Halifax. July 1.
11 *ibid* no. 198, Shepherd to Halifax. July 1.
12 *ibid* no. 212, Phipps to Halifax. July 1.
13 *ibid* no. 211, Henderson to Halifax. July 1.
14 *ibid* Appendix IV (i), Notes on Second Interview. July 8.
15 *ibid* Appendix I (i), Henderson to Cadogan. June 13.
16 *ibid* vol. VII, no. 241, Henderson to Halifax. August 24.
17 *ibid* vol. VI, Appendix I (ii), Henderson to Sargent. June 16.
18 Vansittart, p. 536.
19 Brit. Docs. 3, vol. VI, no. 223, Norton to Cadogan. July 3.
20 *ibid* vol. VII, no. 158, Henderson to Cadogan. August 22.
21 *ibid* vol. VI, no. 224, Norton to Sargent. July 3.
22 *ibid* no. 289, Norton to Cadogan. July 10.
23 *ibid* no. 224, Norton to Sargent. July 3.
24 *ibid* no. 231, Halifax to Norton. July 5.
25 *ibid* no. 234, Halifax to Loraine. July 5.
26 *ibid* no. 235, Norton to Halifax. July 5.
27/28 *ibid* no. 236, Norton to Halifax. July 5.
29 *ibid* no. 289, Norton to Cadogan. July 10.
30 *ibid* no. 176, Halifax to Kennard. June 29.
31 *ibid* no. 222, Halifax to Norton. July 3.
32/33 *ibid* no. 245, Norton to Sargent. July 5.
34 *ibid* no. 374, Norton to Halifax. July 20.
35 *ibid* no. 445, Norton to Halifax. July 25.
36 Szembeck, pp. 483-5.
37 Brit. Docs. 3, vol. VI, no. 327, Norton to Halifax. July 15.
38 *ibid* no. 222, Note 2.
39 *ibid* no. 334, Halifax to Norton. July 17.
40 *ibid* no. 341, Norton to Halifax. July 18.
41 *ibid* no. 343, Halifax to Norton. July 18.
42 Germ. Docs. D, vol. VI, no. 714, Memo by Wohltat. July 24.
43 Brit. Docs. 3, vol. VI, no. 463, Sargent to Norton. July 26.
44 *ibid* no. 319, Halifax to Henderson. July 13.
45 *ibid* no. 317, Chamberlain to Daladier. July 13.
46 *ibid* no. 337, Henderson to Halifax. July 17.
47 *ibid* no. 372, Memo by Roberts. July 20.
48 *ibid* no. 382, Halifax to Shepherd. July 21.
49 *ibid* no. 386, Halifax to Norton. July 21.
50 *ibid* Appendix I (xii), Henderson to Halifax. July 24.
51 *ibid* Appendix I (xiii), Henderson to Halifax. July 25.
52 *ibid* Appendix I (xiv), Henderson to Halifax. July 28.

53 *ibid* no. 448, Sargent to Holman. July 25.
54 *ibid* no. 461, Norton to Halifax. July 26.
55 *ibid* no. 511, Holman to Kirkpatrick. August 1.
56 *ibid* no. 461, Norton to Halifax. July 26.
57/58 *ibid* no. 460, Henderson to Halifax. July 26.
59 *ibid* no. 492, Norton to Sargent. July 29.

CHAPTER 17
Pledges to Poland

1 Brit. Docs. 3, vol. VI, no. 510, Kennard to Sargent. August 1.
2 *ibid* no. 507, Halifax to Osborne. August 1.
3 *ibid* no. 585, Henderson to Halifax. Received 2 P.M. August 8.
4 *ibid* no. 594, Henderson to Cadogan. August 8.
5 *ibid* no. 587, Kennard to Halifax. Received 6 P.M. August 8.
6 *ibid* no. 599, Kennard to Halifax. August 9.
7 *ibid* no. 595, Kennard to Sargent. August 8.
8 *ibid* no. 604, Halifax to Shepherd. August 10.
9 *ibid* no. 659, Visit of Burckhardt to Hitler. Minute by Makins. August 14.
10 *ibid* vol. VII, no. 3, Halifax to Shepherd. August 15.
11 *ibid* no. 4, Halifax to Kennard. August 15.
12 *ibid* no. 37, Henderson to Strang. August 16.
13 Ciano, p. 126.
14 Brit. Docs. 3, vol. VII, no. 27, Campbell to Halifax. August 16.
15 *ibid* no. 52, Kennard to Halifax. August 18.
16 *ibid* no. 70, Kennard to Halifax. August 19.
17 *ibid* no. 87, Kennard to Halifax. August 20.
18 *ibid* no. 90, Kennard to Halifax. August 20.
19 *ibid* no. 108, Kennard to Halifax. August 21.
20 *ibid* no. 119, Kennard to Cadogan. August 21.
21 *ibid* no. 137, Halifax to Kennard. 2:40 P.M. August 22.
22 *ibid* no. 158, Henderson to Halifax. August 22.
23 *ibid* no. 159, Henderson to Halifax. August 22.
24 *ibid* no. 37, Henderson to Strang. August 16.
25 *ibid* no. 140, Halifax to Kennard. 6:50 P.M. August 22.
26 *ibid* no. 214, Loraine to Halifax. August 24.
27 *ibid* no. 206, Halifax to Kennard. August 23.
28 *ibid* no. 227, Kennard to Halifax. August 24.
29 *ibid* no. 228, Kennard to Halifax. August 24.
30 *ibid* no. 241, Henderson to Halifax. August 24.
31 *ibid* no. 263, Kennard to Halifax. August 25.
32 *ibid* no. 237, Minute by Roberts. August 24.

33 *ibid* no. 271, Henderson to Halifax. Received 12:45 P.M. August 25.
34 *ibid* no. 270, Kennard to Halifax. Received 2 P.M. August 25.
35 *ibid* no. 293, Henderson to Halifax. Sent 9:30 P.M. August 25.
36 *ibid* no. 278, Halifax to Phipps. August 25.
37 Command Paper, 6144 (Treaty Series no. 58), 1939.
38 Roberts, *The Nazi Claim to Colonies*, Introduction by Duff Cooper. July, 1939.
39/40 Command Paper, 6616, 1945.
41 Brit. Docs. 3, vol. VII, no. 309, Halifax to Kennard para. 2. August 24.
42 *ibid* para. 3. August 25.

CHAPTER 18
Coercing the Poles

1 Brit. Docs. 3, vol. VII, no. 265, Kennard to Halifax. 2:59 A.M. August 25.
2 *ibid* no. 354, Halifax to Kennard. August 26.
3 *ibid* no. 284, Henderson to Halifax. August 25.
4 *ibid* no. 327, Halifax to Loraine. August 26.
5 *ibid* no. 297, Halifax to Kennard. 11 P.M. August 25.
6 Germ. Docs. D, vol. VII, no. 226, Mackensen to Weizsäcker. August 23.
7 *ibid* no. 271, Mussolini to Hitler. August 25.
8 *ibid* no. 301, Mussolini to Hitler. August 26.
9 *ibid* no. 320, Mackensen to Foreign Ministry. August 26.
10 Brit. Docs. 3, vol. VII, no. 296, Halifax to Loraine. 11 P.M. August 25.
11 *ibid* no. 389, Halifax to Loraine. 9:20 P.M. August 27.
12 Germ. Docs. D, vol. VII, no. 417, Mussolini to Hitler. August 29.
13 *ibid* no. 307, Hitler to Mussolini. August 26.
14 *ibid* no. 405, Memo by Likus. August 28.
15 Brit. Docs. 3, vol. VII, no. 397, Minute by Kirkpatrick. August 27.
16 Germ. Docs. D, vol. VII, no. 322, Bräuer to Foreign Ministry. August 26.
17 *ibid* no. 324, Daladier to Hitler. August 26.
18 *ibid* no. 351, Bräuer to Foreign Ministry. August 27.
19 Brit. Docs. 3, vol. VII, no. 203, Campbell to Halifax. August 23.
20 *ibid* no. 344, Phipps to Halifax. August 26.
21 *ibid* no. 452, Loraine to Halifax. August 29.
22 *ibid* no. 480, Halifax to Loraine. August 29.
23 *ibid* no. 313, Henderson to Cadogan. August 25.
24 *ibid* no. 472, Henderson to Halifax. August 29.
25 *ibid* no. 455, Note 8, Memo by Kirkpatrick. August 29.

26 *ibid* vol. VI, no. 201, Halifax to Shepherd. July 1, 1939.
27 *ibid* vol. VII, no. 262, Loraine to Halifax. 2:30 A.M. August 25.
28 *ibid* no. 357, Kennard to Cadogan. August 26.
29 *ibid* no. 367, Kennard to Halifax. August 27.
30 Hore-Belisha, p. 220.
31 *ibid* p. 221.
32 Brit. Docs. 3, vol. VII, no. 349, Note 7, Minute by Roberts. August 26.
33 *ibid* Note 7.
34 *ibid* no. 402, Note 2, Points made verbally on August 27.
35 *ibid* no. 402, Ogilvie Forbes to Halifax. 6:25 A.M. August 28.
36 *ibid* no. 402, Note 3.
37 Hore-Belisha, p. 222.
38 Brit. Docs. 3, vol. VII, no. 406, Ogilvie Forbes to Halifax. August 28.
39 *ibid* no. 411, Halifax to Kennard. August 28.
40 *ibid* no. 418, Ogilvie-Forbes to Halifax. August 28.
41 Foreign Relations of the United States. Kennedy to Cordell Hull. August 23.
42 Brit. Docs. 3, vol. VII, no. 420, Kennard to Halifax. August 28.
43 *ibid* no. 501, Henderson to Halifax. August 29.
44 *ibid* no. 426, Halifax to Ogilvie Forbes. August 28.
45 *ibid* no. 455, Henderson to Halifax. August 29.
46 *ibid* no. 455, Note 8, Memo by Vansittart. August 29.
47 *ibid* no. 545, Halifax to Henderson. 9 P.M. August 30.
48 *ibid* no. 455, Henderson to Halifax. August 29.
49 *ibid* no. 472, Henderson to Halifax. August 29.
50 *ibid* no. 489, Kennard to Halifax. August 29.
51 *ibid* no. 436, Halifax to Kennard. August 28.
52 *ibid* no. 508, Henderson to Halifax. 2:30 A.M. August 30.
53 *ibid* no. 508, and 565, Henderson to Halifax. August 30.
54 Henderson, *Failure of a Mission*, p. 266.
55 Brit. Docs. 3, vol. VII, no. 514, Report by Dahlerus. August 30.
56/57 *ibid* no. 519, Note of Telephone Conversation between Dahlerus and Göring. August 30.
58 *ibid* no. 520, Henderson to Halifax. August 30.
59 *ibid* no. 523, Henderson to Halifax. August 30.
60/61 *ibid* no. 526, Osborne to Halifax. August 30.

CHAPTER 19
Henderson Versus Kennard

1 Brit. Docs. 3, vol. VII, no. 504, Halifax to Henderson. 2 A.M. August 30.

2   *ibid* no. 493, Henderson to Halifax. Received 10:25 P.M. August 29.
3   *ibid* no. 501, Henderson to Halifax. August 29.
4   *ibid* no. 510, Henderson to Halifax. Received 3:30 A.M. August 30.
5   Henderson, pp. 267-8.
6   Brit. Docs. 3, vol. VII, no. 512, Kennard to Halifax. Received 10 A.M. August 30.
7   *ibid* no. 520, Henderson to Halifax. Received 1 P.M. August 30.
8   *ibid* no. 537, Henderson to Halifax. Received 6:30 P.M. August 30.
9   Foreign Relations of the United States. Kennedy to Cordell Hull. August 30.
10 Hore-Belisha, pp. 223-4.
11 Brit. Docs. 3, vol. VII, no. 538, Halifax to Henderson. 6:50 P.M. August 30.
12 *ibid* no. 539, Halifax to Kennard. 7 P.M. August 30.
13 *ibid* no. 543, Halifax to Henderson. 7:40 P.M. August 30.
14 *ibid* no. 547, Halifax to Henderson. 9:50 P.M. August 30.
15 Henderson, p. 270.
16 Brit. Docs. 3, vol. VII, no. 571, Henderson to Halifax. Received 2:45 A.M. August 31.
17 Henderson, p. 270.
18/19 Brit. Docs. 3, vol. VII, no. 574, Henderson to Halifax. Written 5:15 A.M. August 31.
20/21 *ibid* no. 575, Henderson to Halifax. Written 5:15 A.M. August 31.
22 *ibid* no. 578, Minute by Henniker Major. August 31.
23 Germ. Docs. D, vol. VII, no. 466, Weizsäcker Memo. August 31.
24 Alan Bullock, *Hitler*, p. 500.
25 Brit. Docs. 3, vol. VII, no. 581, Received 11:24 A.M. August 31.
26 *ibid* no. 582, Henderson to Halifax. Received 11:33 A.M. August 31.
27 *ibid* no. 587, Henderson to Halifax. Received 12:20 P.M. August 31.
28 *ibid* no. 597, Henderson to Halifax. Received 1:50 P.M. August 31.
29 *ibid* no. 589, Minute by Cadogan, Annex by Wilson. August 31.
30 *ibid* no. 592, Halifax to Henderson. 1 P.M. August 31.
31 *ibid* no. 587, Henderson to Halifax. Received 12:20 P.M. August 31.
32 *ibid* no. 596, Halifax to Kennard. 1:45 P.M. August 31.
33 *ibid* no. 591, Halifax to Henderson. 1 P.M. August 31.
34 *ibid* no. 627, Minute by Halifax. August 31.
35 *ibid* no. 590, Minute by Halifax. August 31.
36 Germ. Docs. D, vol. VII, no. 478, Memo by Schmidt. September 1.
37 Ciano, p. 141.
38 Brit. Docs. 3, vol. VII, no. 621, Loraine to Halifax. Received 11 P.M. August 31.
39 *ibid* no. 618, Kennard to Halifax. Received 10:25 P.M. August 31.
40 *ibid* no. 628, Henderson to Halifax. August 31.
41 *ibid* no. 632, Halifax to Kennard. 12:50 P.M. September 1.
42 *ibid* no. 650, Kennard to Halifax. Received 12:15 P.M. September 1.

PART FIVE
CHAPTER 20
War Without War

1 Hore-Belisha, p. 244.
2 Brit. Docs. 3, vol. VII, no. 637, Reuter to Halifax. 6:35 A.M.
3 *ibid* no. 638, Kennard to Halifax. 8:30 A.M.
4/5 *ibid* no. 639, Record of Conversation with Dahlerus, by Spencer. 9:50 A.M.
6 *ibid* no. 689, Halifax to Kennard, concerning 10:30 A.M.
7 *ibid* no. 644, Henderson to Halifax. 10:45 A.M.
8 *ibid* no. 645, Henderson to Halifax. 10:50 A.M.
9 *ibid* no. 648, Minute by Orme Sargent. Exact time not known.
10 *ibid* no. 649, Note from the French Embassy. 10:15 A.M.
11/12 Ciano, *Dairy*, p. 142.
13 Brit. Docs. 3, vol. VII, no. 651, Minute by Cadogan. 12:20 P.M.
14 *ibid* no. 652, Minute by Cadogan. 1:25 P.M.
15 *ibid* no. 655, Kennard to Halifax. 2 P.M.
16 *ibid* no. 658, Henderson to Halifax. 3:45 P.M.
17 *ibid* no. 662, Kennard to Halifax. 4 P.M.
18 Henderson, p. 279.
19 Brit. Docs. 3, vol. VII, no. 663, Record of Conversation with M. Dahlerus 4:25 P.M.
20 *ibid* no. 664, Halifax to Henderson. 4:45 A.M.
21 *ibid* no. 669, Halifax to Henderson. Sent 5:45 P.M.
22 *ibid* no. 682, Henderson to Halifax. 9:30 P.M.
23 *ibid* no. 684, Henderson to Halifax. 11:30 P.M.
24 Lady Diana Cooper, p. 257.

CHAPTER 21
The Revolt of Conscience

1 Brit. Docs. 3, vol. VII, no. 595, Kennard to Halifax. Received 5 A.M.
2 *ibid* no. 693, Kennard to Halifax. Received 9:30 A.M.
3 Ciano, p. 143.
4 Brit. Docs. 3, vol. VII, no. 749, Minute by Makins.
5 *ibid* no. 693, Kennard to Halifax. Received 9:30 A.M.
6 *ibid* no. 696, Phipps to Halifax. Received 9:35 A.M.
7 *ibid* no. 699, Halifax to Phipps. Para. 1. 11:55 A.M.
8 *ibid* para. 2.
9 *ibid* no. 709, Minute by Loraine. Para. 1.
10 *ibid* para. 6.

11 Ciano, *Diary*, p. 143.
12 Brit. Docs. 3, vol. VII, no. 710, Minute by Harvey.
13 *ibid* no. 716, Minute by Cadogan. 4 P.M.
14 *ibid* no. 705, Kennard to Halifax. Received 4:20 P.M.
15 Hore-Belisha, p. 225.
16 *ibid* p. 226.
17 Brit. Docs. 3, vol. VII, no. 718, Record, probably by Strang. About 5 P.M.
18 Spears, *Prelude to Dunkirk*, p. 18.
19 Brit. Docs. 3, vol. VII, no. 719, Henderson to Halifax. Received 5:15 P.M.
20 *ibid* no. 720, Kennard to Halifax. Received 5:20 P.M.
21 *ibid* no. 727, Minute by Cadogan. 6 P.M.
22 *ibid* no. 728, Minute by Jebb. 6:38 P.M.
23 *ibid* no. 731, Minute by Loraine. 7:22 P.M.
24 De Monzie, *Ci Devant*, p. 157.
25 Spears, p. 20.
26 *Hansard*, September 2.
27 Amery, vol. III, p. 324.
28 Dalton, p. 264.
29 Duff Cooper, p. 259.
30 Dalton, p. 265.
31 Hore-Belisha, p. 226.
32 Not recorded in *Hansard*. Heard by all present. Spears, p. 21, Duff Cooper, p. 259.
33 *Hansard*, September 2.
34 *Hansard*, September 3.
35 Amery, vol. III, p. 324.
36 Spears, p. 22.
37 Amery, vol. III, p. 324.
38 Hore-Belisha, p. 226-7.
39 Brit. Docs. 3, vol. VII, no. 734, Kennard to Halifax. Received 8 P.M.
40 *ibid* no. 735, Halifax to Henderson, 8:20 P.M.
41 B. Dahlerus, *The Last Attempt*, p. 103 et seq.
42 Duff Cooper, p. 259.
43 *ibid* p. 259.
44 Churchill, *The Gathering Storm*, p. 314.
45 Duff Cooper, p. 260.
46 Private information.
47 Churchill, *The Gathering Storm*, p. 314-15.
48 Lady Diana Cooper, p. 257.
49 Halifax, p. 210.
50 Hore-Belisha, p. 227.
51 Brit. Docs. 3, vol. VII, no. 739, Loraine to Halifax. Received 9:30 P.M.

52 *ibid* no. 740, Minute by Cadogan. 9:50 P.M.
53 Germ. Docs. D, vol. VII, no. 558, Hesse and Kordt for Hitler and Ribbentrop. September 3, 1939.
54 Brit. Docs. 3, vol. VII, no. 751, Halifax to Kennard.
55 Hore-Belisha, p. 227.
56 Brit. Docs. 3, vol. VII, no. 741, Minute by Cadogan. 10:30 P.M.
57 Kirkpatrick, p. 143-4.
58 *ibid* p. 144.
59 Hore-Belisha, p. 227.
60 Brit. Docs. 3, vol. VII, no. 746, Halifax to Henderson. 11:50 P.M.
61 *ibid* no. 743, Halifax to Kennard. 11 P.M.
62 *ibid* no. 752, Halifax to Henderson. September 3, 12:25 A.M.
63 Kirkpatrick, p. 144.
64 Ciano, p. 143.
65 Bonnet, *Fin d'un Europe*, p. 364.
66 Ciano, p. 143.
67 Brit. Docs. 3, vol. VII, no. 754, Kennard to Halifax. September 2, 1939. Sent 2:27 A.M. Received 4:10 A.M.
68 *ibid* no. 755, Sent 3:26 A.M. Received 12:30 P.M.
69 *ibid* no. 762, Note 1, Minute by Roberts.
70 *ibid* no. 762, Minute by Cadogan.
71 Dahlerus, p. 109.

CHAPTER 22
Leaflets Versus Bombs

1   Namier, *Diplomatic Prelude*, p. 62.
2   Wedgwood, *Last of the Radicals*, p. 232.
3   Feiling, p. 418. September 10, 1939.
4   Spender, *World Within World*, p. 262.
5   Dalton, p. 274.
6   Amery, vol. III, p. 330.
7   Spears, *Prelude to Dunkirk*, pp. 31-2.
8   Amery, vol. III, p. 330.
9   Dalton, p. 276.
10 Amery, vol. III, p. 330, Note 1.
11 Spears, p. 29.
12 Dalton, p. 274.
13 *ibid* p. 277.
14 Bryant, *Turn of the Tide*, p. 51.
15 Dalton, p. 273.
16 *ibid* p. 282.
17 Hoare, p. 405, Hoare to Lothian. October 7, 1939.

18 Amery, vol. III, p. 335.
19 Spears, pp. 38-9.
20 Feiling, p. 440.
21 Wheeler-Bennett has discussed some of them in *Nemesis of Power*.
22 Germ. Docs. D, vol. VII, no. 74, Note by Rosenberg. August 16, 1939.
23 *ibid* no. 151, Note by Rosenberg. August 21, 1939.
24 *ibid* vol. VIII, no. 134, Note, presumably by Rosenberg. September 25, 1939.
25 *ibid* no. 235, Unsigned note. October 10, 1939.
26 Henderson, p. 85.
27 Ellis, *War in France and Flanders*, p. 2.
28 *ibid* p. 3.
29 Brit. Docs. 3, vol. III, no. 325, Record of Anglo-French Conversation.
30 Hoare, p. 377.
31 Lockhart, *Friends, Foes and Foreigners*, pp. 192-3.
32 Dalton, p. 292.
33 Ellis, pp. 30-31.
34 Hoare, p. 428.
35 Germ. Docs. D, vol. X, no. 188.
36 Germ. Docs. D, vol. VIII, no. 235, Unsigned. October 10.
37 Germ. Docs. D, vol. VIII, no. 318, Unsigned and undated.
38 Hore-Belisha, p. 251.
39 Spears, p. 65.
40 Shinwell, *Conflict Without Malice*, pp. 137-8.
41 Kirkpatrick, p. 145.
42 Germ. Docs. D, vol. VIII, no. 138, Memo by Schmidt. September 26, 1939.
43 L. B. Namier, *In the Nazi Era*, p. 98.
44 Germ. Docs. D, vol. VIII, no. 138. September 26, 1939.
45 Hoare, p. 405, Hoare to Lothian. October 7, 1939.

CHAPTER 23

"Decayed Serving Men"

1 Bryant, *Turn of the Tide*, p. 70.
2 Germ. Docs. D, vol. VIII, no. 337, Wied to Foreign Ministry. November 9, 1939.
3 *ibid* no. 346, Ribbentrop to Swedish Legation. November 11, 1939.
4 *Lord Derby*, Randolph Churchill, p. 608, September 24, 1939.
5 Dalton, p. 277.
6 Germ. Docs. D, vol. VIII, no. 285, Schulenburg to Foreign Ministry. October 20, 1939.

7 *ibid* no. 375, Weizsäcker Memo. November 20, 1939.
8 *ibid* no. 348, Weizsäcker Memo. November 11, 1939.
9 *ibid* no. 472, Renthe-Fink to Foreign Ministry. December 19, 1939.
10 J. K. Galbraith, *Interrogation of General Thomas* (Unpublished).
11 Macleod, p. 281.
12 Feiling, p. 434.
13 Hore-Belisha, Chapter XXI, pp. 185-200.
14 *ibid* p. 263.
15 J. C. W. Reith, *Into the Wind*, p. 365.
16 Hore-Belisha, p. 269.
17 Macleod, p. 286.
18 *ibid* pp. 285-6.
19 Hore-Belisha, p. 287.
20 Josiah Wedgwood, p. 244.
21 Macleod, p. 291.
22 Reith, p. 382.
23 Private information.
24 Dalton, p. 321.

Bibliography

For cases in which an American edition of a British book has been published, the reference to the American publisher appears after the British reference within the parentheses.

1. DOCUMENTS (published)

Documents on British Foreign Policy 1919-1939, edited by E. L. Woodward and Rohan Butler. HMSO, 1947-.
Second Series: Vols. I-VI. 1931-34.
Third Series: Vols. I-VII. March, 1938—September, 1939.

Documents on German Foreign Policy 1918-1945. Various editors. HMSO.
Series C: Vols. I-II.
Series D: Vols. I-XI.
Contain essential material on Anglo-German conversations and contacts.

Foreign Relations of the United States: 1937, 1938, 1939.
Contain full reports by American Ambassadors in Europe to the U.S. Secretary of State.

New Documents on the History of Munich, Orbis-Prague, 1958.
Additional information on the diplomacy of 1938, especially on Russo-Czech relations.

Documents and Materials relating to the Eve of the Second World War, Moscow, 1947.
A small volume devoted to Anglo-German contacts, 1938-1939. Largely superseded by the relevant volumes of English and German documents.

Dirksen Papers, Moscow, 1948.
A volume of documents found in the files of the former German Ambassador to Britain.

2. DOCUMENTS (unpublished)

German Foreign Ministry Archives, Foreign Office Library, London. Vols. 2005; 2791; 5841H.

An indispensable source for British-German relations; especially for economic matters.

Gilbert Murray Papers, Bodleian Library, Oxford.

Lothian Papers, Scottish Record Office, Edinburgh.

H. A. L. Fisher Papers, Bodleian Library, Oxford.
These private collections contain a number of letters to and from prominent personalities.

Letters to Duff Cooper on his resignation, Foreign Office Library, London.

Private Information

3. NEWSPAPERS

The Times, A consistent supporter of Chamberlain's foreign policy. *Daily Telegraph, Daily Mail, Daily Herald, News Chronicle, Manchester Guardian, Daily Express* (hostile to the Poles, and to Anglo-Polish commitments), *Sunday Times, Observer, Sunday Dispatch, Evening Standard, The Week* (critical of appeasement), *Truth* (critical of Jews), *Anglo-German Review* (critical of those who opposed closer Anglo-German relations).

4. OTHER SOURCES

Hansard
Indispensable for any study of foreign affairs in this period.

Dictionary of National Biography
Useful sketches of dead men. Often by those who knew them well, and often critical.

Survey of International Affairs, and *Documents on International Affairs*. Published by the Royal Institute of International Affairs (Chatham House). Detailed and accurate. Chronicle rather than criticism.

5. MEMOIRS AND BIOGRAPHIES: CABINET MINISTERS

AVON, Earl of (Anthony Eden)
 Facing the Dictators (Cassell, 1962; Houghton Mifflin, 1962)
 Informative and detailed; but tells much less than he knew.

DUFF COOPER, Alfred
 Old Men Forget (Hart-Davis, 1953; E. P. Dutton, 1954)
 An excellent autobiography; contains important material on the Cabinet in 1938, and the activities of the Conservative dissidents in 1939.

FEILING, Keith
Life of Neville Chamberlain (Macmillan, 1946; St. Martin's Press, 1946)
The official biography; contains informative extracts from his diary and letters; essential.

HALIFAX, Lord
Fulness of Days (Collins, 1957; Dodd, Mead, 1957)
Little of interest from a leading appeaser; contains an account of his visit to Hitler in 1937. Otherwise trivial — Vansittart is mentioned only once, as the participant in a Foreign Office entertainment. The facts of life are omitted.

JOHNSON, A. C.
Viscount Halifax (Robert Hale, 1941; Ives Washburn, 1941)
An adequate and compendious contemporary biography.
Sir Anthony Eden (Robert Hale, 1955; *Eden: The Making of a Statesman*, Ives Washburn, 1955)
Similar to the above. Superseded by the relevant volume of memoirs.

LONDONDERRY, Lord
Ourselves and Germany (Robert Hale, 1938; Famous Books, 1938)
Argues in favor of friendship with Germany. Includes some of his correspondence with Nazi leaders.

MACLEOD, Iain
Neville Chamberlain (Muller, 1961; Atheneum Publishers, 1962)
A disappointing book with little material not previously published by Keith Feiling.

MAUGHAM, Viscount
The Truth about the Munich Crisis (Heinemann, 1944)
Unhelpful.

MINNEY, R. J.
Private Papers of Hore-Belisha (Collins, 1960; Doubleday & Co., 1960)
Deals principally with his three years as War Minister, 1937-1940. Much valuable material on dissensions within the Cabinet during the Munich and Polish crises. Evidence of the role played by Horace Wilson in attempting to forestall conscription.

REITH, J. C. W.
Into the Wind (Hodder & Stoughton, 1949)
Describes the relationship between the Government and the BBC; much material about Horace Wilson.

SIMON, Lord
Retrospect (Hutchinson, 1952)
The least useful of all contemporary memoirs. Vague and dull.

SWINTON, Lord
I Remember (Hutchinson, 1948)
Less than he knew.

TEMPLEWOOD, Lord (Samuel Hoare)
Nine Troubled Years (Collins, 1954)
A somewhat labored apology for appeasement. Does much to illuminate the dark corners of an appeaser's mind. Full of detail; essential.

6. MEMOIRS AND BIOGRAPHIES: OTHER ENGLISH POLITICIANS

AMERY, L. S.
My Political Life, Vol III (Hutchinson, 1955)
A brilliantly written first-hand account of pre-war events; contains indispensable material on the Conservative opposition to Chamberlain.

BOOTHBY, R.
I Fight to Live (Gollancz, 1947)
A lively study of pre-war politics by an anti-appeaser.

BROWN, W. J.
So Far (Allen and Unwin, 1943)
The autobiography of an Independent with an intense mistrust of Horace Wilson. Of little importance for foreign policy.

BUTLER, J. R. M.
Lord Lothian (Macmillan, 1960; St. Martin's Press, 1960)
Contains many letters to and from a prominent appeaser; details of his visits to Hitler.

CHURCHILL, Randolph
Lord Derby (Heinemann, 1959; G. P. Putnam's Sons, 1960)
The life and letters of Oliver Stanley's father.

CHURCHILL, W. S.
The Gathering Storm (Cassell, 1948; Houghton Mifflin, 1948)
The first informed criticism of appeasement. Points out the loss England sustained by the early death of Ralph Wigram. Its inspired guesswork must be supplemented by material available since its publication.

DALTON, Hugh
The Fateful Years, 1931-1945 (Muller, 1957)

An exciting autobiography by an Etonian who sought to protect the Labour Party from its pacifist element. Essential.

OWEN, Frank
Tempestuous Journey; Lloyd George, His Life and Times (McGraw-Hill, 1955)
Lloyd George (Hutchinson, 1954)
Contains an important letter from Lloyd George to Conwell-Evans.

SHINWELL, E.
Conflict without Malice (Odhams, 1955)
Of marginal importance; rarely discusses foreign affairs.

SPEARS, E. L.
Prelude to Dunkirk (Heinemann, 1954)
Assignment to Catastrophe, Vol. I (A. A. Wyn, 1954)
An excellent, well-informed, and critical account of the "Phoney War" and the not-so-phoney war.

WEDGWOOD, C. V.
The Last of the Radicals (Cape, 1951; The Macmillan Co., 1951)
The story of Josiah Wedgwood.

WEDGWOOD, Josiah
Memoirs of a Fighting Life (Hutchinson, 1941)
Stimulating criticism of the appeasers by the "Last of the Radicals."

WILSON, Sir Arnold
Walks and Talks Abroad (Oxford, 1939)
An appeaser's travels in Germany.
More Thoughts and Talks (Longmans, Green, 1939)
More of the same.

WOOLTON, Lord
Memoirs (Cassell, 1959)
Interesting sketches of Horace Wilson.

7. MEMOIRS AND BIOGRAPHIES: DIPLOMATS

ASHTON-GWATKIN, F. T. A.
The British Foreign Office (Syracuse University Press, 1949)
A stimulating account of the relations between the Foreign Office and the politicians.

HENDERSON, Nevile
Failure of a Mission (Hodder & Stoughton, 1940; G. P. Putnam's Sons, 1940)
A revealing, but at times inaccurate account of Henderson's mis-

sion to Berlin. Largely superseded by the published documents, but still essential reading.
Water under the Bridges (1945)
Diplomatic reminiscences of the period before he went to Berlin. Includes a short apologia for Munich.

KIRKPATRICK, Ivone
 The Inner Circle (Macmillan, 1959)
 The memoirs of a "disinterested" public servant; contains a useful description of Halifax's visit to Hitler, and the meetings at Godesberg. Otherwise disappointingly barren.

LOCKHART, R. Bruce
 Friends, Foes and Foreigners (Putnam, 1957)
 Contains revealing sketches of Orme Sargent, Brendan Bracken, and Eden.

SARGENT, Orme
 Nevile Henderson, Eric Phipps (Dictionary of National Biography)
 Short, critical assessments by a perceptive fellow-diplomat.

SELBY, Walford
 Diplomatic Twilight (Murray, 1953)
 A description of the decline of Foreign Office influence in the inter-war years.

STRANG, Lord
 At Home and Abroad (Deutsch, 1956)
 Contains a first-hand account of the Czech crisis, and of the Anglo-Russian negotiations of 1939.
 Britain in World Affairs (Faber-Deutsch, 1961; Frederick A. Praeger, 1961)
 Four hundred years of British foreign policy. Critical of Chamberlain. Puts Munich in its historical perspective.

VANSITTART, Lord
 Bones of Contention (Hutchinson, 1945; Alfred A. Knopf, 1945)
 Lessons of My Life (Hutchinson, 1943; Alfred A. Knopf, 1943)
 The Mist Procession (Hutchinson, 1958)
 A first-class account of the inter-war years. Few people read this magnificent autobiography. Contains sketches of all the leading diplomats and politicians. The considered judgment of a remarkable man.

DODD, W. E., Jr., and Martha Dodd (Eds.)
 Ambassador Dodd's Diary (Gollancz, 1941; Harcourt, Brace, 1941)

A revealing account of diplomatic life in Berlin in the thirties. Very critical of appeasement.

HESSE, Fritz
Das Spiel um Deutschland (Munich, 1953)
Contains much interesting but unverifiable information on Anglo-German contacts.
Hitler and the English (Wingate, 1954)
An abridged English version of the above.

KORDT, Erich
Wahn und Wirklichkeit (Stuttgart, 1948)
Nicht aus den Akten (Stuttgart, 1950)
Describes the activities of the Opposition to Hitler within the German diplomatic corps. Contains much information about otherwise elusive figures (e.g.: Conwell-Evans).

MAISKY, Ivan
Origins of the Second World War (Moscow, 1961)
Three broadcast talks with little new material.

WEIZSAECKER, Ernst
Memoirs (Gollancz, 1951; Henry Regnery Co., 1951)
A few useful details; much self-justification.

8. MEMOIRS AND BIOGRAPHIES: FOREIGN POLITICIANS

BECK, J.
Dernier Rapport (La Baconniere, 1951; *Final Report*, Robert Speller, N.Y., 1958).
An account of his career which deals only briefly with the crisis of 1939.

BONNET, Georges
Fin d'un Europe (Geneva, 1948)
Given the dearth of French documents, a useful summary of his policy.

GAFENCU, G.
Last Days of Europe (Muller, 1948; Yale University Press, 1948)
A shrewd, often bitter view of Western policy, seen by an East European politician.

CIANO, Galeazzo
Diary 1937-38 (Methuen, 1952)
Diary 1939-43 (Heinemann, 1947; Doubleday & Co., 1947)
Details of Italian mediation.
Accurate and cynical.

HITLER, Adolf
Mein Kampf (Hurst & Blackett, 1938; Houghton Mifflin, 1942)
A little read but informative account of the Nazi leader's opinions.

DE MONZIE
Ci-Devant (Paris, 1942)
Details of the final French Cabinet crisis before the outbreak
of war.

NOEL, L.
L'Aggression Allemande contre La Pologne (Flammarion, 1949)
Details from the French Ambassador in Warsaw. Not always ac-
curate or complete.

PAUL-BONCOUR, J.
Entre Deux Guerres (Paris, 1945)
Contains a short but useful account of the Rhineland crisis. Must
be used with Lord Avon's account in *Facing the Dictators*.

RIPKA, H.
Munich, Before and After (Gollancz, 1939)
The critical assessment of a Czech politician.

SCHACHT, Hjalmar
My First Seventy-Six Years (Wingate, 1955)
Confessions of the Old Wizard (Houghton Mifflin, 1956)
The biography of a German economic expert who tried to per-
suade Hitler to accept Britain's offer of colonies.

SZEMBEK, J.
Journal, 1933-39 (Plon, 1952)
Details of Anglo-Polish relations, and conversations with Kennard
and Norton.

SCHWARZ, P.
This Man Ribbentrop (Julian Messner, 1943)
Interesting gossip about Ribbentrop's English friends.

9. JOURNALISTS

BARTLETT, Vernon
Nazi Germany Explained (Gollancz, 1933)
Inadequate as an explanation, it supports German rearmament.

COCKBURN, Claud
In Time of Trouble (Hart-Davis, 1956)
Discord of Trumpets (Simon & Schuster, 1956)
The memoirs of a journalist on *The Times* and the *Daily Worker*;
Editor of *The Week*.

DELMER, Sefton
Trail Sinister (Secker & Warburg, 1961)
The memoirs of the Daily Express correspondent well-acquainted with the Nazi leaders.

EINZIG, Paul
World Finance, 1938-39 (Routledge, and Kegan Paul, 1939; The Macmillan Co., 1939)
Appeasement (Macmillan, 1941; The Macmillan Co., 1942)
About economic appeasement, accurate and perceptive.
In the Centre of Things (Hutchinson, 1960)
The memoirs of a financial journalist; contains information about the Czech gold scandal of 1939.

GEDYE, G. E. R.
Fallen Bastions (Gollancz, 1939)
Austria and Czechoslovakia: The Fallen Bastions (Harper & Brothers, 1939)
A brilliant and bitter attack from an eye-witness in Central Europe. Graphic description of the fall of Austria and Czechoslovakia. Essential.

KENNEDY, A. L.
Britain Faces Germany (Cape, 1937; Oxford University Press, 1937)
A Times writer who advocated closer Anglo-German relations.

KIRKPATRICK, Helen
This Terrible Peace (Rich & Cowan, 1938)
An American journalist's account of the Munich crisis.

REED, Douglas
Insanity Fair (Cape, 1938; Random House, 1939)
Disgrace Abounding (Cape, 1939)
A Prophet at Home (Cape, 1941)
A trilogy of journalistic experience. Bitterly anti-appeasement, and somewhat anti-semitic.

10. OTHER CONTEMPORARY WORKS

BRYANT, Arthur
The Turn of the Tide (Collins, 1957; Doubleday & Co., 1957)
The diaries of Lord Alanbrooke.

CATO (pseudonym)
Guilty Men (Gollancz, 1940; Frederick A. Stokes, 1940)
A bitter attack on the appeasers. The most famous British political pamphlet of the twentieth century. Deals with Horace Wilson. Deserves to be read.

COOPER, Diana
The Light of Common Day (Hart-Davis, 1959; Houghton Mifflin, 1959)
An entertaining and perceptive account of the prewar years by Duff Cooper's wife.

DAHLERUS, Birger
The Last Attempt (Hutchinson, 1948)
The detailed activities of an "interloper in diplomacy." Many meetings with Henderson, Ogilvie Forbes, and members of the Cabinet in August, 1939.

HAXEY, Simon
Tory MP (Gollancz, 1939)
England's Money Lords (Harrison-Hilton, 1939)
A contemporary *exposé* of the Anglo-German Fellowship. An attack on "nepotism" in the House of Commons.

JONES, Thomas
Diary with Letters, 1931-50 (Oxford, 1954)
A full account of weekends at Cliveden; description of his visit to Hitler. Mostly about Baldwin.

KEYNES, J. M.
The Economic Consequences of the Peace (Harcourt, Brace, 1920)
A criticism of the Versailles Treaty which influenced postwar opinion.

SARTRE, J. P.
The Reprieve (Hamilton, 1948; Alfred A. Knopf, 1947)
A novel set during the Munich crisis. Inside information obtained from St. John Perse, the pseudonym of Alexis (St. Léger) Léger.

WRENCH, Evelyn
Geoffrey Dawson and Our Times (Hutchinson, 1955)
An illuminating account of Dawson's views and activities. Explains the pro-German policy of *The Times*.

11. THE COLONIAL PROBLEM

AMERY, L. S.
The German Colonial Claim (Chambers, 1939; Longmans, Green, 1940)
Opposes the return of colonies to Germany.

ANGELL, Norman
The Defence of Empire (Hamilton, 1937; Appleton-Century, 1937)

BENNETT, B.
Hitler over Africa (Werner Laurie, 1939)
Details of Nazi activity in Africa.

JOELSON, F. S.
Germany's Claim to Colonies (Hurst & Blackett, 1939)

JOHANNSEN, G. K. and KRAFT, H. H.
Germany's Colonial Problem (Thornton Butterworth, 1937)

ROBERTS, G.
Nazi Claim to Colonies (Murray, 1939)
Introduction by Duff Cooper. Critical of colonial appeasement.

12. SECONDARY WORKS

BURCKHARDT, Karl
Meine Danziger Mission 1937-1939 (Munich, 1960)
Essential for a study of the Danzig problem. Details of British intrigue.

ELLIS, L. F.
The War In France and Flanders (HMSO, 1953)
The Official War History.

GUILLEBAUD, C. W.
Economic Recovery of Germany, 1933-39 (Macmillan, 1939)
More impressed by the effects of the recovery than by the methods used.

NAMIER, L. B.
Diplomatic Prelude 1938-39 (Macmillan, 1948)
The first postwar attempt to make use of memoirs and contemporary documents in the writing of prewar history.
Europe in Decay, 1936-40 (Macmillan, 1950)
In the Nazi Era (Macmillan, 1952; St. Martin's Press, 1952)

NICOLSON, Harold
Peacemaking 1919 (Constable, 1933; Houghton Mifflin, 1933)
Why Britain is at War (Penguin, 1939)
Sound contemporary analysis. See also *The Background and Issues of the War*, Essays by H. A. L. Fisher, Gilbert Murray, Harold Nicolson and others. (Oxford, 1940)

ROWSE, A. L.
All Souls and Appeasement (Macmillan, 1961)
Appeasement; A Study in Political Decline (W. W. Norton, 1961)
Interesting, but does not tell the full story.

SETON-WATSON, R. W.
  Britain and the Dictators (Cambridge, 1938; The Macmillan Co., 1938)
  From Munich to Danzig (Methuen, 1939)
  Czechoslovak Broadsheets (1938)
  Pamphlets produced in the summer and autumn of 1938.

TAYLOR, A. J. P.
  The Troublemakers (Hamilton, 1957)
  Two hundred years of dissent over foreign policy. Lively and perceptive.
  The Origins of the Second World War (Hamilton, 1961; Atheneum Publishers, 1962)
  Stimulating, controversial, and seldom wrong when dealing with British policy. Based on the available documents. Often criticised before it is read.

The Times, History of (Printing House Square, 1952)
  Volume IV, Part II
  An important source. Critical of Dawson and Barrington-Ward.

WHEELER-BENNETT, J.
  Munich, Prologue to Tragedy (Macmillan, 1948; Duell, Sloan & Pearce, 1948)
  Written with intimate knowledge of many of the people concerned. Critical and acute.
  Nemesis of Power (Macmillan, 1953; St. Martin's Press, 1954)
  A brilliant study of the German Opposition to Hitler, included in a history of the German Army in politics. Contains material on the peace moves of 1939-40.

The Partitioning of CZECHOSLOVAKIA 1938

G E R M A N Y

Silesia

P O L A N D

Bavaria

Asch
Eger
SUDETEN
Prague
Bohemia
SMD
Teschen
Cracow

Miles
0   100

Moravia
Brno
S l o v a k i a
Ruthenia
(Carpatho-
Ukraine)

Danube
Vienna
Bratislava
Occupied by Hungary
on 14 March 1939

Austria
H U N G A R Y
Budapest
R U M A N I A

▦ Czech territory ceded to Germany at Munich, 30 September 1938	░ Czech territory given to Hungary by Germany and Italy at Vienna. 2 October 1938
⧄ Czech territory siezed by Poland in September 1938 and formally annexed on 1 November 1938	

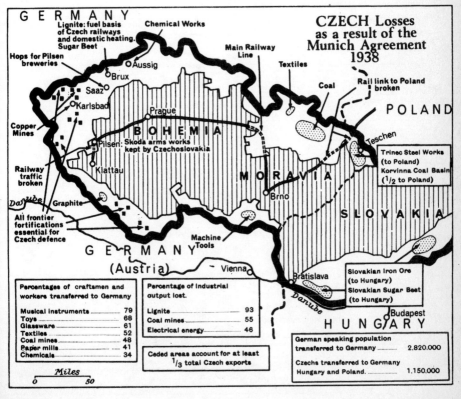

CZECH Losses as a result of the Munich Agreement 1938

G E R M A N Y

Lignite: fuel basis
of Czech railways
and domestic heating.
Sugar Beet

Chemical Works

Hops for Pilsen
breweries

Main Railway
Line

Textiles

Coal

Rail link to Poland
broken

Aussig
Brux
Saaz
Karlsbad
Prague
POLAND

Copper
Mines
BOHEMIA
Teschen

Pilsen: Skoda arms works
kept by Czechoslovakia
Trinec Steel Works
(to Poland)
Korvinna Coal Basin
(1/2 to Poland)

Railway
traffic
broken
Klattau
MORAVIA

Danube
Graphite
Brno
S L O V A K I A

All frontier
fortifications
essential for
Czech defence

G E R M A N Y
(Austria)
Machine
Tools
Vienna

Bratislava
Slovakian Iron Ore
(to Hungary)
Slovakian Sugar Beet
(to Hungary)

Danube

H U N G A R Y
Budapest

German speaking population
transferred to Germany 2,820,000

Czechs transferred to Germany
Hungary and Poland. 1,150,000

Percentages of craftsmen and workers transferred to Germany	
Musical instruments	79
Toys	68
Glassware	61
Textiles	52
Coal mines	48
Paper mills	41
Chemicals	34

Percentage of industrial output lost.	
Lignite	93
Coal mines	55
Electrical energy	46

Ceded areas account for at least
1/3 total Czech exports

Miles
0   50

German Peacetime Expansion 1919-1939

■	Germany 1919
▨	Areas gained by Plebiscite 1920-1921
▨	Saar: plebiscite 1935
▤	Rhineland: demilitarised 1919-1936
▥	Austria: annexed March 1938
▨	Sudetenland: annexed October 1938
▦	Bohemia and Moravia: Protectorate established March 1939
▨	Memel: annexed March 1939
∿∿∿	German eastern frontier in 1914

HOLLAND · BEL · LUX · FRANCE · Cologne · Frankfurt · SAAR · SWITZERLAND · ITALY · GERMANY · Berlin · Sudetenland · Eger · BOHEMIA · Prague · MORAVIA · Vienna · AUSTRIA · YUGOSLAVIA · HUNGARY · SLOVAKIA · Memel · LITHUANIA · EAST PRUSSIA · Danzig · Poznan (Posen) · Warsaw · POLAND · RUSSIA · RUSSIA

Miles 0 100

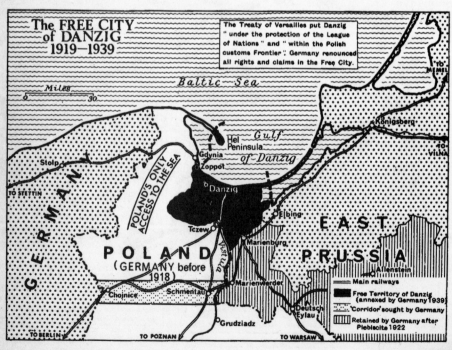

The FREE CITY of DANZIG 1919-1939

The Treaty of Versailles put Danzig "under the protection of the League of Nations" and "within the Polish customs Frontier". Germany renounced all rights and claims in the Free City.

Baltic Sea

Miles 0 30

GERMANY · TO STETTIN · Stolp · POLAND (GERMANY before 1918) · Chojnice · Schmentau · Grudziadz · TO BERLIN · TO POZNAN · Gdynia · Zoppot · Hel Peninsula · Gulf of Danzig · Danzig · Tczew · Vistula · Marienburg · Marienwerder · Deutsch Eylau · TO WARSAW · Elbing · EAST PRUSSIA · Allenstein · Königsberg · Memel · TO VILNA · POLAND'S ONLY ACCESS TO THE SEA

▬	Main railways
■	Free Territory of Danzig (annexed by Germany 1939)
∷	'Corridor' sought by Germany
⫴	Retained by Germany after Plebiscite 1922

Index

Abetz, Otto, 249
Addison, Christopher, 213
Admiralty, 332-33
Aga Khan, 182, 334
Air Ministry, 332, 333, 337
Alexander, King of Yugoslavia, 49
Allen of Hurtwood, Lord, 35, 84, 87, 131, 355
Amery, Leopold Stennett, 355-56; and the German colonial problem, 80, 81n., 85, 89; and the problem of Czechoslovakia, 106, 112; suggests Czechoslovakia declare neutrality, 145; on House reaction to Chamberlain speech, 316, 317; discusses bombing with Kingsley Wood, 328; sense of frustration, 330; urges end of Chamberlain Government, 349-50; mentioned, xi, 90n., 174
Anderson, Sir John, 124, 318, 321, 322
Anglo-German Association, 32
Anglo-German Coal Agreement, 202
Anglo-German Fellowship, 32, 41
Anglo-German Naval Agreement, 178, 179
Anglo-German Review, 32
Anglo-Polish Declaration, 248
Anglo-Polish Treaty of Mutual Assistance, 267-69, 270, 276, 301
Anti-semitism, 10-12, 348

Ashton-Gwatkin, Frank, 356-57; and the Runciman Mission, 133, 134, 136; at Munich, 177; sent to Prague, 178; and economic appeasement, 195-96, 199; exploratory talks in Berlin, 204; and Wohltat, 216-17
Asquith, Lady Margot, 30, 180, 231
Astor, Nancy Whitcher (Viscountess Astor), 357; dislike of the French, 8; as leader of "Cliveden set," 30, 46; luncheon party given by, 119; mentioned, 54
Astor, Waldorf (Viscount Astor), 30, 40, 42, 46, 96, 357
Attlee, Clement, 47, 84, 351
Attolico, 172, 297
Auden, W. H., poem by, 299
Aue, Captain, 47-48
"Augur," correspondent, 119
Austria: Lothian and Hitler discuss, 39-40; discussed by Jones, Ribbentrop, Lothian, 46-47; German annexation of, 101, 108; British inquiry into post-*Anschluss* conditions in, 126; gold and foreign assets given to Germany, 209n.

Baldwin, Stanley, sympathetic to Germany, 20; on Thomas Jones, 30; embarrassed by Phipps and Vansittart, 37; Cliveden set tries to influence, 42; Hitler desires to

meet, 44; urged to meet with
Hitler, 44-45, 62; retires, 51; and
Henderson's appointment to Berlin, 62; on Eden at Cliveden, 71

Balfour, Harold, 319

Ball, Sir Joseph, 216, 224, 227, 358

Barrington-Ward, Robert
McGowan, 8, 67, 74, 358

Bartlett, Vernon, 21, 22, 358

Bastianini, 344-45

Beck, Colonel, determined to maintain high level of German-Polish understanding, 237; French distrust of, 238; in no hurry to aid Rumania, 239-41; offered British guarantee, 241-42; refuses to agree to 4-power declaration with Russia, 242-43; discussions with Chamberlain, 243-45; uninformative about Polish policy, 248; and the Danzig problem, 248, 249; varying opinions of character of, 252; asks alteration of Chamberlain statement, 253; and British financial negotiations, 255; distrusts Russia, 263, 264; anxious for signing of Anglo-Polish treaty, 265; seeks British military support, 267; knows of Secret Protocol re Danzig, 268; reports to Kennard on German attack, 305; rejects Italian proposal for conference, 308; asks for British air support, 318; rebukes Kennard for British lack of action, 324

Belgium, invasion of, 351

Beneš, Edouard, warns against British and French intervention, 108; Newton talks with, 114; Runciman exerts pressure on,

136; rejects idea of surrendering Egerland, 146; feels guarantees valueless, 148; Anglo-French pressures on, 149, 150; Newton and de Lacroix argue with, 150; Hitler attacks in broadcast, 165; accepts British plan in principle, 175; resigns as President, 181

Bergerson, Professor, 219

Beyen, Dr., 210

"Big Four," 58, 65

Bismarck, Prince, 117

Blickling, meeting at, 40-41

Blomberg, General, 95

Blum, Léon, 107, 109, 112, 113

Bohle, E. W., 83

Bonnet, Georges, Halifax talks with, 113, 114, 115; and problem of Czechoslovakia, 135, 141, 142; reports Litvinov ready to go to League, 146; meets "Big Four," 146; questioned by Chamberlain, 161; agrees to concerted Anglo-French action, 169; favors postponement of British elections, 225; anticipates German aggression in Rumania, 234, 239-40; convinced Hitler will move on Rumania, 235; distrust of Russia, 240; sends French declaration re Danzig to Ribbentrop, 251; demands Beck consent to Russian terms, 263; and negotiations re Poland, 275; eager to impose fewest conditions on Germans, 309; interests Halifax in idea of conference, 310, 311, 312; believes negotiations still possible, 318; final attempt to secure withdrawal of German troops, 323-24

Boothby, Robert, 123, 211, 320

Bower, Commander Robert, 339
Bracken, Brendan, 90n., 211, 320, 352, 358-59
Brand, R. H., 189
Brauchitsch, General, 342, 346
Brest-Litovsk, Treaty of, 82
Bridges, Edward, 146
British Broadcasting Company, 57
British Ex-Servicemen's Association, 160
British Federation of Industry, 200
British Plan, 168-69
Brooke, General Alan, 329, 343
Brüning, Heinrich, 10, 74
Bullitt, William C., 36, 51, 94
Burckhardt, Karl, 138, 139, 235, 262
Bürger, Friedrich, 131
Burgin, Leslie, 213
Butler, R. A., 359; succeeds Cranborne in Government, 77; calls at German Embassy, 77-79; and the Sudeten crisis, 128; interviews Litvinov at Geneva, 154; becomes Home Secretary, 182; suggested as mediator, 213; and Kordt, 228; drafts reply to Hitler offer re Poland and Danzig, 278; talks with Maisky and Bastianini, 344-45
Butler, Rohan, xiii
Buxton, Charles Roden, 227

Cabinet Ministers, list of, 353-54
Cadogan, Alexander, 359; interested in Temperley memorandum, 15; replaces Vansittart, 68; on Paul-Boncour, 109; meets with "Big Four," 146; angered at Phipps telegram, 159; urges

return of Danzig and Corridor, 278; opposed to negotiating with Germany, 304; misleads Bastianini, 345; mentioned, 182, 252
Cambon, Roger, 303
Cameroons, 80, 85, 95
Carson, Sir Edward, 59
Casey, 137
Cassel, Sir Ernest, 34
Cecil, Lord Robert, 109
Chamberlain, Sir Austen, on Nazism, 26; opposed to anti-communism as basis for Anglo-German activity, 28-29; on contradictory positions, 45; deplores visit to Hitler, 46; death, 53; and the German colonial problem, 86; signs Parliamentary protest, 90n.
Chamberlain, Joseph, 51, 115
Chamberlain, Neville, 359-60; and aims of appeasement, xii-xiii; careful not to offend Germany, 42; dislikes Eden's insistence on treating dictators firmly, 45; French nickname for, 51; becomes Prime Minister, 51; dislikes Russia, 51-52; seeks Germany's friendship, 52; appoints Simon to Exchequer, 53; treatment of Ministers, 54; dependence on Sir Horace Wilson, 55-57; Inner Cabinet, 58; Cabinet, 61, 62, 353-54; speech at July, 1937, rally, 70; on Halifax, 72-73; attacks League, 77; offers help to Germans, 79; and the German colonial problem, 89, 97, 98, 99, 100, 101; and Czechoslovakia, 107, 108, 132, 133, 140-41; on the French govern-

Duff Cooper, Alfred, xi, 362; resignation of, xii, 182-83; moves to Admiralty, 54; in Chamberlain Cabinet, 54, 61, 77; on Kingsley Wood, 61; urges more friendly gesture towards France, 113; opposes Government attitude on Germany, 140, 141; on Runciman's report, 146; and the Czech mobilization crisis, 155; protests "war with dishonour," 160; and mobilization of the fleet, 163n., 170; suggests parliamentary supervisory council, 226; on the Anglo-Polish agreement, 246; on lack of decision, 268; describes scene in Commons, 174; outraged at Duke of Westminster, 307; furious at Chamberlain announcement of further negotiations, 316; and Cabinet reaction to Chamberlain's announcement, 319-20

Dufferin, Lord, 198

Dunglass, Lord, 173, 177, 182, 218, 362-63

Düsseldorf, meeting of industrialists at, 207-8

Ebbutt, Norman, 66-67

Economist, 87

Eden, Anthony, 363; sees no threat in Hitler's occupation of Rhineland, 41; taken aback by French attitude, 42; urges reliance on League of Nations, 45; on Chamberlain as Prime Minister, 54; ignored by Chamberlain, 55; in Chamberlain Cabinet, 61; and Vansittart, 69; views diverge from Chamberlain's, 70-71; seeks

collective action to strengthen League, 76; resigns from Chamberlain Cabinet, 76, 78; visits Hitler, 85-86; and the problem of the German colonies, 90, 93, 96, 97, 98; letter to Basil Newton, 106-7; and the problem of Czechoslovakia, 108; urges Chamberlain to heed German anti-Nazis, 163; reaction to Chamberlain's announcement of plans to go to Munich, 174; suggests mutual security agreements, 233; reaction to Chamberlain announcement of further negotiations, 320; in Chamberlain Government, 329; insists on Anglo-French staff talks, 336; on defeatism, 346; mentioned, xi, 8

Egerland, 146, 153

Einzig, Paul, 190, 197, 210, 211, 212

Eliot, T. S., quoted, 187

Elizabeth, Queen of England, 166

Elliott, Walter, 155, 318, 321

Epp, Ritter von, 91

Etzdorf, Hasso von, 340

Evening Standard, 72

Fauchet, General, 184

Financial News, 197, 210

Fisher, H. A. L., 27n., 32, 180

Fournier, 210

France: blamed for harshness of Versailles Treaty, 3; English dislike of, 8-9; Hitler plans to attack, 343

Franco, Francisco, 65

Franco-Polish military protocol of May 19, 1939, 342

versations with Wohltat, 219, 222-24; and the Anglo-Polish coal agreement, 256

Huene, 334n.

Hugenberg, 82

Hull, Cordell, 33, 289

I. G. Farben, 190

Illustrated London News, 94

Inskip, Sir Thomas, 365; visits Lothian, 40; at Sandwich, 46; Churchill on, 60-61; in Chamberlain Cabinet, 61; Hudson seeks resignation of, 198

Ironside, General Sir Edmund, 213, 255, 302, 347

Jaksch, Wenzel, 151, 184-85

Jebb, Gladwyn, 196

Jews, Nazi persecution of, 10-12, 196

Jodl, General, 342

Joint Parliamentary Committee on Closer Union in East Africa, 80

Jones, Thomas, 8, 366; on diplomats and hatred, 20; on Hitler, 21; attacks Vansittart's hatred of Nazism, 30; visits to Hitler, 35n., 42-44; urges Phipps be replaced, 37-38, 61-62; pro-German sentiments, 40; impressed by Toynbee's views on Hitler, 42; urges Baldwin and Chamberlain visit Hitler, 44-45, 62; meets Ribbentrop again, 46; on Halifax's visit to Göring, 50-51; on Chamberlain as Prime Minister, 54; on split between Henderson and Eden, 71; on rearmament and foreign trade, 193; on dissatisfaction with Chamberlain, 346

Journal of the Royal African Society, 91

Karlsbad Program, 114, 136

Keitel, General von, 342

Kelly, David, 338

Kennard, Sir Howard, xi, 366: urges Beck to consider 4-power declaration, 239; and negotiations over guarantees to Poland, 241, 261, 262, 264, 266, 277, 280, 281, 295; and the Danzig crisis, 248, 249; opposes putting pressure on Poland, 288-89, 290; telegram to Halifax, 297-98; informed of German air attacks on Poland, 305, 306, 308, 313; emphasizes need for action, 311; hopes for British declaration of war, 318, 324

Kennedy, A. L., 22-23

Kennedy, Joseph, 238, 281, 289

Kent, Duke of, 49; and Duchess, 173

Keyes, Sir Roger, 90n., 350

Keynes, J. M., 3, 5

Kirkpatrick, Helen, 174-75

Kirkpatrick, Ivone, 366; concerned about German foreign policy and rearmament, 36, 37; opposed to appeasement, 46; on Aue's withdrawal from Germany, 48; shows Wigram evidence of German rearmament, 68; and the German colonial problem, 84, 90; and the Czech problem, 117; Germans incredulous at remarks of, 119; at Godesberg meetings, 152; returns from Godesberg, 159; sees Hitler, 165, 166-67; critical of O'Neill, 184; on re-

to Hitler, 38-39, 39-40; and Ribbentrop, 39; second visit to Hitler, 39; Dodd scandalized by, 40;
reported to have congratulated
Hitler on Rhineland occupation,
41; at Sandwich, 46; visits Hitler, 66, 91-92; Dawson relies on,
67; and the German colonial
problem, 85, 87, 91, 92; wants
Hitler to give Czechs their independence, 217
Lubienski, 244, 249, 250
Lukasiewicz, 328

MacDonald, Ramsay, 13, 23-24, 52,
53, 59
Mackensen, 72
Macmillan, Harold, 336, 351
MacNeice, Louis, poetry by, 103,
185
Maginot Line, tours of, 330
Maisky, 51, 52; on the "Cliveden
set," 31; interviewed by Butler
and de la Warr, 154; and R. A.
Butler, 344
Makins, Roger, 269, 308
Malkin, Sir William, 152, 280
Mandel, Georges, 184, 312n.
Margesson, Captain David, 316
Martin, Kingsley, 113
Mary, Queen of England, 173
Masarik, Hubert, 177, 178
Masaryk, Jan, 109, 112, 137, 160-
61
Mason-Macfarlane, Colonel, 158,
207
Mastny, 177, 178
Maurice, Lt.-Gen. Sir Frederick,
160
Mein Kampf, 13, 22, 27

Memel, annexation of, 234
Milner, Lord, 59; "Kindergarten,"
38
Mitford, Unity, 63
Moltke, General von, quoted, 56
Mommsen, 81n.
"Monsieur J'aime Berlin," French
title for Chamberlain, 51
Montreal Star, 119
Moore, Sir Thomas, 31, 84, 369
Morrison, Herbert, 145, 350
Morrison, W. S., 190
Mount Temple, Lord, 32, 34
Müller, 209
Munich: as a "bought" year, xi-
xii; significance of, xii
Munich Agreement, signing of, 178
Murray, (George) Gilbert, 11, 369;
pleads for individual liberty, 12;
on the Nazis, 14-15; denies communism a greater danger than
Nazism, 29; sees Munich as betrayal, 180; quoted, 231
Mussolini, Benito, admiration for,
7; ascribes female appeasement
to sexual frustration, 29-30; invited to Munich, 172-73; at Munich, 177; speculations on intentions of, 235; seen as peaceful influence on Hitler, 257; as
go-between for Halifax, 271-73;
as Hitler ally, 272; French in
touch with, as mediator with Hitler, 275; proposes conference to
revise Versailles, 296

Namier, L. B., 327
National Liberal Foundation, 29
"Nazi Moderates," 190-91
"Nazi-Soviet" pact, 264
Nazism, Rumbold sees evils of, 9-

sidered "hysterical," 52; and Henderson's appointment, 62; and Wigram, 67; made Chief Diplomatic Adviser, 68-69; fails to frighten Henlein, 107; and Czechoslovakia, 112; urges Chamberlain to heed German anti-Nazis, 163; Bonnet believes responsible for Foreign Office communiqué, 164; on Beck, 240, 252; on Chamberlain, 243; on the dangers of Henderson's answer to Hitler, 282; mentioned, xi, 17, 146

Versailles, Treaty of, 3; criticism of, 5; revision advocated, 6; provisions of Articles 42 to 44, 41n.; provisions re Danzig, 246-47

Victoria, Queen of England, 25

Wallace, Euan, 319
Walshe, 94
Warner, George, 139
Wedgwood, Josiah, on Nevile Henderson, 59; on gas masks and ARP, 170; letter to Duff Cooper, 183; wager on bombing of London, 333; on Hore-Belisha's dismissal, 348n.; opposed to Chamberlain Government, 350; sings "Rule, Britannia," 351
Weigel, Major, 83
Weizsäcker, on Henderson, 62; on the German colonial problem, 93-94; and Henderson, 121, 122, 218; receives British proposals re Runciman Mission, 129-30; and the Czech problem, 133, 138, 139, 149; receives British plan from Henderson, 170; aids in drafting Munich memorandum,

177; on the Hesse memorandum, 193; and the Danzig problem, 250; mentioned, 199
Welczeck, 115, 116
Wells, H. G., 32
Wenner-Gren, 280
West, Rebecca, quoted, 1
Westminster, Bendor, Duke of, 307
Wheeler-Bennett, J., 13, 173
Wiedemann, Captain, 128
Wiehl, 199, 201, 203, 204
Wigram, Ralph, 17, 18, 67-68
William II, Emperor of Germany, 10, 25, 66n.
Willingdon, Lord, 124
Wilson, Sir Arnold, 31, 32, 173
Wilson, Sir Horace, xiv, 376-77; aide to Chamberlain, 55-57; active in securing Vansittart's replacement, 69; influence stressed by Butler, 79; on Halifax and the German colonial problem, 101; conversations with Wohltat, 127, 213, 216, 219-20, 225, 226; reprimands Lord Woolton, 127; suggests Dirksen interview with Chamberlain, 129; views on the Czech problem, 132, 133; and Theo Kordt, 132, 133, 139; urges Chamberlain visit Hitler, 141; trip to Berchtesgaden, 143, 144; goes to Munich with Dirksen, 145; at meeting of "Big Four," 146; at Godesberg, 152, 154; visits Hitler, 163, 165, 166; instructed to warn Hitler of French support to Czechoslovakia, 164; takes Hitler's final concession to England, 168; reports to Cabinet, 170; at Munich, 177, 178; approves Drummond-Wolff trip,

201; and economic problems, 201, 202; discussions with Dirksen, 228; suggests Anglo-Polish pact "superfluous," 257; and the Danzig dilemma, 258; and Poland, 278, 295, 321; Jones on, 347; infuriated at Kingsley Wood's betrayal, 351; snubbed by Bracken and Randolph Churchill, 352

Wilson Memorandum, 220-21; 227

Windsor, Duke of, 334

Winn, Antony, 141, 184

Winterton, Lord, 198

Wise, Alfred R., 89, 90

Woermann, 69, 117, 196

Wohltat, Staatstrat, on the expansion of German sovereignty in Europe, 127; and discussions of Anglo-German cooperation, 204, 205; conversations with Wilson, 213, 216, 219-20, 225-26; and

Hudson, 219, 222; and Ball, 224, 227; mentioned, 256

Women, as appeasers, Mussolini on, 29-30

Wood, Sir Kingsley, 377-78; fails to achieve air parity with Germany, xii; Churchill on, 60, 61; in Chamberlain Cabinet, 61; on Chamberlain's reaction to Czech mobilization, 155; views on bombing, 328; opposed to Dalton's going to Poland, 329; and the Air Ministry, 333, 337; favors delay in military action, 336; on the "truth raids," 337; tells Chamberlain he must resign, 351; in Churchill Government, 352

Woodward, E. L., xiii

Woolton, Lord, 56, 126-27

World Economic Conference, 82

Wrench, Evelyn, 67